THE PICADOR BOOK OF

SPORTSWRITING

Edited by Nick Coleman
and Nick Hornby

PICADOR

First published 1996 by Picador

This edition published 1997 by Picador
an imprint of Macmillan Publishers Ltd
25 Eccleston Place, London SW1W 9NF
and Basingstoke

Associated companies throughout the world

ISBN 0 330 34459 5

1 3 5 7 9 8 6 4 2

A CIP catalogue record for this book is available from
the British Library.

Typeset by SetSystems Limited, Saffron Walden, Essex
Printed by and bound in Great Britain by
Mackays of Chatham plc, Chatham, Kent

THE PICADOR BOOK OF SPORTSWRITING

NICK COLEMAN is a journalist and broadcaster.
He is currently an editor at the *Independent*.

NICK HORNBY worked as a teacher before becoming a full-time writer.
He is the author of *Fever Pitch* and *High Fidelity*.

Contents

WHAT'S IT WORTH?

THE MOMENT

ALI, ALI

Editor's Acknowledgements

The editors would like to thank the following for their help in the making of this book: Hugh McIlvanney, Tony Brook, John Gausted, D. J. Taylor, Derek Hornby, Roger Coleman, Matthew Engel, Derek Chapman, Russell Bulgin, Steve Grant.

Introduction

These are good times for English sportswriting: there has been a lot more of it over the last few years, and peculiarly (an increase in quantity does not often signify an increase in quality) almost all of this increase in input has come from the classier end of the media. Most of the Sunday broadsheets, and a couple of the dailies, now have designated sports sections, and they need meaty pieces to fill it. *GQ*, *Esquire* and the other glossy men's magazines provide another new canvas for sportswriters, or writers who are sports fans, who want to paint the big picture. Somewhat belatedly, our publishers are beginning to grasp that not all sports enthusiasts are people who cannot read without their lips moving; football books in particular are no longer the sole preserve of ageing players, their agents and their ghostwriters, partly because football fanzines have raised the profile of the literate fan. And John Gaustad's Sportspages bookshops, which provided a meeting place for these literate fans, have had an influence way beyond their size, by demonstrating conclusively that there was a market for the kind of books they sold. This seemed like a good time to reflect and celebrate this recent sportswriting renaissance, and we make no apology for the contemporaneity of much of the writing here.

Yet those who write about sport still create a whole set of problems for themselves in Britain, many of them relating, predictably, to the subject of class. Sport in Britain has all sorts of class associations apparently absent elsewhere in the world. Cricket and (English, rather than Welsh) rugby union are 'posh' sports, played and watched by 'posh' people, and it is therefore acceptable to write in a 'posh' way about them; but anyone who dares to write about the more traditional working-class sports – football or rugby league, say – in a way that recognizes the existence of polysyllabic words, or metaphors, or even ideas, is asking for trouble, or at the very least a great deal of suspicion. From one side comes the accusation that the writer is a middle-class interloper who knows nothing about the sport and its traditions; from the other the supposition that the writer is slumming it, attaching himself or herself to the sport as a quick and easy way of gaining credibility. (Sometimes the supposition is even more basic: that the writer is simply a semi-literate oaf.)

This pincer movement has all kinds of knock-on effects. Some writers affect an exaggerated one-of-the-boys prose style, full of matey, jocular vulgarisms intended to ingratiate its practitioner with a readership assumed to be distrustful of any voice more refined than this; others borrow wholesale the language and idioms of the tabloids, but use them 'ironically', just to let you know that they could do better than this if they really wanted to. This is not only frustrating, but also patronizing, because it makes the same old assumptions about sports fans, their intelligence and their reading habits. Yet another group seem to suffer from chronic sports insecurity, and pepper their reports and profiles with quotations from Proust, chunks of Italian and anything else they might find lying around in their intellectual larder.

Maybe distance lends enchantment, but it seems from here that Americans experience very few of these difficulties. The class inflections are absent, at least from the major sports themselves, and people like Roger Angell have long accustomed readers to the idea that a love of literature and a love of sport are not mutually exclusive. And – ironically in a country notorious for its flag-waving – the lack of international sporting activity means that there is none of the dubious nationalism that corrupts so many of the things pertaining to sport here: no Tebbit cricket tests, no dumb *Wisden* articles about black players and commitment, no hysterical abuse directed at those who run our national teams. Sport is much more comfortably bedded into popular culture than it is here – and we are only just beginning to learn how to write about popular culture anyway.

Maybe one of the most crucial differences between sports culture in the US and the UK is that very few Englishmen and -women describe themselves as *sports* fans. Football fans, cricket fans, rugby fans, sure. But *sports* fans? Over the other side of the Atlantic, it is not uncommon to find people who care about the New York Giants *and* the Nicks *and* the Yankees *and* the Rangers; but in England there are simply not enough thriving professional sports to sustain that kind of devotion. Most rugby union fans would kill for a ticket to England v. Scotland at Twickenham, but wouldn't cross the road to watch Bath v. Wasps, and while the whole country stops to watch or listen to the Test matches, county cricket is for the most part a poor, bedraggled thing. Only football and rugby league draw in the big crowds on a week-by-week basis. In America, by contrast, the nearest they get to international sport is the World Series; the pro leagues in the major sports are everything. Maybe this is why they have sports fans and we have cricket fans, or rugby fans, or boxing fans who enjoy a spot of football on the side.

And if the whole sporting culture is different, it stands to reason that the sportswriting will be different too. England has yet to sustain a magazine like *Sports Illustrated*, although many (including Robert Maxwell) have tried and failed; one can only presume that aficionados of golf or Formula 1 don't want articles about Ryan Giggs and Mike Atherton cluttering up the magazine. There is no doubt that English sportswriting has suffered as a result. American sportswriters have always had opportunities to stretch out a bit, mull things over, use the room that a three- or four-thousand-word piece will buy them; our best sports journalists, by contrast, have traditionally been chained to the treadmill of daily journalism – eight-hundred-word responses to yesterday's or today's sporting events. It is hard to transcend that sort of limitation and produce a piece that will endure, especially if you work for the *Sun*, but sportswriters like Hugh McIlvanney – although admittedly there are not many sportswriters like Hugh McIlvanney, who in the opinion of the editors of this book is the best in Britain – do it routinely. If there is a lot of American sportswriting in this book, it is because American sportswriters have set the pace.

Even if you are a sport rather than a sports fan, we feel that the strength of the pieces here overcome prejudices and antipathies. We certainly have no interest in body-building, for example, but set against Paul Solotaroff's extraordinary, stomach-churning account of Steve Michalik's chemical diet, this kind of indifference is rather beside the point. Our guiding principle here was the prose, not the sport.

For similar reasons we grouped the pieces by underlying theme rather than by subject-sport. A common misapprehension about sport is that, in itself, it stands as a metaphor for real life; that we play, watch and read about sport because we want the rest of our lives to be illuminated by sport's special allegorical language, as if sport has something to tell us in the same way that art does. The editors beg to suggest that this is tosh. Sport is not a metaphor for the rest of life, it is indivisible from the rest of life. That's its magic. It is not a description of something, it is, simply, what it is, in the same way that sex, food and washing-up are what they are. We don't get messages from sex, food and washing-up; we get on and do them, whether we like them or not. Hence, sport's particular appeal to the writer. It has all of life's business in it and no meaning.

Sport, then, does not exist to enlighten. It exists to be experienced – its pleasures, its pains, its ironies, its tragedies and its comedies. So we have organized this book along those thematic lines. We have, for instance, a section on how sport is shaped by recollection. We have one on the pathology of being a fan. We have a lengthy chapter on what it's like to actually *do* sport. And we consider sport briefly as an agent of epiphany. We finish with a section on Muhammad Ali, who made an awful lot out of the ordinary business of his life and on the way became not only *the* sporting archetype but also the inspiration to a lot of wonderful writers to do their best work.

We decided at an early stage that there should be no fiction in the collection, with the honourable exception of Molesworth, who in our view has long since ceased to be a fictional character, on the basis that we would end up excluding 'proper' sportswriters in an attempt to include some better-known names (and because fictional games, full of players you have never heard of, results you can't remember, and teams with made-up names, are always unsatisfactory); we decided that boxing must be given a disproportionate amount of space, simply because something about it – its glamour and its brutality, possibly – have provoked writers to their best work. It has attracted people of the calibre of Joyce Carol Oates and Norman Mailer, and, in the extraordinary writing of A. J. Liebling, given rise to one of the juiciest literary styles you could hope to read anywhere. We were also particularly keen to choose pieces from some recent sports books that we feel have been unjustly neglected. Charles Sprawson's *Haunts of the Black Masseur*, for example, is an extraordinary and scholarly account of swimming through the ages, written by someone who has been swimming obsessively all his life; David Craig's *Native Stones*, ostensibly a book about climbing, is reminiscent of the work of Raymond Williams. Laura Thompson's *The Dogs* and Andy Martin's *Walking On Water* (greyhounds and surfing), both published in the 1990s, demonstrated, to us at least, that it is not necessary to love a sport before you can love its literature.

They're coming thick and fast now, books like *The Dogs*, *Haunts of the Black Masseur* and *Walking On Water*, books written with care and passion and skill: several more have been published since we finished our selection, and I doubt whether that would have been the case had we been putting this book together five years ago. (I doubt whether anyone would have *asked* us, or anyone like us, to put this book together five years ago.) Long may this trend continue: sport contains as much pleasure, pain, irony, tragedy and comedy as a writer will ever need.

Nick Coleman and Nick Hornby

Tom Stoppard

The Real Thing

HENRY: This thing here, which looks like a wooden club, is actually several pieces of particular wood cunningly put together in a certain way so that the whole thing is sprung, like a dance floor. It's for hitting cricket balls with. If you get it right, the cricket ball will travel two hundred yards in four seconds, and all you've done is give it a knock like knocking the top off a bottle of stout, and it makes a noise like a trout taking a fly ... (*He clucks his tongue to make the noise.*) What we're trying to do is to write cricket bats, so that when we throw up an idea and give it a little knock, it might ... *travel* ... (*He clucks his tongue again and picks up the script.*) Now, what we've got here is a lump of wood of roughly the same shape trying to be a cricket bat, and if you hit a ball with it, the ball will travel about ten feet and you will drop the bat and dance about shouting 'Ouch!' with your hands stuck into your armpits. (*Indicating the cricket bat.*) This isn't better because someone says it's better, or because there's a conspiracy by the MCC to keep cudgels out of Lord's. It's better because it's better.

ON REFLECTION

C. L. R. James

The Window

Tunapuna at the beginning of this century was a small town of about three thousand inhabitants, situated eight miles along the road from Port of Spain, the capital city of Trinidad. Like all towns and villages on the island, it possessed a recreation ground. Recreation meant cricket, for in those days, except for infrequent athletic sports meetings, cricket was the only game. Our house was superbly situated, exactly behind the wicket. A huge tree on one side and another house on the other limited the view of the ground, but an umpire could have stood at the bedroom window. By standing on a chair a small boy of six could watch practice every afternoon and matches on Saturdays – with matting one pitch could and often did serve for both practice and matches. From the chair also he could mount on to the window sill and so stretch a groping hand for the books on the top of the wardrobe. Thus early the pattern of my life was set. The traffic on the road was heavy, there was no fence between the front yard and the street. I was an adventurous little boy and so my grandmother and my two aunts, with whom I lived for half the year, the rainy season, preferred me in the backyard or in the house where they could keep an eye on me. When I tired of playing in the yard I perched myself on the chair by the window. I doubt if for some years I knew what I was looking at in detail. But this watching from the window shaped one of my strongest early impressions of personality in society. His name was Matthew Bondman and he lived next door to us.

He was a young man already when I first remember him, medium height and size, and an awful character. He was generally dirty. He would not work. His eyes were fierce, his language was violent and his voice was loud. His lips curled back naturally and he intensified it by an almost perpetual snarl. My grandmother and my aunts detested him. He would often without shame walk up the main street bare-footed, 'with his planks on the ground', as my grandmother would report. He did it often and my grandmother must have seen it hundreds of times, but she never failed to report it, as if she had suddenly seen the parson walking down the street barefooted. The whole Bondman family, except for the father, was unsatisfactory. It was from his mother that Matthew had inherited or absorbed his flair for language and invective. His sister Marie was quiet but bad, and despite all the circumlocutions, or perhaps because of them, which my aunts employed, I knew it had something to do with 'men'. But the two families were linked. They rented from us, they had lived there for a long time, and their irregularity of life exercised its fascination for my puritanical aunts. But that is not why I remember Matthew. For ne'er-do-well, in fact vicious character, as he was, Matthew had one saving grace – Matthew could bat. More than that, Matthew, so crude and vulgar in every aspect of his life, with a bat in his hand was all grace and style. When he practised on an afternoon with the local club people stayed to watch and walked away when he was finished. He had one particular stroke that he played by going down low on one knee. It may have been a slash through the covers or a sweep to leg. But, whatever it was, whenever Matthew sank down and made it, a long, low 'Ah!' came from many a spectator, and my own little soul thrilled with recognition and delight.

Matthew's career did not last long. He would not practise regularly, he would not pay his subscription to the club. They persevered with him, helping him out with flannels and white shoes for matches. I remember Razac, the Indian, watching him practise one day and shaking his head with deep regret: how could a man who could bat like that so waste his talent? Matthew dropped out early. But he was my first acquaintance with that genus *Britannicus*, a fine batsman, and the impact that he makes on all around him, non-cricketers and cricketers alike. The contrast between Matthew's pitiable existence as an individual and the attitude people had towards him filled my growing mind and has occupied me to this day. I came into personal contact with Matthew. His brother was my playmate and when we got in Matthew's way he glared and shouted at us in a most terrifying manner. My aunts were uncompromising in their judgements of him and yet my grandmother's oft-repeated verdict: 'Good for nothing except to play cricket,' did not seem right to me. How could an ability to play cricket atone in any sense for Matthew's abominable way of life? Particularly as my grandmother and my aunts were not in any way supporters or followers of the game.

My second landmark was not a person but a stroke, and the maker of it was Arthur Jones. He was a brownish Negro, a medium-sized man, who walked with quick steps and active shoulders. He had a pair of restless, aggressive eyes, talked quickly and even stammered a little. He wore a white cloth hat when batting, and he used to cut. How he used to cut! I have watched county cricket for weeks on end and seen whole Test matches without seeing one cut such as Jones used to make, and for years whenever I saw one I murmured to myself, 'Arthur Jones!' The crowd was waiting for it, I at my window was waiting and as soon as I began to play seriously I learnt that Arthur was waiting for it too. When the ball hit down outside the off-stump (and now, I think, even when it was straight) Jones lifted himself to his height, up went his bat and he brought it down across the ball as a woodsman puts his axe to a tree. I don't remember his raising the ball, most times it flew past point or between point and third slip, the crowd burst out in another shout and Jones's white cap sped between the wickets.

The years passed. I was in my teens at school, playing cricket, reading cricket, idolizing Thackeray, Burke and Shelley, when one day I came across the following about a great cricketer of the eighteenth century:

> It was a study for Phidias to see Beldham rise to strike; the grandeur of the attitude, the settled composure of the look, the piercing lightning of the eye, the rapid glances of the bat, were electrical. Men's hearts throbbed within them, their cheeks turned pale and red. Michael Angelo should have painted him.

This was thrilling enough. I began to tingle.

> Beldham was great in every hit, but his peculiar glory was the cut. Here he stood, with no man beside him, the laurel was all his own; it seemed like the cut of a racket. His wrist seemed to turn on springs of the finest steel. He took the ball, as Burke did the House of Commons, between wind and water – not a moment too soon or late. Beldham still survives . . .

By that time I had seen many fine cutters, one of them, W. St. Hill, never to this day surpassed. But the passage brought back Jones and childhood memories to my mind and anchored him there for good and all. Phidias, Michelangelo, Burke. Greek history had already introduced me to Phidias and the Parthenon; from engravings and reproductions I had already begun a lifelong worship of Michelangelo; and Burke, begun as a school chore, had rapidly become for me the most exciting master of prose in English – I knew already long passages of him by heart. There in the very centre of all this was William Beldham and his cut. I passed over the fact which I noted instantly that the phrase 'He hit the House just between wind and water' had been used by Burke himself, about Charles Townshend in the speech on American taxation.

The matter was far from finished. Some time later I read a complicated description of the mechanism and timing of the cut by C. B. Fry, his warning that it was a most difficult stroke to master and that even in the hands of its greatest exponents there were periods when it would not work, 'intermittent in its service', as he phrased it. But, he added, with some batsmen it was an absolutely natural stroke, and one saw beautiful cutting by batsmen who otherwise could hardly be called batsmen at all. When I read this I felt an overwhelming sense of justification. Child though I was, I had not been wrong about Jones. Batsman or not, he *was* one of those beautiful natural cutters. However, I said earlier that the second landmark in my cricketing life was a stroke – and I meant just that – one single stroke.

On an awful rainy day I was confined to my window, Tunapuna CC was batting and Jones was in his best form, that is to say, in nearly every over he was getting up on his toes and cutting away. But the wicket was wet and the visitors were canny. The off-side boundary at one end was only forty yards away, a barbed-wire fence which separated the ground from the police station. Down came a short ball, up went Jones and lashed at it, there was the usual shout, a sudden silence and another shout, not so loud this time. Then from my window I saw Jones walking out and people began to walk away. He had been caught by point standing with his back to the barbed wire. I could not see it from my window and I asked and asked until I was told what had happened. I knew that something out of the ordinary had happened to us who were watching. We had been lifted to the heights and cast down into the depths in much less than a fraction of a second. Countless as are the times that this experience has been repeated, most often in the company of tens of thousands of people, I have never lost the zest of wondering at it and pondering over it.

It is only within very recent years that Matthew Bondman and the cutting of Arthur Jones ceased to be merely isolated memories and fell into place as starting points of a connected pattern. They only appear as starting points. In reality they were the end, the last stones put into place, of a pyramid whose base constantly widened, until it embraced those aspects of social relations, politics and art laid bare when the veil of the temple has been rent in twain as ours has been. Hegel says somewhere that the old man repeats the prayers he repeated as a child, but now with the experience of a lifetime. Here briefly are some of the experiences of a lifetime which have placed Matthew Bondman and Arthur Jones within a frame of reference that stretches east and west into the receding distance, back into the past and forward into the future.

My inheritance (you have already seen two, Puritanism and cricket) came from both sides of the family and a good case could be made out for predestination, including the position of the house in front of the recreation ground and the window exactly behind the wicket.

My father's father was an emigrant from one of the smaller islands, and probably landed with nothing. But he made his way, and as a mature man worked as a pan-boiler on a sugar estate, a responsible job involving the critical transition of the boiling cane juice from liquid into sugar. It was a post in those days usually held by white men. This meant that my grandfather had raised himself above the mass of poverty, dirt, ignorance and vice which in those far-off days surrounded the islands of black lower middle-class respectability like a sea ever threatening to engulf them. I believe I understand pretty much how the average sixteenth-century Puritan in England felt amidst the decay which followed the dissolution of the monasteries, particularly in the small towns. The need for distance which my aunts felt for Matthew Bondman and his sister was compounded of self-defence and fear. My grandfather went to church every Sunday morning at eleven o'clock wearing in the broiling sun a frock coat, striped trousers and top hat, with his walking stick in hand, surrounded by his family, the underwear of the women crackling with starch. Respectability was not an ideal, it was an armour. He fell grievously ill, the family fortunes declined and the children grew up in unending struggle not to sink below the level of the Sunday-morning top hat and frock coat.

My father took the obvious way out – teaching. He did well and gained a place as a student in the Government Training College, his course comprising history, literature, geometry, algebra and education. Yet Cousin Nancy, who lived a few yards away, told many stories of her early days as a house-slave. She must have been in her twenties when slavery was abolished in 1834. My father got his diploma, but he soon married. My two aunts did sewing and needlework, not much to go by, which made them primmer and sharper than ever, and it was with them that I spent many years of my childhood and youth.

Two doors down the street was Cousin Cudjoe, and a mighty man was he. He was a blacksmith, and very early in life I was allowed to go and watch him do his fascinating business, while he regaled me with stories of his past prowess at cricket and critical observations on Matthew, Jones and the Tunapuna CC. He was quite black, with a professional chest and shoulders that were usually scantily covered as he worked his bellows or beat the iron on the forge. Cudjoe told me of his unusual career as a cricketer. He had been the only black man in a team of white men. Wherever these white men went to play he went with them. He was their wicketkeeper and their hitter – a term he used as one would say a fast bowler or an opening bat. When he was keeping he stood close to the wicket and his side needed no longstop for either fast bowling or slow, which must have been quite an achievement in his day and time. But it was as a hitter that he fascinated me. Once Cudjoe played against a team with a famous fast bowler, and it seemed that one centre of interest in the match, if not the great centre, was what would happen when the great fast bowler met the great hitter. Before the fast bowler began his run he held the ball up and shook it at Cudjoe, and Cudjoe in turn held up his bat and shook it at the bowler. The fast bowler ran up and bowled and Cudjoe hit his first ball out of the world. It didn't seem to matter how many he made after that. The challenge and the hit which followed were enough. It was primitive, but as the battle between Hector and Achilles is primitive, and it should not be forgotten that American baseball is founded on the same principle.

At the time I did not understand the significance of Cudjoe, the black blacksmith, being the only coloured man in a white team, that is to say, plantation owners and business or professional men or high government officials. 'They took me everywhere they went – everywhere,' he used to repeat. They probably had to pay for him and also to sponsor his presence when they played matches with other white men. Later I wondered what skill it was, or charm of manner, or both, which gave him that unique position. He was no sycophant. His eyes looked straight into yours, and an ironical smile played upon his lips as he talked, a handsome head on his splendid body. He was a gay lad, Cudjoe, but somehow my aunts did not disapprove of him as they did of Bondman. He was a blood relation, he smiled at them and made jokes and they laughed. But my enduring memory of Cudjoe is of an exciting and charming man in whose life cricket had played a great part.

My father too had been a cricketer in his time, playing on the same ground at which I looked from my window. He gave me a bat and ball

on my fourth birthday and never afterwards was I without them both
for long. But as I lived a great deal with my aunts away from home,
and they did not play, it was to Cudjoe I went to bowl to me, or to sit
in his blacksmith's shop holding my bat and ball and listening to his
stories. When I did spend time with my parents my father told me
about cricket and his own prowess. But now I was older and my
interest became tinged with scepticism, chiefly because my mother
often interrupted to say that whenever she went to see him play he was
always caught in the long field for very little. What made matters
worse, one day when I went to see him play he had a great hit and was
caught at long on for seven. I remembered the stroke and knew
afterwards that he had lifted his head. Joe Small, the West Indian Test
player, was one of the bowlers on the opposite side. However, I was to
learn of my father's good cricket in a curious way. When I was about
sixteen my school team went to Tunapuna to play a match on that
same ground against some of the very men I used to watch as a boy,
though by this time Arthur Jones had dropped out. I took wickets and
played a good defensive innings. Mr Warner, the warden, a brother of
Sir Pelham's, sent for me to congratulate me on my bowling, and some
spectators made quite a fuss over me for I was one of them and they
had known me as a child wandering around the ground and asking
questions.

Two or three of the older ones came up and said, 'Your father used
to hit the ball constantly into that dam over there,' and they pointed
to an old closed-up well behind the railway line. I was taken by
surprise, for the dam was in the direction of extra cover somewhat
nearer to mid-off, and a batsman who hit the ball there constantly was
no mean stroke-player. But as my father always said, the cares of a wife
and family on a small income cut short his cricketing life, as it cut
short the career of many a fine player who was quite up to intercolonial
standard. I have known intercolonial cricketers who left the West
Indies to go to the United States to better their position. Weekes, the
left-hander who hit that daring century in the Oval Test in 1939, is one
of a sizeable list. And George Headley was only saved for cricket
because, born in Panama and living in Jamaica, there was some
confusion and delay about his papers when his parents in the United
States sent for him. While the difficulties were being sorted out, an
English team arrived in Jamaica and Headley batted so successfully
that he gave up the idea of going to the United States to study a
profession.

West Indian cricket has arrived at maturity because of two factors: the rise in the financial position of the coloured middle class and the high fees paid to players by the English leagues. Of this, the economic basis of West Indian cricket – big cricket, so to speak – I was constantly aware, and from early on. One afternoon I was, as usual, watching the Tunapuna CC practise when a man in a black suit walked by on his way to the railway station. He asked for a knock and, surprisingly, pads were handed to him, the batsman withdrew and the stranger went in. Up to that time I had never seen such batting. Though he had taken off his coat, he still wore his high collar, but he hit practically every ball, all over the place. Fast and slow, wherever they came, he had a stroke, and when he stopped and rushed off to catch his train he left a buzz of talk and admiration behind him. I went up to ask who he was and I was told his name was MacDonald Bailey, an old intercolonial player. Later my father told me that Bailey was a friend of his, a teacher, an intercolonial cricketer and a great all-round sportsman. But, as usual, a wife and family and a small income compelled him to give up the game. He is the father of the famous Olympic sprinter. Mr Bailey at times visited my father and I observed him carefully, looking him up and down and all over so as to discover the secret of his athletic skill, a childish habit I have retained to this day.

Perhaps it was all because the family cottage was opposite to the recreation ground, or because we were in a British colony and, being active people, gravitated naturally towards sport. My brother never played any games to speak of, but as a young man he gave some clerical assistance to the secretary of the local Football Association. In time he became the secretary. He took Trinidad football teams all over the West Indies and he was invited to England by the Football Association to study football organization. I met him in the United States trying to arrange for an American soccer team to visit Trinidad. In 1954 he brought the first team from the West Indies to play football in England, and before he left arranged for an English team to visit the West Indies. He has at last succeeded in organizing a West Indies Football Association, of which he is the first secretary.

Even Uncle Cuffie, my father's elder brother, who, like the old man from Bengal, never played cricket at all, was the hero of a family yarn. One day he travelled with an excursion to the other end of the island. Among the excursionists was the Tunapuna CC to play a match with Siparia CC, while the rest of the visitors explored Siparia. Tunapuna was a man short and my father persuaded – nay, begged – Cuffie to fill the gap, and Cuffie reluctantly agreed. Siparia made forty-odd, not a bad score in those days, and Cuffie asked to have his innings first so that he could get out and go and enjoy himself away from the cricket field. Still wearing his braces and his high collar, he went in first, hit at every ball and by making some thirty runs not out won the match for his side by nine wickets. He quite ruined the game for the others. He had never even practised with the team before and never did afterwards.

The story of my elder aunt, Judith, ends this branch of my childhood days. She was the English Puritan incarnate, a tall, angular woman. She looked upon Matthew Bondman as a child of the devil. But if Matthew had been stricken with a loathsome disease she would have prayed for him and nursed him to the end, because it was her duty. She lost her husband early, but brought up her three children, pulled down the old cottage, replaced it with a modern one and whenever I went to see her fed me with that sumptuousness which the Trinidad Negroes have inherited from the old extravagant plantation owners. Her son grew to manhood, and though no active sportsman himself, once a year invited his friends from everywhere to Tunapuna where they played a festive cricket match. This, however, was merely a preliminary to a great spread which Judith always prepared. One year Judith worked as usual from early morning in preparation for the day, doing everything that was needed. The friends came, the match was played and then all trooped in to eat, hungry, noisy and happy. Judith was serving when suddenly she sat down, saying, 'I am not feeling so well.' She leaned her head on the table. When they bent over her to find out what was wrong she was dead. I would guess that she had been 'not feeling so well' for days, but she was not one to let that turn her aside from doing what she had to do.

I heard the story of her death thousands of miles away. I know that it was the fitting crown to her life, that it signified something to me, above all people, and, curiously enough, I thought it appropriate that her death should be so closely associated with a cricket match. Yet she had never taken any particular interest. She or my grandmother or my other aunt would come in from the street and say, 'Matthew made fifty-five,' or 'Arthur Jones is still batting,' but that was all. Periodically I pondered over it.

My grandfather on my mother's side, Josh Rudder, was also an immigrant, from Barbados, and also Protestant. I knew him well. He used to claim that he was the first coloured man to become an engine driver on the Trinidad Government Railway. That was some seventy years ago. Before that the engineers were all white men, that is to say, men from England, and coloured men could rise no higher than fireman. But Josh had had a severe training. He came from Barbados at the age of sixteen, which must have been somewhere around 1868. He began as an apprentice in the shed where the new locomotives were assembled and the old ones repaired, and he learnt the business from the ground up. Then he would go out on odd jobs and later he became a regular fireman on the engines between San Fernando and Princes Town. This proved to be a stroke of luck. His run was over a very difficult piece of track and when the white engine driver retired, or more probably died suddenly, there arose the question of getting someone who understood its special difficulties. That was the type of circumstance in those days which gave the local coloured man his first opportunity, and Josh was appointed. He took his job seriously and, unless something had actually broken, whenever his engine stopped he refused to have it towed into the shed but went under and fixed it himself.

Josh was a card. In 1932 I went to say goodbye before I left for England. He was nearing eighty and we had lunch surrounded by the results of his latest marriage, some six or seven children ranging from sixteen years to about six. After lunch he put me through my paces. I had been writing cricket journalism in the newspapers for some years and had expressed some casual opinions, I believe, on the probable composition of the West Indies team to visit England in 1933. Josh expressed disagreement with my views and I took him lightly at first. But although in all probability he hadn't seen a cricket match for some thirty years, it soon turned out that he had read practically every article I had written and remembered them; and as he had read the other newspapers and also remembered those, I soon had to get down to it, as if I were at a selection-committee meeting. Apart from half a century, the only difference between us that afternoon was that in his place I would have had the quoted papers to hand, all marked up in pencil.

I had never seen nor heard of any racial or national consciousness in Josh. He was a great favourite with everybody, particularly with the white men, managers, engineers and other magnates of the sugar estates. They often travelled between San Fernando and Princes Town on his train and always came up to talk to him. In fact, whenever one of them was talking to Josh, and my mother was anywhere near, Josh was very insistent on her coming up to be introduced, to her own considerable embarrassment and probably to theirs as well. Josh, after all, was a man of inferior status and fifty years ago you did that sort of thing only when you couldn't avoid it. Josh, however, here as elsewhere, was acting with his usual exuberance. And yet there was more to Josh than met the eye.

One Sunday afternoon near the end of the century he was sitting in the gallery of his house in Princes Town when he noticed, from certain peculiarities in the whistles and the smoke from the chimney, that the engines of one of the big sugar-estate factories had failed. Whenever this took place it caused a general crisis. During the season the factories ground cane often twenty hours a day. The cane was cut sometimes miles away and piled on to little open trucks which ran on rails to the factory and emptied on to the moving belt which took it to the grinders. Once the cane was cut, if it was not ground within a certain time, the quality of the juice deteriorated. So that if the big engines stopped and were not repaired pretty quickly the whole process was thrown out of gear, and if the break continued the cutters for miles around had to be signalled to stop cutting, and they sat around and waited for hours. I have worked on a sugar estate and the engineers, usually Scotsmen, walked around doing nothing for days; but as soon as there was the slightest sign of anything wrong the tension was immediately acute. The manager himself, if not an engineer, was usually a man who understood something about engines. There were always one or two coloured foremen who had no degrees and learnt empirically, but who knew their particular engines inside out. All these worked frantically, like men on a wrecked ship. And if the engine stayed dead too long engineers from other factories around all came hurrying up in order to help. Whenever she (as they called the machinery) came to a stop, and the stop lasted for any length of time, the news spread to all the people in the neighbourhood, and it was a matter of universal excitement and gossip until she started off again.

Well, this afternoon Josh sat in his gallery, knowing pretty well what was going on, when suddenly an open carriage-and-pair drew up in front of the house. He recognized it, for it belonged to the manager of the factory who used to drive it to and from the railway station. The groom jumped down and came in and Josh knew what he wanted before he spoke.

'Mr —— has asked you to come round at once,' said the groom. 'He has sent his carriage for you.'

'All right,' said Josh, 'I'll come.'

He drove over the few miles to the factory, and there they were, the usual assembly of engineers, foremen and visitors, by this time baffled and exhausted, while the factory workers sat around in the yard doing nothing, and in the centre the distracted manager. When Josh drove in everyone turned to him as if he were the last hope, though few could have believed that Josh would be able to get her going.

Now, on his way to the factory Josh may have dug up from his tenacious memory some half-forgotten incident of an engine which would not go, or he may have come to the conclusion that if all of these highly trained and practised engineers were unable to discover what was wrong the probability was that they were overlooking some very simple matter that was under their very noses. Whatever it was, Josh knew what he was about. When the manager invited him to enter the engine room and, naturally, was coming in with him (with all the others crowding behind) Josh stopped and, turning to all of them, said very firmly, 'I would like to go in alone.' The manager looked at him in surprise, but, probably thinking that Josh was one of those who didn't like people around when he was working, and anxious to do anything which might get the engines going again, he agreed. He turned round, told the others to stand back and Josh entered the engine room alone. No one will ever know exactly what Josh did in there, but within two minutes he was out again and he said to the astonished manager, 'I can't guarantee anything, sir, but try and see if she will go now.' The foreman rushed inside, and after a few tense minutes the big wheels started to revolve again.

An enthusiastic crowd, headed by the manager, surrounded Josh, asking him what it was that had performed the miracle. But the always exuberant Josh grew silent for once and refused to say. He never told them. He never told anybody. The obstinate old man wouldn't even tell me. But when I asked him that day, 'Why did you do it?' he said what I had never heard before. 'They were white men with all their MICE and RICE and all their big degrees, and it was their business to fix it. I had to fix it for them. Why should I tell them?'

In my bag already packed was the manuscript of what the next year was published as *The Case for West Indian Self-Government*. I recognized then that Josh was not only my physical but also my spiritual grandfather. The family strains persist. I continue to write about cricket and self-government. Some time ago I saw in a West Indian newspaper that the very week that final decisions were being taken about West

Indian Federation in Jamaica, my younger brother was also in Jamaica, putting finishing touches to the West Indian Football Association. A few years ago he was appointed the chief accountant of Josh's Trinidad Government Railway – as far as I know, the first coloured man to hold that post.

Josh was no Puritan, but when his first wife died early it was noteworthy that he sent my mother to live with some maiden ladies, Wesleyans, who kept a small establishment which they called a convent. Convent it was. As far as I could gather, she was not taught much scholastically, but she gained or developed two things there. We were Anglicans, but from these Wesleyans my mother learnt a moral nonconformism of a depth and rigidity which at times far exceeded Judith's. She was a tall handsome woman of elegant carriage and beautiful clothes, but her principles were such that she forbade my playing any sort of game on Sundays, or even going to hear the band play. I was fascinated by the calypso singers and the sometimes ribald ditties they sang in their tents during carnival time. But, like many of the black middle class, to my mother a calypso was a matter for ne'er-do-wells and at best the common people. I was made to understand that the road to the calypso tent was the road to hell, and there were always plenty of examples of hell's inhabitants to whom she could point. She was not unkind, and before I grew up I understood her attitude better when some neighbours of ours defied the elementary conventions to such a degree that she and my father had to pack my young sister off to stay with our aunts until the temperature cooled down somewhat.

There was, however, another side to my mother which she brought from her convent. She was a reader, one of the most tireless I have ever known. Usually it was novels, any novel. Scott, Thackeray, Dickens, Hall Caine, Stevenson, Mrs Henry Wood, Charlotte Brontë, Charlotte Braeme, Shakespeare (she had her own copy which I read to pieces), Balzac, Nathaniel Hawthorne, a woman called Mrs E. D. E. N. Southworth, Fenimore Cooper, Nat Gould, Charles Garvice, anything and everything, and as she put them down I picked them up. I remember her warning me not to read books by one Victoria Cross, but I found the books hidden in one of her dressers and read them just the same.

My mother's taste in novels was indiscriminate, but I learnt discrimination from my father. He was no reader, except for books connected with his teaching, but as a man of some education he knew who, if not what, the classics were. Our bookseller was an itinerant who came once a fortnight carrying a huge pack on his shoulders. He heaved it off and spread his wares, the *Review of Reviews, Tit-Bits, Comic Cuts, The Strand Magazine, Pearson's Magazine,* sixpenny copies of the classics. '*The Pickwick Papers,*' my father would say, taking up the book. 'By Charles Dickens. A great book, my boy. Read it.' And he would buy it. If he took me to a department store he would do the same. And so I began to have my own collection of books as well as my own bat and balls. But in those magazines, particularly *Pearson's,* appeared, periodically, cricketing stories. There would be also articles on the great cricketers of the day, W. G. Grace, Ranjitsinhji, Victor Trumper, C. B. Fry. My father held forth on W. G. Grace and Ranjitsinhji, but he knew little of the others. I found out for myself. I knew about them before I knew the great cricketers of the island. I read about them from paper to paper, from magazine to magazine. When we moved into Port of Spain, the capital, I read two daily papers and on Sundays the green *Sporting Chronicle* and the red *Sporting Opinion.* I made clippings and filed them. It served no purpose whatever, I had never seen nor heard of anyone doing the like. I spoke to no one about it and no one spoke to me.

Side by side with this obsession was another – Thackeray's *Vanity Fair.* My mother had an old copy with a red cover. I had read it when I was about eight, and of all the books that passed through that house this one became my Homer and my Bible. I read it through from the first page to the last, then started again, read to the end and started again. Whenever I finished a new book I turned to my *Vanity Fair.* For years I had no notion that it was a classic novel. I read it because I wanted to.

So there I was, way out in the West Indies, before I was ten, playing games and running races like other little boys, but almost in secret devoting my immense energies to the accumulation of facts and statistics about Grace and Ranjitsinhji, and reading *Vanity Fair* on the average once every three months. What drew me to it? I don't know, a phrase which will appear often in this book. As I dig into my memory I recall that the earliest books I could reach from the window sill when I had nothing to do, or rain stopped the cricket or there was no cricket, were biblical. There was a series of large brightly coloured religious pamphlets telling the story of Jacob and the Ladder, Ruth and Naomi and so forth. There was a large book called *The Throne of the House of David.* One day somebody must have told me, or I may have discovered it from listening to the lessons being read in church, that these stories could be found in the many Bibles that lay about the house, including the large one with the family births and deaths. Detective-like, I tracked down the originals and must have warmed the souls of my aunts and grandmother as they saw me poring over the Bible. That, I had heard often enough, was a good book. It fascinated me. When the parson read the lessons I strove to remember the names and numbers, second chapter of the Second Book of Kings, the Gospel according to St Matthew, and so on, every Sunday morning. Revd Allen had a fine voice and was a beautiful reader. I would go home and search and read half aloud to myself. (In school I was still fooling about with Standards 1 or 2: 'Johnny's father had a gun and went shooting in the forest.') Somewhere along the way I must have caught the basic rhythms of English prose. My reading was chiefly in the Old Testament and I may have caught, too, some of the stern attitude to life which was all around me, tempered, but only tempered, by family kindness.

I must have found the same rhythms and the same moralism when I came to *Vanity Fair*. Certainly of the lords and ladies and much of the life described, as a West Indian boy of eight, I hadn't the slightest idea. When I later told people how and when I had read the book some were sceptical and even derisive. It was not to me an ordinary book. It was a refuge into which I withdrew. By the time I was fourteen I must have read the book over twenty times and I used to confound boys at school by telling them to open it anywhere, read a few words and I would finish the passage, if not in the exact words at least close enough. I can still do it, though not as consistently and accurately as before.

Me and my clippings and magazines on W. G. Grace, Victor Trumper and Ranjitsinhji, and my *Vanity Fair* and my puritanical view of the world. I look back at the little eccentric and would like to have listened to him, nod affirmatively and pat him on the shoulder. A British intellectual long before I was ten, already an alien in my own environment among my own people, even my own family. Somehow from around me I had selected and fastened on to the things that made a whole. As will soon appear, to that little boy I owe a debt of gratitude.

I find it strange, and the more I think of it the stranger I find it. If the reader does not find it strange then let him consider what has happened since.

When I was ten I went to the Government secondary school, the Queen's Royal College, where opportunities for playing cricket and reading books were thrown wide open to me. When I was fifteen, the editor of the school magazine, a master, asked me to write something for it. Such was my fanaticism that I could find nothing better to write about than an account of an Oxford and Cambridge cricket match played nearly half a century before, the match in which Cobden for Cambridge dismissed three Oxford men in one over to win the match by two runs.

I retold it in my own words as if it were an experience of my own, which indeed it was. The choice was more logical than my next juvenile publication. At the end of term, during the English composition examination, I was very sleepy, probably from reading till the small hours the night before. I looked at the list of subjects, the usual stuff, 'A Day in the Country', etc., etc., including, however, 'The Novel as an Instrument of Reform'. Through the thorough grounding in grammar given me by my father and my incessant reading, I could write a good school composition on anything, and from the time I was about eight my English composition papers usually had full marks, with once every three or four weeks a trifling mistake. I sat looking at the list, not knowing which to choose. Bored with the whole business, I finally wrote each subject on a piece of paper, rolled them, shook them together and picked out one. It was 'The Novel as an Instrument of Reform'. For me it seemed just a subject like any other. But perhaps I was wrong. Literature? Reform? I may have been stimulated. But I drew on my knowledge and my long-ingrained respect for truth and justice, and I must have done very well, for at the beginning of the following term the English master called me and surprised me by telling me that he proposed to print the 'very fine' essay in the school magazine. Still more to my astonishment, when the magazine appeared I was constantly stopped in the street by old boys and the local literati, who congratulated me on what they called 'this remarkable essay'. I prudently kept the circumstances of its origin to myself.

As I say, those were the first two printed articles. Nearly forty years have passed, and very active and varied years they have been. In the course of them I have written a study of the French Revolution in San Domingo and a history of the Communist International. I went to the United States in 1938, stayed there for fifteen years and never saw a cricket match, though I used to read the results of Tests and county matches which the New York Times publishes every day during the season. In 1940 came a crisis in my political life. I rejected the Trotskyist version of Marxism and set about to re-examine and reorganize my view of the world, which was (and remains) essentially a political one. It took more than ten years, but by 1952 I once more felt my feet on solid ground, and in consequence I planned a series of books. The first was published in 1953, a critical study of the writings of Herman Melville as a mirror of our age, and the second is this book on cricket. The first two themes, 'The Novel as an Instrument of Reform' and 'Cobden's Match', have reappeared in the same close connection after forty years. Only after I had chosen my themes did I recognize that I had completed a circle. I discovered that I had not arbitrarily or by accident worshipped at the shrine of John Bunyan and Aunt Judith, of W. G. Grace and Matthew Bondman, of *The Throne of the House of David* and *Vanity Fair*. They were a trinity, three in one and one in three, the Gospel according to St Matthew, Matthew being the son of Thomas, otherwise called Arnold of Rugby.

Laura Thompson

The High Life

Derby night at White City was hot with atmosphere. I feel sorry for Wimbledon, which took over the running of the race in 1985, because no one who ever went to the Derby at White City thinks that anywhere else can *really* stage it. 'Ah,' we say, 'the atmosphere, the elegance, that a terrible day when they closed the place down – bastards – nothing's ever been the same since, has it?' White City connected the Derby with the past in a way that Wimbledon can never do. The racecard was engraved with signifiers of tradition: the trophies named by Major Brown after barely remembered champion dogs of the 1930s, the Fret Not Stakes, the Long Hop Chase, or after the little Olympic runner, the Dorando Marathon. When the dogs paraded around the track before the race, their bodies, iridescent beneath the light, were streaked and shot and shimmering with the ghosts of other greyhounds: Mick the Miller, Pigalle Wonder, dogs who in some unimaginable time had been not myths but had paraded this track, had run this Derby, had inhabited this here-and-now.

White City rose to the occasion of the Derby in the way that those rare greyhounds do. Sporting occasions sometimes feel like a quest for atmosphere: one formulates excitement, watches Mexican waves through a haze of indifference, finally abnegates oneself from all that showing off and self-expression. But some events one falls into head first, helplessly and drunkenly. One knows that they are the real thing. One knows that all present are unified by a tacit comprehension of the significance of the occasion. They do not have to tell themselves that the Derby is an event, they do not have to try to make themselves more important than the Derby in order to make it an event; they *know* that the Derby is what matters, and this knowledge, this willingness to subsume themselves into the event, makes the event significant. These mysteries, these myths, these great traditions, great occasions: one cannot partake of their power by enveloping them in bear-hugs, by French kissing them, by dancing around on top of them and hoping that other people are watching this close congress. The only way in which to partake of them is to submit oneself to them, to be humble with them.

And so, entering White City on Derby night, one knew that one was both partaking of, and contributing to, an event. One was an actor upon a stage, playing a part, swelling a procession, watching one's own performance, watching the piece of theatre that it was helping to create. To attend was to feel the ties that bind: all the dog world was here, celebrating the night on which the greatest greyhounds ran in the greatest race at the greatest stadium; all bowed down before all that greatness. All *wanted* to bow down before it. Their eyes glinted proudly with subservience to the occasion.

Derby night in the restaurant meant black tie and, at the end of June, with the sun flooding painfully through the vast glass frontage, the early part of the evening was always cruelly hot. My first Derby was in 1976; on that night the last part of the evening was hot as well, though in a different, less evil, more exhausting way. The drought and the heatwave had a fearsome hold on the White City restaurant.

But I had wanted to go to that 1976 Derby so much. Since 1960 the race had been shown on television, for as far back as I can remember on *Sportsnight*, when lights like creamy suns melted and burned behind a beaming Harry Carpenter – *he* knew it was an event – but for some reason I didn't see the 1975 final. Perhaps it was ousted from the television by a friendly football match – England versus the Faeroe Islands or some such, but at about seven the next morning I was in my parents' bedroom demanding a result. 'If I give you five guesses, you won't get it,' said my father, which was ridiculous, because it was a five-dog race and anyway he'd given it away with that answer. Clearly, the dog that could not win had won. 'Tartan Khan!' I said, bouncing around gleefully, asking for details of starting prices (25/1), did my parents back the dog (no), how had he won the race (easily), what had happened to all the other dogs that were supposedly so much better than he (they weren't). The romance, the *wit*, of this win by Tartan Khan strengthened my desire for complicity in this occasion.

The 1975 final had been thought to belong to Myrtown, the odds-on favourite who had run second in 1974; but these races are not run to a preordained scenario, they are shockingly, staggeringly of the here-and-now. And this here-and-now had been shocking and staggering. Only one other dog has ever won the Derby at such long odds (Duleek Dandy won in 1960 at 25/1). If Tartan Khan had been the invention of a storyteller, one would have dismissed him as a foolish fantasy: he had been third in practically every round of the competition, and at the beginning of 1975, White City had asked his trainer to take the dog away from them when he lost eight races in a row. He scarcely won more than twice in his whole racing career. However, the two races that he won were the final of the Derby and the final of the St Leger.

After the first of these wins, every dog man in the country quested for an explanation for the sudden explosion of greatness from this mysterious greyhound. Eventually one was found. Tartan Khan's trainer had, prior to the final, walked him regularly by the railway line at Cheddington (where the Great Train Robbery took place), believing that the noise of the trains would prepare him for the noise of the crowd. Certainly on Derby night the dog had nerves as loose and easy as Ronald Biggs's.

The noise of the crowd, what is called in the dog world the 'Derby roar', does terrorize some greyhounds. It is for them like hitting a wall of sound, built by gamblers. As the dogs parade the track, the wall is being laid in place, brick by brick, welded together by the hunger of the crowd for the occasion that is now almost upon them, oh so near, they can feel it coming, they are being encircled ever more tightly by the waves of its energy, in a few minutes, in a minute, in a few seconds they will hear the words – 'and now the hare's running' – and the encircling waves of energy will constrict them in a vice from which the only release is to shout and shout. When the hare passes by the traps the individual voices of the crowd become one. When the traps open the dogs hit the wall of sound. Some of them balk at it in fear. Some of them crash through it like heroes. Tartan Khan was such a hero.

And the next year I got to the Derby, and sat in one of my ballerina dresses, in heat that beat as intensely as in a summer garden at midday, encircled by waves of energy, my heart jumping a tiny chasm every time I looked at my watch and saw that 10.45 p.m. this evening was becoming first a possibility, then an inevitability. How well I remember that evening – not clearly, but powerfully. What I remember are the pink tables, the bread rolls like big shells, the curls of butter set in ice, the angled sashay of waiters with one arm aloft; the buzz of dog talk made unnaturally electric by the vibrating timbre of each individual voice; the quality of the early evening light outside, promising such a night, such a summer; the quality of the air inside, soggy with heat, watery with electric light, bright, heavy, filmy, trailing cigarette smoke; the slow building of the wall of sound; the slow encroachment of the floodlights upon the sun; Mutt's Silver, the 6/1 winner of the Derby final, dropping to the ground like a boneless puppy and rolling luxuriously upon his pristine victor's coat; the occasion playing upon the terraces, the bars, the restaurant and The Box as if it were a strong and gentle hand, strumming the strings of a guitar and leaving them separate, tensile, reverberating and harmonious.

When it was there, it seemed as if it would be there for ever. I regret intensely the fact that I scarcely bothered to go to White City after my last Derby there in 1980; but I know that if I had never gone there at all then it would be almost impossible to write this book, ignorant as I would be of this place whose high definition, whose easy grandeur, whose self-possession and self-assurance were at the heart of greyhound racing: the proud, and now buried, heart. Nor should I have in my possession the two vital codewords which can unite the most disparate band of dog people. Say that you went to White City, that you saw the Derby there, that you owned greyhounds there – and that's it, you are in. At the sound of the two codewords, hardened dog men relent and relax. Understanding, of a shared past, of shared priorities, flashes dimly but indestructibly. One day I may meet a dog man who does not respond to the code: 'I always hated the bloody place,' he will say, 'give me Walthamstow any day.' But he will be as rare a creature as a Derby winner. White City has become an icon, a temple, a touchstone. To the dog men its obliteration caused a pain as inexpressibly deep as the razing of Lord's would cause to a cricket lover; except that Lord's would be mourned and eulogized by a world beyond cricket, and White City never has been. White City *was* the world, but those who never went there never knew it.

Charles Sprawson

Haunts of the Black Masseur

It was, though, in 1956, from a chance reading of a report in *The Times*
when a very junior boy at school, that I first became aware of a
Homeric dimension to swimming. It was the year of the Melbourne
Games. At the time Australian men and women dominated every
stroke, and every day news came through of some record broken. Their
outstanding swimmer was Murray Rose. He had already won the 400
metres when they lined up for the start of the longest event, in a race
that brought together in fierce rivalry representatives of the three
leading swimming nations of this century, America, Australia, and
Japan:

> It was the men's 1,500 meres final that drew most attention under the
> arc lights tonight and it proved the outstanding triumph of all the
> Australian swimmers. Two days ago Breen from America, immensely
> strong but with an ugly style, had depressed the supporters of the
> English-born Rose by the impressive way in which he beat the latter's
> world record by nearly seven seconds in his heat. On that occasion
> Breen went out in front of his comparatively poor opposition after 50
> metres and stayed ahead of the record schedule all the way. It was feared
> that tonight he would burn off the slender, seemingly less strong Rose
> in the first 800 metres but, as it happened, Breen could never break
> away from the close attentions of the young Australian and Yamanaka.
>
> It was even more tense than usual at the start as the eight finalists
> crouched forward on their starting stands and then the gun, as shocking
> as ever in this great echoing hall, sent them swooping away in racing
> dives. Breen off best and touching for the first time half a length ahead
> of Yamanaka with Rose only inches behind in third place. After eight
> laps (400 metres) these three had broken away from the others and the
> time was 4 min. 36.6 sec., nearly four seconds ahead of Breen's world
> record schedule on Wednesday. Just after 800 metres, with the time now
> one and a half seconds behind the world record, Rose, who had been
> lying nicely poised, smoothly went into the lead and from then on was
> never led again. Breen kept thrashing along just behind in his ungainly
> way for another six laps and then Rose went away from him by a length.
> At 1,200 metres Yamanaka had overtaken Breen for second place and

then, as the American began to slip back, started to make ground on Rose. With two laps to go Rose was two lengths in front but Yamanaka was overhauling him rapidly and the last lap was swum to a great roar of encouragement, on one side from Australian spectators and wild cries from the other from feverishly excited Japanese supporters and journalists. It was Rose who had swum the most intelligent race, however, and it was he who eventually got home fairly comfortably, though another length would have given a different result.

As I searched through back numbers of *The Times* thirty-five years later and read again the account, I wondered why it had made such an impression at the time. I had never in my life so much as glanced at *The Times*, and it was the only newspaper to describe the race at length. In fact no other paper mentioned it at all. I knew no other boy in the school would have read the report, or if they had, reacted with any interest. Perhaps it was the air of distinction lent by *The Times*, the fact that it endorsed and reflected an arcane obsession on my part that was impossible to communicate, as it was to a large extent the product of a childhood and experiences that were essentially different. At an age when one looks out for heroes, I was drawn to the determined performance of Rose, poised and smooth, 'slender, seemingly less strong', flanked by two rugged and uncompromising competitors, a David among Goliaths. I admired too the softness of his name, his cool intelligence, the quiet control he seemed to exert from the start, his graceful easy style. He was swimming, I was to learn later, in conditions that he favoured, by night in a floodlit pool.

Four years on I happened to switch on the television late one night during the Rome Olympics, and there on the speckled screen was the faintly discernible figure of Rose, gripping the rails in emerging modestly from the pool after having won another gold medal. He was not one to punch the air in triumph. Blond and classically built, he seemed to me, as a mawkish adolescent lately returned from my first visit to the museums of Greece, everything I was not. 'Don't worry,' I remember my mother remarking without much conviction, 'perhaps you have more brains.' Rose's mother was to write that his most prized possessions as a boy were his 'much worn' books by Ancient Greek writers. 'These he studied and thought about constantly,' while she brought him up on a diet of seaweed, sesame, and sunflower seeds, to imbue him with the 'Greek reverence for a disciplined mind and a perfected physique.'

On a recent visit to Los Angeles I was amazed to hear from Richard

Lamparski, a popular chronicler of the declining fortunes of Hollywood
stars, that Rose was living there, in fact just down the road from him.
Now married to an ex-principal dancer of the Joffrey Ballet, he had
been awarded a scholarship by USC after his Olympic triumphs, where
he had taken the part of Hamlet in a college production, then played
some minor roles in the 'beach' films of the early 60s. We arranged to
meet for a game of squash and a swim in the venerable Los Angeles
Athletic Club, among the office blocks and skyscrapers of the downtown area. After a frantic game I left him to swim for an hour, then
proposed a four-length race. He had eyed me swimming and realized I
would present no challenge, so he just stood casually in the shallows
and motioned me to start whenever I liked. He would follow. At the
halfway mark I might almost have been ahead, but then he just glided
in front with his graceful, effortless style and won easily. So he should
have. American coaches described him as the greatest swimmer there
has ever been, greater even than Weissmuller. Only recently he had
been swimming faster times than he had in the Olympics. He still
looked much as he did in his prime, and I noticed he had the long
hands and feet that all the best swimmers seem to possess.

We went on for a meal to the garden of Butterfields, once the home
of Errol Flynn, on the corner of Sunset and Olive. Rose no longer
adhered to seaweed, sesame, and sunflower seeds. Among the orange
trees he talked quietly about his early memories as a boy in Australia,
when he swam in the Manly reservoir, the natural pool on Bondi
Beach, where the waves came over the sides as he raced and propelled
him to extraordinary fast times in one direction. The most intense
experiences were early morning bathes in Sydney Harbour, where the
water was smooth, its texture silky, when swimming seemed like an
'adventure into a different world', particularly during Christmas when
the swollen 'King' tides rolled in from the Pacific. It was in these
conditions that he felt he had swum his fastest times, with a sense of
exhilaration that he never quite experienced in a man-made pool. For
Rose swimming was an intensely sensuous involvement, a rhythmic
succession of sounds as the hands cut through the water that passed
under the body and formed a wave against the side of the face. Rhythm
reduces effort. Before a race he would listen to particular music that
was close to the rhythm of his stroke. Glenn Miller's 'In the Mood'
coincided exactly.

The principal quality, he continued, demanded of a swimmer is a
'feel for water'. He should use his arms and legs as a fish its fins, and

be able to feel the pressure of the water on his hands, to hold it in his palm as he pulls the stroke through without allowing it to slip through his fingers. Rose believed that like water-diviners, only those succeed who have a natural affinity for it. Sometimes water can become an obsession, as in the case of Rick de Mont, a beautiful stylist who won a gold medal in 1972, only for it to be taken away when traces of a drug were found in his system that had been prescribed by the team doctor for asthma. Now he lives in Tucson, on the edge of the Arizona desert, and devotes himself to a 'spiritual quest for water'. He can sense like a diviner where desert streams are likely to appear suddenly after rain, and records their momentary presence in watercolour. Large oil paintings, inspired by dreams, reveal dim shapes of prehistoric fish swimming through jungle rivers. He loves the sound of water, the feel of it on his hands and legs. For de Mont, the streams and dreams 'force' interpretation.

In order to intensify this feel for water, Australian swimmers of the 50s started shaving down their legs before important races. The idea spread to America in 1960 when Rose moved to Los Angeles. American swimmers began to shave, as well as their legs, their arms, chests and heads. Minutes were knocked off times over the longer distances. It was not so much the elimination of the hundreds of minute air-bubbles which cling to hair and slow down movement that counted as its psychological effect. Rose described the immediate sensual awareness of water as he dived in, the feeling that he was suspended, united with the element, the sudden surge of power like that experienced by ballet dancers who remove their hair to activate their nerve-endings. When a swimmer achieves a good time, the first question invariably asked is 'shaved or unshaved?' The problem then arises of how often shaving is possible. If one can delay it till after trials or preliminary heats, it then becomes a psychological advantage over one's rival. Shaving has become a complex science. The secret is not to overdo the shaving or the thrill is lost, to restrain the shaves so more hair comes off when required. Before a race some swimmers are observed rubbing their hands on the rough matting of diving-boards, in the way that a safe-cracker sands the tips of his fingers to increase their sensitivity. The East German women took shaving a stage further when they adopted the 'skin suit', made from a single layer of stretch nylon that appeared to be glued to the body. At first embarrassed television cameramen would only film them from the neck up, but now they are universally accepted. The Australian Dawn Fraser claimed she could have broken every record in the book if allowed to swim naked. Nudity originated in the Greek Olympics when Orsippus dropped his loincloth and was seen to gain a distinct advantage thereby.

Olympic swimmers are subject to conditions unique to them. They remain isolated in their lanes. There is no convergence or contact as with runners. Chance plays a considerable part even at the highest level. A swimmer can be far ahead at the finish, yet mistime his final stroke, or be drawn in a lane where he is forced to breathe on his 'wrong' side up the final length. A photograph from 1936 shows the Japanese Uto well ahead towards the finish, yet losing to the lunging American outside him. If a swimmer can remain on his rival's hip, he can be carried along in his surge, inherit the other's momentum, and also act as an anchor on the man in front. 'I just surfed in on his wake,' was Armstrong's answer to reporters who wondered how he had ever beaten Biondi.

Nor are the physiques of swimmers like those of other athletes. The best swimmers rarely excel at other sports, as their bodies are too finely tuned to adapt. A swimmer's muscles are long and pliable. 'You can't do anything violently or suddenly in water,' observed Bachrach, the great Chicago coach of the 20s, 'it even takes time for a stone to sink. Things must be done with relaxation and undulation like that of a snake.' From observing the superior speed of long slim fish like the sandpike and pickerel, he looked for 'snaky' swimmers and felt he had found the perfect streamlined form in the elastic Weissmuller.

Bachrach insisted that in swimming one must ignore rivals: 'In most sports they have a physical effect on your performance, in swimming only psychological. If you worry about what your rival is doing, you take your mind off what you are doing and so fail to concentrate on your performance.' Once the swimmer hits the water he is his own man and immune from outside influence, but before the race begins much can be done to disturb his state of mind. Even the way a swimmer acknowledges the crowd and removes his tracksuit by the starting blocks can be significant. 'I was scared,' remarked a fellow-finalist when confronted by Gross, 'this monster of a guy swings his arms in your face. I tried not to look at him before the race, he's such a dominating figure.' The changing room is a particularly emotional area. One Australian used to sit in front of her principal rival and just stare into her eyes. Schollander describes how before one Olympic semi-final he broke the nerve of the Frenchman Gottvalles, the world record holder, by moving gradually closer to him on the bench as they changed, then when in desperation Gottvalles dashed to the urinal, Schollander followed and stood behind him waiting although there were others free.

Bachrach was aware of various 'mental hazards, psychology kinks' among his leading swimmers in Chicago, who held almost all the world records in the 20s. There were many, he felt, who might be real champions, 'if only they could straighten out those kinks'. The swimmer's solitary training, the long hours spent semi-submerged, induces a lonely, meditative state of mind. Much of a swimmer's training takes place inside his head, immersed as he is in a continuous dream of a world under water.

Harold Pinter

Hutton and the Past

Hardstaff and Simpson at Lord's. Notts. versus Middlesex. 1946 or
1947. After lunch Keeton and Harris had opened for Notts. Keeton
swift, exact, interested; Harris Harris. Harris stonewalled five balls in
the over for no particular reason. Keeton and Harris gave Notts. a fair
start. Stott at number three, smacked the ball hard, was out in the early
afternoon. Simpson joined Hardstaff. Both very upright in their stance.
They surveyed the field, surveyed themselves, began to bat.

The sun was strong, but calm. They settled into the afternoon, no
hurry, all in order. Hardstaff clipped to midwicket. They crossed.
Simpson guided the ball between mid-off and the bowler. They
crossed. Their cross was a trot, sometimes a walk, they didn't need
to run. They placed their shots with precision, they knew where they
were going. Bareheaded. Hardstaff golden. Simpson dark. Hardstaff
off-drove, silently, Simpson to deep square leg. Simpson cut. Hardstaff
cut, finer. Simpson finer. The slips, Robertson, Bennett, attentive.
Hardstaff hooked, immaculate, no sound. They crossed, and back.
Deep square leg in the heat after it. Jim Sims on at the pavilion end
with leg-breaks. Hardstaff wristed him into the covers. Simpson to fine
leg. Two. Sims twisting. Hardstaff wristed him into the covers, through
the covers, fielder wheeling, for four. Quite unhurried. Seventy in
ninety minutes. No explosions. Batsmanship. Hardstaff caught at slip,
off Sims.

Worrell and Weekes at Kingston on Thames. 1950. The Festival.
Headley had flicked, showed what had been and what remained of
himself, from the 30s. Worrell joined Weekes with an hour to play.
Gladwin and Jackson bowling. Very tight, very crisp, just short of a
length, jolting, difficult. Worrell and Weekes scored ninety before close
of play. No sixes, nothing off the ground. Weekes smashed, red-eyed,
past cover, smashed to long leg, at war, met Gladwin head on, split
midwicket in two, steel. Worrell wanted to straight drive to reach his
fifty. Four men at the sight-screen to stop him. He straight drove,
pierced them, reached his fifty. Gladwin bowled a stinging ball, only
just short, on middle and leg. Only sensible course was to stop it.

Worrell jumped up, both feet off, slashed it from his stomach, square cut for four, boundary first bounce.

MCC versus Australians. Lord's 1948. Monday. On the Saturday the Australians had plastered the MCC bowling, Barnes 100, Bradman just short. On Monday morning Miller hit Laker for five sixes into the Tavern. The Australians passed 500 and declared. The weather darkened. MCC 30 minutes batting before lunch. The Australians came into the field chucking the ball hard at each other, broad, tall, sure. Hutton and Robertson took guard against Lindwall and Miller. Robertson caught Tallon off Miller. Lindwall and Miller very fast. The sky black. Edrich caught Tallon off Miller. Last ball before lunch. MCC 20 for 2.

After lunch the Australians, arrogant, jocular, muscular, larking down the pavilion steps. They waited, hurling the ball about, eight feet tall. Two shapes behind the pavilion glass. Frozen before emerging a split second. Hutton and Compton. We knew them to be the two greatest English batsmen. Down the steps together, out to the middle. They played. The Australians quieter, wary, tight. Bradman studied them. They stayed together for an hour before Compton was out, and M. P. Donnelly, and Hutton, and the Australians walked home.

First Test at Trent Bridge. The first seven in the English batting order: Hutton, Washbrook, Edrich, Compton, Hardstaff, Barnett, Yardley. They'll never get them out, I said. At lunch on the first day, England 78 for 8.

Hutton.

England versus New Zealand 1949. Hutton opened quietly, within himself, setting his day in order. At the first hour England 40 for none. Hutton looking set for a score. Burtt, slow left hand, took the ball at the Nursery end, tossed it up. To his first ball Hutton played a superb square drive to Wallace at deep point. Wallace stopped it. The crowd leaned in. Burtt again. Hutton flowed into another superb square drive to Wallace's right hand. Wallace stopped it. Back to the bowler. Burtt again, up. Hutton, very hard a most brilliant square drive to Wallace's left hand. Wallace stopped it. Back to the bowler. The crowd. Burtt in, bowled. Hutton halfway up the pitch immediately, driving straight. Missed it. Clean bowled. On his heel back to the pavilion.

Hutton was never dull. His bat was part of his nervous system. His play was sculptured. His forward defensive stroke was a complete statement. The handle of his bat seemed electric. Always, for me, a sense of his vulnerability, of a very uncommon sensibility. He never just went through the motions, nothing was glibly arrived at. He was never, for me, as some have defined him, simply a 'master technician'. He attended to the particular but rarely lost sight of the context in which it took place. But one day in Sydney he hit 37 in twenty-four minutes and was out last ball before lunch when his bat slipped in hitting a further 4, when England had nothing to play for but a hopeless draw, and he's never explained why he did *that*. I wasn't there to see it and probably regret that as much as anything. But I wasn't surprised to hear about it, because every stroke he made surprised me.

I heard about Hutton's 37 on the radio. Seven a.m. Listened to every morning of the 1946/47 series. Alan McGilray talking. Always England six wickets down and Yardley 35 not out. But it was in an Irish kitchen in County Galway that, alone, I heard Edrich and Compton in 1953 clinch the Ashes for England.

Those were the days of Bedser and Wright, Evans, Washbrook and Gimblett, M. P. Donnelly, Smailes and Bowes, A. B. Sellers, Voce and Charlie Barnett, S. M. Brown and Jim Sims, Mankad, Mushtaq Ali, Athol Rowan, even H. T. Bartlett, even Hammond and certainly Bradman.

One morning at drama school I pretended illness and pale and shaky walked into Gower Street. Once round the corner I jumped on a bus and ran into Lord's at the Nursery end to see through the terraces Washbrook late cutting for 4, the ball skidding towards me. That beautiful evening Compton made 70.

But it was 1950 when G. H. G. Doggart missed Walcott at slip off Edrich and Walcott went on to score 165, Gomez with him. Christiani was a very good fielder. Ramadhin and Valentine had a good season. Hutton scored 202 not out against them and against Goddard bowling breakbacks on a bad wicket at the Oval.

It was 1949 when Bailey caught Wallace blindingly at still mid-on. And when was it I watched Donnelly score 180 for the Gents versus Players? He went down the afternoon with his lightning pulls.

Constantine hitting a 6 over fine leg into the pavilion. Talk of a schoolboy called May.

Roddy Doyle

Charlie Cooke

There was a boy a few years older than me who used to go from back door to back door swapping comics. There was a knock on the door; you could see him through the glass. His ears were the giveaway. 'Any swaps?' he'd say. He did it every week, like the insurance man or the milkman. He was a Spurs supporter. When he was asked what he wanted to be when he grew up the answer was quick and always the same. 'Pat Jennings.' He didn't want to be like Pat Jennings, the goalkeeper from Newry with the foot-long hands and the Apache chin and haircut. He wanted to *be* Pat Jennings. We laughed, but I understood.

When I was eleven I wanted to be Charlie Cooke.

'Osgood. Now Hutchinson. Cooke! . . . And OsGOOD!. . .

Charlie Cooke played for Chelsea. My team. I'd chosen them because everyone else followed Leeds or Manchester United, and because my best friend followed them. I went through a lot of best friends then; the Chelsea supporter lasted two weeks and four days. I stayed loyal to Chelsea after I'd dumped him and he'd dumped me. We didn't support teams: we followed them. 'Who do you follow?' 'Chelsea.' 'Crap.' In fact, I followed them nowhere. I'd never been to London; I'd never been anywhere except Wexford and Kerry. I'd never been inside a football stadium. I hadn't even walked past one. But I was stuffed with football. Chelsea came out my ears; I left Chelsea stains on everything I touched. I had a Chelsea scarf. My mother'd knitted it for me. The blue wasn't quite right but it didn't matter; it was a Chelsea scarf, the only one in Kilbarrack. Someone in the school yard tried to pull it off me. It scorched the back of my neck; the skin was crispy back there for days after. All for Chelsea. I could name the team and the subs. I knew their dates of birth. I knew how much they'd cost. I knew the names of their wives and children. I could put my hand over the top of the team photograph on the bedroom wall and tell all the names by the shape of their legs. Ian Hutchinson cost £5,000. Peter Bonetti was born in Putney. Charlie Cooke was five foot eight.

Charlie Cooke.

Charlie Cooke was a winger. He was brilliant. He was a genius. He was as good as Georgie Best and he didn't mess around with women. He was five foot eight, twelve stone two. He came from Fife. He was born there on the 14th of October, 1942. 'He was a wonderful dribbler,' it says in *Chelsea: A Complete Record* by Scott Cheshire, 'often leaving a series of bemused opponents in his wake.' It's true; it was like that. Often, the opponents were bemused before he even got to them. They just let him trot by.

'Osgood. Now Hutchinson. Cooke!'

He was five foot eight. He made himself look smaller; modesty and cunning. It was the height I wanted to be; I'd be happy if I reached it. I was eleven and just over five foot. I thought I could make it. His hair was long but not that long; it was a length mothers didn't object to, my mother didn't object to. He was Scottish, I was Irish; both of us weren't English. He'd be thirty-two by the time I was sixteen, and I'd sign apprentice forms for Chelsea. He'd be a big brother to me. I'd clean his boots. We'd share digs. My mother would like him. He'd come to our house for Christmas because his parents were dead. I'd save his life. He'd come to my funeral.

When I played in the back garden I was Charlie Cooke. I walloped a burst ball against the wall. 'Cooke! Yes!' One of my friends commentated on matches while we were playing them on the road. He was very good, very fair – considering he was playing as well. We had to tell him who we were before the start, 'Best.' 'No, I'm Best.' 'You're not; I am.' 'Charlie Cooke,' I'd say, always. No one minded. He was mine. I was him. I missed a sitter. 'Oh, no!' I said it with a Scottish accent. 'And, my word,' said the commentator, 'Charlie Cooke holds his head in despair.' I missed a lot of sitters. That was the difference between me and Charlie Cooke: he was brilliant and I was shite. I was good at holding my head in despair. I practised it.

Chelsea played Leeds in the FA Cup Final in 1970. The first match was a 2–2 draw. The replay was eighteen days – ages – later, on a Wednesday night. I prayed for bad weather. Good weather meant high pressure and bad television reception. The day stayed cloudy and mucky for me. I got my homework out of the way. I couldn't eat my dinner. I sat in front of the telly with my scarf ready, a one-man terrace. For most of the game Chelsea were 1–0 down. It was going to stay that way; I felt it crawling through me. I was very tired and cold. Then—

'Osgood. Now Hutchinson. Cooke! . . . And OsGOOD . . .!'

Hutchinson stepped over the ball, Osgood kept running, Cooke took the ball and chipped – it took for ever – and Osgood dived and headed, and they'd scored. I ran out into the garden; the house wasn't big enough for me. They were going to win; they were going to win.

They won.

My father shook my hand. He congratulated me. 'Well done, old son.' I'd won the FA Cup. It was one of the great moments of my life. I still think that. Made by Charlie Cooke.

He left Chelsea for Crystal Palace in 1972, came back and left again in 1976. He ended his career playing for American teams called Los Angeles Aztecs, Memphis Rogues and – this one really upsets me – California Surf. I hate to think of him playing on the beach, watched by the cast of *Baywatch*.

'Yo, Charlie!' 'Way to go, Charlie-ie-ie!'

Jesus.

I don't know where Charlie Cooke is now. I hope he's well. I hope he's twelve stone two. I hope he's still leaving bemused opponents in his wake.

FANS' NOTES

Roger Angell

The Silence

July 1981

Last week my wife and I came uptown late one night in a cab after having dinner with friends of ours in the Village. We wheeled through the warm and odorous light-strewn summer dark on the same northward route home we have followed hundreds of times over the years, I suppose: bumping and lurching up Sixth nonstop, with the successive gateways of staggered green lights magically opening before us, and the stately tall streetlights (if you tipped your head back on the cab seat and watched them upside down through the back window of the cab: I had drunk a bit of wine) forming a narrowing golden archway astern; and then moving more quietly through the swerves and small hills of the Park, where the weight and silence of the black trees wrapped us in a special summer darkness. The cab driver had his radio on, and the blurry sounds of the news—the midnight news, I supposed—passed over us there in the back seat, mixing with the sounds of the wind coming in through the open cab windows, and the motion of our ride, and the whole sense of city night. All was as always, I mean, except that now it came to me, unsurprisingly at first but then with a terrific jolt of unhappiness and mourning, that this radio news was altered for there was no baseball in it. Without knowing it, I had been waiting for those other particular sounds, for that other part of the summer night, but it was missing, of course—no line scores, no winning and losing pitchers, no homers and highlights, no records approached or streaks cut short, no "Meanwhile, over in the National League," no double-zip early innings from Anaheim or Chavez Ravine, no Valenzuela and no Rose, no Goose and no Tom, no Yaz, no Mazz, no nothing.

The strike by this time was more than a week old, and I had so far sustained the shock of it and the change of it with more fortitude and patience than I had expected of myself. The issues seemed far removed from me—too expensive or too complicated, for some reason, for me to hold them clearly in my mind for long, although I am an attentive and patient fan. I would wait, then, with whatever composure I could find, until it was settled, days or weeks from now, and in some fashion or other I would fill up the empty eveningtimes and morningtimes I had once spent (I did not say "wasted;" would never say "wasted") before the tube and with the sports pages. It might even be better for me to do without baseball for a while, although I could not imagine why. All this brave nonsense was knocked out of me in an instant, there in the cab, and suddenly the loss of that murmurous little ribbon of baseball-by-radio, the ordinary news of the game, seemed to explain a lot of things about the much larger loss we fans are all experiencing because of the strike. The refrain of late-night baseball scores; the sounds of the televised game from the next room (the room empty, perhaps, for the moment, but the game running along in there just the same and quietly waiting for us to step in and rejoin it when we are of a mind to); the mid-game mid-event from some car or cab that pulls up beside us for a few seconds in traffic before the light changes; the baseball conversation in the elevator that goes away when two men get off together at the eleventh floor, taking the game with them; the flickery white fall of light on our hands and arms and the scary sounds of the crowd that suddenly wake us up, in bed or in the study armchair where we have fallen asleep, with the set and the game still on—all these streams and continuities, it seems to me, are part of the greater, riverlike flow of baseball. No other sport, I think, conveys anything like this sense of cool depth and fluvial steadiness, and when you stop for a minute and think about the game it is easy to see why this should be so. The slow, inexorable progression of baseball events—balls and strikes, outs and innings, batters stepping up and batters being retired, pitchers and sides changing on the field, innings turning into games and games into series, and all these merging and continuing, in turn, in the box scores and the averages and the slowly fluctuous standings—are what make the game quietly and uniquely satisfying. Baseball flows past us all through the summer—it is one of the reasons that summer exists—and wherever we happen to stand on its green banks we can sense with only a glance across its shiny expanse that the long, unhurrying swirl and down-flowing have their own purpose and direction, that the river is headed, in its own sweet time, toward a downsummer broadening and debouchment and to its end in the estuary of October.

River people, it is said, count on the noises and movement of nearby water, even without knowing it, and feel uneasy and unaccountably diminished if they must move away for a while and stay among plains inhabitants. That is almost the way it is for us just now, but it is worse than that, really, because this time it is the river that has gone away—just stopped—and all of us who live along these banks feel a fretful sense of loss and a profound disquiet over the sudden cessation of our reliable old stream. The main issue of the baseball strike, I have read, concerns the matter of compensation for owners who have lost a player to free-agency, but when this difficulty is resolved and the two sides come to an agreement (as they will someday), what compensation can ever be made to us, the fans, who are the true owners and neighbors and keepers of the game, for this dry, soundless summer and for the loss of our joy?

Frederick Exley

A Fan's Notes

On the subway going up to the Polo Grounds, I was remembering that meeting and contemplating the heavy uneasiness of it all anew when suddenly, feeling myself inordinately cramped, I looked up out of my reverie to discover that the car was jammed and that I had somehow got smack among the members of a single family—an astonishing family, a family so incredible that for the first time in my life I considered the possibility of Norman Rockwell's not being lunatic. They were a father, a mother, a girl about fifteen, and a boy one or two years younger than she. All were dressed in expensive-looking camel's-hair coats; each carried an item that designated him a fan— the father two soft and brilliantly plaid wool blankets, the mother a picnic basket, the girl a half-gallon thermos, and the boy a pair of field glasses, strung casually about his neck—each apparently doing his bit to make the day a grand success. What astonished me, though, was the almost hilarious similarity of their physical appearance: each had brilliant auburn hair; each had even, startlingly white teeth, smilingly exposed beneath attractive snub noses; and each of their faces was liberally sprinkled with great, outsized freckles. The total face they presented was one of overwhelming and wholesome handsomeness. My first impulse was to laugh. Had I not felt an extreme discomfort caused by the relish they took in each other's being—their looks seemed to smother each other in love—and the crowdedness that had caused me to find myself wedged among them, separating them, I might have laughed. I felt not unlike a man who eats too fast, drinks too much, occasionally neglects his teeth and fingernails, is given to a pensive scratching of his vital parts, lets rip with a not infrequent fart, and wakes up one morning to find himself smack in the middle of a *Saturday Evening Post* cover, carving the goddam Thanksgiving turkey for a family he has never seen before. What was worse, they were aware of my discomfort; between basking in each other's loveliness they would smile apologetically at me, as though in crowding about me they were aware of having aroused me from my reverie and were sorry for it. Distressed, I felt I ought to say something—"I'm sorry I'm alive" or something—so I said the first thing that came to my mind. It was a lie occasioned by my reverie, one which must have sounded very stupid indeed.

"I know Steve Owen," I said.

"Really!" they all chimed in high and good-natured unison. For some reason I got the impression that they had not the foggiest notion of what I had said. We all fell immediately to beaming at each other and nodding deferentially—a posture that exasperated me to the point where I thought I must absolutely say something else. Hoping that I could strike some chord in them that would relieve the self-consciousness we all were so evidently feeling, I spoke again.

"I know Frank Gifford, too."

"Really!" came their unabashed reply. Their tone seemed so calculated to humor me that I was almost certain they were larking with me. Staring at them, I couldn't be sure; and we all fell back to smiling idiotically and nodding at each other. We did this all the way to the Bronx where, disembarking, I lost contact with them—for the moment at least—and felt much relieved.

It seems amazing to me now that while at USC, where Gifford and I were contemporaries, I never saw him play football; that I had to come three thousand miles from the low, white, smog-enshrouded sun that hung perpetually over the Los Angeles Coliseum to the cold, damp, and dismal Polo Grounds to see him perform for the first time; and that I might never have had the urge that long-ago Sunday had I not once on campus had a strange, unnerving confrontation with him. The confrontation was caused by a girl, though at the time of the encounter I did not understand *what* girl. I had transferred from Hobart College, a small, undistinguished liberal arts college in Geneva, New York, where I was a predental student, to USC, a large, undistinguished university in Los Angeles, where I became an English major. The transition was not unnatural. I went out there because I had been rejected by a girl, my first love, whom I loved beyond the redeeming force of anything save time. Accepting the theory of distance as time, I put as much of it between the girl and myself as I could. Once there, though, the prospect of spending my days gouging at people's teeth and whiffing the intense, acidic odour of decay—a profession I had chosen with no stronger motive than keeping that very girl in swimming suits and tennis shorts: she had (and this, sadly, is the precise extent of my memory of her) the most breath-taking legs I had

ever seen—seemed hideous, and I quite naturally became an English
major with a view to reading The Books, The Novels, and The Poems,
those pat reassurances that other men had experienced rejection and
pain and loss. Moreover, I accepted the myth of California the
Benevolent and believed that beneath her warm skies I would find
surcease from my pain in the person of some lithe, fresh-skinned, and
incredibly lovely blonde coed. Bearing my rejection like a disease, and
like a man with a frightfully repugnant and contagious leprosy, I was
unable to attract anything as healthy as the girl I had in mind.

Whenever I think of the man I was in those days, cutting across the
neat-cropped grass of the campus, burdened down by the weight of
the books in which I sought the consolation of other men's grief, and
burdened further by the large weight of my own bitterness, the whole
vision seems a nightmare. There were girls all about me, so near and
yet so out of reach, a pastel nightmare of honey-blonde, pink-lipped,
golden-legged, lemon-sweatered girls. And always in this horror, this
gaggle of femininity, there comes the vision of another girl, now only a
little less featureless than all the rest. I saw her first on one stunning
spring day when the smog had momentarily lifted, and all the world
seemed hard bright blue and green. She came across the campus
straight at me, and though I had her in the range of my vision for
perhaps a hundred feet, I was only able, for the fury of my heart, to
give her five or six frantic glances. She had the kind of comeliness—
soft, shoulder-length chestnut hair; a sharp beauty mark right at her
sensual mouth; and a figure that was like a swift, unexpected blow to
the diaphragm—that to linger on makes the beholder feel obscene. I
wanted to look. I couldn't look. I had to look. I could give her only the
most gaspingly quick glances. Then she was by me. Waiting as long as
I dared, I turned and she was gone.

From that day forward I moved about the campus in a kind of
vertigo, with my right eye watching the sidewalk come up to meet my
anxious feet, and my left eye clacking in a wild orbit, all over and
around its socket, trying to take in the entire campus in frantic split
seconds, terrified that I might miss her. On the same day that I found
out who she was I saw her again. I was standing in front of Founders'
Hall talking with T., a gleaming-toothed, hand-pumping fraternity
man with whom I had, my first semester out there, shared a room. We
had since gone our separate ways; but whenever we met we always
passed the time, being bound together by the contempt with which we
viewed each other's world and by the sorrow we felt at really rather

liking each other, a condition T. found more difficult to forgive in himself than I did.

"*That?*" he asked in profound astonishment to my query about the girl. "*That?*" he repeated dumbly, as if this time—for I was much given to teasing T.—I had really gone too far. "*That,*" he proclaimed with menacing impatience, "*just happens to be Frank Gifford's girl!*"

Never will I forget the contempt he showered on me for asking what to him, and I suppose to the rest of fraternity row, was not only a rhetorical but a dazzlingly asinine question. Nor will I forget that he never did give me the girl's name; the information that she was Gifford's girl was, he assumed, quite enough to prevent the likes of me from pursuing the matter further. My first impulse was to laugh and twit his chin with my finger. But the truth was I was getting a little weary of T. His monumental sense of the rightness of things was beginning to grate on me; shrugging, I decided to end it forever. It required the best piece of acting I've ever been called upon to do; but I carried it off, I think, perfectly.

Letting my mouth droop open and fixing on my face a look of serene vacuousness, I said, "Who's Frank Gifford?"

My first thought was that T. was going to strike me. His hands tensed into fists, his face went the color of fire, and he thrust his head defiantly towards me. He didn't strike, though. Either his sense of the propriety of things overcame him, or he guessed, quite accurately, that I would have knocked him on his ass. All he said, between furiously clenched teeth, was: "*Oh, really, Exley, this has gone too far.*" Turning hysterically away from me, he thundered off. It had indeed gone too far, and I laughed all the way to the saloon I frequented on Jefferson Boulevard, sadly glad to have seen the last of T.

Frank Gifford was an All-America at USC, and I know of no way of describing this phenomenon short of equating it with being the Pope in the Vatican. Our local *L'Osservatore Romano, The Daily Trojan,* was a moderately well-writton college newspaper except on the subject of football, when the tone of the writing rose to an hysterical screech. It reported daily on Gifford's health, one time even imposing upon us the news that he was suffering an upset stomach, leading an irreverent acquaintance of mine to wonder aloud whether the athletic department had heard about "Milk of Magnesia, for Christ's sake." We were, it seems to me in retrospect, treated daily to such breathless items as the variations in his weight, his method of conditioning, the knowledge that he neither smoked nor drank, the humbleness of his beginnings,

and once we were even told the number of fan letters he received daily
from pimply high-school girls in the Los Angeles area. The USC
publicity man, perhaps influenced by the proximity of Hollywood press
agents, seemed overly fond of releasing a head-and-shoulder print
showing him the apparently proud possessor of long, black, perfectly
ambrosial locks that came down to caress an alabaster, colossally
beauteous face, one that would have aroused envy in Tony Curtis.
Gifford was, in effect, overwhelmingly present in the consciousness of
the campus, even though my crowd—the literati—never once to my
knowledge mentioned him. We never mentioned him because his being
permitted to exist at the very university where we were apprenticing
ourselves for Nobel Prizes would have detracted from our environment
and been an admission that we might be better off at an academe more
sympathetic with our hopes. Still, the act of not mentioning him made
him somehow more present than if, like the pathetic nincompoops on
fraternity row, we spent all our idle hours singing his praises. Our
silence made him, in our family, a kind of retarded child about whom
we had tacitly and selfishly agreed not to speak. It seems the only thing
of Gifford's we were spared—and it is at this point we leave his
equation with the Bishop of Rome—was his opinion of the spiritual
state of the USC campus. But I am being unkind now; something
occurred between Gifford and me which led me to conclude that he
was not an immodest man.

Unlike most athletes out there, who could be seen swaggering about
the campus with *Property of USC* (did they never see the ironic,
touching servility of this?) stamped indelibly every place but on their
foreheads, Gifford made himself extremely scarce, so scarce that I only
saw him once for but a few brief moments, so scarce that prior to this
encounter I had begun to wonder if he wasn't some myth created by
the administration to appease the highly vocal and moronic alumni
who were incessantly clamoring for USC's Return to Greatness in, as
the sport writers say, "the football wars." Sitting at the counter of one
of the campus hamburger joints, I was having a cup of chicken noodle
soup and a cheeseburger when it occurred to me that he was one of a
party of three men seated a few stools away from me. I knew without
looking because the other two men were directing all their remarks to
him: "Hey, Frank, how about that?" "Hey, Frank, cha ever hear the one
about ..." It was the kind of given-name familiarity one likes to have
with the biggest man on the block. My eyes on my soup, I listened to
this sycophancy, smiling rather bitterly, for what seemed an eternity;

when I finally did look up, it was he—ambrosial locks and all. He was dressed in blue denims and a terry-cloth sweater, and though I saw no evidence of *USC* stamped anyplace, still I had an overwhelming desire to insult him in some way. How this would be accomplished with any subtlety I had no idea; I certainly didn't want to fight with him. I did, however, want to shout, "Listen, you son of a bitch, life isn't all a goddam football game! You won't always get the girl! Life is rejection and pain and loss"—all those things I so cherishingly cuddled in my self-pitying bosom. I didn't, of course, say any such thing; almost immediately he was up and standing right next to me, waiting to pay the cashier. Unable to let the moment go by, I snapped my head up to face him. When he looked at me, I smiled—a hard, mocking, so-you're-the-big-shit? smile. What I expected him to do, I can't imagine—say, "What's your trouble, buddy?" or what—but what he did do was the least of my expectations. He only looked quizzically at me for a moment, as though he were having difficulty placing me; then he smiled a most ingratiating smile, gave me a most amiable hello, and walked out the door, followed by his buddies who were saying in unison, "Hey, Frank, what'll we do now?"

My first feeling was one of utter rage. I wanted to jump up and throw my water glass through the plate-glass window. Then almost immediately a kind of sullenness set in, then shame. Unless I had read that smile and that salutation incorrectly, there was a note of genuine apology and modesty in them. Even in the close world of the university Gifford must have come to realize that he was having a fantastic success, and that success somewhat embarrassed him. Perhaps he took me for some student acquaintance he had had long before that success, and took my hateful smile as a reproach for his having failed to speak to me on other occasions, his smile being the apology for that neglect. Perhaps he was only saying he was sorry I was a miserable son of a bitch, but that he was hardly going to fight me for it. These speculations, as I found out drinking beer late into that evening, could have gone on forever. I drank eight, nine, ten, drifting between speculations on the nature of that smile and bitter, sexually colored memories of the girl with the breath-taking legs back East, when it suddenly occurred to me that she and not the girl with the chestnut hair was the cause of all my anger, and that I was for perhaps a very long time going to have to live with that anger. Gifford gave me that. With that smile, whatever he meant by it, a smile that he doubtlessly wouldn't remember, he impressed upon me, in the rigidity of my embarrassment, that it is unmanly to burden others with one's grief. Even though it is man's particularly unhappy aptitude to see to it that his fate is shared.

Leaving the subway and walking toward the Polo Grounds, I was remembering that smile and thinking again how nice it would be if Gifford had a fine day for Owen, when I began to notice that the red-headed family, who were moving with the crowd some paces ahead of me, were laughing and giggling self-consciously, a laughter that evidently was in some way connected with me. Every few paces, having momentarily regained their composure, they would drop their heads together in a covert way, whisper as they walked, then turn again in unison, stare back at me, and begin giggling all anew. It was a laughter that soon had me self-consciously fingering my necktie and looking furtively down at my fly, as though I expected to discover that the overcoat which covered it had somehow miraculously disappeared. We were almost at the entrance to the field when, to my surprise, the father stopped suddenly, turned, walked back to me, and said that he was holding an extra ticket to the game. It was, he said, the result of his maid's having been taken ill, and that he—no, not precisely he, but the children—would deem it an honour if I—"knowing Owen and all"—sat with them. Not in the least interested in doing so, I was so relieved to discover that their laughter had been inspired by something apart from myself—the self-consciousness they felt at inviting me—that I instantaneously and gratefully accepted, thanked him profusely, and was almost immediately sorry. It occurred to me that the children might query me on my relationship with Owen—perhaps even Gifford—and what the hell could I say? My "relationship" with both of these men was so fleeting, so insubstantial, that I would unquestionably have had to invent and thereby not only undergo the strain of having to talk off the top of my head but, by talking, risk exposure as a fraud.

My fears, however, proved groundless. These people, it soon became evident, had no interest in me whatever, they were so bound up in their pride of each other. My discomfort was caused not by any interest they took in me but by their total indifference to me. Directing me by the arm, father seated me not with the children who, he had claimed, desired my presence, but on the aisle—obviously, I thought, the maid's seat (accessible to the hot dogs)—and sat himself next to me, separating me from his wife and children who had so harmoniously moved to their respective seats that I was sure that the family held season tickets. Everyone in place, all heads cranked round to me and displayed a perfect miracle of gleaming incisors.

It had only just begun. The game was no sooner under way when father, in an egregiously cultivated, theatrically virile voice, began—to my profound horror—commenting on each and every play. "That's a delayed buck, a play which requires superb blocking and marvelous timing," or, "That, children, is a screen pass, a fantastically perilous play to attempt, and one, I might add, that you won't see *Mr* Conerly attempt but once or twice a season"—to all of which the mother, the daughter, and the son invariably and in perfect unison exclaimed, "Really!" A tribute to father's brilliance that, to my further and almost numbing horror, I, too, soon discovered I was expected to pay—pay, I would expect, for the unutterable enchantment of sitting with them. Each time that I heard the *Really!* I would become aware of a great shock of auburn hair leaning past father's shoulder, and I would look up to be confronted by a brilliant conglomeration of snub noses, orange freckles, and sparkling teeth, all formed into a face of beseechment, an invitation to join in this tribute to Genius. I delayed accepting the invitation as long as I could; when the looks went from beseechment to mild reproachment, I surrendered and began chiming in with *Really!* At first I came in too quickly or too late, and we seemed to be echoing each other: *Really! Really!* Though this rhythmical ineptness chafed me greatly, it brought from the family only the most understanding and kindly looks. By the end of the first quarter I had my timing down perfectly and settled down to what was the most uncomfortable afternoon of my life.

This was a superb Detroit team. It was the Detroit of a young Bobby Layne and an incomparable Doak Walker, of a monstrously bull-like Leon Harte and a three-hundred-and-thirty-pound Les Bingaman, a team that was expected to move past the Giants with ease and into the championship of the Western Division. Had they done so—which at first they appeared to be doing, picking up two touchdowns before the crowd was scarcely settled—I might have been rather amused at the constraints placed on me by the character of my hosts. But at one thrilling moment, a moment almost palpable in its intensity, and unquestionably motivated by the knowledge of Owen's parting, the Giants recovered, engaged this magnificent football team, and began to play as if they meant to win. Other than the terrible fury of it, I don't remember the details of the game, save that Gifford played superbly; and that at one precise moment, watching him execute one of his plays, I was suddenly and overwhelmingly struck with the urge to cheer, to jump up and down and pummel people on the back.

But then, there was father. What can I say of him? To anything resembling a good play, he would single out the player responsible and say, "Fine show, Gifford!" or "Wonderful stuff there, Price!" and we would chime in with "Good show!" and "Fine stuff!" Then, in a preposterous parody of cultured equanimity, we would be permitted to clap our gloved right hands against our left wrists, like opera-goers, making about as much noise as an argument between mutes. It was very depressing. I hadn't cheered for anything or anybody in three years—since my rejection by the leggy girl—and had even mistakenly come to believe that my new-found restraint was a kind of maturity. Oh, I had had my enthusiasms, but they were dark, the adoration of the griefs and morbidities men commit to paper in the name of literature, the homage I had paid the whole sickly aristocracy of letters. But a man can dwell too long with grief, and now, quite suddenly, quite wonderfully, I wanted to cheer again, to break forth from darkness into light, to stand up in that sparsely filled (it was a typically ungrateful New York that had come to bid Owen farewell), murderously damp, bitingly cold stadium and scream my head off.

But then, here again was father—not only father but the terrible diffidence I felt in the presence of that family, in the overwhelming and shameless pride they took in each other's being and good form. The game moved for me at a snail's pace. Frequently I rose on tiptoe, ready to burst forth, at the last moment restraining myself. As the fury of the game reached an almost audible character, the crowd about me reacted proportionately by going stark raving mad while I stood still, saying *Really!* and filling up two handkerchiefs with a phlegm induced by the afternoon's increasing dampness. What upset me more than anything about father was that he had no loyalty other than to The Game itself, praising players, whether Giants or Lions, indiscriminately. On the more famous players he bestowed a *Mister*, saying, "Oh, fine stuff, *Mr* Layne!" or, "Wonderful show, *Mr* Walker!"—coming down hard on the *Mister* the way those creeps affected by The Theater say *Sir* Laurence Olivier or *Miss* Helen Hayes. We continued our *fine shows* and *good stuffs* till I thought my heart would break.

Finally I did of course snap. Late in the final period, with the Giants losing by less than a touchdown, Conerly connected with a short pass to Gifford, and I thought the latter was going into the end zone.

Unable to help myself, the long afternoon's repressed and joyous tears
welling up in my eyes, I went berserk.

Jumping up and down and pummeling father furiously on the back,
I screamed, "Oh, Jesus, Frank! Oh, Frank, *baby! Go! For Steve! For
Steve! For Steve!*"

Gifford did not go all the way. He went to the one-foot line. Because
it was not enough yardage for a first down, it became fourth and inches
to go for a touchdown and a victory, the next few seconds proving the
most agonizingly apprehensive of my life. It was an agony not allayed
by my hosts. When I looked up through tear-bedewed eyes, father was
straightening his camel's-hair topcoat, and the face of his loved ones
had been transfigured. I had violated their high canons of good taste,
their faces had moved from a vision of charming wholesomeness to
one of intransigent hostility; it was now eminently clear to them that
their invitation to me had been a dreadful mistake.

In an attempt to apologize, I smiled weakly and said, "I'm sorry—I
thought *Mr* Gifford was going all the way," coming down particularly
hard on the *Mister*. But this was even more disastrous: Gifford was new
to the Giants then, and father had not as yet bestowed that title on
him. The total face they presented to me made me want to cut my
jugular. Then, I thought, *what the hell*; and because I absolutely refused
to let them spoil the moment for me, I said something that had the
exact effect I intended: putting them in a state of numbing
senselessness.

I said, my voice distinctly irritable, "Aw, c'mon, you *goofies. Cheer.
This is for Steve Owen! For Steve Owen!*"

The Giants did not score, and as a result did not win the game.
Gifford carried on the last play, as I never doubted that he would.
Wasn't this game being played out just as, in my loneliness, I had
imagined it would be? Les Bingaman put his three hundred and thirty
pounds in Gifford's way, stopping him so close to the goal that the
officials were for many moments undetermined; and the Lions, having
finally taken over the ball, were a good way up the field, playing ball
control and running out the clock before my mind accepted the
evidence of my eyes. When it did so, I began to cough, coughing great
globs into my hands. I was coughing only a very few moments before
it occurred to me that I was also weeping. It was a fact that occurred
to father simultaneously. For the first time since I had spoken so
harshly to him, he rallied, my tears being in unsurpassably bad taste,
and said, "Look here, it's *only* a game."

Trying to speak softly so the children wouldn't hear, I said, *"Fuck you!"*

But they heard. By now I had turned and started up the steep concrete steps; all the way up them I could hear mother and the children, still in perfect unison, screeching *"Father!"* and father, in the most preposterously modulated hysteria, screeching *"Officer!"* I had to laugh then, laugh so hard that I almost doubled up on the concrete steps. My irritation had nothing to do with these dead people, and not really—I know now—anything to do with the outcome of the game. I had begun to be haunted again by that which had haunted me on my first trip to the city—the inability of a man to impose his dreams, his ego, upon the city and for many long months had been experiencing a rage induced by New York's stony refusal to esteem me. It was foolish and childish of me to impose that rage on these people, though not as foolish, I expect, as father's thinking he could protect his children from life's bitterness by calling for a policeman.

Giles Smith

In Off the Post: Chelsea 1973/4

You can search long and hard for a word to describe the kind of season Chelsea had in 1973/4, but nothing serves quite so well as 'crap'. They got off to their worst start since the war. They got off to one of their worst middles, too, picking up just two points in the whole of December. And their end wasn't up to much either. By contriving to scrape a couple of dodgy 0–0 draws late on, the team crawled to seventeenth place, five points off relegation. There had been unfathomable humiliations away to Leicester and at home to Ipswich. They had gone out of the League Cup in the second round and the FA Cup in the third. Their two biggest stars had walked out halfway through, the manager was rumoured almost hourly to be poised for the sack and the ground looked like war-torn Poland because building work on the new East Stand was running a year behind schedule – not bad for a project which was only meant to take ten months in the first place. The *Chelsea Football Book*, the annual club publication and normally a source of unflagging optimism and relentless propaganda, referred to it as 'the season that lasted for years'. It was that crap.

But from where I was sitting, things didn't look bad at all. In fact, I had a great season, the season of my life. I played a blinder from start to finish. I was Mr 100 Per Cent. I look back now at the programmes, removing them gingerly from my official Chelsea Football Club programme binder – a piece of folded cardboard clad in white leather-look sticky-back plastic, with a stiff paper pocket gummed to the inside. The spine is blue and stamped with duff gold lettering, in the manner of Reader's Digest condensed books. It says 'Chelsea Football Club – Official Programmes' and there's a picture of the club's lion insignia. And below that, where it says 'Season', I have positioned the printed paper sticker (supplied) – '1973/4'. You've never seen anything so cheap in your life – though of course it was hideously expensive, setting me back 50p in times when you could buy a complete club strip for £2.70.

Still, because of the binder, these programmes are in pristine condition, even now. Not a page that's been creased, not an ear that's been dogged. No fingerprints, no smudges, no coffee or meat-pie stains, all the way from Sheffield United on Saturday 1 September (lost 1–2) to Stoke City on Saturday 27 April (lost 0–1). The covers are still a convincingly bright blue and white, and they're all here, every first team home fixture – twenty-one league games, one FA Cup match (our pathetic Cup form played into my hands there) and two testimonials. Yes, testimonials! I was in deep. I was committed. I raise these pages to my nose, but none of the original print odour remains to spin me back in the approved Proustian manner. After all this time, they smell faintly of dust and cardboard box. But the words and pictures are enough. They bring the whole thing back. And to think I wasn't at a single one of these games.

In 1973 I was eleven, and where I was sitting was in fact Colchester, in Essex. I had never been to Stamford Bridge in my life. Actually, I had never seen Chelsea play anywhere at all. London was just an hour away on the train – unless you had parents as strict as mine, in which case it was an hour and several years. My father used British Rail to get to work every day, so he knew what football fans were like. He'd stepped into enough charred carriages, recently vacated by Manchester United supporters, to realize that a) there was no way he was letting me go near this kind of action and b) there was no way he was risking his own safety by taking me near it. (Actually, he didn't need much dissuading: with the exception of the night he came home and proudly announced he'd said hello to Sir Alf Ramsey on Ipswich Station, my father never expressed a second's interest in football.) But I wasn't going to let a small matter like the impossibility of my ever watching the team prevent me from getting involved. Chelsea and I kept in touch. In 1973/4, we wrote to each other constantly.

I should say the content of my letter barely varied. 'Dear Sir/ Madam,' it began. 'Please send one copy of the following home programme.' Then would come the name of the opponent, the date and even – with a precision which was, on reflection, worryingly neurotic – the time of kick-off. 'I enclose a postal order for 5p and a stamped addressed envelope.' Then I would sign off with the mildly previous but clearly essential, 'Thanking you in advance, Yours faith-fully.' (I'd checked with my father on that crucial faithfully/sincerely distinction because, after all, this was Chelsea I was writing to: etiquette was important.) I must have written this letter twenty times that season. As correspondences go, it wasn't exactly Flaubert to George

Sand. But I bet George Sand was never as excited to hear from Flaubert as I was to get a letter from Chelsea.

To be accurate, our correspondence pre-dated the '73/4 season. I had first written to Chelsea during 1971/2, my second full season as a Chelsea fan. Like many of my generation, I had latched on to the team because my period of kicking a ball around a playground and looking for things to have in common with (and hold against) my peers had coincided exactly with Chelsea's period of glory – their 1970 FA Cup win over Leeds and their 1971 European Cup Winners' Cup triumph over Real Madrid. And of course, like everybody else, I was duped. Since then, we've had twenty years of trophy-free despair, excluding periodic Second Division Championships and the occasional lucky streak in no-hoper tournaments named after office equipment. Even so, I still stand by the principle on which I chose my team. I know people who support the teams of the towns in which they grew up. I know people who support Colchester United for this reason (there could hardly be any other). It has always baffled me that one could base this essential life-decision on something as random as the circumstances of one's birth. My method – though destined to backfire horribly – was at least rigorously scientific. The Chelsea of the early 1970s, the Chelsea of Peter Osgood, Charlie Cooke, Alan Hudson and Peter Bonetti, was magnetically successful.

The first time I sent a letter to Chelsea, it was addressed to Peter Bonetti. Looking back, it was recklessly forward of me to assume I could write directly to the Chelsea goalkeeper without going through a secretary or an assistant, or even through the manager, Dave Sexton. But having acquired, at Christmas 1971, a pair of Bonetti-endorsed goalkeeping gloves – thin and green with a velvet finish – I felt we were already to some extent acquainted. In the light of subsequent events, it strikes me as richly significant that I was forced to say postally what ordinary fans, who could hang around outside the dressing room after games, said in person. 'Dear Peter Bonetti,' I wrote. 'Can I have your autograph, please? I enclose a stamped addressed envelope.' The letter ended, 'Thanking you in advance, Yours sincerely.'

I had figured I should send him something to sign, in case he didn't have a piece of paper handy wherever he was when he opened the letter. (And where exactly was he going to open it? At home, with a sackful of others? On the team coach? In the dressing room before a game? I wondered about this a lot.) I went back to the red folder containing my nascent collection of Chelsea cuttings – arranged chronologically where possible and consisting largely of neat clippings from *Shoot!*, with a sizeable number of match reports from my father's *Times* and my aunt's *Sunday Express*, plus some archive material, retrieved without permission from my elder brother's collection of old *Goal!* magazines. Given that the success of my Bonetti autograph quest was by no means guaranteed, I was naturally reluctant to risk any of my colour material. I settled eventually for a black and white image taken from *Shoot!*. It was about three inches tall and two inches wide and showed 'the Cat' jumping at a striking angle to palm away the ball. Judging by the completely static attitude of the crowd visible behind the goal, the picture had been taken during a pre-match kick-about. It also had a drawing-pin hole in the centre at the top, bearing witness to a period of exposure on the pinboard in my bedroom. (I operated a rotating display policy, rather like the Tate, in which pictures would go on loan to the board for a fortnight before being returned to the main collection in the red folder.) If it all went wrong, the picture would be a loss, but not a desperate one. I put it in the envelope with the letter.

I reckoned on a long wait before I would hear back from Peter, recognizing even in my naïvety that he probably had more pressing things to do than turn his attention immediately to signing tiny, pin-holed pictures of himself warming up. In fact, clearly he didn't, because the stamped addressed envelope came back to me, if not by return of post, then within five days, and inside was the picture, signed 'Peter Bonetti' in biro across the ground beneath his feet. As I writhed with delight on the hall carpet, a great truth came home to me: you could write to Chelsea and Chelsea wrote back.

I pasted the Bonetti picture in an autograph book, which only otherwise contained the signatures of friends and members of my family. My cherishing this item, my returning to it repeatedly for several years, seems normal enough in the circumstances; my treasuring the envelope in which it had arrived – an envelope on which, you will realize, I had written the address myself – looks a touch more desperate. But this was contact with a world which, though it clearly existed, might as well have been Narnia as far as I was concerned. I was tantalized by anything which had passed that way.

Writing off for match programmes seemed the obvious next step. Thanks to my Uncle Frank, I already owned two Chelsea programmes. Uncle Frank had been, until the 1970/71 season, a linesman and referee.

Even before my Chelsea obsession caught fire, I was impressed by a photo on Frank's sitting-room wall showing him at some sort of dinner dance with Bobby Moore. (I don't think he'd gone to the dinner dance with Bobby Moore. I suspect he went with my aunt. But clearly Bobby Moore represented the rarer photo opportunity.) Frank had obviously at some point passed on a pile of old football programmes to one of my brothers, who had in turn passed them on to a cardboard box in the attic. When I raided this, during some idle weekend or other, I uncovered a programme for the Chelsea home League game against West Bromwich Albion on 30 January 1971 – 'Linesman (Red Flag): Mr E. F. Merchant (Colchester)' – and one for the 1967 FA Cup Final between Chelsea and Spurs, which my uncle must have attended in an unofficial capacity. I was faint with excitement. These were the very objects that people who had actually been to games guarded jealously, tokens of an experience to shore up against the passing of time. And for me – who carried them down from the attic and made them my own – they became an almost unbearably vivid reminder of occasions with which I had had absolutely nothing to do.

'Dear Sir/Madam,' I now wrote. 'Please send one copy of the following home programme. Versus Manchester United, Wednesday 18 August 1971, kick-off 7.30 p.m. I enclose a postal order for 5p and a stamped addressed envelope.' We were by now nearing the spring of 1972, but for my first tentative mail-order programme purchase, I had elected to go back to the beginning of the season and the first home fixture. I say tentative, but I had already conceived some breathtaking scheme to work forwards from there, acquiring each of the back numbers, catching up with myself towards the end of April, and seeing the season out as the jubilant owner of an unbroken home collection. In the event, funds restricted me to a handful (Crystal Palace, Stoke City, Jeunesse Hautcharage of Luxembourg in the Cup Winners' Cup First Round, Second Leg), the incompleteness of which was a source of nervy frustration at the time. What is it about small boys and completion? I could say I was displaying a precocious interest in the aesthetics of wholeness, but the truth is I was just being preposterously anal. Small boys are pushed that way by the makers of bubblegum cards, by the designers of petrol station promotions, by Stanley Gibbons and countless others who encourage us to 'collect the set' and are never made to answer for the psychological implications of what they do.

Needless to say, though, that Manchester United programme was a gripper. I was lucky to be getting involved at a time when clubs were beginning to exploit the publicity possibilities of programmes, turning out miniature magazines rather than the old-style programmes, which were basically nothing grander than a team sheet, a lucky number and an advert for the local tandoori. The ugly but not entirely euphemistic phrase 'Matchday Magazine' would not appear on the front of a Chelsea programme until 1976/7, but even in 1971 Chelsea pro-grammes were twenty pocket-sized pages long and entirely without advertising. On page three of the Manchester United one our chairman Brian Mears offered a few words of welcome to the season, making sure to thank 'everybody connected with the club for their valued contribution', an address which seemed to me thrillingly personal and immediate, even though it had been published some seven months previously and not directed at me at all.

In the 1972/3 season, I wrote to Chelsea eleven times asking for programmes (an advance on my '71/2 performance, but still only really a warm-up for my devastating '73/4 form). My twelfth didn't come through the post, though. It came direct from *someone who had actually been to the game*. More than that, it came from *someone who had actually been to the game who was related to me*. One of my brothers was at a teacher-training college in London. At home for a weekend, he casually mentioned to me that the next Tuesday night he and a couple of friends were going to watch Chelsea at home to Wolves, 'just for a laugh'. I knew then the bitterness of the cuckold. It struck me as tragic that my brother was about to fulfil what for me would have been a lifetime's ambition, but what for him was merely the obligation to occupy an evening. Still, he said he'd bring me back a programme.

To be frank, I was rather anxious about this. During the last year or so, the absolutely flawless condition of my programmes had become paramount. I wanted nothing creased or damaged and, while I was waiting for them to arrive in the post, I would endure sustained anxiety attacks at the thought of any GPO-inflicted violence. What if the postman took it into his head to crease the package down the middle, or leave it wedged in the letter box, its contents irretrievably scored? (Luckily, our front door had a capacious and easy horizontal flap: if we'd had one of those small, upright tin-trap models, I would probably have gone through the entire first half of the 1970s without sleep.) For people who go to games, the wear and tear on a programme can tell a heart-warming narrative. Much as people grow attached to the scratches on their records, which indicate a history of use, so a programme virtually papier-mâchéd by rain or wrecked in a shocking turnstile incident might bring back all kinds of memories about the game. But obviously all of that had absolutely no relevance to me at this time. I wanted my programmes undistressed, properly characterless.

Strangely this respect for the programme as a physical entity persisted for some time after I had begun going to games (at Colchester United first, and then much later at Chelsea). It became something of a mission to make it back home with the programme still box-fresh, unscathed by the weather or the terrace crush or the return journey. I remember a Colchester match against Peterborough at which a small fight broke out and the crowd I was part of shifted uneasily to the side, and, in that moment, I experienced fear: but what I feared for most was the safety of my programme. I have to say, I became stunningly skilful at protecting my interest. I still possess the programme from the Colchester v. Ipswich pre-season friendly, dated 10 August 1976. It is a cumbersome, single sheet of only slightly stiffened paper. And it is utterly without blemish.

So I was nervous when I went to my brother's bedroom on his next weekend at home, and he dug down into his bag for the programme – Tuesday 6 March, Wolverhampton Wanderers, kick-off 7.45 p.m. But I had to hand it to him – he'd got the thing out of there in mint condition. As my heart expanded I examined the cover – sharp-edged, clean cut, no foxing or stippling, no distress marks around the staples. Perfect. And then I opened it. On page three, beneath the team lists, my brother had written in black ink the score (Chelsea 0 Wolves 2) and the scorers (Dougan, Richards). I was astounded. You don't *write* in programmes. And to think this person was going to become a teacher.

There are no ink stains on my '73/4 set. I was in complete control. I knew this was going to be my season and I rapidly devised a routine to smooth the path to victory. On Saturday mornings on home match days, I would cycle to the post office and buy the necessary postal order and stamps. If there had been an evening game in the intervening fortnight, I would double up. This way, my order would be on Sir/Madam's desk first thing on Monday morning. I could probably have taken out a subscription and spared myself the effort, but I doubt I would have been able to find the lump sum. As it was, my programme habit would eat deep into my resources, forcing me to supplement my income by washing an aunt's car on a fortnightly basis, even when it wasn't dirty, and, when the weather allowed, hoisting a Flymo over my godmother's handkerchief-sized lawn for an inflated fee.

We kicked off against Sheffield United. Of course, I have no detailed idea of what this game was like. But I do know the programme contained an extraordinary picture of Ian Hutchinson going up for a high ball in the previous weekend's game at Derby, and that chairman Brian Mears devoted a page to asking us for our continued patience with respect to the building work on the East Stand. Take as long as you like, I wanted to say. Against Birmingham City, the programme ran a double-page squad picture – twenty players, and only one of them (Peter Houseman) with a plausible haircut. And David Webb answered '20 Chelsea Questions', revealing that he lived in a detached bungalow in Chigwell and that his business interests included a dress shop and a mini-market. It may seem far-fetched to say such details were magically detaining, but it was the case. Later in the season, I devoted hours to thinking about John Hollins – his dachshunds, Sweep and Jack, and his peculiar Sunday lunch habit: 'Yorkshire pudding and gravy first, then the roast beef and veg.' But in the absence of any actual football, what else was there for me to attach myself to?

Against Coventry, Alan Hudson said he'd be spending this year's holiday in Cornwall, and Peter Bonetti was shown 'having the game of his life' against Liverpool at Anfield. There he was, springing to catch a Kevin Keegan penalty, pushing out a Steve Heighway cross, smacking away an Emlyn Hughes volley. And against Wolves, Bonetti was saving another penalty against Coventry, Chelsea were thumping four goals past Birmingham and Steve Kember was remarking, 'If I ruled the world – I'd bring back hanging.' Nice hearing from you, Steve.

At home to Ipswich there were fabulous rain-drenched pictures from QPR and the Club Shop was advertising 'a new range of Stainless Steel souvenirs'. (I wasn't tempted.) Peter Houseman's Testimonial was played against Fulham, and against Leicester City Ron 'Chopper' Harris maintained that his biggest anxiety was 'getting injured', which was pretty rich coming from him. Versus Leeds, John Hollins was shown actually splitting the net with a penalty at home to Leicester, and against West Ham on Boxing Day, that squad photo was back again, but this time in colour and marked 'Season's Greetings'. It was the most touching Christmas card I had ever received.

At home to Liverpool, I was able to observe the building progress on the new East Stand (embarrassingly slow). But then, this was the year of the three-day week – that desperate government ploy to conserve energy in the face of mining and travel strikes – and it hit football, as well as football stands. Chelsea's home fixture against Burnley took place on a Wednesday afternoon, to comply with power regulations. Of course, the only significant repercussion from my point of view was an enforced reduction in the number of programme pages. A note in the QPR programme on 5 January apologized for the meagre sixteen-page offering. 'We hope to resume a 20-page issue as soon as conditions allow.' But conditions never allowed again for the rest of the season.

By now, things were extremely recessionary on the pitch, too. Or so I read. For the away game at Sheffield United on New Year's Day, Dave Sexton attempted to reverse the team's decline by the bizarre tactic of dropping Bonetti, Osgood, Hudson and Baldwin, and in effect signed the death warrant for the Chelsea we once knew. Both Osgood and Hudson protested by refusing to train with the first team. The club suspended them and put them both on the transfer list. I read with alarm the soggy, cliché-strewn announcement in the Derby County programme: 'There comes a time in everyone's life – at work, within families, in sport – when there is a clash of personalities, and it is evident that for some time such a situation has existed at Stamford Bridge between the manager and one or two players.' Hudson went to Stoke, Osgood to Southampton. I carried on buying the programmes. But I can't pretend my confidence wasn't dented.

We did at least welcome back Charlie Cooke, re-signed from Crystal Palace, in the Manchester City programme on 9 February. But my faith wasn't fully restored until Eddie McCreadie's Testimonial against Manchester United at the season's end. I had to pay 10p for this, the final piece in the jigsaw, but it was worth that alone for the page entitled 'Eddie McCreadie – Poet.' 'For several years Eddie has written poetry for his personal enjoyment and not for other eyes. We asked him whether he might like any of his poems published in his Testimonial Match programme, and he decided he would like to share the following with Chelsea Supporters tonight.' And below were five short poems from the Chelsea and Scotland full back, the last of which – 'It Might Be Cold Tomorrow' – seemed an eerily appropriate note for my season to end on:

> I've never felt so happy
> And yet sad,

I love you today,
It might be cold tomorrow.

Now that I live in London, I can go regularly to Chelsea's home games.
I get to a few aways, too. I always buy a programme and can still
experience an irritating sense of inconclusiveness on the rare occasions
when they're sold out or unavailable. And though I no longer store
them in an Official Programme Binder, there is something about my
reluctance to throw them away and my tendency to leave them mock-
casually in prominent places – on the chair in the bathroom where
visitors might notice them, or on my desk at work – which suggests
they still serve as some sort of psychologically suspect talisman for me.
In fact, I have sometimes wondered whether my entire purpose in
going to games wasn't simply to acquire a programme to keep
afterwards.

But these days, in the words of the poet Eddie McCreadie, 'I tread
the cold ice of reality' ('Winter Thoughts'). I go to games with my
friend, Ben. We were introduced two seasons ago by someone who
knew that we both went miserably alone to Chelsea games and who
thought we might enjoy pairing up and going miserably together.
Which we do. But Ben and Chelsea really go back. He grew up in
London, just across the river from the ground, and he was present at
the games that I could only fantasize about and appreciate postally. He
has a glorious store of first-hand experiences of which I can only be in
awe. He was there on the day Wolves fans built a bonfire on the away
terracing. He once went to a game wearing seven Chelsea scarves and
came away with none. He was involved in a pitch invasion at the
conclusion of a Second Division match against Hull City and was
actually knocked to the Stamford Bridge turf by a fleeing member of
the victorious Chelsea side.

But that says it all about me and Chelsea in those early days. Some
of us were going shoulder-to-shoulder with Graham Wilkins just
outside the centre circle: some of us were at home, filling out postal
orders.

A. J. Liebling

A New Yorker's Derby

May 29, 1955

The ways of Epsom on Derby Day take a good deal of knowing, and since I get there only at seven-year intervals, I don't suppose I shall ever know them well.

This is all the more likely because I began in 1948, when I was already a fair age. I have learned, however, that it is always wise, on entering Tattersalls, to rent binoculars at the booth behind the big stand. They guarantee no prospect more interesting than the backs of grey top hats, which come into your line of vision whenever you level up a horse. But the five-pound deposit you are required to leave on the binoculars assures the means of dignified retreat if your calculations go amiss. It is the best of savers. It is of course essential not to retrieve the deposit before the last race. In 1948 I hauled myself back to London by my binocular-straps.

I have learned also that a French horse always wins when I am present, and the Volterra stable owns at last part of the horse. The late M. Volterra had one-and-a-half of the first two past the post in 1948—a half share in My Love, the winner, and all of Royal Drake, the runner-up. Mme Volterra owned only one of the first two horses Wednesday, but it was the right one. It would therefore be madness not to back a French horse, particularly when a Volterra owns even a cutlet. I am not mad.

A third Epsom commonplace is that the English are a deeply kind nation, and that Derby favorites are often a creation of sentiment. Last Wednesday morning, for example, I read pages by experts who really know quite a lot about racing, evoking the probability of a Derby in which Acropolis, an untried colt, would prove himself one of the great race horses of all time. Their reason for believing he would win a stiff race at a mile and a half was that he had run a fast time trial at a mile and a quarter. The emotional basis of it all, I am sure, was that Acropolis was owned by a noblewoman, ninety-three years old, who had selected him as a yearling. The poetic fitness of a win for such a combination had proved first attractive, then irresistible, to the hardened professionals. In 1948, as I remember it, the favorite's chief qualification was that the Maharajah of something or other had named him after his infant son.

Another factor which improves the odds is the British tendency to underrate invaders. I am sure that Harold the Saxon had information from Chantilly that William the Conqueror was very ordinary and couldn't act uphill. As a result a French horse is always likely to be what we transatlantics call an overlay. I failed to convert the night porter at my hotel to this doctrine. He said, "I don't trust them."

The most important Derby Day truth for me is that I have more fun there than at any other race I know. On one side of the course there are the decorative people, consciously and happily picturesque, exercising the English talent for being dressed up and enjoying it. It is a very great talent, whose effects I had no chance of appreciating during the khaki-and-utility war, when I lived here longest.

On the other side of the track there is the endless Crazy Gang routine of the touts: "I said the 'orse wouldn't stay, but 'e *did* stay, 'e stayed in one place." "You couldn't find a better soldier in the British Army than I was—when you could find me." This is the Self-deprecating Tout, who wins his public's confidence by the establishment of his own human frailty.

"I didn't get this motorcar from Godfrey Davis, the 'ire-car man, to impress you for the day. I've *always* 'ad a car. I'm a responsible businessman. In the tel-e-phone book. You can look me up. I don't go racing so often nowadays, but when I *do* go, I 'ave a *reason* for it." This is the Successful Tout, who sells by dynamism. I suppose he would call it the American method.

In the last seven years, I think, there has been a falling-off in the Grotesque Tout. Prince Monolulu, older and mellower, did not shout when he saw me this year, "I've got a 'orse!" He said deferentially, "Could you use a 'orse?" The Rocket Man was similarly subdued. He had discarded his Mae West for a coachman's hat like the doorman at Hatchett's in Piccadilly. The American method seems to get the half-crowns.

With a press badge you can slip back and forth between the two forms of entertainment, regulating the dosage, as if you were producing your own revue. Ten minutes of comedy and then down to the paddock for a touch of "Florodora" flash with the crinoline girls and the Moss Brothers' men's chorus.

One of the things I haven't learned about Epsom—shall I pick it up in 1962 or 1969?—is how to get fed properly. On the grandstand side of the course I found, when I had my first intimations of malnutrition in 1948, that the only visible antidote consisted of wide white expanses of flaccid bread agglomerated around panes of what I took to be cellophane. The *vendeuse* explained it was "Ham, love. We have rationing, love."

I attributed the ignominy, like all others, to Mr Attlee. Last Wednesday I perceived that three years of free enterprise had not thickened the ham in buffet sandwiches by an eighth of a millimeter, and the elegantly draped elbows one receives in the ribs on the way to the buffet are as hard as they used to be in utility garments.

In quest of something more in keeping with the costumes, a *mayonnaise de langouste* and a pheasant, perhaps with a magnum of *sirop de cacao*, I climbed two winding flights of stairs into a kind of belfry marked "Luncheons." Here, with a glow of nostalgic pleasure, I found again my old love, the wartime queue. The racegoers stood in Indian file in a passageway leading, as I supposed, to the luncheon, although from their faces it may well have been the guillotine.

If I had tagged on at the end, I would have been lucky to emerge in time for the St Leger, so I dashed back to the common folk and lunched on a bison—"a bison of eels," was the full title the *garde-manger* at the barrow gave the dish, and I followed it by a red-hot bag of cold fish-and-chips, a mystery of the British cuisine comparable, but not in many ways, to a baked Alaska.

When I had finished, I understood why fish-and-chips is not served in the enclosures. Had I been wearing appropriate headgear, I should not have been able to doff it without greasing the brim. (My early suspicion that the toppers contained vacuum jugs or chafing dishes had been dispelled by observation of the luncheon queue. It was obvious the *incroyables* were as faminous as I.)

I was therefore on the *qui vive*, as the invaders say, for the tip which I eavesdropped from the lips of Mme Volterra herself on the way over from the walking ring to the paddock before the Derby. (It merely confirmed my resolution to do Phil Drake, but without such ante-post support resolutions have been known to waver.) I was not with, but near, Mme Volterra, and, quite naturally, looking at her, when I heard her say to one of her *chevaliers du chapeau gris*, "*Une chose qui est certaine, c'est que mon cheval a bien mangé.*" (Another Epsom axiom is that it is well to understand the raiders' language.) Mme Volterra looked like a woman who doesn't joke about food.

And if, as she said, her horse had eaten well, I knew he was the only living being on Epsom Downs who had done so. I dashed off to put a fiver on his lovely dark nose, and when he turned loose that run in the stretch—from seventeenth place to first—I knew where he got the stamina. It was a triumph for French cooking as well as for French cunning.

HOW IT LOOKS

Neville Cardus

Hutton, Hobbs and the Classical Style

The characteristics of the classical style in cricket, or in anything else, are precision of technique, conservation of energy, and power liberated proportionately so that the outlines of execution are clear and balanced. Hutton is the best example to be seen at the present time of the classical style of batsmanship. He is a model for the emulation of the young. We cannot say as much of, for instance, Worrell, who is the greatest stroke-player of the moment; it would be perilous if a novice tried to educate himself by faithfully observing the play of Worrell. A sudden snick through the slips by Worrell might cause us to lift an eyebrow, but we wouldn't think that something had gone wrong with the element in which Worrell naturally revels; for it is understood that Worrell and all cricketers of his kind live on the rim of their technical scope. A snick by a Jack Hobbs is a sort of disturbance of a cosmic orderliness. It is more than a disturbance; it is a solecism in fact, as though a great writer of prose were to fall into an untidy period, or actually commit bad grammar. The classical style admits of no venturings into the unknown, of no strayings from first principles. A dissonance is part and parcel of romantic excess and effort; all right in Strauss, impossible in Mozart, where not a star of a semi-quaver may fall. The exponent of the classical style observes, and is content to observe, the limitations imposed by law, restraint, taste. He finds his liberty within the confines of equipoise.

I suppose that the three or four exemplars of the truly classical style of batsmanship have been W. G. Grace, Arthur Shrewsbury, Hayward and Hobbs; I can't include MacLaren; for something of a disturbing rhetoric now and then entered into his generally noble and correct diction. Trumper was, of course, all styles, as C. B. Fry has said, from the lyrical to the dramatic. MacLaren once paid, in a conversation with me, the most generous tribute ever uttered by one great player to another. 'I was supposed to be something of a picture gallery myself,' said he. 'People talked of the "Grand Manner" of MacLaren. But compared with Victor I was as a cab horse to a Derby winner . . .'

In our own day, Hutton comes as near as anybody to the classical style, though there are moments when the definition of it, as expounded above, needs to be loosened to accommodate him. Dignity, and a certain lordliness, are the robes and very presence of classicism. Frankly, Hutton many times is obliged to wear the dress or 'overhauls' of utility; moreover, his resort to the passive 'dead bat', though shrewd and tactical, scarcely suggests grandeur or the sovereign attitude. The truth is that the classical style of batsmanship was the consequence of a classical style of bowling – bowling which also observed precision, clarity of outline, length, length, length! It is as difficult to adapt classical calm and dignity of poise to modern in-swingers and 'googlies' as it would be to translate Milton into Gertrude Stein, or Haydn into Tin-pan Alley.

But Hutton, in the present far from classical epoch, follows the line of Hobbs, and if all that we know today of batsmanship as a science were somehow taken from our consciousness, the grammar and alphabet could be deduced from the cricket of Hutton, and codified again; he is all the textbooks in an omnibus edition. Compared with him Bradman, who has been accused of bloodless mechanical efficiency, was as a volcanic eruption threatening to destroy Pompeii.

We need to be careful of what we mean if we call Hutton a stylist, which, we have agreed, he is. Style is commonly but mistakenly supposed to be indicated by a flourish added to masterful skill, a spreading of peacock's feathers. (The peacock is efficiently enough created and marvellously beautiful without that.) Style with Hutton is not a vanity, not something deliberately cultivated. It is a bloom and finish, which have come unselfconsciously from organized technique rendered by experience instinctive in its rhythmical and attuned movements. His drives to the off side have a strength that is generated effortlessly from the physical dynamo, through nerve and muscle, so that we might almost persuade ourselves that the current of his energy, his life-force, is running electrically down the bat's handle into the blade, without a single short circuit or fusing, thence into the ball, endowing it, as it speeds over the grass, with the momentum of no dead material object compact of leather, but of animate life.

His 'follow through' in his drives is full and unfettered. But the style is the man: there is no squandering in a Hutton innings. Bradman, to refer again to the cricketer known as an 'adding-machine', was a spendthrift compared to Hutton, who is economical always, counting every penny, every single, of his opulent income of runs. We shall understand, when we come to consider the way of life that produced him, his habitat, why with Hutton, the style is indeed the man himself.

Some of us are obliged to work hard for our places in the sun; others have greatness thrust upon them. A fortunate few walk along divinely appointed ways, the gift of prophecy marking their courses. Hutton was scarcely out of the cradle of the Yorkshire nursery nets when Sutcliffe foretold the master to come, not rolling the eye of fanaticism but simply in the manner of a shrewd surveyor of 'futures'. But Sutcliffe knew all the time that the apprenticeship of Hutton had been served in that world of vicissitude and distrust which are the most important factors forming the North of England character under the pressure of an outlook which thinks it's as well to 'take nowt on trust' – not even a fine morning. In his first trial for the Yorkshire Second XI, May 1933, he was dismissed for nothing against Cheshire. Four years after, when he was first invited to play for England, he also made nothing, bowled Cowie. Next innings he was 'slightly more successful' – 'c. Vivian, b. Cowie 1'. Though he was only eighteen years old when he scored a hundred for Yorkshire in July 1934 – the youngest Yorkshire cricketer to achieve such distinction – illness as well as the run of the luck of the game hindered his progress, dogged him with apparent malice. When he reappeared on the first-class scene again it was just in time to take part in that dreadful holocaust at Huddersfield, when Essex bowled Yorkshire out for 31 and 99. Hutton's portion was two noughts. In his very first match for Yorkshire at Fenners in 1934 J. G. W. Davies ran him out brilliantly – for nought. Until yesteryear, in fact, the Fates tried him. The accident to his left forearm, incurred while training in a Commando course, nearly put an end to his career as a cricketer altogether.

He has emerged from a hard school. It has never been with Hutton a case of roses all the way; he had to dig his cricket out of his bones; a bat and the Yorkshire and England colours didn't fall into his mouth like silver cutlery. According to the different threads or warp of our nature and being, a different texture is an inevitable consequence. There is no softness in Hutton's psychological or, therefore, in his technical makeup. And there are broadly two ways of getting things done in our limited world. We walk either by faith or by reason. There are, in other words, the born inexplicable geniuses and those we can account for in terms of the skill they have inherited. They are in a way the by-products of skill and experience accumulated and still pregnant in their formative years; their contribution is to develop the inheritance to a further, though rationally definable, stage of excellence. But we know where they come from and how. Hutton is one of the greatest of these. But a Compton, or, better for our illustration, a Trumper, seems to spring into being with all his gifts innate and in full bloom from the beginning. He improves in certainty of touch with experience, but as soon as he emerges from the chrysalis there is magic in his power, something that 'defies augury'; he is a law unto himself, therefore dangerous as a guide or example to others who are encased in mortal fallibility. But I am wandering from a contemplation of classicism and Hutton.

The unique or ineluctable genius isn't, of course, necessarily the great master. No cricketer has possessed, or rather been more possessed by genius, than Ranji; for his mastery was the most comprehensive known yet in all the evolution of the game. Hobbs summed up in himself all that had gone before him in established doctrine of batsmanship. He was encyclopaedic; we could deduce from his cricket not only grammar but history. We could infer from any Hobbs innings the various forces that had produced and perfected his compendious technique over years which witnessed changes which were revolutionary as never before, ranging from the fast bowlers of the post-Grace period, in which Hobbs was nurtured, to the advent of the modern refinements and licences – swerve and 'googly' and all the rest. When Hobbs began his career the attack he faced day by day was much the same in essentials as the one familiar enough to W.G. But very soon Hobbs was confronted by bowling of the new order of disrule, which W.G. couldn't understand; and Hobbs was not only the first to show how the 'googly' should be detected and exposed and how swerve should be played in the middle of the blade; he taught others and led the way. Hobbs was the bridge over which classical cricket marched to the more complex epoch of the present. Hutton is the only cricketer living at the moment who remotely resembles Hobbs by possession of what I shall call here a thoroughly schooled or canonical method. He doesn't commit crudities. The 'wrong' stroke at times – yes, because of an error of judgement. But never an *uninstructed* stroke.

He is a quite thoughtful Yorkshireman, with widely spaced blue eyes that miss nothing. And his batting is quiet and thoughtful; even in his occasional punishing moods, when his strokes are animating as well as ennobling the field, he doesn't get noisy or rampagious. His stance at the wicket is a blend of easeful muscular organization and keen watchfulness. The left shoulder points rather more to the direction of mid-on than would satisfy Tom Hayward; but here again is evidence that Hutton is a creature or rather a creation of his environment; that is to say, he is obliged to solve problems of spin and swerve not persistently put to Hayward day by day. With Hayward and his school, the left leg was the reconnoitring force, the cat's whisker, the pioneer that moved in advance to 'sight' the enemy. With Hutton it is the right leg that is the pivot, the springboard. But often he allowed it to change into an anchor which holds him back when he should be moving out on the full and changing tide of the game. He is perfect at using the 'dead' bat – rendering it passive, a blanket or a buffer, against which spin or sudden rise from the pitch come into contact as though with an anaesthetic. He plays so close to the ball, so much over it that he has acquired a sort of student's slope of the shoulders; at the sight of a fizzing off break he is arched like a cat. Even when he drives through the covers, his head and eyes incline downwards, and the swing of the bat doesn't go past the front leg until the ball is struck. He can check the action of any stroke extremely late, and so much does he seem to see a delivery all the way that we are perplexed that so frequently he is clean-bowled by a length well up to him. From the back foot he can hit straight for four; and all his hits leave an impressive suggestion of power not entirely expended.

We shall remember, after we have relegated his 364 against Australia at Kennington Oval in 1938 to the museum of records in sport rather than to the things that belong to cricket, his innings at Sydney in the second Test match during the 1946/7 rubber; only 37 but so dazzling in clean diamond-cut strokes that old men present babbled of Victor Trumper. He has even while playing for Yorkshire more than once caused some raising of the eyebrows. At Nottingham in 1948 he not only played, but played well, Miller, Johnston and Johnson as though for his own private and personal enjoyment. But usually he subdues his hand to what it works in – Yorkshire cricket. I have heard people say that he is not above 'playing for himself. Well, seeing that he is Yorkshire to the bone's marrow, we should find ourselves metaphysically involved if we tried to argue that he is ever not playing for Yorkshire.

There is romance even in Yorkshire cricket, though they keep quiet about it. Romance has in fact visited the life and career of Hutton. In July 1930, the vast field of Headingley was a scene of moist, hot congestion with, apparently, only one cool, clean, well-brushed

individual present, name of Bradman, who during the five hours'
traffic of the crease, made at will 300 runs, and a few more, before
half-past six. He returned to the pavilion as though fresh from a band-
box; the rest of us, players, umpires, crowd and scorers, especially the
scorers, were exhausted; dirty, dusty and afflicted by a sense of the
vanity of life. In all the heat and burden of this day at Leeds, more
than twenty years ago, a boy of fourteen years was concealed amongst
the boiling multitude; and so many of these thousands seethed and
jostled that one of them, especially an infant in the eyes of the law,
couldn't possibly (you might have sworn) have made the slightest
difference to what we were all looking at, or to the irony of subsequent
history. The solemn fact is that as Bradman compiled the 334 which
was then the record individual score in a Test march, the boy hidden
in the multitude was none other than the cricketer chosen already by
the gods to break this record, if not Bradman's heart, eight years
afterwards.

Tom Callahan

Iron Mike and the Allure of the 'Manly Art'

An explanation for boxing, at least an excuse, has never been harder to summon or easier to see than it is now, simmering in the eyes of Mike Tyson. Muhammad Ali's face, when his was the face of boxing, at least had a note of humor, a hint of remorse, even the possibility of compassion, though he gave no guarantees. Tyson does: brutal, bitter ones.

The usual case for boxing as art or science is rougher to make in the face of this face. Valor can be redeeming; so can grace, poise, bearing, even cunning. But this is a nightmare. The monster that men have worried was at the heart of their indefinable passion, of their indefensible sport, has come out in the flesh to be the champion of the world. Next Monday night, he will be served Michael Spinks.

Perhaps it is anachronistic to mention only men. Maybe boxing is an anachronism: the manly art of self-defense. Take it like a man. Be a man. In Archibald MacLeish's play *J.B.*, Job told the Comforter, "I can bear anything a man can bear—if I can be one." But nobody talks about being a man anymore. When it comes to bloodlust, female gills pant up and down too. In the matter of boxing's fascination for writers, gender has certainly not been disqualifying. Still, the suspicion persists that males secrete some kind of archetypal fluid that makes it easier for them to understand what's at work here.

As a fictional character, Tyson would be an offense to everyone, a stereotype wrung out past infinity to obscenity. He is the black Brooklyn street thug from reform school, adopted by the white benevolent old character from the country who could only imagine the terrible violence done to the boy from the terrible violence the boy can do to others. "I'll break Spinks," Tyson says. "None of them has a chance. I'll break them all." Other sports trade on mayhem, but boxing is condemned for just this: intent.

It is not a sport to Tyson. "I don't like sports; they're social events," he says, though he holds individual athletes in casual esteem. The basketball star Michael Jordan, for one ("Anyone who can fly deserves respect"), or the baseball and football player Bo Jackson. Tyson says of

Jackson, "I love that he's able to do both, but I heard him say that he doesn't like the pain of football. That makes me wonder about him. Football is a hurting business."

If objections to a blood sport were simply medical and not moral, the outsize linemen who blindside diminutive quarterbacks would inspire grim alarms from the American Medical Association instead of cheery press-box bulletins about "mild concussions." The fact of boxing, not the fate of boxers, bothers people. Naturally, the pugilistic brain syndrome of Ali is saddening. And when Gaetan Hart and Cleveland Denny were breaking the ice for the first match of Leonard–Duran, it was regrettable that nearly no one at ringside so much as bothered to look up or today can even very easily recollect which one of them died. Regrettable, but not precisely regretted.

Only the most expendable men are boxers. All of the fighters who ever died—nearly five hundred since 1918, when the *Ring* book started to keep tabs—haven't the political constituency of a solitary suburban child who falls off a trampoline. Observers who draw near enough to fights and fighters to think that they see something of value, something pure and honest, are sure to mention the desperate background and paradoxical gentleness, which even Tyson has in some supply. "I guess it's pretty cool," he says, to be the natural heir to John L. Sullivan, to hold an office of such immense stature and myth, to be able to drum a knuckle on the countertop and lick any man in the house. "If you say so."

Beyond the power and slam, the appeal of boxing may just be its simplicity. It is so basic and bare. In a square ring or vicious circle, stripped to the waist and bone, punchers and boxers counteract. Tyson is already the first, and potentially the second, so the eternal match-up of gore and guile doesn't just occupy him outwardly, it swirls inside him as well. Modern moviemakers are good at capturing the choreography of fights—they understand the Apache dance. But in their Dolby deafness they overdo the supersonic bashing and skip one of the crucial attractions: the missing. Making a man miss is the art. Fundamentally, boxers are elusive. They vanish one moment, reappear the next, rolling around the ring like the smoke in the light.

If the allure of boxing is hazy, the awe of the champion is clear. Regional vainglories like the World Cup or the World Series only aspire to the global importance of the heavyweight champion. Sullivan, Jack Dempsey, Joe Louis and Ali truly possessed the world—countries that couldn't have picked Jimmy Carter out of a lineup recognized Ali at a distance—to the extent that, in a recurring delusion, the world had trouble picturing boxing beyond him. When Dempsey went, he was taking boxing with him. If Louis surrendered, the game would be up. Without Ali, it was dead. Wiser heads, usually balanced like towels on the shoulders of old trainers, always smiled and said, "Someone will come along." Tyson's place in the line is undetermined, but he is certainly the one who came along.

In what is now a two-barge industry Spinks will also have something to say about lineage. The fight is in Atlantic City instead of Las Vegas, which might be called the aging champion of fight towns if the challenger were not so decrepit. Atlantic City forces its smiles through neon casinos that, like gold crowns, only emphasize the surrounding decay. Similarly, Tyson is the younger party involved, but it hardly seems so. The boardwalk age guessers would be lucky to pick his century. He is twenty-one.

All over Tyson's walls at the Ocean Club Hotel are the old sepia photographs out of which he has stepped, going back to Mike Donovan, Jack Blackburn and Joe Jeannette, who in 1909 fought a forty-nine-rounder that featured thirty-eight knockdowns. Louis, Rocky Marciano and Ali are there, but Jack Johnson, Jim Jeffries and Stanley Ketchel are more prominent. (John Lardner told Ketchel's 1910 fate in a pretty good sentence: "Stanley Ketchel was twenty-four years old when he was fatally shot in the back by the common-law husband of the lady who was cooking his breakfast.") The repeaters in Tyson's gallery are Joe Gans and Battling Nelson. In a seventy-nine-year-old picture, Nelson is posing after a knockout with his gloves balanced defiantly on his hips. Tyson struck that same attitude five months ago over the horizontal remains of Larry Holmes.

"I like them all," says the curator from Brownsville and Bedford-Stuyvesant, completing his tour, "but Nelson and Gans are special. Both of them great fighters [lightweights] and fellow opponents near their peak at the same time. That's always special."

In this at least, Michael Spinks can concur. Though ten years older than Tyson, he has managed to register three fewer professional bouts—thirty-one to thirty-four—and only four of those against heavyweights. All told, the two men share sixty-five victories and uneven parts of the mystical championship. While Tyson owns the various belts, Floyd Patterson says, "Spinks has the real title, my old title, the one handed down from person to person." Spinks was first to get to Holmes (whom he outpointed twice), the acknowledged champion for seven years. Patterson forgets, though, that Holmes's branch of the title originated when Michael's older brother Leon skipped a mandatory defense in order to preserve a lucrative rematch with Ali. Holmes won his championship from Ken Norton, who won it from no one. He was assigned the vacated title on the strength of a slender decision over Jimmy Young that may have represented a backlash against the creaking mobster Blinky Palermo. Boxing is a dazzling business.

Cus D'Amato, the manager who stood up to the fight mob in the 1950s, who defied the murderous Frankie Carbo and helped break the monopolist Jim Norris, died in 1985 at seventy-seven and left Tyson in his will. "More than me or Patterson," says D'Amato's other old champion, the light heavyweight José Torres, "Tyson is a clone of Cus's dream. Cus changed both of us, but he made Mike from scratch." In Brooklyn, Tyson had drawn the absent father and saintly mother, the standard neighborhood issue. "You fought to keep what you took," he says, "not what you bought." His literary pedigree is by Charles Dickens out of Budd Schulberg. When Tyson wasn't mugging and robbing, he actually raised pigeons, like Terry Malloy. A tough amateur boxer named Bobby Stewart discovered Tyson in the "bad cottage" of a mountain reformatory and steered him to D'Amato's informal halfway house at Catskill, NY.

Torres recalls the very sight of Tyson at thirteen: "Very short, very shy and very wide." D'Amato pegged him for a champion straight off, though the resident welterweight Kevin Rooney was dubious. "He looked like a big liar to me; he looked old." Hearing that he was destined to be champ, Tyson shrugged laconically. But before long, everyone in the stable began to see him out of Cus's one good eye. "If he keeps listening," Rooney thought, "he's got a chance." The fighters' gym has a fascination of its own: the timeless loft, the faded posters, the dark and smelly world of the primeval man.

To D'Amato, the punching and ducking were rudimentary. Hands up, chin down. Accepting discipline was harder, and controlling emotion was hardest of all. "Fear is like fire," he never tired of saying. "It can cook for you. It can heat your house. Or it can burn it down." D'Amato's neck-bridging exercises enlarged Tyson's naturally thick stem to nearly twenty inches, and the rest of him filled out in concrete blocks. Like every old trainer, D'Amato tried to instill a courtliness at the same time as he was installing the heavy machinery. "My opponent was game and gutsy," the seventeen-year-old Tyson remarked after dusting a Princeton man during the Olympic trials of 1984. "What round did I stop the gentleman in, anyway?"

But in two tries Tyson could not quite best the eventual gold-medal winner, Henry Tillman, who fought him backing up (Spinks's style, incidentally). When the second decision was handed down, Tyson stepped outside the arena and began to weep, actually to bawl, a cold kind of crying that carried for a distance. He was a primitive again. As the US boxing team trooped through the airport after the trials, a woman mistakenly directed her good wishes to the alternate, Tyson. "She must mean good luck on the flight," said the super heavyweight Tyrell Biggs, a future Tyson opponent who would rue his joke.

Turning pro in 1985, Tyson knocked out eighteen men for a start, twelve of them within three minutes, six of those within sixty seconds. He did not jab them; he mauled them with both hands. They fell in sections. His first couple of fights were in Albany, on the undercard of the welterweight Rooney, at an incubator suitably titled "the Egg." Rooney worked Tyson's corner and then fought the main events. Knowing time was short, D'Amato thought to leave a trainer too. "We were fighters together first," says Rooney, thirty-two, who has not warred in three years (his delicate face is practically healed) but never officially retired. "That's my advantage as Mike's trainer, knowing how a fighter thinks. We're a legacy: he's the fighter; I'm the trainer. We're not in Cus's league, but we're close enough." At any mention of D'Amato, Tyson is capable of tears.

For a time, boxing people questioned whether Tyson was tall enough, scarcely five feet eleven inches. "My whole life has been filled with disadvantages," he replied in a voice incongruously high and tender. Tyson's provocative description of himself as a small child is "almost effeminate-shy." But no one doubted the man was hard enough. He wanted to drive Jesse Ferguson's "nose bone into his brain." Civilized fighters like Bonecrusher Smith might choose to hang on in hopes of a miracle, but Tyson wearily informs every opponent, "There are no miracles here." When the circle finally came round to Biggs, the Olympic jester, Tyson "made him pay with his health. I could have knocked him out in the third round [rather than the seventh], but I wanted to do it slowly so he could remember this a long time."

Even for boxing, what this depicts is stark. But Tyson doesn't wince; he shrugs. "Basically I don't care what people think of me. I would never go out of my way to change someone's mind about me. I'm not in the communications business." This was made particularly clear to a wire-service reporter whose hand proffered in greeting was met with the chilling response, "One of your trucks ran over my dog." Tyson had confused UPI with UPS.

In contrast, Michael Spinks cares how he is perceived. He keeps a dictionary handy, and privately speaks it into a tape recorder, since the time he was embarrassed by an unfamiliar word. As for communications, he is willing even to puzzle out cryptograms. From across the ring before Spinks's first Holmes fight, he studied the vacant figure of Ali, trundled in for ceremonial purposes. Ali's hands were at his sides and the fingers of one of them were jumping around in a pathetic way that even Spinks took for palsy. "Then I realized what he was doing. He was telling me, 'Stick, stick, stick, side to side, stick, feint, move.' I nodded my head, yes." Do softer sports have sweeter stories?

The little brother of Leon Spinks was obliged to be a fighter, since hand-me-down grudges were the uniforms of their neighborhood, the fiercest project in St Louis. "What was it meant for me to do in this life?" Michael often wondered. "I was one hell of a paper salesman: the *Post-Dispatch*. Didn't win awards but made a lot of money, at least what we considered a lot. An honest dollar, my mother kept saying, and I liked it. I was seventeen, still working at papers—tall too. 'What are you doing?' the guys would ask. 'Uh, I'm just helping my brother.' I was one of the best dishwashers, then one of the best potwashers, you ever set your eyes on." But he never figured out what was meant for him to do in this life.

Following his 165-pounds victory in the 1976 Olympics, Spinks resisted the pros instinctively. "It's a strange business, where the guy who takes all the licks ends up with the least. Eventually, though, I decided I might as well try to cash in on the gold medal. Being it was such a dirty business, I had this idea that, together, Leon and I could fight the promoters and maybe come out of it with something." In 1978, Leon won and lost the heavyweight championship quicker than anyone ever had, and began tooling the wrong way up one-way streets with his teeth out. "Leon went haywire," Michael says kindly. "It was a circus. It was a jungle. Leon was Tarzan and everyone was after him."

A younger brother cannot decently talk to an older brother like a father, so Michael could only watch and sigh. He loves Leon, who was still losing thirty-three-second fights as recently as last month. By 1981, Michael had quietly won one of the several light heavyweight championships from Eddie Mustafa Muhammad, and within another two years he consolidated all of the titles in a fifteen-round decision over

Dwight Muhammad Qawi. Ten weeks before the Qawi fight, Spinks's common-law wife, the mother of their two-year-old daughter, was killed in an automobile accident. Spinks cried almost all the way to the ring. The old trainer Eddie Futch despaired. But the moment Spinks arrived he seemed different. Leon was sitting at ringside in a cockeyed Stetson. "Straighten your hat, Lee," Michael said coldly.

Futch, a bouncy little man of seventy-seven, was a Golden Gloves teammate of Joe Louis's in 1934. Though only 140 pounds, he often sparred with Louis. "Always, on the last day before a fight, he wanted to be with me," Futch says happily. "I was difficult to hit." Eddie trained Joe Frazier, who was easy to hit. "The pressure Frazier exerted wore men down and made them make mistakes. He was perpetually in motion, always moving, bobbing and weaving. Tyson will go along and then explode. He probably hits as hard as Joe, though."

Norton, another Futch fighter, was as unorthodox as Spinks but less adaptable. "Most heavyweights are locked into a habit," says the sparring partner Qawi, co-champion no more. "But Michael can adjust." Even when Spinks is shadowboxing, Futch says, "I can see he's thinking, working out his plan, and changing it, and changing that." Spinks pledges, "I'll take something in with me, but I'll react to what I find in there."

Showing a modest manner uncommon among the unbeaten, Spinks explains, "I decided to become a heavyweight when I realized there was no money in being a light heavyweight." The fight is promising his side $13.5 million. The new bulk of 208 pounds becomes Spinks as well as his old 175, but he concedes, "I've been hit harder by the bigger men and have found no pleasure in it." (He will spot Tyson maybe 10 pounds; Tyson will return four inches in height and five inches in reach.) On the chance that history was right about light heavyweights never being able to step up, Spinks had left his daughter home from the first Holmes fight. "The second is the one she shouldn't have seen," he says, acknowledging a near-loss. In boxing, this qualifies as breathtaking honesty.

Spinks's fellow Olympian, Sugar Ray Leonard, laughs at that. "He always seems so cynical and pessimistic," Leonard says. "First doom, then gloom, and finally he prevails. At the Olympics, I remember Michael Spinks as a guy who did things that worked, though they happened to be wrong. He'd step right, step left, cross his feet and hit you. He'd always set you up for the punch he wouldn't throw. And he seemed forever to be looking for something."

Not Tyson, surely. "He's a very powerful young man," whistles Spinks through an air-conditioned smile. "The majority of the guys he's fought have worried about getting hit—I worry about it too. He's got such an advantage; he's so strong. But he does things that are mistakes that he might have to pay for." Is Spinks afraid? "Sure, I've got to have my fear," he says. "I refuse to go into the ring without it." But he also says, "I have a nice grip on my pride: I boss it around. I wear it when I should. I throw it in the corner when I don't need it." He'll need it sometime Monday night.

"This is the first time Tyson is going to meet some talent; Spinks is a thinking fighter," says the venerable trainer Ray Arcel, eighty-nine, who carted thirteen opponents to Louis before beating him with Ezzard Charles. ("And you know something? As happy as I was for my guy, that's how sad I was for Joe.") Nothing can touch boxing for beautiful old men. "Tyson is learning how to think too," Arcel says. "He's picked up a lot from those old films he studies, including a little Jack Dempsey." He first saw Dempsey in 1916 in New York City, against John L. Johnson.

"John *Lester* Johnson," Tyson yawns. "No decision. Just ten rounds, I think. Dempsey wasn't a long-fight guy. He would break you up." A puzzlement curls his eyebrows. "When you're a historian, you know things, and you don't even know why you know them." Preparing for the day's sparring, greasing himself like a Channel swimmer and admiring the reflection in a long mirror, he sounds almost bookish, until Rooney turns up a copy of Plutarch's *Lives* and Tyson inquires archly, "Who wrote that? Rembrandt?"

In his own field, he is erudite. "Howard Davis was middle class, wasn't he?" Tyson muses idly, referring to another Olympian on Spinks's team. "Davis was a real good boxer. You can come from a middle-class background and be a real good boxer. But you have to know struggle to be the champ." Without socks, robe or orchestra, wearing headgear as spare as a First World War aviator's, Tyson hurries out to demonstrate his point against an unsteady corps of clay pigeons with perfect names like Michael ("the Bounty") Hunter and Rufus ("Hurricane") Hadley. The slippery leather thuds reverberate through the hall.

Not much like Rembrandt, Tyson fights by the numbers. "Seven-eight," Rooney calls the tune, signaling for combinations. "Feint, two-one. Pick it up, six-one. There you go, seven-one. Now make it a six." The savage sight of Tyson advancing on his sparring partners recalls the classic moan of an early matchmaker: "He fights you like you stole something from him." Uppercuts are especially urgent. "If you move away too much," says Oliver McCall, the best gym fighter of the nine revolving lawn sprinklers, "he'll punch your hipbone and paralyze you in place." Hurricane comes out of the ring still spinning. "He hit me on the top of my head," he whines. "It burns."

In training-camp workouts and at ringside on fight night, the cauliflower reunions fill in another piece of the picture. They are bittersweet delights. Few of the usual suspects favor Spinks. Jake LaMotta thinks Tyson "is gonna go down as one of the greatest fighters of all times, and he's gonna break all records, and he's gonna be around a long, long time, and he's gonna make over $100 million. I could be wrong, but that's my opinion." Billy Conn, the patron saint of overblown light heavyweights, says, "I think Tyson will fix him up in a couple of rounds." Ali likes Spinks, but then Ali liked Trevor Berbick, whom Tyson knocked down three times with one punch. "I don't think Tyson will even be able to hit Spinks," Ali says. "He's like rubber."

Nobody speaks it with huge conviction, but the most promising theory on behalf of Spinks holds that the real world has recently descended on Tyson in the forms of a famous wife, a flamboyant mother-in-law, a $4.5 million mansion in Bernardsville, NJ, a parade of luxury cars (including a dinged one worth $180,000 that he tried to give away to the investigating officers) and a custody battle that pits the well-cologned manager Bill Cayton against the understated promoter Don King. Last August, once Tyson had all the belts, King threw a coronation for history's youngest heavyweight champion. The melancholy scene recalled King Kong crusted with what the promoter called "baubles, rubies and fabulous other doodads." Beholding the dull eyes and meek surprise under the lopsided crown and chinchilla cloak, King said he was reminded "of Homer's Odysseus returning to Ithaca to gather his dissembled fiefdoms." Sighs Tyson: "It's tough being the youngest anything."'

According to Patterson, "When you have millions of dollars, you have millions of friends." The Tyson camp's slice of this fight is $22 million, bringing his bundle so far to more than $40 million. "I originally picked him, and I still do," Patterson allows, "but now I give Spinks a chance." Torres looks at it the other way: "Who knows? It could be good. After all, doesn't he come from turmoil?" A little overwhelmed, Tyson says, "When I'm out of boxing, I'm going to tell everyone I'm bankrupt." In a sepia mood again he adds that "Damon

Runyon never wrote about fighters beating up their wife or getting into car accidents."

Before Tyson arranged to meet Robin Givens, twenty-three, the television actress (Head of the Class) who took him for a husband in February, he once said, "I look in the mirror every day. I know I'm not Clark Gable. I wish I could find a girl who knew me when I was broke and thought I was a nice guy." Following the wedding ceremony, auditors and lawyers started to arrive. In Givens' estimation, "he's strong and sensitive and gentle. I feel protected, but he's so gentle that sometimes I think I have to protect him." Among her previous heartthrobs were Michael Jordan and the comedian Eddie Murphy. Tyson likes to say, "I suaved her." But he mentions, "It's no joke, I'll tell you. If you're not grown up and you want to grow up real quick, get married." In a slightly different context, but only slightly, he says, "So many fighters have been called invincible. Nobody's invincible."

Almost alone among boxers, Tyson has no entourage. It seems to be the only cliché he has avoided. He does his predawn roadwork by himself on the boardwalk, grateful for the solitude. "I don't have any friends. I get paranoid around a lot of people. I can't relax." Besides Rooney and Cutman Matt Baranski, only Steve Lott is admitted to the inner sanctum. "I'm the spit-bucket man," Lott says with shining eyes. "I would give my life for that." He was a handball buddy of Jimmy Jacobs, an honored player who died at fifty-eight last March, reportedly of leukemia. Jacobs and his business partner Cayton, keepers of the most extensive film archives in boxing, were longtime benefactors of D'Amato's teacherage and comanaged Tyson. Lott is essentially a public relations liaison, but is as devoted as Tyson to the flickering images of history, and seems astounded that they suddenly include him.

"To be in the corner!" Lott exclaims. "To be in the dressing room! In that room before the fight, just the four of us, our heartbeats are deafening. When it gets really quiet, it's almost a despair. I don't know what it is. Maybe we don't want it to be over." Coming to life on the subject, Tyson says, "That's my favorite time, just before. I'm so calm. The work is over. You fight and you go home. Before or after, I don't respect any of them more than another. What they look like doesn't really matter. I never dwell on what's to be done or what's been done. I just don't think of stuff like that. In my heart, I know what to do."

He is referring to horror, and a good many people do not want it done. In the regular processes of human cruelty, nobody is arguing against competition or any of the subtler forms of combat. It's just that using brains to extinguish brains seems a little direct. Developing balance to knock somebody off balance, honing eyesight to administer shiners, marshaling memory and ingenuity and audacity and dexterity—and coordinating all of them against themselves, and against coordination—seems self-destructive to a society.

Speaking in Japan some time ago, José Torres was asked why Puerto Rico had so many boxing champions and Japan so few. "You can't have champions in a society that is content," he answered. "My kids can't be champions. I spoiled them." Ken Norton's son has become a pro football player. "You have to know struggle," Tyson says.

Of course, those who would take boxing away from the strugglers offer no plan to replace it. And no one wants to acknowledge that it may be irreplaceable. The high-minded view is that boxing will exist only as long as whatever it reflects in mankind exists, although picturing Spinks slaughtering Tyson is easier than imagining a world without men who ball their fists for pleasure or prizes. The big fight doesn't come along so often any more, defined as the kind that can get in people's stomachs and occasionally have trouble staying there. But here it is again, for twelve rounds or less.

Perhaps the true horror is that there has always been a class poor enough for this, and maybe that's why so many people avert their eyes. Why others have to watch is a perplexity, and why some have to cheer is personal.

Derek Birley

Cardus and The Aesthetic Fallacy

The association of aesthetic pleasure in cricket with romantic images and English traditions was, of course, the trade mark of Neville Cardus. widely regarded as the greatest modern writer on the game. His Edwardian version of the Victorian apotheosis of cricket had fewer moral overtones – and indeed some irony and a deal of comic skill. It is thus a more insidious form of the 'more-than-a-game' argument and, despite its underlying social attitudes, a much more attractive one. Cardus was scarcely a man of the people, and as he grew older even his staunchest admirers began to think that, as Warner said of Lord Hawke, he was sometimes inclined to dwell too much in the past.

Nevertheless, because of his rejection – often quite explicitly – of conventional moral postures he presents a more credible picture of cricket as a game. He is conscious on the one hand of the elements of display and ritual and style; yet on the other he is aware of the fierce demands of the contest. He looks on them amorally. In this he resembles Ernest Hemingway on the subject of bullfighting and at his best he can be almost as compelling. There are no stylistic similarities, of course. Cardus is too fond of what Hemingway called 'ten-dollar words' and has intellectual pretensions to match.

These pretensions seem sometimes to get him into a muddle. Though Cardus talks much of 'philosophy' it is doubtful if he had one himself – or, if he had, he could produce a new one every day. In 1920 in a piece grandly entitled 'The Cricketer as Artist' we find him claiming that 'love of technique for technique's sake is a characteristic in English cricket today,' and contrasting this with the Hambledon days when folk were simply, and without sophistication, concerned about winning. (That this was not true is not the immediate point.) The attitude in 1920, he suggests, was: 'Who cares about the tussle for championship points if a Ranji be glancing to leg?' As never before cricket was full of artists, forever trying to do things the hard way – 'the divine discontent of the artist'. The danger was that specialism would lead cricketers to become so obsessed with artistic technique that they would forget about the basic principles on which winning matches depend. 1920 was, he felt, the heyday of the 'cricketer-artist'. Yet in 1923 he was rebuking the counties, suggesting that cricket was in danger of becoming cannily utilitarian with too much of an eye to the main chance.

Nor, for all his pretensions, does he make any serious effort to consider the nature of art or to spell out what he means by it. Instead he describes some of the characteristics of certain aspects of art and uses this as the basis for comment on one or other of his favourite characters or themes. What he is usually describing is style, which, though it is a thing all artists have, is not itself art. Thus, on his favourite lay-figure, Frank Woolley: 'Art, when all is said and done, is simply the expression of personality, through a stylish technique, making for our pleasure. Is not then Woolley an artist?'

Style, technique, expressing personality, giving pleasure: are these all that is needed to constitute art? Not unless we are content with a definition of art so loose as to be meaningless. As R. G. Collingwood put it: 'The terms "art", "artist" and "artistic" and so forth are much used as courtesy titles: the thing which most constantly demands and receives the courtesy title of art is the thing whose real name is amusement or entertainment. The vast majority of our literature in prose and verse, our painting and drawing and sculpture, our music and dancing and acting and so forth, is quite plainly and often quite explicably designed to amuse, but is called art. Yet we know there is a distinction.'

Cardus deserves special attention, not only because of the reverence accorded his writings, but because his use of artistic courtesy titles has distinct social overtones. For one thing in cricket he was apt to confuse style with pedigree. For another, despite all the rhetorical flourishes, he gives the distinct impression that he is merely using cricket as a vehicle for his own loftier purposes. His autobiographies suggest that he may even have felt he was slumming, culturally speaking, when he was at Old Trafford rather than at Hallé concerts or the theatre. So he needed to elevate cricket by highbrow comparisons with the world of art.

An interesting comparison with the kind of vibrant prose Cardus was writing in the 1920s can be found in an essay from a more substantial contemporary. J. B. Priestley has no very lofty notions about cricket: he suggests 'that after all there are other things than games, and England is not ruined just because sinewy brown men from a distant colony sometimes hit a ball oftener than our men do'.

However. in the same spirit, he defends the claims of Herbert Sutcliffe to the same artistic status as himself. Priestley purports to admonish friends who believe that 'a man should not play a game for money though they do not object to my method of earning a living. They do not seem to see', he continues, 'that if it is ridiculous that a man should play cricket for money, it is still more ridiculous that a man should air his feelings for money, that a professional batsman is less absurd than a professional sonneteer.'

Priestley promises more than he actually delivers in this diverting essay. 'The fact is', he writes, 'that these friends of mine are unjust to Sutcliffe and his fellow professionals because they have not grasped the simple fact that sport and art are similar activities.' But the point he goes on to make, though fair enough, is a side issue: 'that none of us, whether we are batsmen or poets, bowlers or essayists, work away in our fields or our studies for the money itself. We bat or write because we have a passion for batting or writing and only take the money so that the butcher and baker may be paid while we are so happily engaged.' And again, having got under the ball, as it were, he drops the catch. Priestley tells us that compared with himself Sutcliffe is 'the better performer. Not for long years, if ever at all, shall I achieve in this prose the grace, the lovely ease, that shines through innings after innings of his.' But he offers no exploration of the tension between function and beauty. All he is saying, in effect, is that both writers and batsmen have something we call style.

In Cardus, of course, the cricketer's style is part of something at once more mystical aesthetically and more significant socially. As a result, for all his repeated and conscious efforts, he takes us no further than Priestley, who in his one brief look at cricket was not even trying to go further, in developing the implicit notion that cricket is a performing art. This is unfortunate, for that is what cricket seems to be if it is art at all. Cardus obscures the issue by his descents into vague generalized aestheticisms, spiced with cultural name-dropping. At one point he asks provocatively: 'Why do we deny the art of a cricketer and rank it lower than a vocalist's or a fiddler's?' But in the context of the preceding sentence – 'And Spooner's cricket in spirit was kin with sweet music, and the wind that makes long grasses wave, and the singing of Elizabeth Schumann in Johann Strauss, and the poetry of Herrick' – the thrust of the question is lost.

In his well-known comparisons of cricket with music Cardus seems more concerned with what the neighbours might think than with the actual music. In itself the comparison with music seems to fit cricket better than comparison with literature: unlike the writer the cricketer has no artefact at the end of his innings. This is true of the musician, though not of the composer. It seems unlikely that Cardus had any such distinction in mind when he wrote: 'You will find on every pavilion in the country today men who speak of Gunn's batting as musicians speak of Mozart.' Was he writing metaphorically, meaning 'as musicians speak of a great performance of Mozart's music'? In any event the comparison does not tell the whole story. The cricketer is less than a composer because there is no artefact but more than an interpreter of someone else's artistic creation. In fact he is more like a jazz soloist than either Mozart or his interpreter because he is creating, improvising, as well as performing, and his art is as ephemeral as that of Louis Armstrong.

Ronald Mason, though contrasting the cricketer with those who create artefacts, aligns him with the actor, which unless he is an actor who makes up his own lines seems not quite a true parallel: 'The writer and the painter and the composer live as long as their works are allowed to live. Wren lives in St Paul's, Shakespeare at the Old Vic, Rembrandt at the National Gallery, Mozart at Sadler's Wells. The actor and the games player, every bit as popular and accomplished in their lifetimes, have no personal power of survival.'

The actor and the games player have indeed much in common. For one thing they are both, if successful, likely to find themselves the subject of adulation. Elsewhere Ronald Mason reminds us of the 'formidable army of middle-aged men in whom the memory of Jack Hobbs is ineffaceable by time. I was one of them; in the words of Whitman, I was the man, I suffered, I was there; I took part in this intense and prolonged relationship between a public and its hero.' Here the actor and the games player share a kind of relationship with the public that writers, painters and composers do not usually have.

But the element of originality and improvisation of the jazz musician is lacking. The dancer may be nearer the mark, in this respect, than the actor. C. B. Fry thought the dance was the basis of all worthwhile games: 'The Greeks knew the secret. A game was not worth the trouble it put you to unless it was first and last a physical fine art. Cricket was a dance with a bat in your hand, or with the encumbrance of a ball. What was exquisite and memorable was the lyric movement of the artist in action. What was incidental was the score that came about from his handling of the ball.' However, the very exposition shows the weakness of this and all other comparisons outside games. Fry may give a very good reason for taking up dancing or a very good description of what he got from cricket. The dance may be a sort of game, but it is not the same sort as cricket. Cricket with nobody caring about runs or wickets may be a good dance, but is no longer a game and, surely, no longer cricket.

An obvious point of contrast is in the significance of the rules in games and in art forms. There are rules and conventions in the performing arts, for the benefit of performer and public, but these are acknowledged to be of lesser importance than the style of the performance: innovation and challenge to the accepted order is often the hallmark of talent. In games it is different: there can be innovations in technique or equipment but they must be within the rules. However well he bowls, the bowler will achieve nothing unless he keeps his foot behind a certain white line. Though rules may need to be changed – for instance to accommodate new techniques or equipment – it is essential that they be observed while they do exist and that the star performer does not set them aside or think himself above them. He has to try to win, legally. In cricket he also has to remember that he is a member of a team.

Neville Cardus, some years after his earlier and contentious description, gave a different opinion about early cricket. Presumably he had read Nyren in the meantime: at any rate he came nearer historical accuracy: 'Hambledon cricket was as satisfying to the aesthetic senses as it was stimulating to the combative instincts. In the pages of Nyren we can find as many allusions to the gracefulness of Hambledon cricket as to its skill.' This is the display element that was once greatly admired in cricket and other team games but nowadays tends to be subordinated to competition and excitement. J. M. Kilburn shows how the two elements can coexist for the spectator in this description of Hammond's 240 at Lord's in 1938: 'The mind's eye captured and the heart treasured pictures of drives from the front foot, drives from the back foot scorching through the covers to be greeted with "Oo-oh" and "Aa-ah" of wonder before acknowledgement by crackle of clapping. The clapping applauded the effectiveness of the stroke, its product in runs; the spontaneous cries of wonderment were tribute to the magic in the stroke's creation. Such response is the accolade of the cricket spectator and is rarely given because it is drawn from a quality of batting rarely presented.'

Cardus misses out, of course, the other element in Hambledon cricket: that usually a great deal of money was at stake. This must have given another dimension to the emotions of those involved and an extra edge to the combative element. It is true that many with an eye for beauty have found things to admire in the game, but that does not necessarily mean that it is an art form. Many men with an eye for beauty devote their attention to pretty girls but to think of girls as an art form is, most people would think, to miss the point. With cricket, as with girls, there is more to it than that; and furthermore that something more is what determines what the cricket-lover or the girl-lover thinks is beautiful.

So far as spectators are concerned we must allow for the fact that individuals may take from the game whatever they are seeking from it. But it seems unlikely that Robert Lynd spoke for the majority when he wrote about Bradman: 'Secure conscious mastery of this kind is the crown of genius. By the time he had scored 50 I am sure that even the most ardent pro-English spectator in the ground would have been bitterly disappointed if he had gone out.' The 1977 Test series between England and Australia was chiefly notable for English victories built upon long, patient, disciplined innings by Geoffrey Boycott received in rapture by the crowds. Australia's defeat was assisted by the low scores of their captain Greg Chappell, a much more stylish player (and also a faster scorer) than Boycott. But very few English people would have preferred flamboyance to victory.

Nor can style, in itself, be the most important thing to the cricketer. We can hardly follow Cardus up the garden path in this eulogy of MacLaren. 'I always think of him today as I saw him once playing forward to Blythe beautifully, a majestic rhythm governing the slightest movement. He was clean bowled on the occasion I have in mind for none, but nobody other than a giant of the game could have made a duck so immaculately.' If we are to take this literally MacLaren must have been one of the very few cricketers who ever succeeded in looking and feeling anything other than pretty foolish when bowled through the forward defensive stroke. But even on its own fanciful level this is hard to take: making ducks beautifully is not what cricket is about and if MacLaren had made many of them the selectors would have preferred somebody who could make a few runs, in however ungainly a fashion. His magnificent centuries were fortunately more frequent than his immaculate ducks.

It is no criticism of Tom Richardson, who was one of the great bowlers by any standards, to suggest that his marvellous style was an

optional extra. 'His action moved one like music because it was so
rhythmical,' writes Cardus. On the other hand Sammy Woods tells us
of the Demon Spofforth: 'He delivered every ball with the same action,
and as he looked all legs, arms, and nose, it was very hard to distinguish
what ball was coming along next.'

For the player the best style is that which achieves its objective most
effectively, and the objective must usually be winning. We can leave
out of account exhibition games, virtuoso performances when nothing
is at stake, because they are not typical and would not exist without
the staple of the normal competitive basis of the game, and (also)
because even in a festival match the star performer, if he is to make his
fifty entertaining runs before adjourning to the bar, must keep the ball
out of his stumps.

A batsman's style may be like Sutcliffe's or Bradman's, highly
functional but not elegant; and an elegant style may be none the less
functional. A. G. Gardiner, in asserting the supremacy of Ranji's
technique, writes of his refinement of style, 'which seems to have
reduced action to its barest terms ... It is not jugglery or magic; it is
simply the perfect economy of means to end.' Now this is of course a
widely held tenet of design theory, that reduction to essentials is the
basis of good style, but it is not the only view. C. B. Fry, on Victor
Trumper, puts it slightly differently: 'He had no style, yet he was all
style. He had no fixed economical method of play, he defied all the
orthodox rules, yet every stroke he played satisfied the ultimate
criterion of style – the minimum of effort, the maximum of effect.'

But not all genius is effortless. If Fry had written 'apparent'
minimum of effort he would have made allowance for the perspiration
as well as the inspiration that is also a legitimate part of building up a
style. Many apparently brilliant impromptu speeches have been carefully learned and polished. Furthermore in human movement the
apparently simple and logical may not actually be so. The early time-
and-motion study experts who produced rationalized movement charts
found that the theoretically best system was not necessarily the best for
everyone. The individual has a natural rhythm which may require
peculiarities of movement, and unless these are allowed for the result
may be quicker fatigue, or muscle strain, and lower production. A
cricketer's style, as any good coach will tell you, is unlikely to stand up
to crisis pressures or tests of endurance unless it is based on natural
tendencies.

Whether it looks good is a matter of taste, often depending on the fashion of the day. 'I don't like thy writing, Mester Cardus,' the dour Yorkshire batsman Arthur Mitchell is reported to have said. 'It's too fancy.' 'Well, that's more than anybody could say about thy batting, Arthur,' said Maurice Leyland, putting the matter into perspective. There is more than one good style.

There is also, to return to an earlier point, more to art than style. To refer to the contemporary debate in the groves of academe about aesthetics and sport is to risk entering a morass. But we need to tiptoe around its edges. Style is one thing that may often be thought important to both art and games. But it is not the only thing in either, and if a performer possesses a good style that does not make him, in either sphere, an artist. Professor L. A. Reid, in a thoroughly sensible contribution to a somewhat mixed collection of *Readings in the Aesthetics of Sport*, points out that even if the terms used to describe the many ingredients of art and of sport were used precisely there are many hazards in the path of those who want to link the two. 'Because strategy, design, feeling, skill, grace, beauty, sometimes ritual, are common to both art and games, it does not follow that games are art or works of art ... To argue from some resemblances between art and games to the affirmation that games *are* art is to commit the formal logical fallacy of the undistributed middle.' Even more illogical, we might add, to argue from one pet resemblance, style.

Reid reminds us that when people talk about a great footballer or tennis player as 'artists' it may well be their *craft* that is meant. It may be significant that in cricket the mythology evokes loftier associations. C. L. R. James, in the same collection of *Readings*, identifies style as the essential artistic element in cricket. 'Another name for the perfect flow of motion is style, or, if you will, significant form,' he tells us; and again, 'Significant form at its most unadulterated is permanently present. It is known, expected, recognized and enjoyed by tens of thousands of spectators. Cricketers call it style.'

Whether James is being profound or merely pretentious, cricket seems to attract such statements as a honey pot attracts bees. In part this may be because a greater element of display is intrinsic to cricket than to other games. But there also seem to be social connotations. In the English tradition gentlemen have been considered as a category more stylish than players. And the notion is bound up with reverence for the past.

R. C. Robertson-Glasgow, one of the best of cricket writers, puts it well: 'It is the joy of the critics, when appraising a great player, to say why he is not quite to be compared with this or that hero of the past. When all else fails, they bring up the question of style. "Wonderful," they cry, "yes, very wonderful, but not so beautiful as so-and-so." So-and-so, in his day, of course had the same thing said about him. Thus, elusive perfection is chased ever back. Maybe Adam had an off-drive that made the Serpent weep for very delight.'

His description of Bradman is worth any amount of rhapsody: 'At the wicket, Bradman saw what needed to be done sooner than the others, and did it with more precision. He may or may not have equalled Trumper, Ranji, Macartney, Hobbs, Woolley, in sheer artistry. Such things are arguable. He was not Jovian, like Doctor Grace. He had not the splendour, the mien, of Hammond, who came from the pavilion like the *Victory* sailing to destroy Napoleon. But Bradman went on. He had one eye, as it were, on the heavens and the other on the ledger-book. In the whole game, he was the greatest capitalist of skill. Poetry and murder lived in him together. He would slice the bowling to ribbons, then dance without pity on the corpse. It has been objected that Bradman was fallible on a damaged pitch. He was. This is like saying that a man may slip when walking on ice. But the critics condemn him on one act of rashness against Verity. Verity himself knew better, and told me how Bradman, for over after over at Sheffield in 1938, played his sharpest spinners on a sticky pitch in the middle of the bat.'

Robertson-Glasgow offers an interesting comparison with his near-contemporary Cardus. He shares with him the rejection of cricket as a powerful moral force. 'I have never regarded cricket as a branch of religion. I have met, and somehow survived, many of its blindest worshippers. I have staggered, pale and woozly, from the company of those who reject the two-eyed stance as Plymouth Brethren reject all forms of pleasure except money-making. I have never believed that cricket can hold Empires together, or that cricketers chosen to represent their country in distant parts should be told, year after year, that they are Ambassadors. If they are, I can think of some damned odd ones.'

On the other hand Robertson-Glasgow extended his scepticism to fine writing, too: 'The air of holy pomp started from the main temple at Lord's, and it breathed over the press like a miasma. "Procul, O Procul Este, Profani!" We are not as other men. Sometimes I look back at reports of games in which I took part, and I have thought: "And are these arid periphrases, these formal droolings, these desiccated shibboleths really supposed to represent what was done and how it was done? What has become of that earthy striving, that comic, tragic thing which was our match of cricket?"'

Cardus, by contrast, though never desiccated or arid, could periphrase and drool with the best of them. In this mood he is a blatant purveyor of debased romantic imagery. He is capable of shameless, if sometimes skilful, assemblages of emotive language. Often it dissolves on analysis: 'That day we had watched Woolley in all his glory, batting his way through a hundred felicitous runs . . . Whenever I am in love with cricket's beauty and sentiment I always think of the game as I saw it go to an end that day, in Kent, as though to the strain of a summer's cadence.' And, with more cadences: 'Some of Woolley's innings stay with us until they become like poetry which can be told over and over again . . .

> Lovely are the curves of the white owl sweeping
> Wavy in the dusk lit by one large star.

I admit, O reader, that an innings by Woolley has nothing to do with owls and dusk and starlight. I am trying to talk of an experience of the fancy; I am talking of cadences, of dying falls common to all the beauty of the world.'

In the real world, according to Arthur Mailey, Woolley moved rather awkwardly because he was slightly knock-kneed. This apart, Robertson-Glasgow approached the task of writing about him somewhat differently from Cardus: 'Frank Woolley was easy to watch, difficult to bowl to, and impossible to write about. When you bowled to him there weren't enough fielders; when you wrote about him there weren't enough words. In describing a great innings by Woolley, and few of them were not great in artistry, you had to go carefully with your adjectives and stack them in little rows, like pats of butter or razor-blades. In the first over of his innings, perhaps, there had been an exquisite off-drive, followed by a perfect cut, then an effortless leg glide. In the second over the same sort of thing happened, and your superlatives had already gone. The best thing to do was to assume that your readers knew how Frank Woolley batted and use no adjectives at all.'

Perhaps to readers of the *Manchester Guardian* in 1938 the daring imagery of their cricket correspondent seemed comparable to the striking juxtapositions of Donne, Andrew Marvell or other metaphysical poets of the seventeenth century. Perhaps it was possible to thrill to this description of Hammond: 'The wrists were supple as the fencer's steel; the light, effortless, yet thrilling movements of his bat suggested that he had now reached the cadenza of his full-toned and full-sized concerto with orchestra.' To the irreverent 1970s it may, on the other hand, seem merely bogus. At its worst Cardus's writing is like advertising copy. He exploits the nostalgic, white-on-green, rustic bliss, dreaming spires and village inn images that can be relied upon to evoke deep and satisfying emotions in cricket-lovers, just as a television commercial exploits sex or greed.

There were other sides to Cardus, of course. In terms of our theme, however, which is to compare cricket's mythology with its reality, this aspect has a special importance. The grandiose in all its forms has found a spiritual home in cricket. This hankering after aesthetic significance is, compared with other archetypal attitudes, harmless and often enjoyable. Any connection with cricket though, is often, as cautious fiction writers used to say, purely coincidental. Consider A. G. Gardiner rhapsodizing over the art of Ranjitsinhji – 'It is the great etcher who with a line finds infinity. It is the art of the great dramatist who with a significant word shakes the soul' – or Francis Thompson on Vernon Royle fielding at cover: 'Slender and symmetrical, he moved with the lightness of a young roe, the flexuous elegance of a leopard.'

It is only fair to point out that though it is the English who have most freely conferred the courtesy title of art on cricket they have not been entirely alone in this. C. L. R. James we have already observed bestowing the accolade. Another most distinguished art buff was the late Sir Robert Menzies, the delightful former Prime Minister of Australia and self-confessed cricket addict. He was not only sure that cricket was an art but one that compared favourably with the more conventional sort: 'Indeed, the art of cricket,' he wrote in the Centenary *Wisden*, 'unlike some others, retains its hold upon the art-lover of all generations because its basic elements do not go out of fashion. He does not suffer the puzzlement and frustration of the man who has learned to love and to live with the great works of the Impressionist painters and is then called upon to bow (for fashion's sake) before the abstractionists of the modern school.'

This marvellously question-begging claim illustrates well two points touched on earlier. The first is that when cricket-lovers confer the courtesy title of art it is usually style to which they are referring. The second is that Robertson-Glasgow was right in suggesting that such references are usually part of an argument about the good old days, evocations of Hornby and Barlow long ago, part of the dream-world.

It is a process that, in self-fulfilling prophecy, eliminates from consideration all aspects that do not fit the chosen image. Thus Sir Robert Menzies chides certain of the growing number of cricket writers for missing the point of it all: 'They include far too many who live for sensation and, if possible, scandal; to whom cricket is a sort of warfare to be conducted on, and, principally perhaps, off the field; who are incapable of understanding art; who think in headlines.'

We shall turn, in the next chapter, to the warfare and consider whether or not it is an invention of the media. Here the question is rather whether Sir Robert's somewhat arbitrary encapsulation of art is good enough. Without labouring the point unduly it seems reasonable to suggest that if we are to bestow the courtesy title at all, it must be as a performing art and that we must leave the Impressionists and their modern supplanters out of it. Further, the art must be seen as the chance by-product of the contest .

One thing the aesthetic school tends to forget is that the artistic is not to be equated with the beautiful. The vivid, the dramatic, the comic or the epic may be anything but beautiful, but they are all part of art. And they are very much part of cricket. There was nothing beautiful – unless you were an Australian – about the way Lindwall in 1953 with the darkness of the Headingley stand behind him shattered Hutton's stumps with the second ball of the match, but it was dramatic all right, from the hushed expectancy of the crowd as the bowler began his run to their stunned silence afterwards. For many it seemed like the end of the match.

Nor was there anything beautiful about the sight of Cyril Washbrook's jutting backside when in the corresponding match in 1956, with three England wickets swept away for a handful of runs, the veteran recalled to the colours marched out to face the music. But that was dramatic, too, and it stayed so throughout the whole of the day until that marvellous stand was finally broken when May was caught at long leg by a great catch off Lindwall.

Robertson-Glasgow's spectrum – 'that earthy striving, that comic, tragic thing' – is more convincing than cadences or great etchers. The comic in particular must have its due (as of course Cardus and Menzies were both, in less exalted moments, fully aware). We should not want to forget some of the memorable moments recalled by Robertson-Glasgow himself: the festival match in 1923 when the umpires announced that they were going to be very generous about l.b.w. decisions, and George Gunn sidled up from mid-on and said to one of the umpires: 'And I suppose, if anyone's bowled [rhyming with 'scowled'] it's just a nusty accident?' Or the time he bowled Maurice Tate and followed through so far that he nearly stood on the batsman's huge feet: 'Why,' said Maurice afterwards, 'you came down the pitch like Abraham.'

Jack Fingleton's story of the old Lancashire spectator might be apocryphal but it could be true; the Lancastrian saw 'a well-clad batsman impeccable in his approach and technique to and at the crease survive a loud appeal for leg-before the first ball and another loud appeal for caught behind off the second; with the third he had his stumps spreadeagled. "Ee, lad," said the gaffer as the downfallen one passed him on the pavilion steps, "thou wert lucky to get a dook." Even more probable is the Yorkshire variant in which Emmott Robinson, reluctantly playing and even more reluctantly bowling against one of the older universities, trundled up and turned his arm over to clean-bowl the resplendent youth first ball. On his way out the young man graciously commends Emmott. 'Jolly good ball, Robinson.' 'Aye,' says Emmott, 'it were wasted on thee.'

Nor should the quest for the aesthetic ignore that memorable occasion when Crossland, the Lancashire bowler whom Lord Harris refused to play against, bowled out the Revd J. R. Napier and shouted 'Over goes yon pulpit,' or words to that effect. Or Sir Timothy O'Brien given out caught off his shoulder and saying to the umpire, 'You must be either a rogue or a fool,' and the umpire saying merely, 'I guess I'm a bit of both, sir.' Or Ted Wainwright, getting underneath one of Albert Trott's biggest hits, as high as Blackpool Tower, and then thinking better of trying to catch it, and Lord Hawke on to him with, 'Ted, why didn't you try to catch it?' and Wainwright replying, 'Well, your Lordship, it were a bit 'igh weren't it?' Or any one of a hundred other stories that reflect the game's history and its true nature.

Perhaps in the end, though, it is the earthy and the physical that remind us best what cricket is really like. Sammy Woods's description of an incident in a Yorkshire match may not be elegant prose but it is the real thing: 'Yorkshire were in trouble, Tunnicliffe split a finger and J. T. Brown put his shoulder out bowling. I took off my boot and tried to put it [the shoulder] in at once, but couldn't manage it, although I had someone to sit on his head and others to hold him down. He was very sweaty from bowling, I couldn't get a firm grip of his arm, so he had to go to hospital and have it done. I am certain to this day that had he kept still it would have saved a lot of trouble. Poor fellow, I don't think he ever bowled again.'

BEING THERE

V. S. Naipaul

England v. West Indies (1963)

The First Day

At Waterloo and Trafalgar Square the underground train begins to fill. Young men in tweed jackets, carrying mackintoshes and holdalls. Older men in City black, carrying umbrellas. At every station the crowd grows. Whole families now, equipped as for a rainy camping weekend. And more than a sprinkling of West Indians. At Baker Street we are like a rush-hour train. It is eleven o'clock on a Thursday morning and we are travelling north. The train empties at St John's Wood. Buy your return ticket now, the boards say. We will regret that we didn't. Later. Now we are in too much of a hurry. We pass the souvenir sellers, the man selling the West Indian newspaper, the white-coated newspaper vendors. The newspaper posters. What billing these cricket writers get!

Then inside. It is wet. Play has not begun. A Barbadian in a blue suit, a tall man standing behind the sightscreen, has lost his brother in the crowd, and is worried. He has been in London for four years and a half. He has the bearing of a student. But: 'I works. In transport.' The groundsmen in vivid green lounge against the wicket covers. Someone rushes out to them with a plate of what looks like cakes. There is applause. Few people have eaten before such a large appreciative audience. Presently, though, there is action. The covers are removed, the groundsmen retreat into obscurity, and the rites begin.

Trueman bowling to Conrad Hunte. Four, through the slips. Four, to midwicket. Four, past gully. Never has a Test opened like this. A Jamaican whispers: 'I think Worrell made the right decision.' A little later: 'It's all right now. I feel we getting on top.' The bowling tightens. The batsmen are on the defensive, often in trouble.

'I think Conrad Hunte taking this Moral Rearmament a little too seriously. He don't want to hit the ball because the leather come from an animal.'

A chance.

The Jamaican says: 'If England have to win, they can't win now.'

I puzzle over this. Then he leans back and whispers again: 'England can't win now. *If* they have to win.'

Lunch. In front of the Tavern the middle-class West Indians. For them too this is a reunion.

'... and, boy, I had to leave Grenada because politics were making it too hot for me.'

'What, they have politics in Grenada?'

Laughter.

'You are lucky to be seeing me here today, let me tell you. The only thing in which I remain West Indian is cricket. Only thing.'

'... and when they come here, they don't even change.'

'Change? Them?'

Elsewhere:

'I hear the economic situation not too good in Trinidad these days.'

'All those damn strikes. You know our West Indian labour. Money, money. And if you say "work", they strike.'

But the cricket ever returns.

'I don't know why they pick McMorris in place of Carew. You can't have two sheet anchors as opening batsmen. Carew would have made 16: 16 and out. But he wouldn't have let the bowling get on top as it is now. I feel it have a lil politics in McMorris pick, you know.'

After lunch, McMorris leg-before to Trueman.

'Man, I can't say I sorry. Poke, poke.'

Hunte goes. And, 65 runs later, Sobers.

'It isn't a healthy score, is it?'

'My dear girl, I didn't know you followed cricket.'

'Man, how you could help it at home? In Barbados. And with all my brothers. It didn't look like this, though, this morning. 13 in the first over.'

'But that's cricket.'

A cracking drive, picked up almost on the boundary.

'Two runs only for that. So near and so far.'

'But that's life.'

'Man, you're a philosopher. It must be that advanced age of yours you've been telling me about.'

'Come, come, my dear. It isn't polite to agree with me. But seriously, what you doing up here?'

'Studying, as they say. Interior decorating. It's a hard country, boy. I came here to make money.' Chuckle.

'You should have gone somewhere else.'

In a doorway of the Tavern:

'If Collie Smith didn't dead, that boy Solomon wouldn'ta get pick, you know.'

'If Collie Smith didn't dead.'

'He used to jump out and hit Statham for 6 and thing, you know.'

'I not so sure that Worrell make the right decision.'

'Boy, I don't know. I had a look through binoculars. It breaking up already, you know. You didn't see the umpire stop Dexter running across the pitch?'

'Which one is Solomon? They look like twins.'

'Solomon have the cap. And Kanhai a lil fatter.'

'But how a man could get fat, eh, playing all this cricket?'

'Not getting *fat*. Just putting on a lil *weight*.'

'O Christ! He out! Kanhai.'

Afterwards, Mrs Worrell in a party at the back of the pavilion:

'Did you enjoy the cricket, Mrs Worrell?'

'All except Frank's duck.'

'A captain's privilege.'

The Second Day

McMorris, the West Indian opening batsman whose failure yesterday was so widely discussed by his compatriots around the ground, was this morning practising at the nets. To him, bowling, Sobers and Valentine. Beyond the stands, the match proper continues, Solomon and Murray batting, according to the transistors. But around the nets there is this group that prefers nearness to cricketers. McMorris is struck on the pads. 'How's that?' Sobers calls. 'Out! Out!' the West Indians behind the nets shout, and raise their fingers. McMorris turns. 'You don't out down the line in England.' Two Jamaicans, wearing the brimless pork-pie hats recently come into fashion among West Indian workers in England, lean on each other's shoulders and stand, swaying, directly behind the stumps.

'Mac, boy,' one says, 'I cyan't tell you how I feel it yesterday when they out you. I feel it, man. Tell me, you sleep well last night? I couldn't sleep, boy.'

McMorris snicks one into the slips from Valentine. Then he hooks one from Sobers. It is his favourite shot.

'I wait for those,' he tells us.

A Jamaican sucks his teeth. 'Tcha! Him didn't bat like that yesterday.' And walks away.

The West Indian wickets in the meantime fall. Enter Wesley Hall. Trueman and he are old antagonists, and the West Indians buzz good-humouredly. During this encounter the larger interest of the match recedes. Hall drives Trueman straight back for 4, the final humiliation of the fast bowler. Trueman gets his own back by hitting Hall on the ankle, and Hall clowningly exaggerates his distress. The middle-class West Indians in the Tavern are not so impressed.

'It's too un-hostile, man, to coin a word. You don't win Test matches with that attitude.'

West Indies all out for 301.

And England immediately in trouble. At ten past one Dexter comes in to face a score of 2 for 1. 20 for 1, lunch nearly due, and Griffith gets another wicket. A Jamaican, drunk on more than the bitter he is holding, talks of divine justice: Griffith's previous ball had been no-balled.

'You know, we going to see the West Indies bat again today.'

'But I want them to make some runs, though, I don't want it to be a walkover.'

'Yes, man. I want to see some cricket on Monday.'

But then Dexter. Tall, commanding, incapable of error or gracelessness. Every shot, whatever its result, finished, decisive. Dexter hooking: the ball seeming momentarily *arrested* by the bat before being redirected. Dexter simplifying: an illusion of time, even against these very fast bowlers.

'If they going to make runs, I want to see Dexter make them.'

'It would be nice. But I don't want him to stay too long. Barrington could stay there till kingdom come. But Dexter does score too damn fast. He could demoralize any side in half an hour. Look, they scoring now at the rate of 6 runs an over.'

'How you would captain the side? Take off Griffith?'

Sobers comes on. And Dexter, unbelievably, goes. West Indian interest subsides.

'I trying to sell a lil insurance these days, boy. You could sell to Barbadians. Once they over here and they start putting aside the couple of pounds every weeks you could sell to them. But don't talk to the Jamaicans.'

'I know. They pay three weeks' premiums, and they want to borrow three hundred pounds.'

In the Tavern:

'You know what's wrong with our West Indians? No damn discipline. Look at this business this morning. That Hall and Trueman nonsense. Kya-kya, very funny. But that is not the way the Aussies win Tests. I tell you, what we need is *conscription*. Put every one of the idlers in the army. Give them discipline.'

The score mounts. Worrell puts himself on. He wants to destroy this partnership between Parks and Titmus before the end of play. There is determination in his run, his delivery. It transmits itself to the West Indian crowd, the West Indian team. And, sad for Parks, who had shown some strokes, Worrell gets his wicket. Trueman enters. But Hall is damaged. There can be no revenge for the morning's humiliation. And matters are now too serious for clowning anyway.

West Indies 301. England 244 for 7.

Afterwards, Mrs Worrell in her party.

'You can still bowl, then, Mrs Worrell. You can still bowl.'

'Frank willed that, didn't he, Mrs Worrell?'

'Both of us willed it.'

'So, Mrs Worrell, the old man can still bowl.'

'Old man? You are referring to my father or my husband?'

The Third Day

Lord's Ground Full, the boards said at St John's Wood Station, and there was two-way traffic on Wellington Road. No one practising at the nets today. And Trueman and Titmus still batting. Hall, recovered this morning, wins his duel with Trueman by clean bowling him. But England is by no means finished. Shackleton is correct and unnervous against Hall and Griffith, Titmus regularly steals a run at the end of the over.

Titmus won't get 50; England won't make 300, won't make 301. These are the bets being made in the free seats, West Indian against West Indian. Lord's has restrained them: in the West Indies they will gamble on who will field the next ball, how many runs will be scored in the over. For them a cricket match is an unceasing drama.

Titmus gets his 50. All over the free stands money changes hands. Then England are all out for 297. More money changes hands. It has worked out fairly. Those who backed Titmus for 50 backed England for 300.

Anxiety now, as the West Indians come out for the second innings. With the scores so even, the match is beginning all over again. 'I feel we losing a wicket before lunch. And I feel that it not going to be McMorris, but Hunte. I don't know, I just have this feeling.' Hunte hits a 6 off a bad ball from Trueman, and alarms the West Indians. 'Trueman vex too bad now.' What opens so brightly can't end well. So it turns out. Hunte is caught by Cowdrey off Shackleton. And in comes Kanhai, at twenty past one, with ten minutes to lunch, and the score 15 for 1. How does a batsman feel at such a time?

I enquire. And, as there are few self-respecting West Indians who are not in touch with someone who is in touch with the cricketers, I am rewarded. I hear that Kanhai, before he goes in to bat, sits silent and moody, 'tensing himself up'. As soon as the first West Indian wicket falls he puts on his gloves and, without a word, goes out.

Now, however, as he appears running down the pavilion steps, bat in one hand, the other hand lifted and slightly crooked, all his tenseness, if tenseness there ever was, has disappeared. There is nothing in that elegant figure to suggest nervousness. And when he does bat he gives an impression of instant confidence.

The crowd stirs just before the luncheon break. There is movement in the stands. Trueman is bowling his last over. McMorris is out! Caught Cowdrey again. McMorris has made his last effective appearance in this match. He goes in, they all go in. Lunch.

For West Indians it is an anxious interval. Will Worrell send in Sobers after lunch? Or Butcher? Or Solomon, the steady? It is Butcher; the batting order remains unchanged. Butcher and Kanhai take the score to 50. Thereafter there is a slowing up. Kanhai is subdued, unnatural, over-cautious. It isn't the West Indians' day. Kanhai is caught in the slips, by Cowdrey again. Just as no one runs down the pavilion steps more jauntily, no one walks back more sadly. His bat is a useless implement; he peels off his gloves as though stripping himself of an undeserved badge. Gloves flapping, he walks back, head bowed. This is not the manner of Sobers. Sobers never walks so fast as when he is dismissed. It is part of his personality, almost part of the grace of his play. And this walk back is something we will soon see.

84 for 4.

'You hear the latest from British Guiana?'

'What, the strike still on?'

'Things really bad out there.'

'Man, go away, eh. We facing defeat, and you want to talk politics.'

It looks like defeat. Some West Indians in the free seats withdraw from the game altogether and sit on the grass near the nets, talking over private problems, pints of bitter between their feet. No need to ask, from the shouts immediately after tea, what has happened. Applause; no hands thrown up in the air; the West Indians standing still. Silence. Fresh applause, polite, English. This has only one meaning: another wicket.

The English turn slightly partisan. A green-coated Lord's employee, a cushion-seller, says to a West Indian: 'Things not going well now?' The West Indian shrugs, and concentrates on Solomon, small, red-capped, brisk, walking back to the pavilion.

'I can sell you a good seat,' the man says. 'I am quite comfortable, thank you,' the West Indian says. He isn't. Soon he moves and joins a group of other West Indians standing just behind the sightscreen.

Enter Worrell.

'If only we make 150 we back in the game. Only 150.'

And, incredibly, in the slow hour after tea, this happens. Butcher and Worrell remain, and, remaining, grow more aggressive.

The latest of the Worrell late cuts.

'The old man still sweet to watch, you know.'

The old man is Worrell, nearly thirty-nine.

The 50 partnership.

'How much more for the old lady?' The old lady is Butcher's century, due soon. And it comes, with two fours. A West Indian jumps on some eminence behind the sightscreen and dances, holding aloft a pint of bitter. Mackintoshes are thrown up in the air; arms are raised and held in massive V-signs. Two men do an impromptu jive.

'Wait until they get 200. Then you going to hear noise.'

The noise comes. It comes again, to mark the 100 partnership. Butcher, elegant, watchful, becomes attacking, even wild.

'That is Mr Butcher! That is Mr Basil Fitzpatrick Butcher!'

And in the end the score is 214 for 5.

'Boy, things was bad. Real bad. 104 for 5.'

'I didn't say nothing, but, boy, I nearly faint when Solomon out.'

In the Tavern:

'This is historic. This is the first time a West Indian team has fought back. The first time.'

'But, man, where did you get to, man? I was looking for a shoulder to lean on, and when I look for you, you gone.'

Many had in fact sought comfort in privacy. Many had joined the plebeian West Indians, to draw comfort from their shouting. But now assurance returns.

'I know that Frank has got everything staked on winning this match, let me tell you. And you know what's going to happen afterwards? At Edgbaston they are going to beat Trueman into the ground. Finish him off for the season.'

Behind the pavilion, the autograph hunters, and some West Indians.

'That girl only want to see Butcher. She would die for Butcher tonight.'

'I just want to see the great Gary and the great Rohan.'

Gary is Sobers, Rohan is Kanhai. These batsmen failed today. But they remain great. West Indies 301 and 214 for 5. England 297.

The Fourth Day

After the weekend tension, farce. We are scarcely settled when the five remaining West Indian wickets fall, for 15 runs. England, as if infected, quickly lose their two opening batsmen. Hall is bowling from the Pavilion end, and his long run is accompanied by a sighing cheer which reaches its climax at the moment of delivery. Pity the English batsmen. Even at Lord's, where they might have thought they were safest, they now have to face an audience which is hostile.

And Dexter is out! Dexter, of the mighty strokes, out before lunch! 3 for 31.

Outside the Tavern:

'I just meet Harold. Lance Gibbs send a message.'

How often, in the West Indian matches, conspiratorial word is sent straight from the players to their friends!

'Lance say,' the messenger whispers, 'the wicket taking spin. He say it going to be all over by teatime.'

Odd, too, how the West Indians have influenced the English spectators. There, on one of the Tavern benches, something like a shouting match has gone on all morning between an English supporter and a West Indian.

'The only man who could save all-you is Graveney. And all-you ain't even pick him. You didn't see him there Thursday, standing up just next to the tea-stand in jacket and tie, with a mackintosh thrown over his arm? Why they don't pick the man? You know what? They must think Graveney is a black man.'

Simultaneously: 'Well, if Macmillan resigns I vote Socialist next election. And – I am a Tory.' The speaker is English (such distinctions are now necessary), thin, very young, with spectacles and tweed jacket. 'And,' he repeats, as though with self-awe, 'I am a Tory.'

In spite of that message from Lance Gibbs, Barrington and Cowdrey appear to be in no trouble.

'This is just what I was afraid of. You saw how Cowdrey played that ball? If they let him get set, the match is lost.'

When Cowdrey is struck on the arm by a fast rising ball from Hall, the ground is stilled. Cowdrey retires. Hall is chastened. So too are the West Indian spectators. Close comes in. And almost immediately Barrington carts Lance Gibbs for two sixes.

'Who was the man who brought that message from Lance Gibbs?'

'Rohan Kanhai did send a message, too, remember? He was going to get a century on Saturday.'

Where has Barrington got these strokes from? This aggression? And Close, why is he so stubborn? The minutes pass, the score climbs. 'These West Indian cricketers have some mighty names, eh: *Wesley* Hall. *Garfield* Sobers. *Rohan* Kanhai.'

'What about McMorris? What is his name?' A chuckle, choking speech. 'Easton.'

Nothing about McMorris, while this match lasts, can be taken seriously.

Now there are appeals for light, and the cricket stops. The Queen arrives. She is in light pink. The players reappear in blazers, the English in dark blue, the West Indians in maroon. They line up outside the pavilion gate, and hands are shaken, to a polite clapping which is as removed from the tension of the match as these courtly, bowing figures are removed from the cricketers we have been watching for four days.

With Barrington and Close settled in, and the score at the end of play 116 for 3, the match has once more swung in England's favour. Rain. The crowd waits for further play, but despairingly, and it seems that the game has been destroyed by the weather.

The Fifth Day

And so it continued to seem today. Rain held up play for more than three hours, and the crowd was small. But what a day for the seven thousand who went! Barrington, the hero of England's first innings,

out at 130, when England needed 104 to win. Parks out at 138. Then
Titmus, the stayer, came in, and after tea it seemed that England,
needing only 31 runs with five wickets in hand, was safely home. The
match was ending in anticlimax. But one shot – May's cover drive off
Ramadhin at Edgbaston in 1957 – can change a match. And one ball.
That ball now comes. Titmus is caught off Hall by – McMorris. And,
next ball, Trueman goes. Only Close now remains for England, with 31
runs to get, and the clock advancing to six. Every ball holds drama.
Every run narrows the gap. Hall bowls untiringly from the Pavilion
end. Will his strength never give out? Will Worell have to bring on the
slower bowlers – Sobers, himself or even Gibbs, whose message had
reached us yesterday? Miraculously to some, shatteringly to others, it is
Close who cracks. 70 his personal score, an English victory only 15
runs away. Close pays for the adventuring which until then had
brought him such reward. He is out, caught behind the wicket.
However, the runs trickle in. And when, two balls before the end,
Shackleton is run out any finish is still possible. Two fours will do the
trick. Or a four and a two. Or a mighty swipe for six. Or a wicket.
Cowdrey comes in, his injured left arm bandaged. And this is the
ridiculous public-school heroism of cricket: a man with a bandaged
arm saving his side, yet without having to face a ball. It is the peculiar
style of cricket, and its improbable appreciation links these dissimilar
people – English and West Indian.

    Day after day I have left Lord's emotionally drained. What other
game could have stretched hope and anxiety over six days? A slow
game, but there were moments when it was torment to watch, when I
joined those others, equally exhausted, sitting on the grass behind the
stands. And what other game can leave so little sense of triumph or
defeat? The anguish and joy of a cricket match last only while the
match lasts. Close was marvellous. But it didn't seem so to me while
he was in. Frustration denied generosity. But now admiration is pure.
This has been a match of heroes, and there have been heroes on both
sides. Close, Barrington, Titmus, Shackleton, Trueman, Dexter.
Butcher, Worrell, Hall, Griffith, Kanhai, Solomon. Cricket a team
game? Teams play, and one team is to be willed to victory. But it is the
individual who remains in the memory, he who has purged the
emotions by delight and fear.

A. J. Liebling

Ahab and Nemesis

Back in 1922, the late Heywood Broun, who is not remembered primarily as a boxing writer, wrote a durable account of a combat between the late Benny Leonard and the late Rocky Kansas for the lightweight championship of the world. Leonard was the greatest practitioner of the era, Kansas just a rough, optimistic fellow. In the early rounds Kansas messed Leonard about, and Broun was profoundly disturbed. A radical in politics, he was a conservative in the arts, and Kansas made him think of Gertrude Stein, *les Six*, and nonrepresentational painting, all novelties that irritated him.

"With the opening gong, Rocky Kansas tore into Leonard," he wrote. "He was gauche and inaccurate, but terribly persistent." The classic verities prevailed, however. After a few rounds, during which Broun continued to yearn for a return to a culture with fixed values, he was enabled to record: "The young child of nature who was challenging for the championship dropped his guard, and Leonard hooked a powerful and entirely orthodox blow to the conventional point of the jaw. Down went Rocky Kansas. His past life flashed before him during the nine seconds in which he remained on the floor, and he wished that he had been more faithful as a child in heeding the advice of his boxing teacher. After all, the old masters did know something. There is still a kick in style, and tradition carries a nasty wallop."

I have often thought of Broun's words in the years since Rocky Marciano, the reigning heavyweight champion, scaled the fistic summits, as they say in *Journal-Americanese*, by beating Jersey Joe Walcott. The current Rocky is gauche and inaccurate, but besides being persistent he is a dreadfully severe hitter with either hand. The predominative nature of this asset has been well stated by Pierce Egan, the Edward Gibbon and Sir Thomas Malory of the old London prize ring, who was less preoccupied than Broun with ultimate implications. Writing in 1821 of a milling cove named Bill Neat, the Bristol Butcher, Egan said, "He possesses a requisite above all the art that *teaching* can achieve for any boxer; namely, *one hit* from his right hand, given in proper distance, can gain a victory; but three of them are positively enough to dispose of a giant." This is true not only of Marciano's right hand but of his left hand, too—provided he doesn't miss the giant entirely. Egan doubted the advisability of changing Neat's style, and he would have approved of Marciano's. The champion has an apparently unlimited absorptive capacity for percussion (Egan would have called him an "insatiable glutton") and inexhaustible energy ("a prime bottom fighter"). "Shifting," or moving to the side, and "milling in retreat," or moving back, are innovations of the late eighteenth century that Rocky's advisers have carefully kept from his knowledge, lest they spoil his natural prehistoric style. Egan excused these tactics only in boxers of feeble constitution.

Archie Moore, the light heavyweight champion of the world, who hibernates in San Diego, California, and estivates in Toledo, Ohio, is a Brounian rather than an Eganite in his thinking about style, but he naturally has to do more than think about it. Since the rise of Marciano, Moore, a cerebral and hyper-experienced light-colored pugilist who has been active since 1936, has suffered the pangs of a supreme exponent of *bel canto* who sees himself crowded out of the opera house by a guy who can only shout. As a sequel to a favorable review I wrote of one of his infrequent New York appearances, when his fee was restricted to a measly five figures, I received a sad little note signed "The most unappreciated fighter in the world, Archie Moore." A fellow who has as much style as Moore tends to overestimate the intellect— he develops the kind of Faustian mind that will throw itself against the problem of perpetual motion, or of how to pick horses first, second, third, *and* fourth in every race. Archie's note made it plain to me that he was honing his harpoon for the White Whale.

When I read newspaper items about Moore's decisioning a large, playful porpoise of a Cuban heavyweight named Nino Valdes and scoop-netting a minnow like Bobo Olson, the middleweight champion, for practice, I thought of him as a lonely Ahab, rehearsing to buck Herman Melville, Pierce Egan, and the betting odds. I did not think that he could bring it off, but I wanted to be there when he tried. What would *Moby Dick* be if Ahab had succeeded? Just another fish story. The thing that is eternally diverting is the struggle of man against history—or what Albert Camus, who used to be an amateur middle-weight, has called the Myth of Sisyphus. (Camus would have been a great man to cover the fight, but none of the syndicates thought of it.) When I heard that the boys had been made for September 20, 1955, at the Yankee Stadium, I shortened my stay abroad in order not to miss the Encounter of the Two Heroes, as Egan would have styled the rendezvous.

In London on the night of September thirteenth, a week before the date set for the Encounter, I tried to get my eye in for fight-watching by attending a bout at the White City greyhound track between Valdes, who had been imported for the occasion, and the British Empire heavy-weight champion, Don Cockell, a fat man whose gift for public suffering has enlisted the sympathy of a sentimental people. Since Valdes had gone fifteen rounds with Moore in Las Vegas the previous May, and Cockell had excruciated for nine rounds before being knocked out by Marciano in San Francisco in the same month, the bout offered a dim opportunity for establishing what racing people call a "line" between Moore and Marciano. I didn't get much of an optical workout, because Valdes disposed of Cockell in three rounds. It was evident that Moore and Marciano had not been fighting the same class of people this season.

This was the only fight I ever attended in a steady rainstorm. It had begun in the middle of the afternoon, and, while there was a canopy over the ring, the spectators were as wet as speckled trout. "The weather, it is well known, has no terrors to the admirers of Pugilism of Life," Egan once wrote, and on his old stamping ground this still holds true. As I took my seat in a rock pool that had collected in the hollow of my chair, a South African giant named Ewart Potgieter, whose weight had been announced as twenty-two stone ten, was ignoring the doctrine of Apartheid by leaning on a Jamaican colored man who weighed a mere sixteen stone, and by the time I had transposed these statistics to three hundred and eighteen pounds and two hundred and twenty-four pounds, respectively, the exhausted Jamaican had acquiesced in resegregation and retired. The giant had not struck a blow, properly speaking, but had shoved downward a number of times, like a man trying to close an overfilled trunk.

The main bout proved an even less grueling contest. Valdes, eager to get out of the chill, struck Cockell more vindictively than is his wont, and after a few gestures invocative of commiseration the fat man settled in one corner of the ring as heavily as suet pudding upon the unaccustomed gastric system. He had received what Egan would have called a "ribber" and a "nobber," and when he arose it was seen that the latter had raised a cut on his forehead. At the end of the third round, his manager withdrew him from competition. It was not an inspiring occasion, but after the armistice eight or nine shivering Cubans appeared in the runway behind the press section and jumped up and down to register emotion and restore circulation. "*Ahora Marciano!*" they yelled. "Now for Marciano!" Instead of being grateful for the distraction, the other spectators took a poor view of it. "Sit down, you chaps!" one of them cried. "We want to see the next do!" They were still parked out there in the rain when I tottered into the Shepherd's Bush underground station and collapsed, sneezing, on a train that eventually disgorged me at Oxford Circus, with just enough time left to buy a revivifying draft before eleven o'clock, when the pubs closed. How the mugs I left behind cured themselves I never knew. They had to do it on Bovril.

Because I had engagements that kept me in England until a few days before the Encounter, I had no opportunity to visit the training camps of the rival American Heroes. I knew all the members of both factions, however, and I could imagine what they were thinking. In the plane on the way home, I tried to envision the rival patterns of ratiocination. I could be sure that Marciano, a kind, quiet, imperturbable fellow, would plan to go after Moore and make him fight continuously until he tired enough to become an accessible target. After that he would expect concussion to accentuate exhaustion and exhaustion to facilitate concussion, until Moore came away from his consciousness, like everybody else Rocky had ever fought. He would try to remember to minimize damage to himself in the beginning, while there was still snap in Moore's arms, because Moore is a sharp puncher. (Like Bill Neat of old, Marciano hits at his opponent's arms when he cannot hit past them. "In one instance, the arm of Oliver [a Neat adversary] received so paralyzing a shock in stopping the blow that it appeared almost useless," Egan once wrote.) Charlie Goldman would have instructed Marciano in some rudimentary maneuver to throw Moore's first shots off, I felt sure, but after a few minutes Rocky would forget it, or Archie would figure it out. But there would always be Freddie Brown, the "cut man," in the champion's corner to repair superficial damage. One reason Goldman is a great teacher is that he doesn't try to teach a boxer more than he can learn. What he had taught Rocky in the four years since I had first seen him fight was to shorten the arc of most of his blows without losing power thereby, and always to follow one hard blow with another—"for insurance"—delivered with the other hand, instead of recoiling to watch the victim fall. The champion had also gained confidence and presence of mind; he has a good fighting head, which is not the same thing as being a good mechanical practitioner. "A *boxer* requires a *nob* as well as a *statesman* does a HEAD, coolness and calculation being essential to *second* his efforts," Egan wrote, and the old historiographer was never more correct. Rocky was thirty-one, not in the first flush of youth for a boxer, but Moore was only a few days short of thirty-nine, so age promised to be in the champion's favor if he kept pressing.

Moore's strategic problem, I reflected on the plane, offered more choices and, as a corollary, infinitely more chances for error. It was possible, but not probable, that jabbing and defensive skill would carry him through fifteen rounds, even on those old legs, but I knew that the mere notion of such a *gambade* would revolt Moore. He is not what Egan would have called a shy fighter. Besides, would Ahab have been content merely to go the distance with the White Whale? I felt sure that Archie planned to knock the champion out, so that he could sign his next batch of letters "The most appreciated and deeply opulent fighter in the world." I surmised that this project would prove a mistake, like Mr. Churchill's attempt to take Gallipoli in 1915, but it would be the kind of mistake that would look good in his memoirs. The basis of what I rightly anticipated would prove a miscalculation went back to Archie's academic background. As a young fighter of conventional tutelage, he must have heard his preceptors say hundreds of times, "They will all go if you hit them right." If a fighter did not believe that, he would be in the position of a Euclidian without faith in the hundred-and-eighty-degree triangle. Moore's strategy, therefore, would be based on working Marciano into a position where he could hit him right. He would not go in and slug with him, because that would be wasteful, distasteful, and injudicious, but he might try to cut him up, in an effort to slow him down so he could hit him right, or else try to hit him right and then cut him up. The puzzle he reserved for me—and Marciano—was the tactic by which he would attempt to attain his strategic objective. In the formation of his views, I believed, Moore would be handicapped, rather than aided, by his active, skeptical mind. One of the odd things about Marciano is that he isn't terribly big. It is hard for a man like Moore, just under six feet tall and weighing about a hundred and eighty pounds, to imagine that a man approximately the same size can be immeasurably stronger than he is. This is particularly true when, like the light heavyweight champion, he has spent his whole professional life contending with boxers—some of them considerably bigger—whose strength has proved so near his own that he could move their arms and bodies by cunning pressures. The old classicist would consequently refuse to believe what he was up against.

The light heavyweight limit is a hundred and seventy-five pounds, and Moore can get down to that when he must, in order to defend his title, but in a heavyweight match each Hero is allowed to weigh whatever he pleases. I was back in time to attend the weighing-in ceremonies, held in the lobby of Madison Square Garden at noon on the day set for the Encounter, and learned that Moore weighed 188 and Marciano 188¼— a lack of disparity that figured to encourage the rationalist's illusions. I also learned that, in contrast to Jack Solomons, the London promoter who held the Valdes–Cockell match in the rain, the IBC, which was promoting the Encounter, had decided to postpone it for twenty-four hours, although the weather was clear. The decision was based on apprehension of Hurricane Ione, which, although apparently veering away from New York, might come around again like a lazy left hook and drop in on the point of the Stadium's jaw late in the evening. Nothing like that happened, but the postponement brought the town's theaters and bars another evening of good business from the out-of-town fight trade, such as they always get on the eve of a memorable Encounter. ("Not a bed could be had at any of the villages at an early hour on the preceding evening; and Uxbridge was crowded beyond all former precedent," Egan wrote of the night before Neat beat Oliver.) There was no doubt that the fight had caught the public imagination, ever sensitive to a meeting between Hubris and Nemesis, as the boys on the quarterlies would say, and the bookies were laying 18–5 on Nemesis, according to the boys on the dailies, who always seem to hear. (A friend of mine up from Maryland with a whim and a five-dollar bill couldn't get ten against it in ordinary barroom money anywhere, although he wanted Ahab.)

The enormous—by recent precedent—advance sale of tickets had so elated the IBC that it had decided to replace the usual card of bad preliminary fights with some not worth watching at all, so there was less distraction than usual as we awaited the appearance of the Heroes on the fateful evening. The press seats had been so closely juxtaposed that I could fit in only sidewise between two colleagues—the extra compression having been caused by the injection of a prewar number of movie stars and politicos. The tight quarters were an advantage, in a way, since they facilitated my conversation with Peter Wilson, an English prize-ring correspondent, who happened to be in the row behind me. I had last seen Mr. Wilson at White City the week before, at a time when the water level had already reached his shredded-Latakia mustache. I had feared that he had drowned at ringside, but when I saw him at the Stadium, he assured me that by buttoning the collar of his mackintosh tightly over his nostrils he had been able to make the garment serve as a diving lung, and so survive. Like all British fight writers when they are relieved of the duty of watching British fighters, he was in a holiday mood, and we chatted happily. There is something about the approach of a good fight that renders the spirit insensitive to annoyance; it is only when the amateur of the Sweet Science has some doubts as to how good the main bout will turn out to be that he is avid for the satisfaction to be had from the preliminaries. This is because after the evening is over, he may have only a good supporting fight to remember. There were no such doubts—even in the minds of the mugs who had paid for their seats—on the evening of September twenty-first.

At about ten-thirty the champion and his faction entered the ring. It is not customary for the champion to come in first, but Marciano has never been a stickler for protocol. He is a humble, kindly fellow, who even now will approach an acquaintance on the street and say bashfully, "Remember me? I'm Rocky Marciano." The champion doesn't mind waiting five or ten minutes to give anybody a punch in the nose. In any case, once launched from his dressing room under the grandstand, he could not have arrested his progress to the ring, because he had about forty policemen pushing behind him, and three more clearing a path in front of him. Marciano, tucked in behind the third cop like a football ball-carrier behind his interference, had to run or be trampled to death. Wrapped in a heavy blue bathrobe and with a blue monk's cowl pulled over his head, he climbed the steps to the ring with the cumbrous agility of a medieval executioner ascending the scaffold. Under the hood he seemed to be trying to look serious. He has an intellectual appreciation of the anxieties of a champion, but he has a hard time forgetting how strong he is; while he remembers that, he can't worry as much as he knows a champion should. His attendants—quick, battered little Goldman; Al Weill, the stout, excite-able manager, always stricken just before the bell with the suspicion that he may have made a bad match; Al Columbo—are all as familiar to the crowd as he is.

Ahab's party arrived in the ring a minute or so later, and Charlie Johnston, his manager—a calm sparrow hawk of a man, as old and wise in the game as Weill—went over to watch Goldman put on the champion's gloves. Freddie Brown went to Moore's corner to watch *his* gloves being put on. Moore wore a splendid black silk robe with a gold lamé collar and belt. He sports a full mustache above an imperial, and his hair, sleeked down under pomade when he opens operations, invariably rises during the contest, as it gets water sloshed on it between rounds and the lacquer washes off, until it is standing up like the top of a shaving brush. Seated in his corner in the shadow of his personal trainer, a brown man called Cheerful Norman, who weighs two hundred and thirty-five pounds, Moore looked like an old Japanese print I have of a "Shogun Engaged in Strategic Contemplation in the Midst of War." The third member of his group was Bertie Briscoe, a rough, chipper little trainer, whose more usual charge is Sandy Saddler, the featherweight champion—also a Johnston fighter. Mr. Moore's features in repose rather resemble those of Orson Welles, and he was reposing with intensity.

The procession of other fighters and former fighters to be intro-duced was longer than usual. The full galaxy was on hand, including Jack Dempsey, Gene Tunney, and Joe Louis, the *têtes de cuvée* of former-champion society; ordinary former heavyweight champions, like Max Baer and Jim Braddock, slipped through the ropes practically unnoticed. After all the celebrities had been in and out of the ring, an odd dwarf, advertising something or other—possibly himself—was lifted into the ring by an accomplice and ran across it before he could be shooed out. The referee, a large, craggy, oldish man named Harry Kessler, who, unlike some of his better-known colleagues, is not an ex-fighter, called the men to the center of the ring. This was his moment; he had the microphone. "Now Archie and Rocky, I want a nice, clean fight," he said, and I heard a peal of silvery laughter behind me from Mr. Wilson, who had seen both of them fight before. "Protect yourself at all times," Mr. Kessler cautioned them unnecessarily. When the principals shook hands, I could see Mr. Moore's eyebrows rising like storm clouds over the Sea of Azov. His whiskers bristled and his eyes glowed like dark coals as he scrunched his eyebrows down again and enveloped the Whale with the Look, which was intended to dominate his will power. Mr. Wilson and I were sitting behind Marciano's corner, and as the champion came back to it I observed his expression, to determine what effect the Look had had upon him. More than ever, he resembled a Great Dane who has heard the word "bone."

A moment later the bell rang and the Heroes came out for the first round. Marciano, training in the sun for weeks, had tanned to a slightly deeper tint than Moore's old ivory, and Moore, at 188, looked, if anything, bigger and more muscular than Marciano; much of the champion's weight is in his legs, and his shoulders slope. Marciano advanced, but Moore didn't go far away. As usual, he stood up nicely, his arms close to his body and his feet not too far apart, ready to go anywhere but not without a reason—the picture of a powerful, decisive intellect unfettered by preconceptions. Marciano, pulling his left arm back from the shoulder, flung a left hook. He missed, but not by enough to discourage him, and then walked in and hooked again. All through the round he threw those hooks, and some of them grazed Moore's whiskers; one even hit him on the side of the head. Moore didn't try much offensively; he held a couple of times when Marciano worked in close.

Marciano came back to his corner as he always does, unimpassioned. He hadn't expected to catch Moore with those left hooks anyway, I imagine; all he had wanted was to move him around. Moore went to his corner inscrutable. They came out for the second, and Marciano went after him in brisker fashion. In the first round he had been throwing the left hook, missing with it, and then throwing a right and missing with that, too. In the second he tried a variation—throwing a right and then pulling a shoulder back to throw the left. It appeared for a moment to have Moore confused, as a matador might be confused by a bull who walked in on his hind legs. Marciano landed a couple of those awkward hooks, but not squarely. He backed Moore over toward the side of the ring farthest from me, and then Moore knocked him down.

Some of the reporters, describing the blow in the morning papers, called it a "sneak punch," which is journalese for one the reporter didn't see but technically means a lead thrown before the other man has warmed up or while be is musing about the gate receipts. This had been no lead, and although I certainly hadn't seen Moore throw the punch, I knew that it had landed inside the arc of Marciano's left hook. ("Marciano missed with the right, trun the left, and Moore stepped inside it," my private eye, Whitey Bimstein, said next day, confirming my diagnosis, and the film of the fight bore both of us out.) So Ahab

had his harpoon in the Whale. He had hit him right if ever I saw a
boxer hit right, with a classic brevity and conciseness. Marciano stayed
down for two seconds. I do not know what took place in Mr. Moore's
breast when he saw him get up. He may have felt, for the moment, like
Don Giovanni when the Commendatore's statue grabbed at him—
startled because he thought he had killed the guy already—or like
Ahab when he saw the Whale take down Fedallah, harpoons and all.
Anyway, he hesitated a couple of seconds, and that was reasonable. A
man who took nine to come up after a punch like that would be doing
well, and the correct tactic would be to go straight in and finish him.
But a fellow who came up on two was so strong he would bear
investigation.

After that, Moore did go in, but not in a crazy way. He hit Marciano
some good, hard, classic shots, and inevitably Marciano, a trader, hit
him a few devastating swipes, which slowed him. When the round
ended, the edge of Moore's speed was gone, and he knew that he
would have to set a new and completely different trap, with diminished
resources. After being knocked down, Marciano had stopped throwing
that patterned right-and-left combination; he has a good nob. "He
never trun it again in the fight," Whitey said next day, but I differ. He
threw it in the fifth, and again Moore hit him a peach of a right inside
it, but the steam was gone; this time Ahab couldn't even stagger him.
Anyway, there was Moore at the end of the second, dragging his
shattered faith in the unities and humanities back to his corner. He
had hit a guy right, and the guy hadn't gone. But there is no geezer in
Moore, any more than there was in the master of the *Pequod*.

Both came out for the third very gay, as Egan would have said.
Marciano had been hit and cut, so he felt acclimated, and Moore was
so mad at himself for not having knocked Marciano out that he almost
displayed animosity toward him. He may have thought that perhaps
he had not hit Marciano *just* right; the true artist is always prone to
self-reproach. He would try again. A minute's attention from his
squires had raised his spirits and slicked down his hair. At this point,
Marciano set about him. He waddled in, hurling his fists with a sublime
disregard of probabilities, content to hit an elbow, a biceps, a shoulder,
the top of a head—the last supposed to be the least profitable target in
the business, since, as every beginner learns, "the head is the hardest
part of the human body," and a boxer will only break his hands on it.
Many boxers make the systematic presentation of the cranium part of
their defensive scheme. The crowd, basically anti-intellectual, screamed

encouragement. There was Moore, riding punches, picking them off, slipping them, rolling with them, ducking them, coming gracefully out of his defensive efforts with sharp, patterned blows—and just about holding this parody even on points. His face, emerging at instants from under the storm of arms—his own and Rocky's—looked like that of a swimming walrus. When the round ended, I could see that he was thinking deeply. Marciano came back to his corner at a kind of suppressed dogtrot. He didn't have a worry in the world.

It was in the fourth, though, that I think Sisyphus began to get the idea he couldn't roll back the Rock. Marciano pushed him against the ropes and swung at him for what seemed a full minute without ever landing a punch that a boxer with Moore's background would consider a credit to his workmanship. He kept them coming so fast, though, that Moore tired just getting out of their way. One newspaper account I saw said that at this point Moore "swayed uncertainly," but his motions were about as uncertain as Margot Fonteyn's, or Arthur Rubinstein's. He is the most premeditated and best-synchronized swayer in his profession. After the bell rang for the end of the round, the champion hit him a right for good measure—he usually manages to have something on the way all the time—and then pulled back to disclaim any uncouth intention. Moore, no man to be conned, hit him a corker of a punch in return, when he wasn't expecting it. It was a gesture of moral reprobation and also a punch that would give any normal man something to think about between rounds. It was a good thing Moore couldn't see Marciano's face as he came back to his corner, though, because the champion was laughing.

The fifth was a successful round for Moore, and I had him ahead on points that far in the fight. But it took no expert to know where the strength lay. There was even a moment in the round when Moore set himself against the ropes and encouraged Marciano to swing at him, in the hope the champion would swing himself tired. It was a confession that he himself was too tired to do much hitting.

In the sixth Marciano knocked Moore down twice—once, early in the round, for four seconds, and once, late in the round, for eight seconds, with Moore getting up just before the bell rang. In the seventh, after that near approach to obliteration, the embattled intellect put up its finest stand. Marciano piled out of his corner to finish Moore, and the stylist made him miss so often that it looked, for a fleeting moment, as if the champion were indeed punching himself arm-weary. In fact, Moore began to beat him to the punch. It was

Moore's round, certainly, but an old-timer I talked to later averred that one of the body blows Marciano landed in that round was the hardest of the fight.

It was the eighth that ended the competitive phase of the fight. They fought all the way, and in the last third of the round the champion simply overflowed Archie. He knocked him down with a right six seconds before the bell, and I don't think Moore could have got up by ten if the round had lasted that long. The fight by then reminded me of something that Sam Langford, one of the most profound thinkers—and, according to all accounts, one of the greatest doers—of the prize ring, once said to me: "Whatever that other man wants to do, don't let him do it." Merely by moving in all the time and punching continually, Marciano achieves the same strategic effect that Langford gained by finesse. It is impossible to think, or to impose your thought, if you have to keep on avoiding punches.

Moore's "game," as old Egan would have called his courage, was beyond reproach. He came out proudly for the ninth, and stood and fought back with all he had, but Marciano slugged him down, and he was counted out with his left arm hooked over the middle rope as he tried to rise. It was a crushing defeat for the higher faculties and a lesson in intellectual humility, but he had made a hell of a fight.

The fight was no sooner over than hundreds of unsavory young yokels with New England accents began a kind of mountain-goat immigration from the bleachers to ringside. They leaped from chair to chair and, after they reached the press section, from typewriter shelf to typewriter shelf and, I hope, from movie star to movie star. "Rocky!" they yelled. "Brockton!" Two of them, as dismal a pair of civic ambassadors as I have seen since I worked on the Providence *Journal & Evening Bulletin,* stood on Wilson's typewriter and yelled "Providence!" After the fighters and the hick delinquents had gone away, I made my way out to Jerome Avenue, where the crowd milled, impenetrable, under the "El" structure.

If you are not in a great hurry to get home (and why should you be at eleven-thirty or twelve on a fight night?), the best plan is to walk up to the station north of the stadium and have a beer in a saloon, or a cup of tea in the 167th Street Cafeteria, and wait until the whole mess clears away. By that time you may even get a taxi. After this particular fight I chose the cafeteria, being in a contemplative rather than a convivial mood. The place is of a genre you would expect to find nearer Carnegie Hall, with blond woodwork and modern functional furniture imported from Italy—an appropriate background for the evaluation of an aesthetic experience. I got my tea and a smoked-salmon sandwich on a soft onion roll at the counter and made my way to a table, where I found myself between two young policemen who were talking about why Walt Disney has never attempted a screen version of Kafka's "Metamorphosis." As I did not feel qualified to join in that one, I got out my copy of the official program of the fights and began to read the high-class feature articles as I munched my sandwich.

One reminded me that I had seen the first boxing show ever held in Yankee Stadium—on May 12, 1923. I had forgotten that it *was* the first show, and even that 1923 was the year the Stadium opened. In my true youth the Yankees used to share the Polo Grounds with the Giants, and I had forgotten that, too, because I never cared much about baseball, although, come to think of it, I used to see the Yankees play occasionally in the nineteen-'teens, and should have remembered. I remembered the boxing show itself very well, though. It happened during the spring of my second suspension from college, and I paid five dollars for a high-grandstand seat. The program merely said that it had been "an all-star heavyweight bill promoted by Tex Rickard for the Hearst Milk Fund," but I found that I could still remember every man and every bout on the card. One of the main events was between old Jess Willard, the former heavyweight champion of the world, who had lost the title to Jack Dempsey in 1919, and a young heavyweight named Floyd Johnson. Willard had been coaxed from retirement to make a comeback because there was such a dearth of heavyweight material that Rickard thought he could still get by, but as I remember the old fellow, he couldn't fight a lick. He had a fair left jab and a right uppercut that a fellow had to walk into to get hurt by, and he was big and soft. Johnson was a mauler worse than Rex Layne, and the old man knocked him out. The other main event, *ex aequo*, had Luis Angel Firpo opposing a fellow named Jack McAuliffe II, from Detroit, who had had only fifteen fights and had never beaten anybody, and had a glass jaw. The two winners, of whose identity there was infinitesimal preliminary doubt, were to fight each other for the right to meet the great Jack Dempsey. Firpo was so crude that Marciano would be a Fancy Dan in comparison. He could hit with only one hand—his right—he hadn't the faintest idea of what to do in close, and he never cared much for the business anyway. He knocked McAuliffe out, of course, and then, in a later "elimination" bout, stopped poor old

Willard. He subsequently became a legend by going one and a half sensational rounds with Dempsey, in a time that is now represented to us as the golden age of American pugilism.

I reflected with satisfaction that old Ahab Moore could have whipped all four principals on that card within fifteen rounds, and that while Dempsey may have been a great champion, he had less to beat than Marciano. I felt the satisfaction because it proved that the world isn't going backward, if you can just stay young enough to remember what it was really like when you were really young.

Pete Davies

The Beautiful Game: England–West Germany

At the stadium on 4 July, Italia '90 News on the Database had gone
into a tailspin, presenting helpful reports dated 2 June about the
Romanians training under the olive trees at Telesa Terme ... confusion
and time slippage reigned, as the end drew nigh. The press centre was
a jammed morass. The telly said the temperature was thirty degrees,
the scoreboards said twenty-seven – we didn't even know how hot it
was any more.

Outside in the parking lots there was not a note of music, not a jot
of the party feeling there'd been when Brazil had played here – it felt
sullen and tense. Tickets changed hands everywhere, on car bonnets, at
stalls, even at the entrance gates in full view of stewards and police –
of whom there were two thousand. The fans were searched again. I
shook my head and stared, feeling the world gone quite beyond belief
or reality, at the sight of an English boy being ordered to unpick the
lettering that named his club from his Union Jack ... supporting
England, for the young and the broke, looked set fair to be the ultimate
joyless rip-off.

Yet in the end, it wasn't. Supporting England, in the end, proved
against all the odds to have been worthwhile, thanks to the one central
thing that mattered more than all the rest – the team and the players.

Because they, and the Germans, were about to give us the best game
of Italia '90.

Inside I wondered where the much-rumoured forty thousand
Germans were. Large sweeps of the lower tier, and great gap-toothed
chunks of the upper two, were empty ... ticketing incompetence and
greed, combined with the hooligan psychosis, had made this semi-final
an absurdly under-attended event. But then, what was new? The stands
had had gaping vacancies in them in many of the twelve cities all down
the track – the only thing that was new here was that the number of
helicopters chattering low overhead had increased. But never mind –
those who'd endured were rewarded.

The English singing was loud and proud, out-noising the Germans.
And the players stormed into the game, as if these opponents were no

more to be feared than the UAE. Mark Wright was playing – could
you ever have stopped him? – and Peter Beardsley was in the hole
between Gary Lineker and midfield, with John Barnes's sad injury
finally denying him any last hope of redemption. Otherwise, it was the
new England we were coming to believe in – with Terry Butcher
sweeping, Des Walker alongside Wright in front of him, Paul Parker
and Stuart Pearce outside, and David Platt, Chrissie Waddle, and Paul
Gascoigne to run the middle.

So it was hot, the sky was bright blue, the Alps looked ravishing
to the north – and we were away. The fans roared out 'God Save The
Queen' – and I thought, there may be some ugly and stupid dimwits
among then, and, no doubt, a few scum and villains too – but *they are
England*.

They get no party, just antagonism; they get no joy, just searches
and batons; but they get their football – and here and now, that'd do.

England won the first corner straight off in the first minute, and
from the clearance coming out, Gazza fired in a rocket of a volley that
looked to be just curving wide – but Illgner lunged to push it away
anyhow, and we had a second corner. And then we had a third ... our
football was surging and relentless – we were playing like the Germans
did, and the Germans didn't like it. Bruises and knocks, sore joints and
worn limbs, forget it – there's no end to the magic hope can work.
Wright had Klinsmann under wraps; Waddle released Parker, Beardsley
went through once, and then again ... Hässler took the Germans' first
serious strike, and it deflected away from Pearce for their first corner –
but Butcher towered up, and headed away. Then Wright picked a
through ball off Klinsmann's feet; the German looked angry and
rattled. You could feel their pace, their threat – but still we had them,
and the first phase was all England.

No question: England could win this.

The press box was buzzing. Gazza tangled with Brehme; he got
another shot in, then broke to the left corner, won a free-kick ...

> Let's all have a disco
> Let's all have a disco.

It was more than a disco, it was history – Butcher of all people played
a nifty back-heel; Gazza nutmegged Matthäus ... half an hour gone,
and it was England, England. The Germans just couldn't find their
way, they were trying so hard, but they were pressured so much. You'd
never know Wright had a head wound – while Beardsley was running

and running, he went through, gave it to Waddle, the cross shaved off Lineker's head, and just past Platt. Gazza worked another opening, and Pearce fired wide. Then Walker ran back with Völler, who he'd been marking off the park, and the German striker fell – he lay wounded on the sideline, and they were down to ten men.

Waddle showed a touch of magic now, when a free-kick had been blown against Platt – he saw Illgner off his line, and chipped him with power from thirty-five yards anyway. The German keeper scrambled back to tip it against the bar – it wouldn't have counted, but that didn't matter – scaring them like that did no harm . . .

It was wonderful football; we were first to everything, and Gazza made Matthäus look ordinary. But Riedle came on for Völler – and the Germans were forcing their way back in. Shilton saved low from Thon; I felt my chest constricting under the terrible tension of the beautiful game, in this beautiful cavern of a stadium . . . as Shilton pulled off a magnificent save from an Augenthaler free-kick, fingers just stretching to edge over for a corner. Beardsley was back tackling; and the Germans were playing fine football themselves now, pass and run, pass and run – another corner, another proud leap from Butcher – and suddenly it was all Germany.

Who says our defenders can't play? They were playing now – they bloody had to. Gazza and Brehme tussled again, on the brink of half-time . . . but came out of it smiling, Gazza ruffling Brehme's hair. As the whistle blew, I felt like I breathed out for the first time in forty-five minutes.

The second half began – and twenty-two men picked up where they'd left off. Beardsley released Pearce, and we won a corner; it came out, Thon broke upfield, and Shilton saved. The German attacks were looking faster and more coherent, they seemed fresher – Matthäus was coming ominously to the boil.

Pearce downed Hässler for a free kick on the edge of the box; the English wall formed up, Paul Parker a yard or two wide on the right-hand end of it. Hässler touched the kick square, Brehme drove the ball in, and, as Parker advanced, the ball ballooned up off him, the deflection looping beyond the reach of desperately back-pedalling Shilton – and into the net.

Shilton sat in his goal in disbelief. Parker had done the right thing, going to charge down the kick, and it was hideously unlucky – no deflection, I think, would have meant no goal – but then it was, to be fair, with the run of play at this stage.

So, fifty-nine minutes gone: 1–0 to Germany.

Platt ran back to pick up the ball, and get us going again – and the England fans roared their deafening support. It was time to ask what we were made of again.

And they dredged up the energy they needed, from somewhere where normal people would have none. A Gazza free-kick glanced just wide off Pearce; Illgner saved from Wright. Then Gazza put Waddle through, with a gem of a ball; and a surging run by Pearce ended in a clattering sandwich on the edge of the area, for another free-kick.

Twenty minutes left. Butcher came off, Trevor Steven came on – and had a shot straight off. Nice first touch ... we'd closed in to four across the back, with Steven going up wide on the right. It was all or nothing, do or die, burning deck, into the breach ... 'God Save The Queen' rang out around the ground.

Brehme went down, and the Germans kicked the ball out of play so they could see to him. From the throw-in, Pearce gave it back to them; they in turn kicked it up for Shilton to restart, all fair and evens – it was that sort of game.

It was, basically, the real World Cup Final ... with only ten minutes left, and the Germans one ahead.

Parker fired over a long cross. Kohler failed to deal with it; Lineker caught it neatly on his thigh as he ran in at full speed and, harried and bumped, swept voraciously past the flailing Augenthaler, past Berthold too – and then fired, with immaculate precision.

England were level.

Lineker looked frenzied, he looked mad with joy, eyes bulging wide and staring all around as he sprinted away, fists and teeth clenched ... and the support of the boys singing in the stands was fantastic. They'd blundered and shoved and banged and barged their single-minded and sleepless way round Italy for a month – and still they were there.

So screw the venom-headed minority – and screw it if even those who don't mean harm can be charmless and boorish and stupid. Because the good and the dim together, they'd been spat at and shot at and shat on all round, they'd been sat down and stood up, they'd been herded over here and marched over there – and still they were singing – because this was their time, in this great bowl of light beneath the Alps, in this raging cavern brought to life against all the odds, against all adversity, by the England football team.

When you walk through the storm
Hold your head up high
And don't be afraid of the dark.
At the end of the storm
There's a golden sky
And the sweet silver sound of the lark.

Walk on, walk on
With hope in your heart
And you'll never walk alone
You'll never walk alone.

Ninety minutes: 1–1. And who goes to applaud them before the restart? Gazza . . .

Walker saved us with a flying last-gasp tackle off Klinsmann's feet; I had to stand, I couldn't take it sitting down any more. Now Shilton saved us, a reflex reaction to Klinsmann again. It was all Germany, attacking, attacking . . . Klinsmann went clear through yet again – and missed by inches.

At the other end, another razor-sharp pass from Gazza went to Beardsley – who lost it. Bully and Macca were warming up on the track; and then Gazza was booked, for the most innocuous of fouls. He'd gone for the ball – but Berthold made a meal of it, diving and rolling; and the German bench were up in noisy protest, making the foul look worse than it was . . . it was Gazza's second booking, he was out of the next game – and the next game might well be the World Cup Final.

He looked mental, torn up, cut to the heart and the knife twisted hard. Lineker was tapping a finger to his temple, warning the bench that Gazza might have lost it – it was the harshest injustice.

We love you Gascoigne, we do
We love you Gascoigne, we do
We love you Gascoigne, we do
Ohhhh, Gascoigne we love you.

He didn't lose it – he threw himself in more fiercely than ever. And Chrissie Waddle hit the post . . . Jesus. You couldn't bear to watch it – and you couldn't tear your eyes from it.

Fifteen minutes left; turn-round time. But the song was still the same.

There's only one Paul Gascoigne
Only one Paaw-uuhl Gaaaaa-uh-scoigne.

Every piece of me was frozen bar the heart that beat and the hand that wrote.

Brehme crunched Gazza, ugly and hard. The English fans rose in a tumult of outrage. Brehme was booked instantly – and Gazza got up, and shook the German's hand.

He'd been threatening to grow up all this time – but there was the moment, booked himself and heartbroken, that he proved that he'd done so. Six months ago he'd have hit him, and got himself sent off.

So whatever happened here now, England could go home knowing that we had on our hands a player who'd come of age, at twenty-three promising to be one of the world's greatest in the 1990s ... and from the free-kick, Platt put the ball in the net.

Offside, offside ... it was disallowed. No matter – Beardsley went through two, and came within an ace of releasing Lineker. It was all England now, forward, forward, finding speed to run and strength to play in their sixth game in twenty-four days, their third extra time in nine days – it was a performance of matchless pride. The fans sounded like they filled the whole stadium.

And we deserved to win this. We'd fought hard, and our hearts were big. Who says they were better than us?

But then, it takes two to make a great game of football – and what I've just written could just as well be written of the Germans.

Shilton saved from Thon; a shot from Brehme went rocketing close over the crossbar; Steven went searing through on a lovely lay-off from Beardsley, and crossed to win a corner; then at the other end, Buchwald hit the post just as Waddle had. So no one deserved to lose here. But after two hours, we'd battled to a standstill – and no one did lose. The score was 1–1 and we had to settle it on a duckshoot instead.

Applause rang out round the whole of the magnificent arena, pure and wholly merited by both sides. In the centre circle, players from both sides shook hands, put arms round each others' shoulders, and exchanged congratulations on the game. Gazza was crying; Robson took time out from organizing the penalty takers to console him. And in London, Bryan Robson said from the heart, 'They should take the camera off him.'

In the VIP box Kissinger watched with Agnelli, the latter wearing the fattest kipper tie on earth.

And the keepers went to the goal; the players sat down in the centre circle.

> There's only one Peter Shilton
> Only one Peter Shilton.

But he didn't make any saves – though he did go the right way all four times. And thirty million English people watched this game; we all know the cruel way it ended.

The penalty shootout's a heartless piece of ersatz TV drama, irrelevant to the game of football ... ah well. Lineker, Beardsley, and Platt all scored; Brehme, Matthäus, and Riedle ditto. Then Pearce fired it straight at Illgner, who, diving left, saved with his legs. Beardsley ran to Pearce as he walked back, and Lineker – but what could you say to him? And Thon scored; then Waddle fired his kick over the top. 4–3 to the Germans.

Nightmare. The black pit of loss opened wide ... and the sound system immediately blared out, 'All English fans are kindly requested to remain in your seats for fifteen minutes. You will then be escorted by security to where your buses are located. All English fans ...'

1984. I mean, how dare they, *how dare they?* It was staggeringly, brutishly insensitive. And there were people with little flags forming up a silly bloody Ciao on the pitch in some naff Turin closing ceremony ... a decent period of silence and respect was called for here. And look what we got instead.

Gazza was crying in the big arms of Terry Butcher. And I was crying too; from a tight chest and an aching head, the tears had been threatening since they sang 'You'll Never Walk Alone'. Robson, putting the bravest imaginable face on it, gulped down his sorrow, and subjected himself to the instant interview. He said, 'This is a cruel situation, but we just have to accept it. We played a big part in the tournament.'

We certainly did, sir. We certainly did.

A Scottish journalist going out, I don't know who he was, saw me crying, staring out blindly over the huge emptying stands. He said, with the softest kindness, 'It's hard for you. It's very hard.'

And it was. Our story was all played out – but how bravely, in the end. How very bravely.

I went down cavernous corridors to where a scrum of press and TV crews waited to be let into the interview area. The COL limit was twenty-five each from England and Germany, twenty Italians, and ten agency men. So what Ecuadorian TV was doing down there I don't know ... but that's Planet Football for you; a jostling ruck, getting sweaty under the hot lights of camera crews.

The War Correspondent pushed through, and we shook hands. He just said, 'The best, the best' – it seemed all he could say, he seemed wordless – and though right then I felt the worst, the worst, I knew also that what he said was right.

Because football is Pelé's beautiful game – and with the Germans we'd played it beautifully – with strength and speed, with courage and skill, with honesty and honour.

The two team buses waited in a dim-lit and cavernous space of concrete. The bulk of the press went, naturally and mercifully, to the Germans. Macca asked me to translate a crucial request to the bus driver: 'Where are the beers?' And out came the Becks from the cold box – I hope they drank a fountain of the stuff.

Beardsley came through, silent, looking cut in half. And as Gazza came then, head still shaking at the ground in anguished disbelief, just wanting to get on the bus, Rob Bonnet shovelled the mike in his face as he got on the steps.

He asked, 'Whatareyourfeelingsonthegame?'

What a stupid question. And what an awful bloody job, for an intelligent man to have to ask it, at this time of all times.

The bustle and squeeze milled about, question and answer echoing dully off the bare dark walls. There was a mob around Platt. Butcher came, smiled, and we talked quietly for a moment, standing a bit apart. It was like, on the bench, he'd had time to work it out – he was thirty-one, it was his third World Cup. And he knew – though it hurt awful to be out in this way, at this stage – that it was still the best, the best.

He joked, 'Every time they bring me off we score. Maybe they should have brought me off earlier.'

Seventy-seven caps; an almighty contribution. And six weeks later, as the new season started with Rangers favourites to win the Scottish League again, Terry Butcher announced his retirement from international football.

Les Walker said, 'It was a good result for English football, and a good tournament for English fans. They've been good as gold in there. I think it's the start of a new era – I really do.'

Robson arrived – the man who'd brought the old era to an end that few had imagined might be so magnificent – and one crew after another was on him, from England and Brazil, from Germany and

Ecuador. And even here, now – with the bus waiting, and his highest hopes so cruelly stolen – still he talked, and signed autographs for people from the other side of the world. He said, 'It's the biggest match we've played in twenty-four years.'

Gary Lineker ended one last interview backing away, looking just bleakly, desperately sad. He'd been once to the quarters, once to the semis – he was twenty-nine. Would he still be there, in four more years? He shook his head, no, no more words – speechlessly sad.

And Platt was all interviewed out – but he did another, and another – until finally, politely and helplessly, he just asked, 'Can't you get it off somebody else?'

Les Walker watched Robson still talking, and smiled with a fond incredulity. Would the man ever stop giving himself to them?

But most of the players and staff were on the bus now, with Stuart Pearce last on, someone keeping him company to try and salve the pain of the missed penalty. And now the German bus was leaving, and the press and the cameras too.

I backed away, against a rough grey wall; one of the last few there, though I wasn't there really, not fully – I was still back in the beautiful game, still watching the weave and weft of the play, the patterns and the passes, the missed chances and the goals, the hope and the grief – still crying and cheering in the stands where the ordinary folk go to watch the men who've got gold in their shoes.

On the bus, the staff were at the front, and the players in their own compact world at the back. Gazza, when he'd got on, had been still barely over his tears; he'd sat down, and for a short while looked silent, and bitterly miserable.

But what the hell, a beer and a sing-song, it's all over now – and it was Gazza who started them singing. Lineker looked back at it, and looked away – then he smiled too – and before long they were all joining in, working some daft little routine with their arms to the song, as the bus pulled away. Because we may have been edged out of this one – but there's always another game down the road, and another season, and another goal to go for.

The last thing I noticed was Bobby Robson standing in the aisle near the front, leaning slightly forward with one hand on the back of a seat, and the other over his eyes. It was the posture of a man drained and shattered – the posture, perhaps, of a man in tears at journey's end.

And in the empty bus park, the small simple words of the War Correspondent came back. Because what had it been like, to follow England to the semi-finals of the World Cup?

It had been the best – just the best.

MEANWHILE, SOMEWHERE ELSE . . .

John Arlott

It Occurs to Me

It occurs to me that a poor South-country man ought never to think that he knows anything about Yorkshire or Yorkshiremen.

I walked into Headingley for the Leeds Test match with the air of one who knows his way around the place. There he was, at his bookstall immediately inside the gate – Smithy. As usual, his cricket shirt was open at the neck, his white coat was catching the breeze, his hair was swept back to the neckline as sharp as a razor slash.

'Hullo, Smithy,' I said, anxious to convince myself that I was not in strange country, 'how are you?' Then, as I noticed a sunburn on him that would have turned a Riviera life-saver green with envy: 'Have you been having some sun in Yorkshire – or where did you get that sunburn?' 'Australia,' he said with a grin.

Now, Smithy sells newspapers and sporting magazines at the Yorkshire cricket grounds. He played cricket as hard as any other Yorkshire boy until he was fifteen, when he was so ill that he never caught up with the other boys again.

He was apprenticed to a plumber, but he wanted to be in cricket, so he started selling newspapers at the cricket grounds round his county – Leeds, Sheffield, Hull, Scarborough, Huddersfield.

It was last summer that Yorkshire matches and even Tests in Yorkshire stopped being enough for him – he wanted to go to Australia. Mrs Smith decided him to go by saying that it was a good idea. He sold the van and the tools which were the stock in trade of part-time winter plumbing business for a hundred pounds, left his wife the newspaper round to keep her and the two children for the winter and bought a ticket to Australia on the *Strathaird*.

Arthur Smith, from Leeds, landed in Perth, Western Australia, with a small trunk, an overnight case, fifteen pounds and two hundred copies of Len Hutton's benefit booklet. He off-loaded the booklets, left his trunk in Melbourne and set off. How he was going to sleep, eat, travel, get into cricket grounds and above all get back to England in the following spring were matters of faith and hope, but not of charity.

He could sell newspapers in England, couldn't he? He wanted to see the MCC's matches in Australia and, to that end, by Heaven, he could sell newspapers in Australia. He could sell souvenirs of the touring team – if he could find the souvenirs and the people who produced them – and if he could persuade them to let him have a stock of them.

The tour rolled on. Sidney Barnes, toughest and most businesslike of Australian cricketers, drove Smithy from Towoomba to Sydney. That trip apart, he flew once, otherwise he took the local transport to the end of the main street and thumbed his way to the MCC's next port of call.

Things were not always easy. So far from money piling up for the return trip to Mrs Smith and the next Yorkshire season – at Canberra he had to sleep in the bus shelter and twice he slept on park benches.

He saw those Test matches and, when an English player – particularly his fellow-countryman, Len Hutton – did well, he could afford to be proudly an Englishman.

In Australia evening newspapers cost threepence each; the seller's commission is twenty-five per cent. But in Melbourne paper-sellers are not allowed to sell inside the ground. So Smithy had to sell his papers outside and buy his way into the ground until the next batch of papers arrived. While the MCC side was in Tasmania Smithy sold papers outside Richmond Station at Melbourne and slowly the £100 built up.

He never had a drink or a cigarette all through that tour. His story spread round Australia and six broadcasts helped to fill his shrewd Yorkshire wallet.

As Len Hutton broke records so did his fellow Yorkshireman Smithy – on the second day of the Adelaide Test with 1,224 newspapers sold in a single day.

He bought his ticket home, presents for his family and friends and landed at Tilbury in time for the new cricket season with seven pounds, a shy, sharp smile and a terrific layer of sunburn to prove that he had been from Leeds to Australia for a cricketing winter.

If you want another proof ask Mrs Smith behind his stall at Headingley whether she is the wife of the man who went from Leeds to Adelaide and back and, if she is not forced to tell you that her husband is too busy to be interrupted, she will be proud to introduce you: I suspect that Mrs Smith is also fond of cricket.

George Plimpton

Golf Caddies

Just about the liveliest place to listen to golf talk, though of a slightly different nature, was along the rail fence where the touring caddies gathered out behind the clubhouse—just off the practice putting green—where they perched upon the fence between the big golf bags they tended, many of them in white coveralls with the identifying numbers and names of their professionals across the shoulder blades. Their rialto was here, and they rocked back and forth on the fence and compared notes and swapped yarns and gossip, and talked of their rounds, particularly about money and how their pro had let them down: "Oh my, we're doin' jes' fine and then my man he goes an' *dies* on me," etc., etc.

There are about forty professional caddies—touring caddies, they're called—some of whom, the fortunate ones, stay with one golfer throughout the winter tour (the PGA does not allow the touring caddy system during the summer months when the high schools are out—at that time a caddy must stick to a home course) while the others, less fortunate, travel uncommitted and hope to pick up a bag, or "pack a bag" as the phrase goes, when they turn up on the eve of a tournament and look to catch a pro's eye and sign up with him for that particular event.

The touring caddies are a wildly individual clan, not at all to be confused with the local caddies. They are a nomadic group (some of the more disapproving professionals refer to them as "The Traveling Brewery") that moves from tournament to tournament, usually four or five to a car, and they suddenly appear around the caddy shacks with the abruptness and aplomb of extremely competent men sent to do an expert job. The local caddies stare at them with as much awe as they work up for the professional golfers. Johnny Pott once told me: "I can't imagine what it's like to travel with the touring caddies. I remember once a car with six of them in it—going cross-country—came through my hometown, and they stopped by to pick up an open-faced driver I had promised one of them. Well, I opened up the trunk of their car to put in the driver and there wasn't anything in there at all—no suitcases, kits, anything. Real Gypsies. They travel in just their shoes."

During the tour I got to know some of them by wandering down and leaning up against the fence and asking questions from time to time. It was very lively listening. Most of the touring caddies are blacks, though there were exceptions, notably Arnold Palmer's caddy, Bob Blair, a loner I never saw with the others, and Jack Nicklaus's regular caddy, Angelo Argea, who was quite a different sort, being a soft-spoken Italian with a pleasant grin who was very popular with the others. In joshing him, they had a number of derogatory nicknames, which he took in good humor. The caddies, as a whole, owned a splendid variety of nicknames: Cut Shot, Violence, Texas Sam, the Wolfman, the Rabbit, the Baron, Cricket, the Rock, Big Ted, the Golfball ... their names peppering their conversation, as in, "Hey, Cricket, you seen the Golfball?" "Hell, no, ask the Wolfman."

Ted Randolph was the one called the Wolfman. He was given that nickname in the Boy Scouts where he had once made, he told me, a very impressionable imitation of a werewolf. The name stuck for a while and was about to fade away. "Then," he said, "I grew me a long beard and I damn near *looked* like a werewolf. So the name stuck for good."

Walter Montgomery was the one they called Violence. He had had his hair straightened. He kept it flattened slick against his skull, so that the sheen of black seemed newly painted on. He was named after his short temper—a characteristic he had worked in recent years at curbing.

"What did you use to do, Violence?" I asked, relishing the odd nickname and the strangeness of it on the tongue. "Hey, Violence?" I asked, grinning at him.

"I've cooled it, baby. It don't make no sense. It don't do no help to the guys I was packing for."

"You mean you took it out on the golfers?" I asked.

"A cat'd make some crazy play like miss a putt of two foot. Now a cat like that, why he's cuttin' my money, making a bad shot, dig? So I go up and kick his bag. I really bang it."

"Well, how did they take that?"

"Like I say, it don't make no sense, 'cause it don't do no good. They start keepin' a side eye on me, like maybe I'm fixin' to lift a shoe into *them* the next time, druther than the bag. It don't do no good for their golf, and then I ... well, they ain't fixin' hard to have me pack for them again."

"What else did you do?"

Violence frowned slightly. "Oh," he said, "I slam the pin back in the cup real hard, jes' to show the guy, y'know, what I think of his messin' up the shot. Threw my cap quite a lot. Once I sailed it across the green and it hit Doug Sanders in the back of the head. But then, like I say, I cool it. I pack for Julius Boros and he like me and he say, 'Man, act like me, very calm, all the time, and you do O.K.' So I do what he say. I'm goin' fine for a good long time now, and it pays good, it's an honest livin' an' I'm gettin' on fine. But the guys remember what I done—y'know, like in San Diego, when we go there for the Open, they say, 'Hey, Violence, baby, so you goin' out on the town? Well, you broke a guy's jaw in this town, you *re*-call,' and they grin, and I say, 'Sure, man, but that was las' year.' They waiting for me to bust someone, they al'ays *lookin'*, but I ain't done nothing like that for a time. 'Course I ain't sayin' when a guy messes a shot, the juices don' get worked up ..."

I said that frankly I was glad he wasn't packing my bag, if he didn't mind my saying so.

He laughed and said oh, yes, he had heard about my golf.

Alfred Dyer, out of New Orleans, was called the Rabbit. He was very self-assured. "You talk to the Rabbit," he said, "an' you're getting the stuff straight from number one. If it's caddyin' you're talkin' 'bout, the Rabbit's your man. Why, at those big Jewish country clubs in the East, it's the Rabbit they's always calling for. 'Where's the Rabbit? Where's the Rabbit?' They say, 'You think I'm takin' one step on this course lessen the Rabbit's packing my bag, you is loco in the *head*.' Why, I make forty dollars a day in the East jes' on my name alone. Autographs? Man, the Rabbit's always signing autographs ..."

At this there was a bit of good-natured hooting from the others down the fence. Someone shouted: "Rabbit, you can't write, man, an X much lessen your name."

I asked: "Rabbit, what do you think you do best as a caddy?"

The Rabbit thought and he said: "Well, calm my man down, I think that's what I do very good. Pull him off to the side when he's got a lot of pressure on him and I tell him, let the Rabbit share it with you. Maybe I get him telling what he done the night before—jes' to get his mind off the pressure and make him relax. 'Course sometimes you got to do jes' the opposite—fire yo' man up. Now take Tom Weiskopf in the Colonial. We're comin' down the stretch with a jes' fine lead, but then Tom bogeys three holes in a row and he comes up on the thirteenth jes' 'bout ready to fall to pieces. He's chokin'. He's got this big ball in his throat. He says, 'Rabbit, we're going to have to play for second place. I'm playing it safe in here.' So the Rabbit says, 'Man, I'm dropping yo' bag right here if you don't go for the flag. You take a two iron and put the ball up there nice an' easy. Smooth,' I said. I can say 'smooth' like you never heard nobody say that word, like silk. Well, he done it."

Quite another different sort of touring caddy was Dale Taylor, Billy Casper's caddy—a soft-spoken polite man in his forties, I would guess, and with very much of a no-nonsense attitude about his profession. He was an excellent golfer, I was told. He told me that he caddied for his man with pleasure because Casper always tended to the business at hand—their rounds together on a golf course had no other purpose.

"That's the point," Dale said. "If you're in the business and you want to make a dollar, you got to play with a man who's got a right attitude. Billy Casper's got a wife and two kids. He goes out on a golf course and he's got their support in mind. He isn't thinking about anything else but his business. That's the attitude I got to have too. We think alike. I'm good for him to have around. He keeps me on the payroll and I babysit for his children, things like that."

I asked: "But don't all golfers go out on the course with that same attitude—that they're going to win?"

"They should," Dale said. "But then you get a golfer like Ken Still, who has this really great talent, this fantastic potential..." He looked around at the other caddies. "That's right, isn't it?" They all nodded. "And yet when he goes out on a golf course, his mind just isn't on what's what. He's interested in sports, Ken Still is, and if there's a ball game going on somewhere, he's thinking about it. He's like to have a transistor plugged in his ear, and sometimes he yells things like, 'Come on, Duke, belt one for ol' Ken.' You ever see Ken walk down a fairway?" The caddies all rocked back and forth, grinning. "Why, he's got that radio goin' in his ear, maybe one in *each* if they got two ball games on, and his feet come down *plop plop* like he's dizzy, and you got to see him wobble from one side of the fairway to the other, his arms waving, and his lips wobbling, too, and then he wanders off, and then his caddy, he's got to say, 'Man, we're over *heah,*' just to get his man back on the track."

"You jivin'," someone said. They were all laughing.

Doug Sanders's caddy, who was called Cricket, spoke up and said that he wished he had transistors to worry about with *his* man, because it was girls, which was worse.

"He looks for 'em in the gallery, and man, he spots one, we gotta lose three strokes."

"It don't take much to make 'em a duck," someone said.

"A what?" I asked.

"A duck."

"Duck" turned out to be a word they used a lot for the young professionals rather than the word *rabbit,* which the golfers used. A caddy would say: "I got me a duck who *faints* on me at Napa—lies down on the course and goes to sleep with two holes to go and we got the cut made cold."

Some of the terms they used were rather arcane. One caddy referred to a golfer as a Union Oil.

"What's that?" I asked. "A Union Oil?"

"He's like those speculative oil stocks," I was told. "He goes up and down jes' like they do—man, he's a sixty-nine one day, and the next, he shoot up to a eighty-nine. So we call him a Union Oil. Or a drugstore pro. Sometime we call him that."

From the earliest days of golf, caddies have been the originators of golfing terms, and also masters of the quip, the laconic remark that seems so often the legacy of menial jobs. I particularly like the caddy's retort to the novice golfer who slices an enormous divot out of the ground, and asks, "What do I do with this?"

"Take it home," the caddy says, "an' practice on it."

Or the golfer who hits his drive toward the end of an imperfect day and peers off into the gloom.

Golfer: "Did that go straight, boy?"

Caddy: "Couldn't see it, but it sounded crooked."

Or this one.

Beginner (after repeated failures): "Funny game, golf."

Caddy: "'Taint meant to be."

Traditionally, caddies have been great showboat characters. In recent times when Johnny Pott sank a chip shot to win the Crosby in 1968, his caddy, Scott, flung his arms up and fell down in a heap. The television cameras caught him in his prostration of pleasure, and he told me that his mother had seen him on national television, and most of the neighborhood, and he had become a celebrity with people coming around and knocking on his mother's window, and smiling in, some of them complete strangers, to indicate they'd seen him and now appreciated his status.

When I spoke to him, and he was reminiscing, he said that he thought he might *patent* his collapse and do it every time he came on the eighteenth with a tournament winner, or even with someone back in the pack if that golfer recorded a great shot on television. "Just throw up my arms," Scott said, "and fall in a heap on the green."

"Scott, do you ever throw up your arms and fall in a heap on an *early* hole—if your man makes a great shot on the third hole, say?"

I sensed his answer and was right: "Oh, I give a good yell," he said. "But for falling down, I save that for the finishing holes and the television. I mean it takes something out of you to fall down like that. It's a question of timing. Of course, the trouble is," he said, "you got to find someone to pack a bag for who's going to do *his* side of the act. I mean, make that shot, baby. I been all set to fall down for some months now but I ain't had no *kind* of cat to give me the opportunity. It seem like I'm fighting to make the cut every time. I dunno," he said mournfully. "Maybe the next time we make the cut I'm goin' to fall down in a heap jes' to keep my hand in . . ."

I asked them about perhaps the most famous contemporary caddy— the one the golfing public would know about from watching TV— Arnold Palmer's Iron Man, the tall, gaunt dean of the caddies at the Masters in Augusta, the caddy everyone remembered for his long, slow, loping walk up the last fairways in the white coveralls, the old, thin face under the cap, and how he sat on the bag at the edge of the green with his knees drawn up under his chin, or stood out behind Palmer where he leaned over and spoke his notions into Palmer's ear as the two of them inspected the lie of the putt on those last huge greens.

A chorus of disapprobation rose, particularly from Scott.

"Iron Man? What he know 'bout packing a bag. He know nothin' man."

"That's right. You get the Iron Man offen the Masters course, an' he *lost*—why he stumble 'round like he gonna be *bit* by something."

Another caddy chimed in: "He been confused since he was two year ol'—shit, man, how you talk about Iron Man?"

"Well," I said, "what about all that advice he gives Palmer. On the green. You see him there, leaning over, advising . . . at least he's whispering things for Palmer to hear."

"He's jes' movin' his lips. He don't know what he sayin'."

"Why, he ain't *got* nothin' to say. He don' know golf enough to say beans."

One of them leaned forward. "I'll tell you what he's saying man. He's leanin' into Palmer's ear an' he's saying: 'Jes' in case you wanna know, Mis' Palmer, it's gettin' on 'bout fo'-fifteen in the afternoon.'"

The caddies all grinned and hee-hawed.

The one caddy all of them spoke creditably of—a hero among them, apparently—was Hagan, semiretired now, they said, who worked out of the Riviera Country Club in Pacific Palisades, California. They spoke of him as being the first caddy who made a scientific art of the craft, checking the course early in the morning for pin positions and pacing off the course and marking distances on a card so that if a golfer asked what the distance was, Hagan would say, looking at his card, "Well, from that tree it's exactly one hundred and thirty-five yards to the center of the green." All of this, when Hagan began the practice, was unknown, and was now widely practiced, not only by the caddies, but by the golfers themselves. Nicklaus relied largely on a card he pulled from his hip pocket with the distances carefully tabulated.

"Tell me more about Hagan," I said.

"He really knew what he was doing," one of the caddies said. The others nodded. "Big pride in his work. There was this time he was working for Tommy Bolt. So Bolt says, 'What do you think?' and Hagan says, 'It's a six iron.' Bolt says, 'No, it's a five.' Hagan says, 'No, it's a six and when you hit it, just hit it firm and don't press.' Bolt says, 'You're crazy, Hagan,' and he takes a five iron and hits it twenty yards over the green. So Bolt takes the five iron and he breaks it over his knee. Well, Hagan, who's been holding the six iron, *he* breaks *it* over *his* knee, and he drops Bolt's bag right there and begins striding off down the fairway. He's done with him. But Bolt comes hurrying on down after him and he's all full of apologies. He says, 'Wait for me, Hagan; ol' Tom's right sorry. You was right. Listen, I'm on the tournament committee and I'm fining myself one hundred and fifty dollars for what I done."

"Do caddies ever get fired?" I asked.

The caddy called the Baron spoke up and said that Bob Goalby had fired him three times on one hole.

"He says to me, 'How far is the flag?' I tell him, and he says, 'You're fired.' Well, I stand around and he comes up with a bad shot and he sees I was right and he looks around and he hires me again. But he's all riled up inside, and when he misses his next shot he bangs his club around and his eye lights on me and he fires me again. So I drop his bag. I stand around. I don't know who else he can hang the bag on. A couple of grandmothers. He don't háve this big gallery. His wife maybe. She was there. Or maybe he'll pack the bag himself. He must be thinking the same thing, 'cause after a while he says, 'Hey, Baron, pick it up,' which means he's hired me again. We get up to the green and we confer on a putt and he misses it real bad—he don't *begin* to do what I tell him. So he wheels around and he fires me again in this big loud voice. That's enough for me. I drop the bag and I head for the caddy shop. His wife comes running after me. She don't want to pack the bag. She says, 'Come back, Baron, please, Bob don't mean none of that, he *needs* you.' She's a great girl. I know he don't mean no harm. Golf does things to people. So I tell her that and I go back and I pick up his bag."

"Does one ever really drop a bag on a pro?"

"Who was it—Tony?—who dropped Finsterwald's bag on the thirteenth at Denver in the Open in '60."

They nodded.

"Yah, Arnold Palmer won that one with a little short white caddy. You recall?"

I never could get a word out of Arnold Palmer's present caddy, Bob Blair. He reminded me of a rancher—quiet, strong-faced. I asked him a few times if he would talk about his job but he always declined, very politely. He kept to himself. The other caddies knew very little about him. Palmer had had some strange ones, one of the caddies told me. For a while he had a caddy who was a Marine Corps colonel on the lam—his wife was trying to sue him. The colonel thought he could lose himself in the nomadic life of the touring caddies, which he imagined, I suppose, as the American equivalent of the Foreign Legion. It worked for a while, until suddenly he was Palmer's caddy, appearing on television, and it rather went to his head. "He tried to pass himself off as a big shot," the caddy said. "Man, he had a terrific wardrobe. Then he begins signing Palmer's name to checks. I don't know what happened to him. He was a big good-looking guy. He turned up at the country club dances in a tuxedo—man, he was more at home in a tuxedo than Arnie, the guy he was caddying for."

"Maybe his wife caught up with him," I said.

"Well, it was sure a funny place to hide," the caddy said. "With the touring caddies. I mean, every Sunday, if his wife catches a look at her

TV set, there her husband would be, most likely—standing in the background there."

"Maybe she never made the connection," I said. "Maybe she saw him and said, 'Well, that reminds me of somebody, that guy . . .' like that theory if you're going to hide something, set it right out in the middle of the room where it's so obvious everyone walks around it and ignores it."

"Well, I don't know about that theory," the caddy said. "More is likely she took one look at the TV set and said, 'So there you is, you mother,' and she jumped in the family car and took off after him. Hell, man, if my wife run off and I look in the TV set and there she is caddying for Jack Nicklaus, I ain't going to be saying to myself, 'Now, let's see, who that remind me of?' Hell, *no.*"

"Well, you sound very convincing," I said.

When I asked the caddies along the fence if there were any players they were not particularly anxious to caddy for, there was a quick reaction.

"Oh, my!"

A chorus of dismay went up.

"Frank Beard!"

"Man, Bert Yancy's got to head that list."

"Baby, I'll tell you, Bobby Nichols sure on that list, and there don't have to be no squeezing to get him on!"

"Cupit!"

"Tommy Aaron!"

"Shut yo' mouth. Richard Crawford, he's the cake. That man, why he's as tight as beeswax!"

"I'm telling you, Frank Beard! Nobody's alive like him—why, I'm telling you he pinches a penny and right between his fingers that thing turn into a BB pellet!"

"You know what Deane Beman give? Why, man, he give ten dollar a day and *three* percent of his winnings. And when he han' that ovah, he look at you like you done stab him in the knee!"

"How about the caddy's friend?" I asked.

The mood grew respectful.

"Dan Sikes, he's sure one, I'll tell you."

"Nicklaus. You know what he did for this caddy, this guy called Pappy?"

"What was that?" I asked.

"Pappy took his winnings at this Las Vegas tournament and he got hot on the crap tables and he had a pile—twenty-two thousand—sitting in front of him. He thought his luck was never going to stop. He was going to take that entire town and stuff it in his back pocket. Well, someone run and get Nicklaus and he come on the double and there's Pappy, the big crowd around him, with this big gleam in his eye and rolling the dice like crazy. Nicklaus says, 'O.K., hand it over, Pappy, 'fore it's gone.' He leaves Pappy two thousand and he takes that twenty grand and invests it for him in Arnold Palmer's equipment company. I tell you that fellow Pappy's sitting pretty these days."

"Dean Martin's a great caddy's friend," one of the others said. "There were these two guys last Fourth of July up to Bel Air Country Club, and they find Dean and they say, 'Dean, we got a good drunk goin' and we ain't got enough to *finish* it.' He looks 'em over and they were telling the truth, you could tell that right smart, and so he reckons twenty dollars ought to be enough to finish what they begun, maybe much less, maybe *two* dollars by the looks of them, but he takes out the twenty and he forks it over."

"I tell you my man Doug Sanders is a caddy's friend," Cricket said. There was general agreement.

"I tell you," someone said, "the caddies' best friends are the golfers who finish in the top fifteen. You don't pack a bag for one of those cats and you like to have troubles."

"You're talking," said Cricket. He reported he had made twenty-seven hundred in a month of Florida tournaments packing Sanders's bag.

They told me that if they finish out of the money, caddies get paid a hundred to a hundred and fifty. Usually they can rely on ten percent of their professional's winnings.

The caddy called Doc stirred and said that when it came to money they were all spoiled. He had been on the tour for twenty-two years. When he started to caddy he was lucky to get two dollars for packing a professional's bag for eighteen holes. Out of the first prize for tournaments in those days—maybe three thousand—why, a caddy'd be pretty lucky to clear a hundred and fifty. Doc's real name was Foster Eubanks. He was called Doc because he carried all his gear—his rainhat and so forth—in a doctor's satchel. He was one of the caddies with a car. Five other caddies drove with him, spelling each other at the wheel. He shook his head thinking of their conduct. "They don't know what a dollar is. The gambling! Those boys from Dallas, I tell you, they'll bet you a hoss fell out of a tree."

Most of the caddies certainly had first-class ideas about high living. Jack Nicklaus told me that Willie Peterson, who caddied him through his first Masters win in 1963, had suddenly, on one occasion, turned up in Columbus, Ohio, the golfer's hometown, to see him to borrow money—traveling first class on the plane and arriving at Nicklaus's door in a taxi with the meter ticking over and the driver waiting—very nattily dressed, according to Nicklaus, in an outfit which included a silk shirt in the twenty-dollar price range, with a straw boater set at a debonair tilt over one eyebrow. "Mr. Jack, I'm here for a loan," he said, just as easily as he might have said "good morning."

Nicklaus paid off the taxi, invited Peterson in, and sat him down to talk finance with him. "I told him I had some friends in Cleveland who could give him a hand, give him a good enough job to keep him going, and that I'd let them know. I suggested he cut down on his standard of living since he just wasn't in the financial bracket to keep it up. He nodded and he said certainly, but he'd better be hurrying on up to Cleveland to see those people I'd told him about. Well, he took a *taxi* to Cleveland—a hundred and forty-nine miles."

Nicklaus laughed and shook his head. "A great character. He was sort of a cheerleader for me—jump up and down and try to get some reaction from the crowds if there had been a good shot. He loved to get his picture in the paper and he was very proud about caddying. He'd say, 'Mr. Jack, I gotta have more than anyone's *ever* been paid.'"

The caddies themselves kept track of each other's fortunes. "You can tell if a caddy's doing O.K. on the tour by his shoes," one of them told me. "If he ain't wearing rubber-sole shoes to get a grip on the hills, and he's wearing his regular shoes with wax paper in them to keep the wet out of his socks and slidin' under those big bags—those big Haigs, hell, they'll weigh over a hundred pounds—and he's wearing a quarter in each ear to keep out the cold out there on the dew patrol—first golfers out in the morning—well, you got a caddy who hasn't got a deal, an' he'll be thinking real low. He'll be starvin' in *Florida*, man, packing for ducks who can't play the game, who won't stand up for you nohow."

A "deal" is what the traveling caddy craves—a steady arrangement with a golfer who finishes consistently in the high money.

I asked how they got started with their pros—those who packed for a pro regularly. One of them, called Leroy, who had talked about being fired, spoke up and said that he had been with Bob Goalby for nine years. He had gone through some tough times with him. And then, this one time, Goalby had this sixty-foot putt to win his first tournament. Goalby said: "Leroy, what do you think?"

"I took a look," Leroy said. "'Bob,' I said to him, 'I think it's goin' to double-break this way, then hump over that way, but you got to make sure it *gets* there.'"

Goalby followed his advice. The putt dropped, and he leaped for Leroy and gave him a big hug, near hauling him down to the green. "You got a job for life!" he shouted.

Some of them got involved just by chance. Angelo Argea, who has been with Nicklaus pretty steadily since 1963, was assigned to him at a Las Vegas tournament in which Nicklaus was not expected to play because of a bursitis attack. Argea was assigned "just in case." Nicklaus did play and won the tournament.

The two had a ritual. Argea was always supposed to say, "Good luck," on the second hole. Sometimes, particularly if they started a round on the back nine, and the second hole was the eleventh, Argea would forget, and Nicklaus would fret and ask leading questions, until finally Argea would remember and say, "Oh, God, yes, good *luck*!".

One of the main topics that the traveling caddies talk about is the Rule. They inveigh against it at any opportunity, and one can hear such odd legal phrases along caddies' row as, "I'm telling you, baby, it's restraint of trade . . . and besides, it ain't fair practices."

The Rule is the condition enforced by the PGA that touring caddies cannot work the tour from June 1 to September 1 when school is out and the caddy forces are largely made up of kids caddying for their summer jobs. The PGA is sympathetic—excessively so, the professional caddies feel—to this group, administering, for example, a scholarship plan known as the Chick Evans Award, which benefits top caddies from each club; of particular dismay to the touring caddies is the PGA's insistence that when the tour arrives at a club in the summer season, its own club caddies should benefit.

Tommy Brown, a caddy they called the Kid, who had been on the tour for three years, said, "Yeah, it's a good life. You travel. You sit around in these nice country clubs. The company is good. You have just about everything. When the Rule hits, though—why these thirteen-year-old kids are depriving me of this good time and my income. The summer months—well, it's hard to sit in one place, in the East there; you count the time when you can get back moving."

"Those kids snap up our bread," the Rabbit said. "Why in San Francisco this one time when they play the tournament there in June, this kid from the Stanford University packs for Billy Casper who makes the playoff and wins it. Kid's name was Stark. Casper says, 'Stark, what's your fee for packing?' And the kid says, 'Seven dollars a day. Five dollars for the playoff 'cause that's extra.' Billy gives him two thousand dollars."

A moan went up along the fence, and the clicking of tongues.

"What can you do to better your cause?" I asked.

"Well, let me say this," one of them said. "Them players, those cats who calls themselves the caddy's bes' friend, what they can do is say that if they can't have their own caddies for the summer months, why, they'll *strike*. Won't play. That's what those cats could do, dig?"

They all nodded their heads. "Man, you jivin'," one of them said.

"We're treated like dogs," one of the caddies said. "We got to park fifty miles over in the woods. The public don't understand this. We got a lot of trouble. We should have credentials just like the touring pros. We're worth it to them. In the seven years I been a touring caddy I can't think of a touring pro who's lost a penalty shot 'cause of some mistake."

It was true that many of the golfers were sympathetic to the caddies' woes. When I asked Doug Sanders about the Rule, he was very insistent.

"I wish they'd waive it," he said. "You have to be lucky to get a good caddy in the summer. I'd as soon put a hundred dollars in a kitty for the high-school kids for the chance to have a touring caddy packing for me. You don't want an intern operating on you; you want a doctor. A great caddy can help you maybe only one shot a week—but that adds up. Try that on the money list. It makes a big difference. An amateur caddy will lose you strokes. I don't mean that he's going to rake a trap with your ball in it, something against the rules that'll penalize you, but you can lose strokes worrying about him. Particularly if you're near winning a tournament. He's never been through an experience like that. It's like combat. You want someone you can really depend on."

Rod Funseth agreed. He said: "You get scared around a trap if your caddy doesn't know the rules. It's a two-stroke penalty if you hit your own bag. Most caddies don't know that. Two strokes if you hit an attended pin. Why I can remember T. B., who caddies for me a lot, having a pin stick on him with a long putt of mine rolling up toward him, and he wrenched at that flag, and he was so anxious he let out this yell, and finally he hauls the whole cup out, the entire metal thing, and just in time too."

"The only thing one can say against the touring caddies," Sanders said, "is that they drink and carry on too much—a bit crazy. Like if a caddy has five hundred dollars a week, he'll spend five-twenty. But then, that's *his* business. I tell you that for my business, which is golf, I want them around. Good caddies are confidence builders and great assets. In fact, if you've got a really good caddy you find yourself playing hard for him. My caddy, Cricket . . . you know him?"

"Yes," I said.

". . . well, this one time I made this really great recovery shot. Cricket says: 'That's a great save, Doug!' I say to him, 'Cricket, I'm right glad to hear what you say 'cause that's the first nice word I've heard you say this round.' And he says: 'Doug, up to now you ain't deserved any comment.'"

Some of the golfers disapproved of the touring caddy arrangement. Tom Nieporte, for example, told me that he thought a team of a professional and his caddy, if they had been together for a long time, might be tempted, well, to "try something." To give an extreme example, a caddy, with or without the knowledge of his pro, might be tempted to edge a ball into a slightly better lie. Nieporte had never heard of this happening on the tour, but his point was that an arrangement should not be condoned that could so easily lead to such a temptation.

I asked the caddies about this, and they were scornful. Cricket said: "It never happen. Man'd be crazy to take a chance like that. You get caught, that's the end, baby. I never heard of such a thing, trying to help or hinder a golfer. You ain't goin' to find any long-toed boys on the tour." When I asked, he said what he meant by "long-toed boys" was in reference to the old-time barefoot caddy who could envelop a ball with his toes and move it to a better lie. "You see these cats at the private clubs. These boys work the Eastern country clubs in the off-season, packin' those big-money amateur foursomes. You always give a good lie for those cats. It don't mean that much. If I step on a player's ball, man, I put it back. But you don' find nothing like that goin' on when the tour rolls aroun'. It ain't the same gig."

The main attribute of the caddy, almost all professionals seemed to agree, is to reinforce their pro's decisions, or even to dispute them, and make the golfer think hard before making his shot. Naturally some golfers feel a caddy's importance is overrated.

Claude Harmon was scornful of a caddy's advice. He said his instruction to them was always very simple: Clean the clubs and the balls and show up on time and be in the right place and always be quiet. "My idea of a caddy is the one I won the Masters with. Never said one word. Hell, he won two other Masters that I know of—with Ben Hogan and Jackie Burke—and I think he won a fourth one. We compared notes and only Burke could remember him saying anything. That was on the seventy-second hole, the last of the tournament, and Burke, who was looking over his putt, heard this calm voice just behind him say: 'Cruise it right in there, Mr. Burke. Cruise it in.' And he did, too."

Harmon said he never could recall asking a caddy's advice. He said: "How can a boy know what you spend your life learning? Take a ball's lie. Just how the ball's sitting on the ground, whether it's hunkered down or sittin' up, can mean a fifty-yard difference in a shot's length using the same club. How's the caddy going to know? Is he good enough to make the right allowances for the weather—that a ball isn't going to go so far in the cold ... that it's going to die up there—he's going to know *that*? And how's he going to know about adrenaline— that great power you get under pressure, that strength, y'know, that allows one-hundred-pound women to lift Cadillacs off children? That's why you get such great pitching performances in the World Series from those speed pitchers—guys like Gibson of the Cards. Why, he throws the ball faster than he ever *knew* he could. In golf the same thing ... you come down those last fairways in contention and you find yourself hitting the ball thirty yards more than you know how. Well, how's a caddy going to judge *your* adrenaline quota? Think of Trevino in the '67 Open. He comes down the stretch just about ready to take the whole thing and he asks his caddy to club him and the guy suggests a five iron. Trevino's all hopped up, crazy strong, and he knows it, so he grabs himself an eight iron and hits the flag with it. Well, imagine where a five iron would have taken him. Right out of the whole caboodle, that's where."

I asked: "Are there golfers who don't have the courage of their convictions? Who really rely on caddies excessively?"

"Well, Sam Snead's too dependent on his caddy, and he's gullible—

which is a combination that can add up to a couple of mental errors a round. I can remember once at Oakmont on a round we come up to the thirteenth hole and we both hit the middle of the green with six irons. Well, the next day we come to the same hole and Sam asks his caddy, 'Boy, what do you think here?' He hasn't got his mind on it, I guess. His caddy clubs him with a five iron and Sam flies the shot over the green. He stares after it, and then he says, 'Hell, boy, that ain't no five-iron shot!' Well, hell, it's Sam should have known about that shot, not the caddy. It's typical of him, though. I always reckon I can have a good time with Sam on match play. I work up a little conversation with my caddy, just pretending to be all-fired confused about a shot, and I take out the three iron, and then the two, and then finally I choke up and hit an easy two that just clears the river and coasts up the green. The fact is, the shot's a natural four iron. Well, Sam steps up and he says, 'Boy, what do you think?' and his caddy, who's been keeping his ears open, knows that I used the two iron, so he says, 'It's a good two, Mr. Snead.' So Sam laces out a two iron and it clears the river, and green, and maybe some trees beyond. And Sam, he stares after it, and he says, 'Hell, boy, that ain't no two-iron shot.' Well, the fact is, you got to learn to depend on yourself. Hagen had the great system for penalizing opponents who eavesdropped on him. He had a jacked-up set of irons—the four iron was marked five, and so forth, and you could get into big trouble relying on him."

Gay Brewer, the 1967 Masters champion, also felt a caddy's value was overrated. It was fine to have his reassurance on club selection, but a professional would be foolish to rely on anything but judgment based on knowledge of his own game. Brewer had a different caddy every week on the tour, never really trying to keep one on a regular basis, and indeed he had won tournaments with boys who had never been on that particular course before. He took the Masters in 1967 but he couldn't remember the name of the caddy with whom he won.

"But I'll tell you when the caddy *is* important," he told me. "In England. The caddy seems more devoted there, and God knows he *has* to be. The weather is such a factor—weird stuff—that the courses can change overnight. You'll have a hole which one day requires a drive and an easy wedge, and the next day it takes a drive and a *three wood* to reach the green. So yardage doesn't mean a thing—I mean, unless the conditions are absolutely perfect and static, which in that country is rare, hell, *unknown.* So you rely more on your caddy. They not only know the course but also how your ball is going to act in the air currents above, and how it's going to bounce and move on the turf. I think I was clubbed on nearly every hole in the tournaments I played there. Those caddies are incredible."

Certainly the English caddies were self-assured. Bobby Cruickshank told me that on his first practice round at Muirfield in 1929 he had a seventy-five-year-old caddy, Willie Black. Cruickshank hit a good drive on the first hole. "Willie," he said, "give me the two iron." "Look here, sir," Willie said. "*I'll* give you the club, *you* play the bloody shot." I've always liked the story about the caddy at St. Andrews who interrupted his "boss" (which was the current term) at the top of his backswing, and shouted, "Stop! We've changed our mind. We'll play the shot with an iron!" Frank Stranahan had a terrible problem with such caddies in one of the British Amateur championships at Muirfield. He fired a number of them, mostly because pride on both sides got the best of the situation. The caddies were furious and sulking because their advice was ignored, and Stranahan was upset and oversensitive because he could not, under the circumstances, keep his mind on his golf game. The climactic moment in their strained relationship came on a hole with the green hidden behind a high ridge. Stranahan sent his caddy up on the ridge to point out the direction of the green, indeed to place himself so that a shot soared over his head would be on the correct line. The caddy went up there with the golf bag, moving around on the ridge, sighting between Stranahan and the green, his head turning back and forth, and finally he waved Stranahan on. Stranahan hit directly over the caddy and then toiled up the hill to discover that the caddy had lined him up with a thick patch of bracken, waist-high, where it would be a miracle if he found the ball, much less knocked it out; the caddy looked at him and very carefully, like a dog laying down a bone, he dropped Stranahan's golf bag at his feet and set out for the golf house, saying over his shoulder, "Now, sir, if you think you know so much about it, let's see you get yourself out of *there.*"

What a tradition caddies come from! I suppose the first of their number who achieved prominence was Scotland's William Gunn of the early nineteenth century. Caddy Willie, he was called—an odd and famous character referred to in the chronicles of the time as "peculiar but harmless." His habit was never to refer to those he caddied for by name, but rather by profession. Mr. Brand, for example, his landlord and an amateur gardener, he called "the man of the cabbage," as in "You'll be needin' a cleek, sure as not, man of the cabbage, to reach the green."

He wore his entire wardrobe on his back, one suit above the other—four or five of them at a time, including their vests. An old worn fur coat was outermost. He wore three bonnet-like hats, each sewed within the other.

He would leave his job for six weeks, hiking up to his Highland home, all those suits on his back, and the hats. One spring in the late 1820s he never came back. His one fear had been that he would end up in a pauper's grave—he had set all his money aside for a proper burial. Those for whom he had caddied comforted themselves that at least he had reached home and had his wish granted; they preferred not to think that he had succumbed on his long trek . . . a small tumble of clothes that could have been discarded from a passing coach.

There were others: "Big" Crawford, who caddied for "Wee" Ben Sayers and used to try to intimidate the opposition by rearing over them and making rumbling sounds in his throat. He once threw a horseshoe at Vardon. Pretense meant nothing to him. He referred to the Grand Duke Michael of Russia as Mr. Michael.

Max Faulkner, himself one of the most colorful personalities in golf, had a series of memorable caddies—Turner, who had a long red beard, and then for years he had a caddy who traveled with him named Mad Mac, who wore three ties but no shirt, and a long shoe-top-length overcoat which he kept on during the hottest weather. From his neck dangled a pair of large binoculars from which the lenses were missing and through which he would peer at the line of a putt and announce, "Hit it slightly straight, sir."

Then, Eddie Lowery, age ten, who carried Francis Ouimet's bag when the young American beat Ray and Vardon for the U.S. Open at Brookline.

Or Vardon's caddy at Prestwick in 1893, who was so disgusted when Vardon disregarded his advice that he turned his back and held out the golf bag behind him for Vardon to choose from.

Or Skip Daniels of Sandwich, who was Walter Hagen's caddy when he twice won the British Open Championship. Gene Sarazen had him in the year 1932—a stooped man who wore an old cap, a celluloid collar, and a black Oxford suit that had never been pressed. He was seventy years old when Sarazen won his 1932 Open with him at Prince's, a course next to Royal St. George's in Sandwich. He was almost blind and Sarazen didn't want to take him. He did more out of nostalgia than anything else, and when he won he had Daniels stand next to him while he accepted the trophy and he gave him a polo coat.

Or the caddy who is reputed to have said to Vardon when asked, "What on earth shall I take now?" "Well, sir, I'd recommend the four-oh-five train."

My favorite caddy, though, is a Frenchman—Vardon tells the story about him—who packed the golf bag of an Englishman playing the course at Pau, just north of the Basque country. The Englishman made a particularly fine approach shot, and he turned to his caddy with a wide smile for some indication of approval. "Well, good heavens! What? What?"

The caddy's English was very limited. He struggled, and offered what he had often heard uttered but did not fully understand. He said, nodding happily in reply: "Beastly fluke!"

Mihir Bose

Keith Boyce: head groundsman

[We sat in the players' dining-room and looked out at what has been described as the most notorious ground in the world.]

I tell you summat. It is probably one of the most exciting jobs you could ever wish to have. I came to Headingley in 1978, and if you look back at records Headingley has always had problems. Going back to the 1930s and 1940s Bradman used to rate it as, possibly, one of the best batting wickets in the world. The wickets just after the War were very good. But during the late 1950s the wickets started to go back. They lost pace, they lost bounce.

We have done a lot of work on the problems of Headingley. I sent samples of these old wickets to be analysed, to see exactly what sort of wickets they were. Why were they good wickets? I wanted to know. The answer I got back from the research people was that the old groundsman used various soils, anything he could get hold of, then he mixed it with marl to give it a bit of strength, and cow dung. What a recipe! This was the mixture that was commonly used. It made good surfaces. But the soil itself on its own, when the wickets were dried out, was not quite strong enough to withstand the impact of the ball. What the old groundsman used to do in them days, he left a very thin, tight-knit, close-laid cover of grass that protected the soil. In the situation of the wicket being dry and rolled out, the wickets played well. Good batting wickets: the ball came on.

But what happened then was that the wickets started to go back. This was in the late 1950s and into the 1960s. There was a gradual decline from then on. They started to lose pace and bounce. In the 1960s cricketers suddenly realized that these thin layers of grass that were being left on the surface, if they were disturbed and the soil exposed to the impact of the ball, the ball would turn. So now we had spinners' wickets, and many very poor wickets were prepared at Headingley. Ray Illingworth and his like were getting 100 wickets a season and Yorkshire were winning the County Championship. I shall say no more. The fact is, wickets were turning.

In the late 1960s when my predecessor, George Cawthrey, started here he saw this fault. He came from Hull and started to import Humber silt, soil that would not break up; soil that had the ability to let the ball hit it without disintegrating. He started to top dress with that at Headingley. He did a temporary patch-up job. But the wickets still had no pace or bounce, and the ball was still going through very low. They weren't good wickets.

Then, in 1972, disaster! A Test match versus Australia all over on the Saturday! In three days. They brought in the old inspector, old Bert Lock, who was at the Oval many years ago. Old Bert dug down and found these old soils and he saw the problems. He said, 'The soil is no use at all, you'll have to dig it out and relay the whole lot. These underlying soils are a problem which we are not going to get over easy.' This was that mixture of various soils, marl and cow dung, and it had started to disintegrate. What happened was, there were very fine layers of grass within these soils and dressings, and they seemed to have like a cushion effect against the impact of the heavy roller. Consequently, you couldn't get the consolidation and compaction into your soil, and as a result the ball would just keep coming through low.

So it was decided that we would have to dig out and rebuild the whole square. An attempt was made and three wickets were taken out. Unfortunately the soil that was then used was a very heavy, silty Surrey loam and it had an adverse impact. Yes, you were able to get it hard; yes, it had pace and bounce. But the soil was uncontrollable. It cracked; you couldn't get grass to grow on it; it lost its strength. Therefore you had an unbalanced soil. Now we had a situation where the ball was flying off at all angles; it bounced, doing all sorts of things.

The wickets were constructed under the advice and guidance of the Sports Turf Research Institute at Bingley. Mr Escritt was the director of soil research there, and he was the one who recommended we use this soil. But it was soil we could not work with. Three wickets were dug out and the rest of the square was top-dressed. When I arrived here in 1978 I had a situation where I had three wickets that had been laid in four inches of this stuff – very difficult to prepare wickets on – and the rest of the square had three-quarters of an inch of top-dressing of this same stuff. And this top-dressing was over poor soils. So I had horrendous problems. It didn't seem to matter how I prepared wickets and what effort I put into making wickets, it was very difficult to get high-class wickets out of the square. You couldn't get roots to grow through this very poor soil. Consequently we had a situation where the square cracked uncontrollably. It gave us some nightmarish problems.

I always believed, when preparing wickets in the early 1980s, that if I got the preparation exactly right on the first morning I could expect three days of reasonable cricket. On the fourth day, however, the bounce became uneven and on the fifth day it would be totally unacceptable. That is an honest opinion of how I classified those wickets. It was vital, vital that I got it exactly right for that first morning. A wicket with maybe a little bit of moisture in it, just to see me through three days. If I misjudged it I had a bad wicket. This is what happened in the 1981 Test when the wicket was too dry.

Botham had a tremendous Test match. It was a Test match that went off bang. But the wicket was not acceptable. We had five days' cricket, magnificent cricket from a spectator's, from everyone's, point of view. But I didn't get carried away by all the glory. I knew before the match we were going to have difficulties because I saw the wicket drying out too quickly. I was running short of moisture. We had got a little bit too near the Test for watering because by now the wicket had started to crack. We can't suddenly start watering two days before a match in this country. I could have held it by putting plastic sheets over it. That would have had a checking effect. And the remaining moisture would have been brought towards the surface and maybe held up. But one of the dangers of putting water on a wicket that has cracked a few days before a match is that the water gets down the cracks. And rather than soften the lump you get a soft edging area around the crack. When the ball hits that you are in real trouble.

The 1981 Test match, my third, was my first in drying conditions and it was like trying to control an ugly beast. You sort of had to work with it, you couldn't just get it back down. The soil used to reject you in a way. We are talking here of the same wicket that was condemned in 1972. The one that should have been dug out but never was. We still had that wicket. In fact, the same wicket was used every year from 1978 to 1984.

This situation was carrying on and I was having to sort out work within this problem area. A lot of people misunderstood the situation. A lot of people felt I was getting it right. A lot of people kept giving me encouragement. But I knew it wasn't what I wanted. I wanted something doing. It was very difficult for me to explain to these people, to get them to truly understand the situation.

We had the 1985 Test against Australia: it was played on the same wicket, the one used for the 1972 and the 1981 Tests. England made their biggest ever Headingley score against Australia – 500 or summat. Robinson got 171. The scoring rate was fantastic, the spectators thoroughly enjoyed it, and the match was over after tea on the last day. Perfect situation for a Test match finish.

I felt as a groundsman that again the wicket was not as it should have been. In 1986 the Indians won on a wicket that was very difficult to get dried, a wicket that had moisture in it. It was a difficult wicket because it was moist all the time and the ball held up and seamed around. It wasn't the irregular bounce, it was the ball that swung in the air and seamed off the wicket.

My nightmare was about the cracks that appeared on the wicket even before a ball was bowled. On these old wickets the soil used to crack because it consisted of loose, crumbly layers. The wicket looked like an almighty jigsaw. It was so loose that you felt that, if you could get your fingers down the side of it, you could pick up all the pieces as in a jigsaw puzzle. But that wasn't the really frightening part. If you have a slice of bread and you leave it for a day or so, what will happen? The edges will curl. That was what was happening on the square. These weren't just flat blocks of soil. The edges were literally falling off, creeping over. You had, like, a wriggly saucer shape. When the ball hit the down slope it kept low, when it hit the up slope it flew. That was frightening – yes – frightening.

But I look back on the India Test and I got something done that I had never expected to be done here at Headingley. Following that Test match I finally got permission to dig out that wicket. People had kept saying it was getting better. To put it mildly, I think ignorance and a lack of understanding of the true situation has been one of the problems here.

I'll always remember the day. It is a day I will never forget in my period as senior groundsman. It was the day I got my biggest break – Monday, 25 August 1986. I dug out the Test wicket on that Monday. It was nine o'clock in the morning. We shovelled it out onto a dumper truck. It was only after a quarter of an hour, half an hour's digging, that I noticed this strange phenomenon: every single spadeful of earth that we threw onto the dumper broke apart at the same place. I watched the other lads doing it, and then I realized we were not able to throw a complete spadeful of earth onto the truck. It would all break. I went down the side of the hole we were digging out to have a closer look. For the first two inches it felt firm. Then between two inches and five inches depth I could literally scrape out the soil with my fingers. These were the old wickets, the cow dung that had disintegrated.

There were cavities there. I am not going to exaggerate and say the cavities were big enough to put a golf ball in. But certainly you could have laid your finger within them. I just couldn't believe it. Now, for the first time, I discovered these poor soils that caused the problem and what the square was condemned for in 1972. No one had said anything to me. I didn't know anything about the soils below the square. I dug it out and I found those soils. It was then that I got them analysed and it was then that I found out what they consisted of. Ten inches out of the wicket, taken out and thrown away. Better soil put back in.

For years I had worked on this square believing that my problems were to do with this heavy Surrey loam – the layer of heavy soil that had been put on the square in the 1970s. In fact, the problem had started in the 1930s. When I dug down and made my discovery I was so elated I had to tell people.

Some of the soil still left was poor; it wasn't good soil. But I felt that if I could convert it from being a loose crumbly soil into something of a uniform nature, I had a chance to improve the wickets. I carried out a big rolling programme. I sat on the roller for hours and hours. In the spring of 1987 we played the first match, versus Hampshire, and I sat back and watched the wicket. The match was not played on the Test match strip but on another wicket on the square. I watched the balls before lunch flying off at varying heights, and I was devastated. I thought the heavy rolling would have solved the problem. Then, in the Somerset match, Roebuck came in and broke a finger. And so it went on until we played Essex. After the Essex match I closed the gates and I got a spade and dug into the square. I found that all the rolling I had done had had no effect through the heavy layer of Surrey loam. The soil was still loose and crumbly below. So I decided I would put an even heavier roller on: I was convinced it still had to be rolled. I brought in this big twin-vibrating roadroller.

Lord's had asked us to go down and explain what was happening. Brian Close went with me and we met the full ground committee. They asked me what we were going to do. I said my mind was turning to bigger rollers. I said that I was still convinced that I could roll it down and that it would get us through until I got the relayings done. It was only a temporary measure. By now I was convinced that the whole square wanted doing. Lord's gave me the support I needed and I came back and got on with the job.

Possibly the initial reaction was a few tut-tuts. After all, I was actually breaking the rule which says that wickets should not have anything bigger than a 2.5 ton roller. At the meeting Jackie Bond said that this ruling was brought in because at the Portsmouth ground a very heavy roller was used and the TCCB decided that 2.5 tons should be the maximum. Anyway, Colin Cowdrey, who chaired the meeting, knew I had problems. He felt that whatever I wanted to do they should support me because ultimately it was for the benefit of Test cricket at Headingley. So I came back and got on with the job. But I knew it was a very radical step and I had a sleepless night over it.

I was sensible enough to know that the damage I could cause would be damage by ridging and distorting levels. That was the danger. If you run a car over wet soil you will see ridges. I could have had that effect on the square. But I was convinced that it had to be rolled out, that it had to be put down. But if I had realized, after putting on a few tons for a short spell of roll, that I was damaging the wicket I would have gone no further; there's no way I would have put the big weight on. I spent all my time on the square. I almost lived on the square. I practically slept there. When the other lads were using the roller I was never off the square. I observed everything. I totally supervised all the work. The roller was only 3 tons dead weight, but because of its vibratory effect you could generate tremendous weight. The experts talking of the equivalent of 12 tons. The roller almost jumped up and down instead of rolling. It was like a set of hammers going up and down, hitting the wicket. It was a very radical step.

It was an operation that took time. I watered for five days and I spiked for five days to get the soil workable. Then I rolled for a day at 1.5 tons. Our roller at the Headingley ground without ballast is 1.5 tons. Then I put ballast – which means filling the roller drum with water – and I rolled for another day at 2.5 tons. Then I gradually increased the weight by using the monster roller at first on its dead weight of 3 tons and then by adding a vibratory system until we were sat on a vibrating road roller generating towards 12 tons. I was starting at six o'clock in the morning, the lads were coming at eight, they worked through till five in the afternoon, then I took over again. We did that for three days. Since that big roller went onto the square I think that, if you look back, you'll find the classification markings by umpires have been a vast improvement. In 1988, when the West Indies won, the wicket played very well: it got above-average marks from the umpires, so that speaks for itself.

They marked it 'satisfactory' and, after what I had produced before, that was a big improvement. The problem had been solved. [The umpires also gave a favourable report after the 1989 Australian Test.]

My aim on the square is to get a good root structure. There's got to be a relationship between top growth and root growth. Everything is being done to stimulate a good, healthy, strong root structure because, when the wickets are dried out, that is what we need. The root structure acts as a reinforcement to hold the soil together. We just hope we don't get this notorious cracking. That problem has been solved by the big roller. It has put the thing down solid. I have two more wickets to do this autumn [1989]. Then I will have relaid the whole square.

The 1988 'drain problem' was something else. I have an understanding with the police that if it starts to rain I want getting out of bed. At 12.55 a.m., on the morning of the West Indies Test in 1988, a policeman knocked on my door. As I got out of bed it had just started raining. I worked with the water hog machine from then until four o'clock in torrential rain. We put the lights on and I pumped off literally hundreds of thousands of gallons of water. I was absolutely knackered. I rang up my deputy head groundsman. I got him out of bed. He lives on the outskirts of Leeds and he came into work and we worked continuously through the rest of the night and morning until the start of the match.

It was a very dull morning. Things got brighter round about ten thirty. People were saying to me, 'What are the chances, Keith?' I reckoned that if we got the sun we should get a start after lunch. Suddenly the sun broke through round about eleven o'clock at the time of the scheduled start of the match. Now you had a situation where there was a fear that you might have to play an extra hour if you didn't start on time. In the previous Test at Lord's they had been playing cricket till seven forty! They were trying to avoid that sort of thing. Though the ground was very wet, people walked over the grassed area and were delighted with it. 'We can play, it is not bad at all.' I said, 'You are going to struggle here, this is not dry.' Richards and Chris Cowdrey walked around on the square, which I had protected, and it was playable. They walked over the bowler's run-up and while it was damp they decided that every effort should be made to get a start before midday. The game started at eleven fifty.

There is a difference between people walking round doing an inspection and somebody like Ambrose coming in at his pace and height. What happened then was that by his foot banging on to the grass, about five yards back from the wicket, it brought up the moisture. But this had nothing whatsoever to do with drains.

[The result was dramatic. *Wisden* notes, 'Play, having started fifty minutes late, was halted after two overs, this time for two hours, when the bowler's run-up at the Rugby Club end was found to be flooded. Umpire Bird has always had a keen eye for dangerous elements above, but this attack from below caught him unawares. The drains had been blocked before the Test to try to retain moisture in the square. But the Yorkshire club insisted that all drains should be functioning properly by the start of the match and put the cause of the trouble onto the volume of overnight rain.']

I don't know where the press got the story of drains. Who gave it to television? I was told by the secretary not to talk to the press. I was told there would be an official statement from the county club. Dickie Bird got very upset with television and said, 'What can I do when the water is coming up?' The drain explanation was totally wrong. The problem was the moisture just below the surface and it was brought up by the feet banging down. People jumped onto this drainage. I could sit back and have a good laugh. The drains are perfect. However, I was very frustrated to hear that reaction after all the hard work, night and day, I had put in on the Test wicket.

The drains are not a problem. The ground is a very good drier. The slope helps us. Can you remember when a game was held up because of wet outfields at Headingley? Never. It doesn't happen.

I am Yorkshire and proud of it. I am responsible for the Rugby League ground too. I believe we have one of the finest stadiums of its type in the world. I don't want to produce wickets that suit Yorkshire. Let Nottingham produce what they like. I shall still have sleepless nights. Actually, I don't know many groundsmen, even on the out-grounds, who don't have sleepless nights. Groundsmen are very poorly rewarded for the efforts we put in and it is all too easy for cricketers and the public to blame the wicket or blame the umpires for the players' dismal performances at times. I think we are all aware that we tend to be used as scapegoats from time to time. Yet I don't think there is a groundsman amongst us, certainly not a senior groundsman, who doesn't realize the very great importance of the wickets we prepare on the result of matches.

I feel the wicket is like a member of my family: it is such a big part of my life. My wife realizes the tremendous work I put in and what it means to be in charge of the Test match pitch. She supports me tremendously. I don't know whether she gets jealous of it. She sometimes thinks I spend too much time with it, particularly round about the time of the Test match. It is a big thing in our house. But people put up with me – just!

I always watch the cricket from side-on at Headingley. I love to watch from the edge. The big thing I like to watch is the bounce. I can assess a wicket before the match and how firm it is, how bouncy it is. I would probably be able to assess a pace factor before the start of play by the rebound and the penetration which I certainly do the evening before. So I have a good indication of how it is going to play. Then I like to sit back and watch. If I find the bounce isn't to my liking then I make a dossier out and if one end is different from the other I am always interested in that.

I check ball marks, I look to a third party being involved, such as tufty grass, or a crack or disintegration. I go out at lunch time on the first day and I rub my fingers over a ball pitching area just to get a feel of it, if it is responding. I try to work out the indentation the ball has made on the wicket, to see if it has been a little bit too much, or to try to judge where the ball was held up by the length of the skid marks of the ball on the wicket. I certainly check all that again in the evening after the spectators have gone.

I put myself under a lot of pressure at times. My wife worries about it, because I don't relax as I should do. Sometimes I allow myself to be trodden on far too much. Maybe I should communicate more. But I find it very difficult to communicate with people who don't understand groundsmanship. Why should I talk to people and convince them? If you want to criticize wickets why should I try to answer you if you know so little about groundsmanship? Why should I bother to reply to you if you haven't got the knowledge to understand what I am going to tell you? So I take that philosophy and keep it all to myself. At times I have got very up-tight. But, cross my fingers, it is all coming right now.

Andre Dubus

Under the Lights

The first professional baseball players I watched and loved were in the Class C Evangeline League, which came to our town in the form of the Lafayette Brahman Bulls. The club's owner raised these humpbacked animals. The league comprised teams from other small towns in Louisiana, and Baton Rouge, the capital. The Baton Rouge team was called the Red Sticks. This was in 1948, and I was eleven years old. At the Lafayette municipal golf course, my father sometimes played golf with Harry Strohm, the player-manager of the Bulls. Strohm was a shortstop. He seemed very old to me and, for a ballplayer, he was: a wiry deeply tanned greying man with lovely blue eyes that were gentle and merry, as his lined face was.

Mrs. Strohm worked in the team's business office; she was a golfer too, and her face was tan and lined and she had warm grey-blue eyes with crinkles at their corners. In the Bulls' second season, she hired me and my cousin Jimmy Burke and our friend Carroll Ritchie as ball boys. The club could not afford to lose baseballs, and the business manager took them from fans who caught fouls in the seats. No one on the club could afford much; the players got around six hundred dollars for a season, and when one of them hit a home run the fans passed a hat for him. During batting practice we boys stood on the outside of the fence and returned balls hit over it, or fouled behind the stands. At game time a black boy we never met appeared and worked on the right-field fence; one of us perched on the left, another of us stood in the parking lot behind the grandstands, and the third had the night off and a free seat in the park. Our pay was a dollar a night. It remains the best job I ever had, but I would have to be twelve and thirteen and fourteen to continue loving it.

One late afternoon I sat in the stands with the players who were relaxing in their street clothes before pregame practice. A young outfielder was joking with his teammates, showing them a condom from his wallet. The condom in his hand chilled me with disgust at the filth of screwing, or doing it, which was a shameful act performed by dogs, bad girls, and thrice by my parents to make my sisters and me;

and chilled me too with the awful solemnity of mortal sin: that season, the outfielder was dating a young Catholic woman, who later would go to Lourdes for an incurable illness; she lived in my neighborhood. Now, recalling what a foolish boy the outfielder was, I do not believe the woman graced him with her loins any more than baseball did, but that afternoon I was only confused and frightened, a boy who had opened the wrong door, the wrong drawer.

Then I looked at Harry Strohm. He was watching the outfielder, and his eyes were measuring and cold. Then with my own eyes I saw the outfielder's career as a ballplayer. He did not have one. That was in Harry's eyes, and his judgment had nothing, of course, to do with the condom: it was the outfielder's cheerful haplessness, sitting in the sun, with no manhood in him, none of the drive and concentration and absolute seriousness a ballplayer must have. This was not a professional relaxing before losing himself in the long hard moment-by-moment work of playing baseball. This was a youth with little talent, enough to hit over .300 in Class C, and catch fly balls that most men could not, and throw them back to the infield or to home plate. But his talent was not what Harry was staring at. It was his lack of regret, his lack of retrospection, this young outfielder drifting in and, very soon, out of the profession that still held Harry, still demanded of him, still excited him. Harry was probably forty, maybe more, and his brain helped his legs cover the ground of a shortstop. He knew where to play the hitters.

My mother and father and I went to most home games, and some nights in the off-season we ate dinner at Poorboy's Restaurant with Harry and his wife. One of those nights, while everyone but my mother and me was smoking Lucky Strikes after dinner, my father said to Harry: "My son says he wants to be a ballplayer." Harry turned his bright eyes on me, and looked through my eyes and into the secret self, or selves, I believed I hid from everyone, especially my parents and, most of all, my father: those demons of failure that were my solitary torment. I will never forget those moments in the restaurant when I felt Harry's eyes, looking as they had when he stared at the young outfielder who, bawdy and jocular, had not seen them, had not felt them.

I was a child, with a child's solipsistic reaction to the world. Earlier that season, on a morning before a night game, the Bulls hosted a baseball clinic for young boys. My friends and I went to it, driven by one of our mothers. That was before seatbelts and other sanity, when you put as many children into a car as it could hold, then locked the doors to keep them closed against the pressure of bodies. By then I had taught myself to field ground and fly balls, and to bat. Among my classmates at school, I was a sissy, because I was a poor athlete. Decades later I realized I was a poor athlete at school because I was shy, and every public act—like standing at the plate, waiting to swing at a softball—became disproportionate. Proportion is all; and, in sports at school, I lost it by surrendering to the awful significance of my self-consciousness. Shyness has a strange element of narcissism, a belief that how we look, how we perform, is truly important to other people.

In the fall of 1947 I vowed—I used that word—to redeem myself in softball season in the spring. I used the word *redeem* too. We had moved to a new neighborhood that year, and we had an odd house, two-storied and brick, built alone by its owner, our landlord. It had the only basement in Lafayette, with a steep driveway just wide enough for a car and a few spare inches on either side of it, just enough to make a driver hold his breath, glancing at the concrete walls rising beside the climbing or descending car. The back wall of the living room, and my sisters' shared bedroom above it, had no windows. So I practiced there, throwing a baseball against my sisters' wall for flies, and against the living-room wall for grounders. In that neighborhood I had new friends and, since they did not know me as a sissy, I did not become one. In autumn and winter we played tackle football, wearing helmets and shoulder pads; when we weren't doing that, I was practicing baseball. Every night, before kneeling to say the rosary then going to bed, I practiced batting. I had learned the stance and stride and swing from reading John R. Tunis's baseball novels, and from *Babe Ruth Comics*, which I subscribed to and which, in every issue, had a page of instructions in one of the elements of baseball. I opened my bedroom door so the latch faced me, as a pitcher would. The latch became the ball and I stood close enough to hit it, my feet comfortably spread, my elbows away from my chest, my wrists cocked, and the bat held high. Then one hundred times I stepped toward the latch, the fast ball, the curve, and kept my eyes on it and swung the bat, stopping it just short of contact.

In the spring of 1948, in the first softball game during the afternoon hour of physical education in the dusty schoolyard, the two captains chose teams and, as always, they chose other boys until only two of us remained. I batted last, and first came to the plate with two or three runners on base, and while my teammates urged me to try for a walk, and the players on the field called, "Easy out, easy out," I watched the softball coming in waist-high, and stepped and swung, and hit it over the right fielder's head for a double. My next time at bat I tripled to center. From then on I brought my glove to school, hanging from a handlebar.

That summer the Bulls came to town, and we boys in the neighborhood played baseball every morning, on a lot owned by the father of one of our friends. Mr. Gossen mowed the field, built a backstop, and erected foul poles down the left and right field foul lines. Beyond them and the rest of the outfield was tall grass. We wore baseball shoes and caps, chewed bubble gum and spat, and at the wooden home plate we knocked dirt from our spikes. We did not have catcher's equipment, only a mask and a mitt, so our pitchers did not throw hard. We did not want them to anyway. But sometimes we played a team from another neighborhood and our catcher used their shin guards and chest protector, and we hit fast balls and roundhouse curves. I don't know about my other friends, but if Little League ball had existed then I would not have played: not with adult coaches and watching parents taking from me my excitement, my happiness while playing or practicing, and returning me to the tense muscles and cool stomach and clumsy hands and feet of self-consciousness. I am grateful that I was given those lovely summer days until we boys grew older and, since none of us was a varsity athlete, we turned to driving lessons and romance.

There were three or four of those baseball seasons. In that first one, in 1948, we went one morning to the Bulls' clinic. The ball field was a crowd of boys, young ones like us, eleven or twelve, and teenagers too. The day began with short drills and instruction and demonstrations; I don't remember how it ended. I only remember the first drill: a column of us in the infield, and one of the Bulls tossing a ground ball to the first boy, then the next boy, and so on: a fast, smooth exercise. But waiting in line, among all those strangers, not only boys but men too, professional ballplayers, I lost my months of backyard practice, my redemption on the softball field at school and the praise from my classmates that followed it, lost the mornings with my friends on our field. When my turn came I trotted toward the softly bouncing ball, crouched, took my eyes off the ball and saw only the blankness of my secret self, and the ball went between and through my legs. The player tossed me another one, which I fielded while my rump puckered as in anticipation of a spanking, a first day at school. Harry Strohm was watching.

So later that summer, amid the aroma of coffee and tobacco smoke at the table at Poorboy's, when he gazed at me with those eyes like embedded gems, brilliant and ancient, I saw in them myself that morning, bound by the strings of my fear, as the ball bounced over my stiffly waiting gloved hand. Harry Strohm said nothing at the table; or, if he did, I heard it as nothing. Perhaps he said quietly: "That's good."

I was wrong, and I did not know I was wrong until this very moment, as I write this. When Harry looked at me across the table, he was not looking at my body and into my soul and deciding I would never be a ballplayer, he was not focusing on my trifling error on that long day of the clinic. He was looking at my young hope and seeing his own that had propelled him into and kept him in this vocation, this game he had played nearly all his life. His skin was deeply, smoothly brown; the wrinkles in his face delineated his skin's toughness. He wore a short-sleeved shirt and slacks. I cannot imagine him in a suit and tie, save in his casket; cannot imagine him in any clothing but a baseball uniform, or something familiar, something placed in a locker before a game, withdrawn from it after the game and the shower, some assembly of cotton whose only function was to cover his nakedness until the next game, the next season. He had once played Triple A ball.

So had Norm Litzinger, our left fielder. A shoulder injury was the catalyst for his descent from the top of the wall surrounding the garden where the very few played major league baseball. I do not remember the effect of the injury on his performance in the Evangeline League. Perhaps there was none, as he threw on smaller fields, to hold or put out slower runners, and as he swung at pitches that most major leaguers could hit at will. He was brown, and broad of shoulder and chest, handsome and spirited, and humorous. He was fast too, and graceful, and sometimes, after making a shoestring catch, he somersaulted to his feet, holding the ball high in his glove. Once, as he was sprinting home from third, the catcher blocked the plate. Litzinger ducked his head and ran into the catcher, who dropped the ball as the two men fell; then Litzinger rose from the tumble and dust, grinning, holding his shoulders sloped and his arms bent and hanging like an ape's, and walked like one into applause and the dugout.

He was in his thirties. At the end of every season he went home, to whatever place in the North. For us, everything but Arkansas above us was the North; everything but California, which was isolate and odd. One season he dated a beautiful woman who sat with another beautiful woman in a box seat behind home plate. I was thirteen or fourteen. Litzinger's lady had black hair and dark skin, her lips and fingernails were bright red, her cheeks rouged. Her friend was blonde, with very red lips and nails. They both smoked Chesterfields, and as I watched them drawing on their cigarettes, marking them with lipstick, and blowing plumes of smoke into the humid and floodlit night air, and daintily removing bits of tobacco from their tongues, I felt the magical and frightening mystery of their flesh. The brunette married Norman Litzinger; and one night, before the game, the blonde married Billy Joe Barrett with a ceremony at home plate.

One season I read a book by Joe DiMaggio. I believe it was a book of instruction, for boys. I only remember one line from that book, and I paraphrase it: If you stay in Class D or C ball for more than one season, unless you have been injured, you should get out of professional baseball. Perhaps DiMaggio wrote the word *quit*. I can't. I've spent too much of my life in angry dread of that word.

How could I forget DiMaggio's sentence? I loved young ballplayers who, with the Bulls, were trying to rise through the minor leagues, to the garden of the elect. I loved young ballplayers who, like the outfielder with the condom, were in their second or third seasons in Class C ball. And I loved old ballplayers, like Harry Strohm; and Bill Thomas, a fifty-year-old pitcher with great control, and an assortment of soft breaking balls, who one night pitched a no-hitter; and once, when because of rain-outs and double headers, the Bulls had no one to pitch the second game of a double header, he pitched and won both of them. And I loved players who were neither old nor young, for baseball: men like Tom Spears, a pitcher in his mid-twenties, who had played in leagues higher than Class C, then pitched a few seasons for us on his way out of professional baseball. He was a gentle and witty man, and one morning, because we asked him to, he came to one of our games, to watch us play.

Late one afternoon Mrs. Strohm gave both my cousin Jimmy and me the night off, and we asked the visiting manager if we could be his batboys. Tom Spears pitched for the Bulls that night. This was a time in baseball when, if a man was pitching a no-hitter, no one spoke about it. Radio announcers hinted, in their various ways. Fans in seats looked at each other, winked, raised an eyebrow, nodded. We were afraid of jinxing it; and that belief made being a fan something deeper than watching a game. An uninformed spectator, a drunk, even a thirteen-year-old boy could, by simply saying the words *no-hitter*, destroy it. So you were connected with everyone watching the game, and everyone listening to it too, for a man alone with his radio in his living room, a man who lacked belief, could say those two sacred words and break the spell.

But Jimmy and I did not know until the night Spears pitched a no-hitter, while we were batboys for the New Iberia Pelicans, that the opposing team transcended their desire to win, and each player his desire to perform, to hit, and instead obeyed the rules of the ritual. We were having fun, and we were also trying to do perfect work as batboys; we did not know Spears was pitching a no-hitter. We sat in the dugout while the Pelicans were in the field, sat with pitchers and the manager and reserve ballplayers. When the Pelicans were at bat we stayed close to the on-deck circle, watched hitter after hitter returning to the dugout without a hit. And no one said a word. Then the last batter struck out on a fast ball, a lovely glint of white, and the crowd was standing and cheering and passing the hat, and the Bulls in the field and from the dugout were running to the mound, to Spears. Then the Pelicans were saying the two words, surrounding them with the obscenities I first heard and learned from ballplayers, and they went quickly to their bus—there were no visiting locker rooms in the league—and left their bats. Jimmy and I thrust them into the canvas bat bag and ran, both of us holding the bag, to the parking lot, to the bus. The driver, a player, had already started it; the team was aboard. "Your bats," we called; "Your bats." From the bus we heard the two words, the obscenities; a player reached down through the door and hoisted in the bag of Louisville Sluggers.

How could I forget DiMaggio's sentence? Our first baseman, in the Bulls' first season, was a young hard-hitting left-hander whose last name was Glenn. We were in the Detroit Tiger system, and after Glenn's season with us, he went up to Flint, Michigan, to a Class A league. I subscribed to *The Sporting News* and read the weekly statistics and box scores, and I followed Glenn's performance, and I shared his hope, and waited for the season when he would stand finally in the garden. At Flint he batted in the middle of the order, as he had for us, and he did well; but he did not hit .300, or thirty home runs. In the next season I looked every week at the names in *The Sporting News*, searched for Glenn in double A and triple A, and did not find him there, or in Class A or B. and I never saw his name again. It was as though he had come into my life, then left me and died, but I did not have the words then for what I felt in my heart. I could only say to my friends: I can't find Glenn's name anymore.

I believed Billy Joe Barrett's name would be part of baseball for years. I believed he would go from us to Flint, then to double and finally triple A, and would have a career there, at the top of the garden wall. And, with the hope that is the essence of belief, I told myself that he would play in the major leagues; that one season, or over several of them, he would discover and claim that instant of timing, or that sharper concentration, or whatever it was that he so slightly lacked, and that flawed his harmony at the plate. In the field he was what we called then a Fancy Dan. He was right-handed and tall, fast and graceful and lithe. He leaped high and caught line drives as smoothly as an acrobat, as though the hard-hit ball and his catching it were a performance he and the batter had practiced for years. On very close plays at first, stretching for a throw from an infielder, he did a split, the bottom of one leg and the top of the other pressed against the earth; then quickly and smoothly, without using his hands, he stood. He stole a lot of bases. He often ended his slide by rising to his feet, on the bag. He batted left-handed and was a line drive hitter, and a good one; but not a great one.

I have never seen a first baseman whose grace thrilled me as Barrett's did; and one night in Lafayette he hit a baseball in a way I have never seen again. He batted lead-off or second and every season hit a few home runs, but they were not what we or other teams and fans or Barrett himself considered either a hope or a threat when he was at the plate. But that night he hit a fast ball coming just above his knees. It started as a line drive over the second baseman, who leaped for it, his gloved hand reaching up then arcing down without the ball that had cleared by inches, maybe twelve of them, the glove's leather fingers. Then in short right field the ball's trajectory sharply rose, as though deflected higher and faster by angled air, and the right fielder stopped his motion toward it and simply stood and watched while the ball rose higher and higher and was still rising and tiny as it went over the lights in right field. Billy Joe Barrett's career ended in Lafayette.

How could I forget DiMaggio's sentence? Before I got out of high school, the Bulls' park was vacant, its playing field growing weeds. The Strohms had moved on, looking for another ball club; and Norm Litzinger and Billy Joe Barrett and their wives had gone to whatever places they found, after Lafayette, and after baseball. I was driving my family's old Chevrolet and smoking Lucky Strikes and falling in love with girls whose red lips marked their cigarettes and who, with painted fingernails, removed bits of tobacco from their tongues; and, with that immortal vision of mortality that youth holds in its heart, I waited for manhood.

DiMaggio was wrong. I know that now, over forty years after I read his sentence. Or, because I was a boy whose hope was to be a different boy with a new body growing tall and fast and graceful and strong, a boy who one morning would wake, by some miracle of desire, in motion on the path to the garden, I gave to DiMaggio too much credence; and his sentence lost, for me, all proportion, and insidiously became a heresy. Which I am renouncing now, as I see Billy Joe Barrett on the night when his whole body and his whole mind and his whole heart were for one moment in absolute harmony with a speeding baseball and he hit it harder and farther that he could at any other instant in his life. We never saw the ball start its descent, its downward arc to earth. For me, it never has. It is rising white over the lights high above the right-field fence, a bright and vanishing sphere of human possibility soaring into the darkness beyond our vision.

Arthur Hopcraft

The Referee

'I've been pig sick when I haven't got a game I thought I ought to have had. I've had to run the line sometimes for someone else when I thought the game was mine by rights. I've said to myself afterwards, "I could have eaten this kid – *eaten* him." But I've still gone to him and shaken his hand, and said, "Well done, son." Well, that's sport. Of course it is.'

The football referee who said that to me revealed much more than the fact that he thought he had not always been sufficiently well rewarded for his sweat. He was speaking for the side of the referee's character which passes barely noticed by either the players or the fans: his place as a competitor in the game.

In English football there are between fifteen thousand and twenty thousand referees. They include boys of sixteen and middle-aged men with paunches and inadequate spectacles. Thousands of them never rise above the lowest class of football in those lumbering Sunday afternoon games on the public recreation grounds which ooze tuftily between the lines of council houses and the ring roads. For thousands more there is, at least at some point in their lives, the real hope that they will win their way through to the *élite* eighty, the ones appointed as Football League referees. A few hundred reach the looming obstacle before that happy goal, which is to be accepted as a League linesman; it is from the linesmen that the final promotion to League referee is made.

Referees regard selection for the most glamorous matches, such as FA Cup Finals and international games, with every bit as much longing and pride as do players. The secretary of the Referees' Association talks about the privilege of 'treading the Wembley turf' with as much awe as I have ever heard from any player. Referees suffer from tension before and during matches, as players do; they admit to jealousy and vindictiveness in their fraternity; they become minor celebrities; they receive letters of praise and sour abuse from people they have never met. They see themselves as part of the action, closer to it than managers. Just as with the players, it is when a referee stops getting letters and is no longer being cheerfully booed outside football grounds that he worries most about his future.

On the face of the matter the referee in top-class football is an anachronistic figure. He is still a part-timer, in fact very nearly an amateur, controlling a match in which the player's wages often total £2,000 and the result of the game may hinge on his decisions. Yet he undergoes only a minimal degree of formal training; in many cases he spends the rest of the week in a position of little importance in some employer's office; and he is paid £10.50 a game, with a choice of sixpence a mile or his first-class train fare for travelling, a maximum allowance for meals of £3 and an extra £4.20 if he has to stay overnight in a hotel. While football has changed dramatically in terms of pace, competitiveness and anxiety for reward, it is still controlled on the field, where it matters most, from the ranks of the clerks and shopkeepers and foremen who turned to the job when they realized, regretfully, that they would never be competent as players.

The case for and against the introduction of professional referees for the top-grade football will be discussed in the last chapter. Here I want to talk about the nature of the job and of the man who chooses it.

There are a few League referees with substantial professional qualifications in their everyday careers and some who run their own businesses; but of the best of them most have had to subordinate ambition, or even effort, in their regular work in order to blow the Acme Thunderer, the standard British referee's whistle, in professional football. Because of the increased speed of the game and the close critical attention nowadays given to refereeing it is accepted that unless a man has reached the League's list of linesmen by his early thirties he will never referee a League match. Every referee must start at the lowest level, and in order to work his way up the promotion ladder, through the town and regional leagues, he must start at the latest before he is out of his early twenties. The League fixes the retiring age at forty-seven.

Maurice Fussey is one of the League's best known referees, attracting attention as much for the obvious jokes that his name invites as by his arresting appearance. He is a tall, galloping-major type of figure, with sparse, sandy hair and a sandy moustache kept uniformly trimmed. Off the field he is relaxed and affable, attentive to questions and ready with inoffensive little stories about the quirks in the characters of famous players and other referees. 'Did you know there's one referee who always takes a hot bath twenty minutes before a game?' he said to me. 'I always tell him it can't be a good thing for his health, but he says it's the only thing that relaxes him.' In action on the field Fussey moves with unforgettable mannerisms.

He is famous for his furious sprints to the scene of dramatic incident. His white knees pump high, and his elbows piston so that his clenched fists jab up and down beside his chin. He is a picture of urgency: authority in a state of tizzy. The crowd often laughs or hoots in encouragement or derision, according to how his decisions have been going for their team. Fussey does not resent this response. For one thing it takes a little of the tension out of the atmosphere. For another his first concern is to reach the spot of the eruption as suddenly as he can manage it, and he does not care that his style is ungainly. He said: 'The thing is that when you blow your whistle for a foul the player's immediate reaction is to turn round and look at you. It's instinct. Now, if you're twenty yards away he's going to argue, because he's got time. But if he turns round and you're right behind him, even if you've just arrived, he's going to think twice.'

Referees are involved in the sweat and the rancour of the game. They are close to the pain and the outrage which can only be observed distantly, and often for that reason imprecisely, by the crowd. Referees are conscious of what the players are saying to each other. They can watch the bitterness develop in a match long before the crowd sees its explosive result.

Referees like to feel that they are respected by players for their astuteness and their fairness; they are, in this respect, like schoolteachers who regard themselves as close to the boys, or police detectives who think that give-and-take with criminals is the best way to deal with them in the long run. Fussey expressed this attitude explicitly when he said, with evident pleasure and pride, that a certain Scottish international player, known for his unpredictable temper, 'doesn't bear me any ill will because I sent him off'. He was confirming the same attitude when he said that another temperamental international 'responds to the right treatment'. This man, he said, was 'a great character, really, and it's no use making a lot of threats'. By and large, Fussey said, he found professional footballers were 'a great crowd', which is generous of him, considering the low opinion players are often prepared to give of referees.

It is striking how closely referees align themselves with players, in contrast with the scorn with which players will detach themselves from connection with the referees. There is no question about who would like to change places with whom. It is a romantic and, it seems to me, most unrealistic view of refereeing to say, as Sir Stanley Rous, the President of FIFA (the international football authority), says: 'It is a job for volunteers, who are doing a service to the country.' Plainly it is not public spiritedness that motivates men into the ambition of controlling big football matches, even if the authorities insist on treating them like servants of duty. As with managers and directors there is undoubtedly a deep absorption in football here, and the material reward is insubstantial to say the least of it. But there is much more satisfying of ego than disinterest in the motive. The referee wants to be recognized in the game, and he wants to feel he is important to it. He even wants to be liked.

Success as a referee requires devotion to the job. A League referee has to keep himself at a level of physical fitness which is far beyond the reach of the average man of his age. In his forties he has to try to keep close contact with the eye of the hurricane in the game, hard on the heels of the central action all the time. A breathless referee is a flustered and inadequate one, open to abuse from the players and hardly in a position to subdue it. Rous insists that it is vital to the game that 'we should get back to the position we used to have, when players always accepted the referee's decision as final'. The point is that some referees command that degree of submission from players and some are clearly not worthy of it. Fussey, like other leading referees, places physical fitness first in his order of essential attributes for effective refereeing.

He is a bachelor with a clerical job with the National Coal Board, and his life is centred on football. He trains two evenings and four lunchtimes a week, mostly at Doncaster Rovers' ground, and on the one Saturday in five when he does not referee a League match he trains in the morning and either watches or referees schoolboy football in the afternoon. He began refereeing when he was twenty-one, and it took him eleven years to reach League matches.

Fussey said that he was seldom conscious of crowd reaction, and only occasionally did spectators' abuse get through to him. It needed a lull in the general clamour for the word 'bastard', which was the most frequent epithet to burn a way through his concentration on the game.

Off the field he wears a large Football League badge on his blazer. Outside grounds on Saturdays, or in the street during the week, he said, people often stopped him to say something like: 'Oh, I remember you. You gave So-and-so a penalty in the Cup in 1962. We'd have won but for you.' The arguments he was mostly called on to settle were those about interpretations of the offside rule. (This rule obsesses some referees as well as spectators. One League referee has named his house 'Offside'.)

Fussey said he was aware of tension at matches but did not think he was unsettled by it. 'But once you step out there you know there's only you who can make the decisions. That's real responsibility, and I feel it. I don't deny it.' When he entered refereeing he was keenly interested, but not immediately imbued with ambition, he said. 'But once I realized I was making progress I knew I had to be a League referee. That was when I got stuck in and really did it properly.'

He named two other qualities for successful refereeing to accompany fitness. A referee ought always to be well turned out, he said, and he had to be naturally tactful: that is, he must not be subject to an impulsive attitude in moments of stress, because it immediately angers people. (Is this not the good policeman again?)

There is a standard uniform for League referees consisting of black shorts and shirt, and Fussey said that people were more likely to defer to a man whose uniform was always clean and well pressed. He said: 'It makes him look as if he's going to take it seriously. You're not going to have respect for him if he's in a dirty pair of shorts and some scruffy old shirt.'

The part-timer who disciplines the professionals is in turn judged by the amateurs. The two teams' directors have to report to the League after every match on the referee's performance. Literally, they 'mark his card'. They are required to score the referee on a scale of nought to ten. (At the start of the 1970/71 season the League introduced a system of second opinions on referees' efficiency: an assessor, always a former referee, is now at each match to score the official on the same scale.)

Referees are divided on the value of this system. (It is not optional to the clubs; they can be fined £5 for failing to submit a report.) The most self-confident referees tend to defend it by silence, dismissing the matter with the observation that good referees have nothing to be afraid of. Others attack the arrogance of the procedure. Some point to the absurdity of being judged by directors of a team which may have had a couple of penalties awarded against it. The argument in favour of the system says, in effect, that between the views of the most disgruntled directors and those of the most pleased a reasonable mean of a referee's ability emerges over the months. But again the point is glaring that there is a vast difference in attitude between the intense preparation of players to contest the game and the crude, rule-of-thumb manner in which authority oversees it. There is absolutely nothing in the League's regulations which guarantees that the directors who are assessing the referees actually know the offside rule.

This is not to say, of course, that there are no clubs which have close connection with refereeing. There are retired referees who become directors, and there are clubs which frequently invite referees to talk to them and their supporters' clubs about the job. But neither the referees nor the League and the FA can influence the clubs in the attention they pay to referees' problems beyond the directors' own degree of interest. The referee is in the unsatisfactory position of a consultant brought in to adjudicate, instructed to brook no interference and then made subject to the criticism of his employers on the grounds that he was not up to the job.

Under these circumstances one of the English referees in the 1966 World Cup, Ernie Crawford, could hardly be said to be overstating the referee's predicament when he said that he needed, above all else, 'a skin like a rhinoceros and to be as deaf as a doornail'. Fire is breathed on him from the crowd, obscenity may be muttered at him by the players and afterwards he can be accused of both laxity and over-zealousness, by directors watching the same game. As Crawford said to me: 'The referee's only got to make one bad mistake and everything else he does in the game is forgotten.'

Crawford reached retiring age after the World Cup, so when I talked to him at his home in Doncaster he was in the mood to review his career as a referee. It is hard to imagine a more explicit example of a competitor in sport suddenly shoved aside by the years. It was his voice I quoted at the beginning of this chapter, remembering his bitter disappointment at not being chosen for a top game. But his years as a referee had their moments of high flame, as well. He said: 'When you get a letter from Lancaster Gate [the FA headquarters] saying you've been picked to referee a game like England versus Young England, well, the walls move in and out and you could rush outside and kiss people in the street. It's like being picked to play for England.'

Crawford, a tiny Yorkshireman with the unnerving vibrato of the drill instructor in his voice, refereed in ten countries and never thought it necessary, or even relevant, to conceal how much he had enjoyed the glamour and the drama of the exhilarating showpiece matches of international football. His only regret was that he had never taken charge of an FA Cup Final; but in his living room he pointed out the shining cups and plaques which filled a glass-fronted showcase with a precise memory of each occasion they marked. He took me round the house, lingering at every souvenir with which it was hung. They decorated nearly every wall and corner. There were china plates, dolls, crystal goblets, a gold whistle, a cigar box, plaques and medals, an ornamented bull, vases. Most of them were gifts from foreign clubs or from rich football patrons whose names meant nothing to him. A delicate coffee set reached him from Italy, addressed simply: 'E. Crawford, The Referee, England.' When he refereed in an inter-clubs contest in Barcelona, which had no British connection beyond his own presence, the loudspeakers silenced the crowd with a full rendering of 'God Save the Queen'. To mark his selection as a World Cup referee Doncaster Corporation gave him a blazer with the borough coat of arms on the breast pocket.

Crawford was a League referee for fifteen years. He turned to the job in response to the prompting of one of the elder statesmen of football in his area soon after he admitted to himself that he would never be able to make a living as a player. He remembers his first assignment as a referee in local football with the same cringing pain that some people show when they recall their first visit to a dentist or first fall off a rock face. The match was a local 'derby' between the two teams of the same mining village. 'It was the worst experience I ever had in my life,' he said. He awarded a penalty in the first five minutes. 'I put the ball on the spot and a chap came up and kicked it away. Well, I spoke to him nice and politely and said he shouldn't do that, and that was how it went on. I was dreadful. The game afterwards was just a shambles. I wanted to see a hole in the ground I could jump into. We changed in the pub, and when we got back there the comments were terrible. They paid me five shillings, and they made it up in all the threepenny bits and pennies and ha'pennies they could find. They followed me all the way to the bus, shouting at me.' He was twenty-two.

When he got home he immediatdy wrote to his mentor, saying that he had refereed his last game. He said to me: 'I told the wife, "I'm not having this, not for five bob a week."' But his anxiety to stay close to football was an ally to authority's persuasion, and his next match was the return encounter between the same teams, the decision made on the same grounds that send high-wire men back up the rope ladder immediately after a fall. He said: 'The advice I was given was to wait for the first chap to open his mouth and then give him some stick. Well, this feller, poor chap, he didn't do anything really, but I tore this strip off him. He didn't know what hit him, and after that it was a wonderful game.'

Crawford reached the League at the time when professional football was still being played on Christmas Day, and he made the point strongly that the privations of referees at the time were far worse than the players' circumstances. A working man without a car in the early 50s, he had to make his own way to Christmas matches when public transport was skeletal. He said: 'This is what I mean by dedication. I've gone to bed at eight p.m. on Christmas Eve so that I could be up to get the only train on Christmas morning. I've landed up at Chesterfield at seven thirty on Christmas Day, wandering about when there's no one around. I was huddling in this doorway when a policeman came up and wanted to know what I was doing. Well, he had a right. I told him who I was, and he took me off to his little kiosk and we had a cup of tea with some whisky in it. He said, "Well, I thought I had a lousy job, but yours is worse."'

Referees who have worked their way through that sort of thing are not likely to be reticent when they are offering their opinions on the ways other men should prepare themselves for the job. Crawford said he was a frequent speaker at referees' gatherings, and he did not think it could be drummed home too often to them that if they were ambitious they had to train without stint. He said: 'I've run round Doncaster Rovers' track in pouring rain with a towel round my head, when the weather's been so bad that the players have been kept inside for talks.' A referee also needed a sense of humour; he would never succeed if he was pompous; finger-wagging and elaborate lecturing of players could irritate more than control. He said, 'I don't know how many players I've sent off. I don't want to know. It's one of the easiest decisions to make, to send a man off. That's not what you're there for. The hard thing is to keep him on sometimes. You do better keeping your voice down. I've run alongside players and said, "Ee, give over, I knew thee when tha was a good player." That hurts more than shaking your finger at a man.'

Crawford was an effective, obeyed referee, probably for the most part because he remembered his own belligerent nature as a young player and had the good sense to keep in mind the fact that youth, impetuosity and the burning will to win go together in a highly combustible package. He said he had been 'a bad lad' as an adolescent player. 'I'd kick anything above the grass,' he said. Recalling his own attitude to authority when he was the age of many of today's professional footballers, he emphasized that all referees should make it a rule never to touch a player. He said: 'A referee jabbed me in the chest once when I was playing, and he was the luckiest man alive. I could have kicked him in the teeth.'

This may not be the tone of voice which the government of football likes to hear. The leadership suggests, in its public utterances on the vexing problem of the growing dissatisfaction with refereeing, that it would prefer a more haughty detachment by referees. This reflects a mistaken belief that the arrogance of authority, as exercised on the school playing field over a captive company, can be extended to the professional game as long as the official is enough of a disciplinarian. Crawford's attitude was that the players knew referees made mistakes; it was no use pretending otherwise. The task was to convince the players that the referee always 'gave what he saw'. Similarly a referee ought to be able quickly to differentiate between the spontaneous expletives of angered players and the malevolent abuse of those trying to intimidate him.

Sir Stanley Rous made his name as a referee before he became secretary of the FA and eventually President of FIFA. Admittedly the football Rous controlled was less explosive than today's, but he and Crawford were at one in the view that an adjustable deafness was a positive asset. Rous did not send off the French captain who once questioned the award of a penalty with a furious, 'Bloody *pourquoi*?' Crawford said that there could be little future for the referee who regularly admitted being sworn at; too many complaints would put him in a similar position to that of a player who shows too readily how he can be hurt. Here again we have the point that the referee sees himself as part of the action, not an agent of authority.

Crawford found that the best team captains quickly understood how much it was in their own interests to support the referee; bitterness over a harsh decision might well linger in a captain's mind, but it was less dangerous to his own success than letting one of his men get himself sent off the field for intransigence. Crawford said: 'I've known a captain threaten to thump one of his own men for arguing with me. I always made a point of letting captains I didn't know very well understand exactly what I'd stand and what I wouldn't. I'd say to them, "Right, now look, we're going to play football; that's why we're all here." Captains always knew with me that they weren't there just for the toss of the coin.'

In a game which creates as much passion and as much demand on a man's resources as does professional football there are bound to be moments when gamesmanship and outright villainy test a referee to his limit. There are also times when he has to decide which of the two is present in the same incident. The good referee is not the man who plays safe with either a blind eye or a public display of moral outrage, but the one who can unobtrusively remove the teeth from the offence. The story goes that one famous referee awarded a penalty in the closing minutes of a cup-tie, when the score was 0–0. As the hot-shot of the visiting side prepared to take the kick the captain of the other team said softly in the hush of the moment: 'Bet you twenty quid you score.' The referee, equally softly, said to the villain: 'Bet you he takes it again if he doesn't.'

DOING IT

Jackie Stewart (with Peter Manso)

Faster

March 8, 1970

Speed: really the whole business is the reverse of speed, how to eliminate it.

In a racing car, speed doesn't exist for me except when I'm driving poorly. Then things seem to be coming at me quickly instead of passing in slow motion. It's the surest sign that I'm off form, the kind of thing that happens whenever I go too fast too early on a strange circuit. For the first lap or two, everything seems too fast. Then once I've learned the course, I see things a long way off, in fine detail. A corner will come toward me very slowly, not unexpectedly. There's plenty of time as I'm closing in on it, plenty of time to brake and balance the car, to turn in, hit the apex, go through and hit the exit, and even look down at the rev counter to see how quickly I've gone around. On the other hand, when I'm driving poorly I'll go into the corner at the same speed, but everything is a great rush. Things are coming at me rather than passing me and I'm all ruffled. None of it's of a piece, my movements are not coordinated; and it's like first learning how to drive.

Speed is therefore what I compete *against*. It's the thing that stops me from conquering a corner because I'm the master of the car and the car is coming along with me, and speed—what I'm calling speed—exists only when the car takes over, when something goes wrong or I'm really not getting down to it.

When some people speak of speed in conjunction with racing, they really don't know what they're talking about. Two hundred or a hundred and eighty miles an hour in a Formula 1 car, if you're plugged in, is literally like eighty or sixty on the highway. The car is made to go that fast. It's stable and very easy to drive in a straight line, and once you're used to it, things don't rush past in an enormous flurry or blur. They're actually very clear. I remember once going down the Masta straight at Spa and there was a marshal sitting in a wheelchair with his leg in a cast, and as I went past him at about a hundred and

ninety I was thinking, "What an idiot! What happens if there's an
accident, what good will he be?" I'll also usually recognize photographers there, even at those speeds, recognize their faces and clothing,
and I'll have time to look over to my right to see who's going up the
hill on the other side of the track, which is all of a mile away. I'll be
able to spot particular cars. Everything is clear, neither hurried nor
distorted, a tableau spread out in front of you, things going past, a new
field coming into view, all of it in sequence, like a slowed-down movie
film.

Through the turns, though, is where the true character of the car
shows itself. A Formula 1 car is really an animal; a machine, yes, of
course, but beyond that an animal because it responds to different
kinds of treatment. A highly bred race horse, a thoroughbred in its
sensitivity and nervousness. To get the best out of it you must coax it,
treat it gently and sympathetically. In a corner it's right on its tiptoes,
finely balanced, on the very edge of adhesion, just fingertips on the
road, and if you dominate it or try to push it around, it will go straight
on or slide off or do any number of things that leave you without
control. So you coax it—gently, very gently—to get it to do what you
want. You point it and coax it into the apex, and even after you've
pointed it and it's all set up, committed to the corner which might still
be fifty or a hundred feet away, you must be tender with it, holding it
in nicely, because it's got an angle on it, an angle of roll, and it's
building to its climax of hitting that apex. You've set a rhythm and
now you must keep it. And as it hits the apex, you take it out nicely;
you don't say, "You've got your apex, now I'll put my boot in it and
drive however I want." No, your exit speed is very important, so you've
got to maintain that balance or rhythm which you've been building all
along. You've got to follow through, let the car fulfill itself.

Obviously, all this suggests that a car is very much like a woman,
and however banal it sounds, the analogy holds. I know of no better.
Cornering is like bringing a woman to a climax. The two of you, both
you and the car, must work together. You start to enter the area of
excitement of that corner, you set up a pace which is right for the car,
and after you've told it that it's coming along with you, you guide it
through at a rhythm which has by now become natural. Only after
you've cleared that corner can you both take pleasure in knowing that
it's gone well. If you do otherwise, alter the car's line, sometimes by no
more than three or four inches, scrape a curbing, give it too much
throttle or fail to feed it in gently, you'll spoil it. You'll ruin it. Through

your own impatience you'd have taken away all the pleasure. It'll be finished, yet there will be something still to come.

March 9, 1970

Yesterday's thoughts continued.

This business of being sensitive to the car, very true, especially with today's Formula 1 car. Any ripple in the road, any small change in the surface, any oil or water or rubber that's been laid down radically affects the car's performance, more than most people would believe. And yet here again the car resembles a woman, if only because it's so unpredictable. You'll be driving well and all of a sudden the car may turn around and do something completely unexpected, shift its mood entirely. It turns on you viciously, abruptly, taking you by surprise, and when this happens it snaps away from you, immediately, spontaneously, and at that moment you've got to work very hard and very fast to bring it back because what's happening is happening so quickly that you don't know where you are. You've stopped thinking about coaxing it through and you're deep into a big recovery job, and now speed is showing itself quite vividly. You've got to stop what's happening and then start all over again, almost from scratch, really, because the car has chosen to protest your relationship.

March 12, 1970

It occurs to me that I ought to tell what I do with myself before a race, since I might overlook this as the season progresses. Because it's now ritual, a veritable countdown, I can talk about it in the abstract.

The process is akin to a deflating ball. The point of it is to shape my mood, really to expel mood, all mood. Beginning the night before, I start to pace myself into an emotional neutrality, a flatness or isolation that is imperative for a good start. By the time I go to bed, I will have obliterated all contact with people around me, Helen included. Usually I'll be reading, lying there beyond anybody's reach, trying to cleanse my mind, empty it of all extraneous thoughts, all impingements, anything that might encroach. Around eleven or twelve, perhaps, I'll go off to sleep. I'll awaken at half-past six or seven, stay in bed, pick up my reading, then probably doze off to reawaken around nine.

Breakfast in my room, always in my room, and usually alone, and perhaps, too, I'll have a massage, if one's available. Then back to sleep, up at noon, dress, and leave for the track.

By now I'm fairly bouncy. After the calm of being alone, the ball has started to inflate again. I'll have thoughts of what I'm going to do on the first lap, where I'm going to pass if someone gets off ahead of me, but immediately I'll then become aware of having to change my mood, of the need to put aside all these thoughts lest I lock myself into a plan that might interfere with my driving. More than anything, I know I need to stay loose, so I force myself to deflate, consciously, concentrating on it. I don't want Helen around me, I don't want to be bugged by reporters or film people or magazine photographers, by people wanting my autograph or by anyone. I'm into it, I need to be alone.

By race time I should have no emotions inside me at all—no excitement or fear or nervousness, not even an awareness of the fatigue that's been brought on by pacing myself. I'm absolutely cold, ice-cold, totally within my shell. I'm drained of feeling, utterly calm even though I'm aware of the many things going on around me, the mechanics, people running about, the journalists and officials and everything else.

Ten minutes or so from the start, I'll walk out to the car. My mechanics will belt me in, do up my seatbelts, and I'll just sit there waiting. If there is a warm-up lap, I'll leave from the pits rather than the grid, go out and bed the brakes, get the temperatures up, using the brakes heavily all the way around, even riding my left foot on the pedal, and I'll also do a few corners very fast to warm up the tires.

Back on the dummy grid, I'll get out of the car and move around a bit, then with four or five minutes to go I'll get back in, again get belted up, and the mechanics will wait there with me, kneeling down beside the car or sitting on one of the tires, not talking. At the two-minute signal I'll start the engine, they'll have to leave, and I'll hold it revving fairly high, somewhere between 5,000 and 7,000, with occasional blips up to about 9,000. A minute to go, they'll move us up to the grid proper and I'll keep the clutch out until the very last before sticking it in gear.

The engines are revving all around you, and you hear them even with your earplugs and helmet, but I'm still in my shell, concentrating on what I'm going to have to do in the next minute. I may be looking around, or down at the instruments, but I'm still concentrating, the ball totally deflated. Thirty seconds left, I'll put it in gear. Twenty seconds, or maybe when the starter begins thinking about lifting the flag, I'll take the revs up to about 8,500 and hold it there, and that's when I take my foot off the clutch.

George Plimpton

Shadow Box

The fight, or exhibition, or what people later called "that time when you . . ." took place in Stillman's Gym, which was a famous and rickety boxers' establishment on Eighth Avenue just down from Columbus Circle. A dark stairway led up into a gloomy vaultlike room, rather like the hold of an old galleon. One heard the sound before one's eyes acclimatized: the *slap-slap* of the ropes being skipped, the thud of leather into the big heavy bags that squeaked from their chains as they swung, the rattle of the speed bags, the muffled sounds of gym shoes on the canvas of the rings (there were two rings), the snuffle of the fighters breathing out through their noses, and, every three minutes, the sharp clang of the ring bell. The atmosphere was of a fetid jungle twilight. When Gene Tunney trained at Stillman's, he wanted to open the windows, which were so caked that it was hard to pick out where they were in the wall. "Let's clear this place out with some fresh air," he had said, and everybody there had looked at him astonished. Johnny Dundee, the featherweight champion at the time, made an oft-quoted remark: "Fresh air? Why, that stuff is likely to kill us!"

The proprietor was Lou Stillman himself. His real name was Lou Ingber, but he had managed Stillman's so long—it was originally opened by a pair of philanthropist millionaires as a charity mission to bring in kids off the street—that he found himself named for the gym that he made famous. His attitude about his place was as follows: "The way these guys like it, the filthier it is, the better. Maybe it makes them feel more at home." He announced this in what Budd Schulberg had once described as a "garbage-disposal voice." He sat up on a high stool under the automatic timer that set off the ring bell.

I remember him for leaning forward off the stool and delivering himself of a succession of tiny spits—oh, the size of BB shots—and though there were signs nailed up everywhere that read NO RUBBISH OR SPITTING ON THE FLOOR, UNDER PENALTY OF THE LAW, Stillman himself expectorated at almost every breath. Perhaps he felt that he was exonerated by the infinitesimal size of his offerings.

I had gone in there to ask him if we could take over the premises for an hour or so; I told him about Archie Moore and what we hoped to do. *Sports Illustrated* would pay him a small sum for the inconvenience. He did not seem especially surprised. An eyebrow might have been raised. It turned out that he condoned almost anything that would break the dreary tedium of the workouts—the never-ending three-minute doomsday clang of the ring bell, the mind-stupefying slamming of the punching-bag equipment—and that in the grim steerage-hold atmosphere much more hanky-panky and joking went on, perhaps as a sort of therapy, than one might have expected. For years the fall guy for practical jokes had been a huge scar-faced black fighter known as Battling Norfolk, employed by Stillman as a rubdown man, who became such a target for a hotfoot, or a bucket of water on the nape of the neck, that as he moved around the gym he *revolved*, turning to make sure no one was coming up on him from behind. They never let up on him. When he answered the phone, an explosive charge would go off; a skeleton was set up in the little cubicle in the back reaches of the gym where he gave his rubdowns, and when he saw it there, glistening in the dull light, he gave a scream and was said to have fainted, crashing up against the wood partition.

Perhaps Stillman saw me as another in the line of Battling Norfolks. He agreed to turn over his premises, though he told me what a businesslike establishment he was running there, and what a considerable inconvenience it was going to be to stop operations for the hour or so of the exhibition. Couldn't *Sports Illustrated* come up with more scratch? I said that I would see what I could do. I told him that, frankly, it was the least of my worries.

As the day of the fight approached, I began to get notes in the mail. I don't know who sent them. Most of them were signed with fighters' names—aphorisms, properly terse, and almost all somewhat violent in tone. I suspected Peter Gimbel, my sparring partner, but he would not fess up.

One of them read, "If you get belted and see three fighters through a haze, go after the one in the middle. That's what ruined me—going after the other two guys."—MAX BAER.

Another, on the back of a postcard that had a cat sitting next to a vase of roses on the front, announced succinctly, "Go on in there, he can't hurt us."—LEO P. FLYNN, FIGHT MANAGER.

Another had the curious words Eddie Simms murmured when Art Donovan, the referee, went over to his corner to see how clear-headed he was after being pole-axed by Joe Louis in their Cleveland fight: "Come on, let's take a walk on the roof. I want some fresh air."

Joe Louis' famous remark about Billy Conn turned up one morning: "He can run, but he can't hide." So did James Braddock's description of what it was like to be hit by a Joe Louis jab: "... like someone jammed an electric bulb in your face and busted it."

One of the lengthier messages was a parody of a type of column Jimmy Cannon occasionally wrote for the New York *Journal-American* in which he utilized the second-person form for immediacy and dramatic effect. "Your name is Joe Louis," a column might start. "You are in the twilight of your career ..." The one I received read as follows: "Your name is George Plimpton. You have had an appointment with Archie Moore. Your head is now a concert hall where Chinese music will never stop playing."

The last one I received was a short description of a fighter named Joe Dunphy, from Syracuse, a fair middleweight, who became so paralyzed considering his prospects against a top middleweight Australian named Dan Creedon that he stood motionless in his corner at the opening bell, his eyes popping, until finally Creedon, carefully, because he was looking for some kind of trick, went up and knocked him down, much as one might push over a storefront mannequin.

Occasionally, someone of a more practical mind than the mysterious message-sender would call up with a positive word of advice. One of the stranger suggestions was that I avail myself of the services of a spellcaster named Evil Eye Finkel. He possessed what he called the "Slobodka Stare," which he boasted was what had finally finished off Adolf Hitler.

"Think of that," I said.

"Evil Eye's got a manager," I was told. "Name of Mumbles Sober. The pair of them can be hired for fifty dollars to five hundred dollars depending—so it says in the brochure—on the 'wealth of the employer and the difficulty of the job.'"

I wondered aloud what the price difference would be between saving my skin in the ring against Archie Moore and what it had cost to preserve the Western democracies from fascism.

"I don't know," I was told. "You'll have to ask Mumbles."

As it was, I picked corner men who were literary rather than evil-eyed, or even pugilistic—composed of the sort of friends one might have as ushers at a wedding (or perhaps, more appropriately, as someone pointed out, as bearers at a funeral) rather than at a boxing showdown in a gymnasium. They were Peter Matthiessen, the novelist and explorer (he appeared on the day of the fight and gave me the tibia of an Arctic hare as a good-luck token—the biggest rabbit's foot I had ever seen); Tom Guinzburg, of the Viking Press; Blair Fuller, the novelist; Bob Silvers, then an editor of *Harpers*: and, of course, George Brown, the only professional among us, who of course had literary connections because of his friendship with Ernest Hemingway. None of them, except Brown, had anything to do, really. I asked them if they would have lunch with me the day of the fight. They could steady me through the meal and get me to eat something. They could distract me with funny stories.

On the morning of the fight, to get a flavor of what the boxer goes through on the day of his bout, I turned up at the offices of the Boxing Commission, just uptown from Madison Square Garden, to get weighed in with the rest of the boxers scheduled to fight on various cards that evening around the City. John Conden, of the Garden, who was in charge of the proceedings, had said he would see to it that I got weighed in along with everyone else. The room was crowded with fighters, their managers, and more press than usual—a boxer-policeman from New Jersey named Dixon had raised considerable public interest.

I got in line. The fighters who were scheduled to fight in the Garden that evening and were staying in local fleabag hotels came ready for quick disrobing—overcoats over a pair of underwear shorts. One or two of them were wearing shoes with the laces already untied, so that all they had to do was shuck their overcoats and step up out of the shoes onto the scales. The official at the scales jiggled the weights and announced the figures. We shuffled forward. I had my overcoat on my arm. I was wearing a Brooks Brothers suit, a vestcoat that I was affecting at the time, a button-down-collared shirt with a striped regimental tie, and a pair of dark scuffed shoes over long calf-length socks.

When I was within eight boxers of the scale I began to take off my clothes. I removed my suit-coat, tossing it and my overcoat on a chair as I passed, and I started taking off my tie, just picking at the knot. But then I saw someone staring at me—one of the journalists, probably—nudging the man next to him to attract *his* attention, the two of them staring at me as surprised as if the boxing commissioner himself had decided to step out of his trousers. That was enough. I could not go through with it. My fingers slipped off the tie, and I rolled my eyes ceilingward to suggest how stifling I felt the room was.

I did not tell my corner men at lunch about my experience that morning at the commissioner's office. It was not appropriate to the temper of the day to dwell on bungles of any sort. We had the lunch at the Racquet Club. My friends stared at me with odd smiles. We ordered the meal out of stiff large menus that crackled sharply when opened. I ordered eggs benedict, a steak diane, and a chocolate-ice-cream compote. Someone said that it was not the sort of place, or meal, one would relate to someone going up against the light heavyweight champion of the world, but I said I was having the meal to quiet my nerves; the elegance of the place, and the food, arriving at the table in silver serving dishes, helped me forget where I was going to be at five that afternoon.

I took out Matthiessen's enormous rabbit foot. "How can I lose with this thing?" I said. We talked about good-luck charms and I said that in the library down the hall I had read that when Tom Sharkey was preparing for a fight against Gus Ruhlin, he was sent a pair of peacocks by Bob Fitzsimmons, the former heavyweight champion. Sharkey was somewhat shaken by the gift, because he said he had heard from an old Irishwoman that an owner of a peacock never had any good luck. But Fitzsimmons was such a good friend that Sharkey didn't want to insult him by sending the birds back. So Sharkey kept them around, walking past their pens rather hurriedly, and indeed when he lost his fight to Ruhlin in the eleventh round, he blamed it on what he called his "Jonah birds."

"You trying to tell me you feel awkward about that hare's foot?" Matthiessen asked.

I had the sense that he had been reluctant to give it up in the first place. It was a *huge* foot, and it probably meant a lot to him.

"Perhaps you could hold it for me," I said.

"You better keep it," he said.

During lunch I kept wondering what Archie Moore was up to. I knew that he was in town, not far away. I thought of him coming closer all the time, physically moving toward our confrontation, perhaps a quarter of a mile away at the moment, in some restaurant, ordering a big steak with honey on it for energy, everybody in the place craning around to stare at him, and a lot of smiles because a month before he had won an extraordinary fight against Yvon Durrelle, a strong pole-axer French Canadian, in which he had pulled himself up off the canvas five times, eventually to win, so that the applause would ripple up from among the tables as he left the restaurant; then he would turn uptown feeling good about things, people nodding to him on the avenues, and smiling, and then he might duck into a Fifth Avenue shop to buy a hat, and afterward perhaps he'd wander up by the Plaza and into the Park where he might take a look at the yak over there in the zoo. Then he'd glance at his watch. That might get him upset. It disturbed the equanimity of the day. Who *was* this guy? The nerve! This creep who had written him a letter. So the distance would be shortened; he was coming crosstown now, then up the stairs of Stillman's, just yards away from me in the labyrinthine gloom of the dressing lockers, and then finally in the ring, just a few feet away, seeing me for the first time, looking at me speculatively, and then when he put a fist in my stomach, there wouldn't be any distance between us at all!

Later I discovered what he *was* doing. At the same time I was having lunch with my entourage, he was sitting in a restaurant with Peter Maas, a journalist friend of mine. Over dessert, Archie Moore asked Peter who I was—this fellow he had agreed to go three rounds with later that afternoon. Maas, who knew about the arrangements—I had invited him to Stillman's—could not resist it: he found himself, somewhat to his surprise, describing me to Moore as an "intercollegiate boxing champion."

Once Peter had got that out, he began to warm to his subject: "He's a gawky sort of guy, but don't let that fool you, Arch. He's got a left jab that sticks, he's fast, and he's got a pole-ax left hook that he can really throw. He's a barnburner of a fighter, and the *big* thing about him is that he wants to be the light heavyweight champion of the world. Very ambitious. And confident. He doesn't see why he should work his way up through all the preliminaries in the tank towns: he reckons he's ready *now*."

Moore arched his eyebrows at this.

"He's invited all his friends," Maas went on gaily, "a few members of the press, a couple of guys who are going to be at the McNeil Boxing Award dinner tonight"—which was the real reason Moore was in town—"and in front of all these people he's going to waltz into the ring and *take* you. What he's done is to sucker you into the ring."

Maas told me all of this later. He said he had not suspected himself of such satanic capacities; it all came out quite easily.

Moore finally had a comment to offer. "If that guy lays a hand on me I'm going to coldcock him." He cracked his knuckles alarmingly at the table.

At this, Peter Maas realized that not unlike Dr. Frankenstein he had created a monster, and after a somewhat hollow laugh, he tried to undo matters: "Oh, Arch, he's a friend of mine." He tried to say that he had been carrying on in jest. But this served to make Moore even more suspicious—the notion that Maas and the mysterious man with the "pole-ax left hook" he was describing were in cahoots of some sort.

At the time, of course, I knew none of this. I dawdled away the afternoon and arrived early at Stillman's. George Brown was with me, carrying his little leather case with the gloves, and some "equipment" he felt he might have to use if things got "difficult" for me up in the ring.

We went up the steps of the building at Eighth Avenue, through the turnstile, and Lou Stillman led us through the back area of his place into an arrangement of dressing cubicles as helter-skelter as a Tangier slum, with George Brown's nose wrinkled up as we were shown back into the gloom and a stall was found. George sat me down in a corner, and, snapping open his kit bag, he got ready to tape my hands. I worried aloud that Archie Moore might not show up, and both George and I laughed at the concern in my voice, as if a condemned prisoner were fretting that the fellow in charge of the dawn proceedings might have overslept. We began to hear people arriving outside, the hum of voices beginning to rise. I had let a number of people know; the word of the strange cocktail-hour exhibition had spread. Blair Fuller arrived. He was the only one of my seconds who seemed willing to identify himself with what was going to go on. The rest said they were going to sit in the back. Fuller was wearing a T-shirt with THE PARIS REVIEW across the front.

Suddenly, Archie Moore himself appeared at the door of my cubicle. He was in his street clothes. He was carrying a kit bag and a pair of boxing gloves; the long white laces hung down loose. There was a crowd of people behind him, peering in over his shoulders—Miles Davis, the trumpet player, one of them; and I thought I recognized Doc Kearns, Moore's legendary manager, with his great ears soaring up the sides of his head and the slight tang of toilet water sweetening the air of the cubicle (he was known for the aroma of his colognes). But all of this was a swift impression, because I was staring up at Moore from my stool. He looked down and said as follows: "*Hmm.*" There were no greetings. He began undressing. He stepped out of his pants and shorts; over his hips he began drawing up a large harnesslike foul-protector. I stared at it in awe. I had not thought to buy one myself; the notion of the champion's throwing a low blow had not occurred to me. Indeed, I was upset to realize he thought *I* was capable of doing such a thing. "I don't have one of those," I murmured. I don't think he heard me. The man I took to be Doc Kearns was saying, "Arch, let's get on out of here. It's a freak show." Beyond the cubicle we could hear the rising murmur of the crowd.

"No, no, no," I said. "It's all very serious."

Moore looked at me speculatively. "Go out there and do your best," he said. He settled the cup around his hips and flicked its surface with a fingernail; it gave off a dull, tinny sound. He drew on his trunks. He began taping his hands—the shriek of the adhesive drawn in bursts off its spool, the flurry of his fists as he spun the tape around them. During this, he offered us a curious monologue, apparently about a series of victories back in his welterweight days: "I put that guy in the hospital, didn't I? Yeah, banged him around the eyes so it was a question about could he ever *see* again." He looked at me again. "You do your best, hear?" I nodded vaguely. He went back to his litany. "Hey, Doc, you remember the guy who couldn't remember his name after we finished with him . . . just plumb banged that guy's name right out of his skull?" He smoothed the tape over his hands and slid on the boxing gloves. Then he turned and swung a punch at the wall of the cubicle with a force that bounced a wooden medicine cabinet off its peg; it fell to the floor and exploded in a shower of rickety slats. "These gloves are tight," he said as he walked out. A roll of athletic tape fell out of the ruin of the cabinet and unraveled across the floor. Beyond the cubicle wall I heard a voice cut through the babble: "Whatever he was, Arch, he was not an elephant."

Could that have been Kearns? An assessment of the opposition? Of course, at the time I had no idea that Peter Maas had built me up into a demonic contender whom they had good reason to check.

"What the hell was that?" I said. I looked at George Brown beseechingly. He shrugged. "Don't let it bother you. Just remember what we've been doing all this time," he said, smoothing the tape on my hands. "Move, and peck at him."

"At least he didn't find out about the sympathetic response," I said.

"What's that?" Brown asked.

"Well, it's that weeping you've noticed when I get cuffed around."

"Maybe he'll think it's sweat," Brown said cheerfully.

After a while he reached for the gloves and said it was time we went out.

The place was packed; the seats stretching back from the ring (a utility from the days when the great fighters sparred at Stillman's) were full, and behind them people were standing back along the wall. Archie Moore was waiting up in the ring, wearing a white T-shirt and a pair of knit boxing trunks like a 1920s bathing suit. As I climbed into the ring he had his back to me, leaning over the ropes and shouting at someone in the crowd. I saw him club at the ring ropes with a gloved fist, and I could feel the structure of the ring shudder. Ezra Bowen, a *Sports Illustrated* editor, jumped up into the ring to act as referee. He provided some florid instructions, and then waved the two of us together. Moore turned and began shuffling quickly toward me.

I had read somewhere that if one were doomed to suffer in the ring, it would be best to have Archie Moore as the bestower. His face was peaceful, with a kind of comforting mien to it—people doubtless fell easily into conversation with him on buses and planes—and to be put away by him in the ring would not be unlike being tucked in by a Haitian mammy.

I do not remember any such thoughts at the time. He came at me quite briskly, and as I poked at him tentatively, his left reached out and thumped me alarmingly. As he moved around the ring he made a curious humming sound in his throat, a sort of peaceful aimless sound one might make pruning a flower bed, except that from time to time the hum would rise quite abruptly, and *bang!* he would cuff me alongside the head. I would sense the leaden feeling of being hit, the almost acrid whiff of leather off his gloves, and I would blink through the sympathetic response and try to focus on his face, which looked slightly startled, as if he could scarcely believe he had done such a thing. Then I'd hear the humming again, barely distinguishable now against the singing in my own head.

Halfway through the round Moore slipped—almost to one knee— not because of anything I had done, but his footing had betrayed him somehow. Laughter rose out of the seats, and almost as if in retribution he jabbed and followed with a long lazy left hook that fetched up against my nose and collapsed it slightly. It began to bleed. There was a considerable amount of sympathetic response and though my physical reaction, the *jab* ("peck, peck, peck"), was thrown in a frenzy and with considerable spirit, the efforts popped up against Moore's guard as ineffectually as if I were poking at the side of a barn. The tears came down my cheeks. We revolved around the ring. I could hear the crowd—a vague buzzing—and occasionally I could hear my name being called out: "Hey, George, hit him back; hit him in the knees, George." I was conscious of how inappropriate the name George was to the ring, rather like hearing "Timothy" or "Warren" or "Christopher." Occasionally I was aware of the faces hanging above the seats like rows of balloons, unrecognizable, many of them with faint anticipatory grins on their faces, as if they were waiting for a joke to be told which was going to be pretty good. They were slightly inhuman, I remember thinking, the banks of them staring up, and suddenly into my mind popped a scene from Conan Doyle's *The Croxley Master:* his fine description of a fight being watched by Welsh miners, each with his dog sitting behind him; they went everywhere as companions, so that the boxers looked down and everywhere among the human faces were the heads of dogs, yapping from the benches, the muzzles pointing up, the tongues lolling.

We went into a clinch; I was surprised when I was pushed away and saw the sheen of blood on Moore's T-shirt. Moore looked slightly alarmed. The flow of tears was doubtless disarming. He moved forward and enfolded me in another clinch. He whispered in my ear, "Hey, breathe, man, breathe." The bell sounded and I turned from him and headed for my corner, feeling very much like sitting down.

Lou Stillman had not provided a stool. "There's no stool," I said snuffily to George Brown. My nose was stopped up. He ministered to me across the ropes—a quick rub of the face with the towel, an inspection of the nose, a pop of head-clearing salts, a predictable word of the old advice ("just jab him, keep him away, keep the glove in his snoot, peck, peck, you're doing fine"). He looked out past my shoulder at Moore, who must have been joking with the crowd, because I could hear the laughter behind me.

For the next two rounds Moore let up considerably, being assured— if indeed it had ever worried him—of the quality of his opposition. In the last round he let me whale away at him from time to time, and then he would pull me into a clinch and whack at me with great harmless popping shots to the backs of my shoulder blades which sounded like the crack of artillery. Once I heard him ask Ezra Bowen if he was behind on points.

But George Brown and Blair Fuller did not like what was going on at all ... I think mostly because of the unpredictable nature of my opponent: his moods seemed to change as the fight went on; he was evidently not quite sure how to comport himself—clowning for a few seconds, and then the humming would rise, and they would grimace as a few punches were thrown with more authority; they could see my mouth drop ajar. In the third round Brown began to feel that Moore had run through as much of a repertoire as he could devise, and that the fighter, wondering how he could finish things off aesthetically, was getting testy about it. I was told Tom Guinzburg, one of my seconds, came up to the corner and threw a towel into the ring ... but whether he was doing it because he was worried or because he knew it would raise a laugh—which indeed it did—I never discovered. But, long after the event, I found out that Brown had reached down and advanced the hand of the time clock. The bell clanged sharply with a good minute to go. Ezra called us together to raise both our arms, and, funning it up, he called the affair a draw. I can remember the relief of its being done, vaguely worried that it had not been more conclusive, or artistic; I was quite grateful for the bloody nose.

"That last round seemed awfully short," I mentioned to Brown.

He dabbed at my face with a towel. "I suppose you were getting set to finish him," George said.

Much of the crowd moved with us back into the cubicle area. In my stall, I was pushed back into a corner. Moore stood in the doorway, the well-wishers shouting at him, "Hey, Arch, hey, Arch!" There was a lot of congratulating and jabber about the great Yvon Durelle fight. I heard somebody ask, "Whose blood is that on your shirt, hey, Arch?" and somebody else said, "Well, it sure ain't his!" and I could hear the guffawing as the exchange was passed along the gloomy corridors beyond the cubicle wall.

The character of the crowd had begun to change. The word had gone around the area that Archie Moore was up in Stillman's, and the fight bars down the avenue had emptied. A whole mess of people came up Stillman's stairs, some of them in time to see the final round, others pushing against the striped-tie crowd leaving. "It's over? What the hell was Arch doin' fightin' in Stillman's?"

"I dunno," one of the others pushing up the stairs said. "I hear he kilt some guy."

"A grudge fight, hey?"

They pushed back into the cubicle area. The cigar smoke rose. I caught sight of Lou Stillman. He was frantic. He had found two women, a mother and daughter, back in the cubicle area, which had flustered him; but the main aggravation was that his place was packed with people who had not paid to come through his turnstile. Someone told me that he had become so astonished at the number turning up for the exhibition, at the quantity of coats and ties, signifying that they *could* pay, that finally venality had overcome him; he rushed to the turnstile and the last twenty or thirty people who crowded in had to pay him two dollars a head. Later, I heard that he had tried to recoup what he had missed by charging people, at least those wearing ties, as they *left*.

I sat on my stool, feeling removed from the bustle and the shouting. While I pecked at the laces of my gloves, suddenly in front of me a man turned—I had been staring at the back of his overcoat—and he said, "Well, kid, what did you get out of it?"

He was an older black man, with a rather melancholy face distinguished by an almost Roman nose; his ears were cauliflowered, though very small.

"So far, a bloody nose," I said.

He smiled slightly. "That's the good way to begin; that's the start."

"I guess that's right," I said.

"There's a lot more to it," he went on.

I must have looked puzzled.

"Stick to it," he said. "You've got a lot to find out about. Don't let it go, hey?"

"No," I said vaguely, "I won't."

I never discovered who he was. I thought of him a couple of times later that evening.

Stillman's cleared out, finally. The fighters, who had been standing along the back wall to watch the strange proceedings, took over the premises again; they climbed up into the rings; the trainers sat down in the front seats, gossiping; things returned to normal.

I was told that at seven o'clock or so the Duchess d'Uzès had arrived. She was not a duchess then (she had a marriage or so to go before she became one) but she had the airs: she was delivered to the door of Stillman's in a Rolls-Royce. She stepped out and hurried up the stairs. She was famous for being late—even at her own extravagant parties, where her guests stood yawning with hunger, waiting for her to come down the long, curved stair and make an entrance—and she paused at the turnstile, a lovely, graceful girl who always wore long light-blue chiffon, on to set off her golden hair.

She peered into the gloom. "Where's everybody?" she called. She had a clear musical voice, perfect for cutting through the uproar of a cocktail party.

Lou Stillman approached. I don't know if he produced one of his infinitesimal spittles. Let us say he cleared his throat.

"Everybody is not here," he said.

Ken Dryden

The Game

I have always been a goalie. I became one long enough ago, before
others' memories and reasons intruded on my own, that I can no
longer remember why I did, but if I had to guess, it was because of
Dave. Almost six years older, he started playing goal before I was old
enough to play any position, so by the time I was six and ready to play,
there was a set of used and discarded equipment that awaited me—
that and an older brother I always tried to emulate.

I have mostly vague recollections of being a goalie at that time. I
remember the spectacular feeling of splitting and sprawling on pavement or ice, and feeling that there was something somehow noble and
sympathetic about having bruises and occasional cuts, especially if they
came, as they did, from only a tennis ball. But if I have one clear image
that remains, it is that of a goalie, his right knee on the ice, his left leg
extended in a half splits, his left arm stretching for the top corner, and,
resting indifferently in his catching glove, a round black puck.

It was the posed position of NHL goalies for promotional photos
and hockey cards at the time and it was a position we tried to reenact
as often as we could in backyard games. There was something that
looked and felt distinctly major league about a shot "raised" that high,
and about a clean, precise movement into space to intercept it. Coming
as it did without rebound, it allowed us to freeze the position as if in a
photo, extending the moment, letting our feelings catch up to the play,
giving us time to step outside ourselves and see what we had done. In
school, or at home, with pencil and paper, sometimes thinking of what
I was doing, more often just mindlessly doodling, I would draw
pictures of goalies, not much more than stick figures really, but fleshed
out with parallel lines, and always in that same catching position. Each
year when my father arranged for a photographer to take pictures for
our family's Christmas card, as Dave and I readied ourselves in our
nets, the shooter was told to shoot high to the glove side, that we had
rehearsed the rest.

To catch a puck or a ball—it was the great joy of being a goalie.
Like a young ballplayer, too young to hit for much enjoyment but old

enough to catch and throw, it was something I could do before I was big enough to do the rest. But mostly it was the feeling it gave me. Even now, watching TV or reading a newspaper, I like to have a ball in my hands, fingering its laces, its seams, its nubby surface, until my fingertips are so alive and alert that the ball and I seem drawn to each other. I like to spin it, bounce it, flip it from hand to hand, throw it against a wall or a ceiling, and catch it over and over again. There is something quite magical about a hand that can follow a ball and find it so crisply and tidily every time, something solid and wonderfully reassuring about its muscular certainty and control. So, if it was because of Dave that I became a goalie, it was the feeling of catching a puck or a ball that kept me one. The irony, of course, would be that later, when I finally became a real goalie instead of a kid with a good glove hand, when I learned to use the other parts of a goaltender's equipment—skates, pads, blocker, stick—it could only be at the expense of what had been until then my greatest joy as a goalie.

I was nineteen at the time. It surely had been happening before then, just as it must before any watershed moment, but the time I remember was the warm-up for the 1967 NCAA final against Boston University. For the first few minutes, I remember only feeling good: a shot, a save, a shot, a save; loose, easy, the burn of nerves turning slowly to a burn of exhilaration. For a shot to my right, my right arm went up and I stopped it with my blocker; another, low to the corner, I kicked away with my pad; along the ice to the other side, my skate; high to the left, my catching glove. Again and again: a pad, a catching glove, a skate, a stick, a blocker, whatever was closest moved, and the puck stopped. For someone who had scooped up ice-skimming shots like a shortstop, who had twisted his body to make backhanded catches on shots for the top right corner, it was a moment of great personal triumph. I had come of age. As the warm-up was ending, I could feel myself becoming a goalie.

Goaltending is often described as the most dangerous position in sports. It is not. Race drivers die from racing cars, jockeys die, so do football players. Goalies do not die from being goalies. Nor do they suffer the frequent facial cuts, the knee and shoulder injuries, that forwards and defensemen often suffer. They stand as obstacles to a hard rubber disc, frequently shot at a lethal speed, sometimes unseen, sometimes deflected; the danger to them is obvious, but it is exaggerated—even the unthinkable: a goalie diving anxiously out of the way of a 100 mph slap shot, the shooter panicking at his own recklessness, the fans "ah"-ing at the near miss. Except for that one, feared time, the time it doesn't happen that way, when the puck moves too fast and the goalie too slow, and, hit in the head, he falls frighteningly to the ice. Moments later, up again, he shakes his head, smiling as others slowly do the same, again reminded that he wears a mask which at other times he sees through and forgets. The danger of playing goal is a *potential* danger, but equipment technology, like a net below a trapeze act, has made serious injury extremely unlikely.

From the time I was six years old, until as a freshman at Cornell I was required to wear a mask, I received fifteen stitches. Since then I have had only four—from a Dennis Hull slap shot that rebounded off my chest, hitting under my chin, in my first playoff year. I have pulled groins and hamstrings, stretched, twisted, and bruised uncounted times various other things, sent my back into spasm twice, broken a toe, and torn the cartilage in one knee. In almost eight years, after more than 400 games and 1,000 practices, that's not much.

Yet, I am often afraid. For while I am well protected, and know I'm unlikely to suffer more than a bruise from any shot that is taken, the puck hurts, constantly and cumulatively: through the pillow-thick leg pads I wear, where straps pulled tight around their shins squeeze much of the padding away; through armor-shelled skate boots; through a catching glove compromised too far for its flexibility; with a dull, aching nausea from stomach to throat when my jock slams back against my testes; and most often, on my arms, on wrists and forearms especially, where padding is light and often out of place, where a shot hits and spreads its ache, up an arm and through a body, until both go limp and feel lifeless. Through a season, a puck hurts like a long, slow battering from a skillful boxer, almost unnoticed in the beginning, but gradually wearing me down, until two or three times a year, I wake up in the morning sore, aching, laughing/moaning with each move I make, and feel a hundred years old. It is on those days and others that when practice comes, I shy away.

The puck on his stick, a player skates for the net. Deep in my crouch, intent, ready, to anyone watching I look the same as I always do. But, like a batter who has been knocked down too many times before, when I see a player draw back his stick to shoot, at the critical moment when concentration must turn to commitment, my body stiffens, my eyes widen and go sightless, my head lifts in the air, turning imperceptibly to the right, as if away from the puck—I bail out, leaving only an empty body behind to cover the net. I yell at myself as others might ("you chicken"). I tell myself reasonably, rationally, that lifting my head, blanking my eyes, can only put me in greater danger; but I don't listen. In a game, each shot controlled by a harassing defense, with something else to think about I can usually put away fear and just play. But in practice, without the distraction of a game, seeing Tremblay or Lambert, Risebrough, Chartraw, or Lupien, dangerous, uncontrolled shooters as likely to hit my arms as a corner of the net, I cannot. In time the fear gradually shrinks back, manageable again, but it never quite goes away.

I have thought more about fear, I have been afraid more often, the last few years. For the first time this year, I have realized that I've only rarely been hurt in my career. I have noticed that unlike many, so far as I know, I carry with me no permanent injury. And now that I know I will retire at the end of the season, more and more I find myself thinking—*I've lasted this long: please let me get out in one piece.* For while I know I am well protected, while I know it's unlikely I will suffer any serious injury, like every other goalie I carry with me the fear of the *one big hurt* that never comes. Recently, I read of the retirement of a race-car driver. Explaining his decision to quit, he said that after his many years of racing, after the deaths of close friends and colleagues, after his own near misses, he simply "knew too much." I feel a little differently. I feel I have known all along what I know now. It's just that I can't forget it as easily as I once did.

Playing goal is not fun. Behind a mask, there are no smiling faces, no timely sweaty grins of satisfaction. It is a grim, humorless position, largely uncreative, requiring little physical movement, giving little physical pleasure in return. A goalie is simply there, tied to a net and to a game; the game acts, a goalie reacts. How he reacts, how often, a hundred shots or no shots, is not up to him. Unable to initiate a game's action, unable to focus its direction, he can only do what he's given to do, what the game demands of him, and that he must do. It is his job, a job that cannot be done one minute in every three, one that will not await rare moments of genius, one that ends when the game ends, and only then. For while a goal goes up in lights, a permanent record for the goal-scorer and the game, a save is ephemeral, important at the time, occasionally when a game is over, but able to be wiped away, undone, with the next shot. It is only when a game ends and the mask comes off, when the immense challenge of the job turns abruptly to immense satisfaction or despair, that the unsmiling grimness lifts and goes away.

If you were to spend some time with a team, without ever watching them on the ice, it wouldn't take long before you discovered who its goalies were. Goalies are different. Whether it's because the position attracts certain personality types, or only permits certain ones to succeed; whether the experience is so intense and fundamental that it transforms its practitioners to type—I don't know the answer. But whatever it is, the differences between "players" and "goalies" are manifest and real, transcending as they do even culture and sport.

A few years ago, at a reception at the Canadian Embassy in Prague, the wife of Jiri Holecek, former star goalie for Czechoslovakia, was introduced to Lynda, and immediately exclaimed, "The players think my Jiri's crazy. Do they [my teammates] think your husband's crazy too?" (No more of the conversation was related to me.) For his book on soccer goalies, English journalist Brian Glanville chose as his title *Goalkeepers Are Different.* It is all part of the mythology of the position, anticipated, expected, accepted, and believed; and in many ways real.

Predictably, a goalie is more introverted than his teammates, more serious (for team pictures, when a photographer tells me to smile, unsmilingly I tell him, "Goalies don't smile"), more sensitive and moody ("ghoulies"), more insecure (often unusually "careful" with money; you might remember Johnny Bower and I *shared* a cab). While a goalie might sometimes be gregarious and outgoing, it usually manifests itself in binges—when a game is over, or on the day of a game when he isn't playing—when he feels himself released from a game. Earlier this season, minutes before a game with the Rangers in the Forum, Robinson looked across the dressing room at me and asked, "Who's playing?" Before I could answer, Shutt yelled back, "I'll give ya a hint, Bird," he said. "Bunny's in the shitter puking; Kenny hasn't shut up since he got here." While teams insist on togetherness, and on qualities in their teammates that encourage it both on and off the ice, a goalie is the one player a team allows to be different. Indeed, as perplexed as anyone at his willingness to dress in cumbrous, oversized equipment to get hit by a puck, a team allows a goalie to sit by himself on planes or buses, to disappear on road trips, to reappear and say nothing for long periods of time, to have a single room when everyone else has roommates. After all, *shrug*, he's a goalie. What can you expect? Flaky, crazy, everything he does accepted and explained away, it offers a goalie wonderful license. It was what allowed Gilles Gratton to "streak" a practice, and Gary Smith to take showers between periods.

In many ways, it is also why my teammates accepted my going to law school.

Good goalies come in many shapes, sizes, and styles. So do bad goalies. A goalie is often plump (Savard, a defenseman, always insists "I like my goalies fat"), sometimes unathletic, and with reflex reactions surprisingly similar to those of the average person (recently at a science museum, with a flashing light and a buzzer I tested my eye–hand reactions against Lynda's; she was slightly faster). While most might agree on what the ideal physical and technical goalie-specimen might look like, it almost certainly would be a composite—the physical size of Tretiak, the elegance of Parent, the agility of Giacomin or Cheevers, the bouncy charisma of Vachon or Resch—with no guarantee that *supergoalie* would be any good. For while there are certain minimum standards of size, style, and agility that any goalie must have, goaltending is a remarkably aphysical activity.

If you were to ask a coach or a player what he would most like to see in a goalie, he would, after some rambling out-loud thoughts, probably settle on something like: consistency, dependability, and the ability to make the big save. Only in the latter, and then only in part, is the physical element present. Instead, what these qualities suggest is a certain character of mind, a mind that need not be nimble or dextrous, for the demands of the job are not complex, but a mind emotionally disciplined, one able to be focused and directed, a mind under control. Because the demands on a goalie are mostly mental, it means that for a goalie the biggest enemy is himself. Not a puck, not an opponent, not a quirk of size or style. Him. The stress and anxiety he feels when he plays, the fear of failing, the fear of being embarrassed, the fear of being physically hurt, all are symptoms of his position, in constant ebb and flow, but never disappearing. The successful goalie understands these neuroses, accepts them, and puts them under control. The unsuccessful goalie is distracted by them, his mind in knots, his body quickly following.

It is why Vachon was superb in Los Angeles and as a high-priced free-agent messiah, poor in Detroit. It is why Dan Bouchard, Tretiak-sized, athletic, technically flawless, lurches annoyingly in and out of mediocrity. It is why there are good "good team" goalies and good "bad team" goalies—Gary Smith, Doug Favell, Denis Herron. The latter are spectacular, capable of making near-impossible saves that few others can make. They are essential for bad teams, winning them games they shouldn't win, but they are goalies who need a second chance, who need the cushion of an occasional bad goal, knowing that they can seem to earn it back later with several inspired saves. On a good team, a goalie has few near-impossible saves to make, but the rest he must make, and playing in close and critical games as he does, he gets no second chance.

A good "bad team" goalie, numbed by the volume of goals he cannot prevent, can focus on brilliant saves and brilliant games, the only things that make a difference to a poor team. A good "good team" goalie cannot. Allowing few enough goals that he feels every one, he is driven instead by something else—the penetrating hatred of letting in a goal.

The great satisfaction of playing goal comes from the challenge it presents. Simply stated, it is to give the team what it needs, when it needs it, not when I feel well-rested, injury-free, warmed-up, psyched-up, healthy, happy, and able to give it, but when *the team* needs it. On a team as good as the Canadiens, often it will need nothing; other times, one good save, perhaps two or three; maybe five good minutes, a period, sometimes, though not often, a whole game. Against better teams, you can almost predict what and when it might be; against the rest, you cannot. You simply have to be ready.

During my first two years with the team, for reasons none of us could figure out, we would start games slowly, outplayed for most of the first period, occasionally for a little longer. It happened so regularly that it became a pattern we anticipated and prepared for, each of us with a special role to play. Mine was to keep the score sufficiently close in the first period, usually to within one goal, so as not to discourage any comeback—their role—that otherwise we would almost certainly make. We were a good combination. I could feel heroically beleaguered the first period, all the time knowing that it would end, that we would soon get our stride, and when we did that I would become a virtual spectator to the game.

That has changed. It began to change the next season, and for the last four years, the change has been complete. A much better team than earlier in the decade, it needs less from me now, just pockets of moments that for me and others sometimes seem lost in a game. But more than that, what it needs now is not to be distracted—by bad goals, by looseness or uncertainty in my play. It needs only to feel secure, confident that the defensive zone is taken care of; the rest it can do itself.

It makes my job different from that of every other goalie in the NHL. I get fewer shots, and fewer *hard* shots; I must allow fewer goals, the teams I play on must win Stanley Cups. Most envy me my job, some are not so sure. Once Vachon, my predecessor in Montreal, in the midst of one of his excellent seasons in Los Angeles, told me that he wasn't sure he would ever want to play for the Canadiens again, even if he had the chance. He said he had come to enjoy a feeling he knew he would rarely have in Montreal—the feeling of winning a game for his team—and he wasn't sure how well he could play without it. In a speech a few years ago, my brother talked about the heroic self-image each goalie needs and has, and is allowed to have because of the nature and perception of his position. "A solitary figure," "a thankless job," "facing an onslaught," "a barrage," "like Horatio at the bridge"—it's the stuff of backyard dreams. It is how others often see him; it is how he sometimes sees himself. I know the feeling Vachon described because I felt it early in my career, when the team wasn't as good as it is now. It is a feeling I have learned to live without.

But something else has changed, something that is more difficult to live without. Each year, I find it harder and harder to make a connection between a Canadiens win and me—nothing so much as my winning a game for the team, just a timely save, or a series of saves that made a difference, that arguably made a difference, that might have made a difference, that, as with a baseball pitcher, can make a win feel mine and ours. But as the team's superiority has become entrenched, and as the gap between our opponents and us, mostly unchanged, has come to seem wider and more permanent, every save I make seems without urgency, as if it is done completely at my own discretion, a minor bonus if made, a minor inconvenience, quickly overcome, if not.

A few months ago, we played the Colorado Rockies at the Forum. Early in the game, I missed an easy shot from the blueline, and a little unnerved, for the next fifty minutes I juggled long shots, and allowed big rebounds and three additional goals. After each Rockies goal, the team would put on a brief spurt and score quickly, and so with only minutes remaining, the game was tied. Then the Rockies scored again, this time a long, sharp-angled shot that squirted through my legs. The game had seemed finally lost. But in the last three minutes, Lapointe scored, then Lafleur, and we won 6–5. Alone in the dressing room afterwards, I tried to feel angry at my own performance, to feel relieved at being let off the uncomfortable hook I had put myself on, to laugh at what a winner could now find funny; but I couldn't. Instead, feeling weak and empty, I just sat there, unable to understand why I felt the way I did. Only slowly did it come to me: I had been irrelevant; I couldn't even lose the game.

I catch few shots now, perhaps only two or three a game. I should catch more, but years of concussion have left the bones in my hand and wrist often tender and sore, and learning to substitute a leg or a stick to save my hand, my catching glove, reprogrammed and out of practice, often remains at my side. Moreover, the game has changed. Bigger players now clutter the front of the net, obstructing and deflecting shots, or, threatening to do both, they distract a goalie, causing rebounds, making clean, precise movements into space— commitments to a single option unmindful of possible deflection or rebound—an indulgence for which a price is too often paid. What I enjoy most about goaltending now is the game itself: feeling myself slowly immerse in it, finding its rhythm, anticipating it, getting there before it does, challenging it, controlling a play that should control me, making it go where I want it to go, moving easily, crushingly within myself, delivering a clear, confident message to the game. And at the same time, to feel my body slowly act out that feeling, pushing up taller and straighter, thrusting itself forward, clenched, flexed, at game's end released like an untied balloon, its feeling spewing in all directions until the next game.

David Craig

Native Stones

The sitting room of our home in Aberdeen, on evenings when I was
nerving myself to tell my father that I planned a trip to the mountains,
used to turn into a chamber two or three times its already ample size,
the light dimmed, red mahogany loomed as dark as sherry, the tall
plum-velvet curtains reared up to the ceiling like trees whose upper
branches were webbed with gloom. I sat there, trying to read my book,
wanting (to bursting-point) to say, 'Daddy, we're thinking of going
hostelling to Inverey, hill-walking in the Cairngorms.' I practised the
words, decided on the diplomatically tentative 'thinking' although the
plan was already firm, didn't specify who 'we' were (it was transparent
anyway), rehearsed counters to his disapprovals, promised myself to
speak after a count of twenty, delayed the start of the count.

Does he know I'm about to make my proposal? Behind the *Scotsman*
his eyes flicker – by chance? or under the stress of his awareness of my
stress? My head is now encased in a special atmosphere which makes
my ears sing slightly. My chair is a pinnacle, on whose top I roost in a
clench of apprehensiveness, hazy unplumbed depths far far below and
all around. In the fireplace consumed coals fall inwards with a clink.
The pulse of the clock on the mantelpiece beats hurriedly.

The pressure grows unbearable. 'Daddy,' I hear my voice saying,
'we're thinking of going hostelling ... in the Cairngorms ... at
Easter ...'

You, the reader, are presuming that I was fourteen or fifteen at the
time. But the date was 1952, and I was twenty.

My father shakes his newspaper to keep it upright. He lets me sweat
for some seconds. 'Won't it be very cold?' he finally asks, not looking
at me. This is the first of a series of questions, most of them negative.
'Will you be able to carry enough food for a week? Isn't it a bit early in
the year? Will the Estate let you have a key?' (to the long moor road to
Derry Lodge, which we'd like to cycle). 'What does Mrs Stephenson
say?' (my girlfriend's mother, my mother-in-law-to-be). Really these
questions are a series of tactical moves that lead up to the final strategic
blockade – the warning pronounced with the whole force of his

prestige as the leading children's physician in Scotland (on call for the royal children when they were at Balmoral): 'Remember what I said about your back.'

Was there anything wrong with my back? (It's still in quite good fettle – aching sometimes but serviceable.) The fact was that I had had iridocyclitis of my left eye in the late spring of 1950. The story was that I would have lost the sight of it had not my father been able to use his position to contact a doctor in America, who had been stationed near Aberdeen during the War, and ask him to send over by plane a supply of the then brand-new drug called adreno-cortico-tropine hormone, ACTH, a cortisone. My eyeball had turned green, the lens muscle was paralysed and I couldn't focus. I was seeing double as I played in a trial for the 1st XI at the start of the season. It was the last game of cricket that I played for twenty years. After some weeks in a hospital bed and a series of injections in the buttock I was pronounced cured. My leg muscles recovered their tone after three weeks' complete disuse, and I spent my last weeks at school wearing a pair of dark glasses with turquoise plastic frames, an eccentricity that gratified me no end, especially when I stepped up onto the platform at assembly and read out choice passages from arcane parts of the Old Testament (Zephaniah or Amos) which I had chosen to air their superb language and irritate the headmaster.

The eye condition is considered minor nowadays. The feeling allowed to permeate the family at that time was that it was dreadfully serious, it had been a near thing, and my father made a connection (validly, no doubt) with our hereditary tendency to arthritis. 'If you go on playing cricket,' he said grimly when I began to chafe at the long lay-off from games, 'your back could go as stiff as a poker – and *stay like that.*' I gave up cricket. Three months later, although I'd been an ardent rugby player, I bowed to his ban on playing for the 3rd XV of the Former Pupils' Club. Golf was all right, a still-ball game played at a walking pace, retired ministers in their seventies could play it, so I went round and round the superb links course of Balgownie just north of Aberdeen, wearing my green-framed shades, until one day, as I hit a drive off the seventeenth tee, an arm of the glasses snapped and I finished the round blinking in the bright marine sunshine. (Two of the old ministers, members of a regular foursome, died on the course not long afterwards.)

Other bans now slid into place under cover of my recent illness. If I 'overdid it' and got very wet or sweaty, the rheumatic tendency might be potentiated. I must be very careful about cold winds or grit in the eyes in case the iritis recrudesced. The fact was that the hellish consequences of 'overdoing it' had overcast our lives for years. In those days it was dangerous to sit on the grass in case you 'caught your death of cold'. If you got 'overheated', the demon pneumonia would seize his chance and get you. My father had only just been saved from what was a killing disease in 1936 by the brand-new May & Baker drugs and 'M&B 693' still rang in our ears like a charm.

So the chains were draped over my shoulders, over my wrists, my legs – lined with the velvet of fatherly concern, forged by the hammer-blows of medical knowledge, weighted extra-heavy by the fact that my elder brother had gone down with rheumatic fever in his eighteenth year, his knees were swollen and useless, his university career cut through in its bright bud. Now he was in bed upstairs and if I went to the mountains I was deserting him, the feckless selfish younger son (and remaining hope of the family) putting *his* health in jeopardy while leaving his worried and saddened parents 'alone' with their ill offspring.

This was my construct. My parents did not put it on me (not in so many words). 'Mind-forg'd manacles' – we compound our own unfreedoms by letting the phobias of others into our selves. An offspring with more hardihood (moral, not physical: I never flinched from the shocks and bruisings of the games field) would have steeled himself to break through those parental binds. Some of my contemporaries did it all the time. Bill Brooker told me recently how he always had to promise his mother, when he started going off to climb on Lochnagar in his early teens, that he would 'not go near Black Spout'. The very name of the huge scree funnel must have sounded infernal to Aberdonian mothers at a time when the rockfaces of that corrie had not been climbed and safety gear was minimal. Bill and his friends had to swear that they would only be going up Red Spout, an easy-angled chute of warm-coloured gravel which can be walked up and down in all conditions. Presently, Bill says, he became an experienced go-between, interceding with other worried parents to let their sons go off to climb in the Cairngorms. But love had nearly smothered me by then. I walked the mountains in summer – in the company of my family. I can still see my father's eyes widen to show the whites, his mouth pursed to draw in a hissing breath, as he warned us against steep drops or deep pools in the burns by simulating the sounds and faces people make when actual danger has just missed them. So I was twenty years old before I was first benighted and slept in a bothy

(Corrour in the Lairig Ghru between Deeside and Speyside), before I first skited off down a refrozen snow slope (on Cairn Toul above the Lairig) and was only saved by my girlfriend sticking in our single ice axe (ex-War Department) and holding me when I fetched up against her. I was twenty-four before I first bivouacked under the night sky (beside the Spey on the way to the Pass of Corrieyairack) with the embers of a cooking fire pulsing red among the river shingle nearby (and on this occasion my father allowed me to see and hear his disappointment that I was leaving my brother 'alone' and gadding off through the Highlands).

But I did, in the autumn of 1952, go up to Lochnagar and Beinn a Bhuird for those two rock climbs. And I can remember no utterly sinking warnings or disapprovals (but plenty of apprehensiveness) when they were mooted. Something else was needed to intensify the deterrence to its crushing maximum. I now believe it was that other, even more inhibiting ban – the taboo that parents seek (or sought) to put upon the girlfriend. Bill Brooker and his friends, the first great wave of rock-and-ice climbers in the Cairngorms, Graham Nicol and Kenny Grassick and Gordon Lillie and the rest – all from my university, mostly from my school – climbed in all-male company. Girls were for necking sessions and hops. Whereas I assumed that whatever I did, I did it with my girlfriend Jill. Therefore to plan a time away in the hills was to propose a time alone with her – in youth hostels or bothies – and what parent was sure of the sleeping arrangements there? When a great friend of mine, precocious in his personal life, arranged to go to the south of France with his girlfriend and I mentioned this choice piece of news to my father, he said with a full dark look into my eyes, 'I would not have *trusted* myself when *I* was his age.' Sex before marriage was wicked. Sex of any kind was unmentionable. My mother never said someone was pregnant, she used the word *enceinte*. When I brought home the unexpurgated edition of *Lady Chatterley's Lover* (published in Sweden), hidden in a road map to hoodwink the Customs at Dover, my father got hold of it and pronounced, after a short inspection, 'Some things should not be written about.' The facts of life were studiously ignored – at the age of seventeen I had no idea how intercourse took place – and this kind of ban gave rise to a whole comedy of concealments. My father always had his bath behind a locked door and the only time I ever went into the bathroom while he was in the water, he sat bolt upright and covered his genitals with his facecloth.

How did we survive? Deformed, is the answer, curtailed and crippled, and especially so if, like me, you let the phobias of your elders invade your head and body. I grew up so shy of women that it felt like a disease and for many years I blushed feverishly when I had to relate to them. The trouble was worse because the bans put on us were not outright prohibitions, enforced with physical punishment or threat of it, which could then have been resisted outright with heroic and self-confirming bloodymindedness. Instead they were solemn pleas, appeals to 'our own' consciences, displays of wounded or affronted love. When my brother and I (intellectually precocious) first defied our father by refusing to go to church at the age of ten or so on atheist grounds, he said with a heavy, tragic face, 'I'm not angry; I'm just disappointed.' I was standing near our playroom window and I remember how the granite windowsill outside grew greyer, the lime tree branches drooped lower. How could we disappoint our father, who loved us so dearly? Presently his own Christian belief failed, although he had been an elder of the Kirk, and the religious issue lost its sting. But the important matters lurked in the future. Would I grow up to be independently and happily sexual? Would I let my agility and daring, my tree-climbing and adoration of wild uplands, carry me up onto the rock faces? Or would the fearfulness I had inherited from my parents compound inside me with the fears they now expressed on my behalf and hold me back and down?

Kafka has the wisdom of the matter, in 'Letter to my Father', when he writes that they were both 'entirely blameless' in what passed (and failed to pass) between them:

I'm not going to say, of course, that I have become what I am only as a result of your influence. That would be very much exaggerated (and I am indeed inclined to this exaggeration). It is indeed quite possible that even if I had grown up entirely free from your influence ... I should probably have still become a weakly, timid, hesitant, restless person ...

Courage, resolution, confidence, delight in this and that, did not endure to the end when you were against whatever it was or even if your opposition was merely to be assumed ...

'Do whatever you like. So far as I'm concerned you have a free hand. You're of age, I've no advice to give you,' and all this with that frightful hoarse undertone of anger ...

I was too docile, I became completely dumb, cringed away from you, hid from you, and only dared to stir when I was so far from you that your power could no longer reach me, at any rate directly ...

[Mother] loved you too much and was too devoted and loyal to you to have been able to constitute an independent spiritual force, in the long run, in the child's struggle.

– *Wedding Preparations in the Country*, 1954, pp. 159–83

I can only wince with admiration at the unsparing lucidity with which this defines my own case. All it lacks is a more modern, genetically-based definition of how the family binds are double: parents frightened of physical danger or sex or nakedness or illness tend to produce offspring whose hereditary excess of frailty or qualm is then reinstilled by the parents' worrying on their behalf ('for their sake').

There is no way out of these twisted bonds except by clarity, of both will and mind. I as a parent must be clear with myself which of my fears are bogeys – projections of my own phobias, not accurate images of dangers in the real world. If I am afraid of heights, and take my children to some beauty spot, Pavey Ark in the Lakes or Malham Cove in the Yorkshire Dales, and spend the afternoon hissing at them, '*Don't* go near that *edge!*', then I am protecting them against a possible fall at the cost of stopping them from using their own perception of space and drop in order to choose their own footholds rationally. Animals do not readily plunge to their deaths. It is true that one-eighth of gibbons in the wild have healed fractures of a limb but they are at risk all the time as they move through the trees. Sheep fall from the crags but they are driven onto irreversibly narrow ledges by over-grazing on scanty hill pastures and further disadvantaged by being bred for wool, which makes them top-heavy and upsets their natural goatlike agility. My own dog, a yellow Labrador, has come to the crags with me hundreds of times and I have never held him back or shouted at him to 'save' him from a drop, not even when he trotted to the very end of the ledge below the climb called Sundance Wall, three hundred feet up the Cove at Malham. At the tapered end he looked down and then backed eight or nine paces until he was able to turn in his own length (to the horror of my companion, who has no pet) and trotted surefootedly along to safety. I have also never held back or shouted deterrently at my children. We left them to see the manifest dangers for themselves. Even when they played cricket hour after hour in a lane sloping down to a main road, I never cautioned them against rushing after the ball when it bounced out into the traffic. And every time they chased it, they paused at the kerb and looked before running out to retrieve it. They were impulsive enough – cannoning into stone dykes when they went downhill too fast on new bikes, injuring knees in headlong rugby tackles. But they were allowed to build up their own working sense of what was too broad a gap to jump, too dark a pool to wade, too sheer a face to climb.

Whenever parents say to their offspring, 'Be careful,' instead of leaving them to discover for themselves that a drop or a depth is dangerous and must be explored with care, they cut at the offspring's sense of balance, their fine control of muscle and digit, their self-reliance, their ability to estimate risk. It is analogous to amputation, or leucotomy. The psychological tendons, the driving-belts between mind and limb, are threatened with severance. You start to look elsewhere rather than into yourself for the faculties that will enable you to survive.

In my own case I was so unnerved by my father's forebodings – or to put it less partially, was unduly frail in myself and therefore shrank from the stress of facing up to his disapprovals – that I went into the mountains far less than I might have done. When I did I was so tense, so ill-at-ease that sometimes my stomach would accept no food all day and I finished up retching with emptiness. And even if I had forced the issue and gone out climbing as much as my contemporaries, would I have been able to find in myself the well-tempered mix of flair and will that climbing calls upon? From seeing my sons at the very thresholds of their climbing lives I would say that to embark on unknown, steep rock demands a certain blithe dash, an unimpaired animal assumption that the thing can be done and you are up to it. I never had that. The baby-reins of upbringing had grown into my tendons, stiffening and holding back – not entirely, or I could not have set off onto the steeps again at the age of forty-one; but I can't climb with a mental poise equal to my muscular capacities. On the hardest rock I can climb physically I need a leader. Hundreds of hours of the keenest and most fundamental comradeship have come of this, and at least one epiphany of tragicomic realization. This occurred on one of Cumbria's most famous climbs, Kipling Groove on Gimmer Crag. The western shoulder of the mountain, visible from our garden thirty miles away as a steeply angled edge, juts towards the big boys across the way, Bow Fell with Sca Fell behind it, as though to say, 'You're bigger than me but I'm as hard as you.' A climber from Bradford called Arthur Dolphin, in the spring of 1948, managed to climb a line here which for years had been focusing the attention of the best local climbers. He called it Kipling Groove because it was 'ruddy 'ard'. Ever since it has been a burning point on the horizon, making us try it, exacting our best efforts.

We first went for it, Pete and I, on a brilliant, breezy June day in 1975. I had climbed nothing of that grade before (Hard Very Severe). Pete's eagerness used to set him off up coveted routes even when other climbers were already on them. This time we were just behind a rope of three men in their early thirties, all of them doctors who, we gathered from their echoing conversations, had had some years' lay-off to graduate, start work, get married, and the like. They were 'rusty', they kept telling each other, and as they clambered rustily upwards Pete had to pause in mid-pitch and wait until the chimney stance (before the severest difficulties) cleared of at least some of the doctors and made room for him. Sixty feet away, in a shirt and squashy tennis pumps, I shivered in the whipping wind, then nodded off to sleep – an escape from fear? After an hour's doldrum Pete went up to the stance, I joined him there, and he climbed out onto the burnished, airy front of Gimmer in his boyishly speedy style. The crux was up there, out in space. On the third ascent, in 1951, Joe Brown had hammered in a piton for protection because the run-out was so long and exposed. The Lancashire climber Mick Burke (later killed on Everest) had made eight attempts before he got past that point. I was well deterred already. When distant shouts signalled to me to move, I climbed up and outwards from the narrowing cleft above the stance feeling as though I was stepping onto an invisible ladder in the midst of the blue air itself. I made three efforts at a high step onto a frighteningly small notch on the arête before shouting up to Pete, 'I've done the crux!'

Shout from above: 'That wasn't the crux.'

With energy fading (more mentally than physically) I stretched way past the rusting stub of Brown's peg – what in hell's the handhold? That smooth-lipped incut far away (a few feet away) to the right? Can't reach that – try and get the palms of my hands on the shelf just above me and mantel upwards – scrabble and press – stretch upwards like a telescope – too far, it's too far – the muscles round my nose squirm with the last spasms of exertion, my feet skid backwards off their little edge, I'm off on a pendulum-swing that faces me outwards – Wrynose Fell, Pike of Blisco, Crinkle Crags, Bow Fell swim past in a slow-motion arc – crunch as my right hip hits rock and the arc reverses itself, majestic, as exhilarating as flying, the best way to see the Lake District...

Pete held me manfully (aged fifteen), I recovered grip on the rock and finished the climb, but I hadn't really climbed it because I had swung Tarzan-style past the main difficulty. Five years later, when Neil was fifteen and felt ready to lead it, I was of course minutely aware of what to do. Too aware. A kind of absurd negative charge, a barrier of fear, had gathered round the pole of that crux and it scattered my mental clarity. When I tried the mantelshelf move again and again found it too hard to get my weight above my hands, instead of traversing a few yards rightwards with my hands first on the shelf and then on the incut I made another scrabbling effort to palm myself upwards, fell off, and dangled about ... This time I collected myself a little more coolly and when the pendule had stopped I duly made the hand-traverse rightwards, with a little help from the rope held taut above me. But Neil knew and I knew that Kipling had defeated me again. As I pulled up the last few feet towards him, he gave me a pawky smile and uttered the most final sentence ever addressed to me: 'Tough luck, Dad – you've run out of sons.'

Brough Scott

My Aintree Nightmare

24 March 1985

Every life has a waking dream that turns into nightmare. Mine happened exactly twenty years ago next Saturday. It was called the Grand National.

Distance is supposed to lend enchantment. Aintree memories are meant to be of heroic days and joshing nights, and when tackled about any pre-race nerves our hero gives a B-movie laugh and says: 'Well there were a few butterflies in the changing-room, but once we were out for the race everything was great.' Not here it wasn't.

Mind you, everybody was very nice to the still pretty innocent Mr B. Scott – the other jockeys, the tough but kindly 'Frenchy' Nicholson as he legged me up, stable lad Barry Davies as he led us out on to the track and even big, thundering Time as he plodded beneath me during the parade.

But the problems now were quite appallingly obvious. All those runners (there were no fewer than fifty-six that year) over those all-too-famous Grand National fences (the obligatory on-foot inspection had been no comfort); and on this horse. Time was a huge, tough old sod, and we'd been through a fairly encouraging run at Cheltenham a fortnight earlier. But the year before, when National favourite, he had kept landing too heavily in the drops, and the idea today was to go more gently, to let him 'fiddle' round, to (oh happy phrase!) 'keep out of trouble'.

Well, Julius Caesar might have liked having fat men around him for reassurance, but the trick at the start of the National is to get beside someone lean and hungry who looks as if they know what they are doing. But just as we got jammed in next to crack jockeys Bill Rees and David Nicholson, old Time contrarily backed out of line, the space was taken and when we finally got back in it was between two nervous-looking amateurs, one of whom, Chris Collins, had wasted so deathly white that I remember giving him last words of unneeded support. He eventually finished third, I ended up in Walton hospital.

Maybe I had read too much Siegfried Sassoon about war in the trenches, but the parallel here had just about everything save the Flanders mud. The long, stamping, cursing line was the 'stand to'. The starter's shout and the tapes flying up was 'over the top'. The grit of the Melling Road was 'through the wire into no man's land'. The long row of fences up ahead were the enemy lines.

And we were straightaway in trouble. Off his legs and at the back of the field, Time landed deep in the drop at the first, and all the way down to Becher's it was a horrible, scrambling struggle to stay in one piece.

We could never get any rhythm, find any passage. There were loose horses everywhere, and even the mounted cavalry were all over the place. A grey horse kept coming leftwards into me. At the fifth fence I'd seemed to have escaped him. The next was Becher's; you could hear the commentary and see the crowds on the far side. Two strides off it, the grey horse came slap across us. For a dreadful doomed moment we blundered completely blind into the fence of fences.

Even in hell you can have moments of love. I loved Time then. For somehow he got over Becher's, survived the steep, steep landing, bulldozed past two fallers and suddenly the first smoke of horror had cleared. Chesterton's donkey might have had his hour 'one far fierce hour and sweet'. Time and I only had about four minutes. But as the fences began to flick by below us, and we began actually to make contact with this race, this Grand National, we had our moment, everything except the palms beneath our feet.

But nightmare, albeit of a simpler kind, was waiting. Going out for the second circuit, Time was steaming along so strongly that the thirty lengths we were off the leaders seemed no great gap. Confidence was growing, but carelessness was close. At the big ditch, I sat still, indecisive. Time galloped slap into it, somersaulted high and heavy, and then I was in the ambulance with the Duke of Albuquerque.

The pay-off put things into perspective. The ambulance went from fence to fence, and stretcher parties brought across the wounded. Eventually we headed back to the racecourse doctor, on to hospital and presumably to anxious orderlies all ready to greet and tend their heroes.

Well, poor Jimmy Morrissey was rushed in to have his smashed head treated. The old duke was put behind a curtain, where he mystified the assembled medics by moaning, '*Mon genou, mon genou.*' But the other two of us, still in breeches, boots and grass-stained jockey sweaters, just sat on the bench next to the granny who had tripped over on the pavement, and the little boy who had cut his hand on a milk bottle.

Eventually a polite little doctor called us forward. The broken collarbone was not difficult to diagnose, but the cause of the accident appeared to be beyond him. 'What have you been doing?' he asked. 'At what races? How long ago?' Maybe it was a dream after all.

Simon Armitage

Great Sporting Moments: The Treble

The rich! I love them. Trust them to suppose
the gift of tennis is deep in their bones.

Those chaps from the coast with all their own gear
from electric eyes to the umpire's chair,

like him whose arse I whipped with five choice strokes
perfected on West Yorkshire's threadbare courts:

a big first serve that strained his alloy frame,
a straight return that went back like a train,

a lob that left him gawping like a fish,
a backhand pass that kicked and drew a wisp

of chalk, a smash like a rubber bullet
and a bruise to go with it. Three straight sets.

Smarting in the locker rooms he offered
double or quits; he was a born golfer

and round the links he'd wipe the floor with me.
I played the ignoramus to a tee:

the pleb in the gag who asked the viscount
what those eggcup-like things were all about –

'They're to rest my balls on when I'm driving.'
'Blimey, guv, Rolls-Royce think of everything' –

but at the fifth when I hadn't faltered
he lost his rag and threw down the gauntlet;

we'd settle this like men: with the gloves on.
I said no, no, no, no, no, no, no. OK, come on then.

Andy Martin

Walking on Water

Betty had given away the Corona. Ted had burned the Excalibur. Bullshit Alan's offer had blown away like smoke. My Willis Brothers Phazer had still not materialized. I was boardless and knew in my heart that I could not boast I had got the North Shore wired. My time was running out and I feared I would be going home defeated. Then another board entered my life.

Louis had been married to Debbie Beecham at some stage in the past. Now they were good friends. He had come over to visit her from California and was crammed into Yvon's room too. About the first thing he said to me was: "Andy, you don't happen to have any socks, do you?"

It was like the time a friend at school with a reputation as a snappy dresser approached me and asked if he could borrow my suit. I had a standard grey two-piece, of the kind that mothers buy their sons. I was flattered that this man of fashion should turn to me. It wasn't till later that I learned he was going to a funeral and didn't have anything dull and sober enough to wear.

I loaned Louis a pair of long Argyle socks, purple with green and yellow flashes from Blazers in Cambridge. He had never seen anything like them before. My footgear was a constant source of wonderment to the shoeless, sockless inhabitants of the North Shore. Louis was so impressed with the socks that he asked to borrow them again. "They caused a sensation at the party," he said.

I was glad to help out: I had a plentiful supply of socks. But there was something faintly depressing about being known as the Man with the Socks. If only someone had asked to borrow my 100 percent Mambos or the shirt with toucans and cockatoos I had picked up at Wild Clothing.

Louis had a beautiful board. It was a remake of a classic 60s malibu: nine feet long, broad in the hip, but light, with a rounded nose and three fins, in deep blue with orange stripes and a crimson rim. It bore the signature of Quigly, a West Coast shaper who had been prominent in the revival of the longboard in the eighties.

I lusted after that Quigly. Thus it was that when Louis wondered if there was anything he could do for me in return for the socks, I mentioned I was currently without a board.

"You want to borrow my Quigly?" he said. It was more a plea than a question. Unscrambled, his message read: "Please don't take my Quigly! It's the love of my life."

I was implacable. "If you can spare it for a few hours," I said.

"Have you surfed much on the North Shore?" he inquired.

"Sure," I said, truthfully. "Jocko's, Freddie's, Haleiwa, Lani's, Backyards. All over." I passed over the details of what had taken place.

"Oh well, I guess that's all right, then." He sounded reassured.

The following morning I steered the Quigly into the car like a kidnap victim and headed for Haleiwa. Bodo and Damon were waiting for me.

"That's a fine board you have there," said Bodo.

"A Quigly," I boasted.

"Wow!" gasped Damon. "They're like gold dust in California."

I had a good feeling about that board. It felt right as I gave it a solid basting of wax and uncurled the leash, and it felt right as I paddled it out: well balanced, smooth through the water, responsive. Bodo called it a "modern tanker": it was a subtle compromise between a gondola and a toothpick, combining the virtues of robustness and sensitivity, stability and speed.

I followed Bodo and Damon out through the channel. The Quigly sliced through the oncoming waves like a knife through butter, so by the time we hit the line-up I was still in good shape. There was a right-hander and further over towards the harbour a left. We opted for the left, which was less crowded. Bodo and Damon drove straight at the peak. But I didn't want to push my luck and followed my usual cautious procedure of testing out the unoccupied shoulder.

I lined myself up with an easygoing four- to five-footer as it ambled into shore, despised by the hunters further out who were stalking bigger game. I got into gear and rammed the Quigly ahead of the swell. Then I felt the wave hook itself under the rear and start to jack it up. I cranked out another couple of strokes and leapt to my feet.

It was almost too easy. It was like riding a bicycle successfully for the first time: you can't understand why you had so much difficulty before, just as before it was impossible to understand how the deed could ever be done. My feet were planted in the textbook position: my left foot halfway up the board, sideways on but angled towards the nose, my right foot slanted across the board at the tail. Surprised to find myself still upright I flung out my arms and crouched, modeling myself on the famous picture of Eddie Aikau. The Quigly planed down the face and, almost without my exerting any effort, began to curve into a leisurely bottom turn. Behind me and to the right, the wave was bursting apart; over my left shoulder was an unbroken section. I leaned over, slid my weight onto my right foot, and the Quigly carved a voluptuous line along the crystal-blue wall, like Michelangelo shaping his Madonna. I had no idea how long I'd been standing up. Chronometrically, it would be insignificant; but I have a mental clock permanently arrested with its hands on that morning and that wave. "No one times how long the ride is," Mark Foo had said to me. "It's so intense, the duration doesn't matter. A second is a long time on the wave."

The breaking wave was like Jean Cocteau's *Le Sang d'un poète,* which opens on a shot of a factory chimney stack as it starts to collapse and finishes as it hits the ground: everything happens in that split-second of demolition. There is a story by Jorge Luis Borges, "The Secret Miracle," which is a mirror-image of that film. Jaromir Hladik is about to be executed by firing squad, and the sergeant has already delivered the order to fire, when God brings the physical universe to a halt, granting Hladik a reprieve of a year in order to finish, in his head, a poetic drama entitled *The Vindication of Eternity.* The last line is completed punctually, the year expires, a raindrop that has remained immobile on Hladik's face for twelve months slides down his cheek, the rifles fire their volley and he slumps dead on the ground at the appointed hour. The wave, similarly, was in a time-zone all of its own: it was set to the time that ticked by in your brain and pulsed through your body, to Bergson's *duration,* not exterior, clock-measured time.

I was whooping with incoherent joy as I raced back to the line-up. Liese was right, I thought: you just have to wait: everything furthers. I knew I would remember this day forever. I latched on to another wave and rode it till it curled up and died. Each wave was already a trophy in my memory. The Quigly was a Venus de Milo among boards: I was head over heels in love with it. How much more pleasure was it possible to experience?

Bodo caught me paddling back out again, looking for my third ride. One more practice run, I reckoned, and I would be ready to join the big boys on the higher hurdles of the main peak.

"Come on over here," he yelled. "I'll find you a wave."

It was a siren voice I couldn't resist: it was the Lieutenant of Lifeguards drumming up business.

"Now listen," said Bodo, "there's just one thing you've got to know about this left-hander. And once you know it, it's simple. You see that booee out there?" I had heard "buoy" pronounced "booee" enough times to know what to look for. I spotted the grey truncated bell-tower bobbing about a quarter of a mile away.

"When you see that booee disappear, you know a set is coming. It gives about twenty seconds' warning. Just keep your eye on that booee and you'll be all right."

I staked out a zone for myself. Bodo was about ten yards away on my inside. I sat up on my Quigly and gazed out to sea. It looked tranquil, dormant, seamless, so blue it was almost colorless, indistinguishable from the azure above. Surfing is like an empty sky intermittently streaked with lightning: it's watching and waiting shot through with flashes of ecstasy and terror. The sea was a landscape without landmarks, an inscrutable mask. It was strange to think there was nothing between me and Alaska. On my right, America; on my left, Asia. Straight ahead, the North Pole. I felt as if I was balanced on the fulcrum of the world, an axis around which North and South, East and West endlessly swung.

I don't know how long it took me to recall that to see nothing was to know everything, that absolute zero of perception was a red flag of danger. But I know that I reacted late. The buoy had vanished, buried beneath an oncoming set. I wondered if I could distantly hear the tolling of a bell. I span the Quigly round, proned myself against it, and struck out madly.

Out of the corner of my eye I glimpsed Bodo powering forwards. But I couldn't rely on his wisdom to guide me: it doesn't matter who you go out with, you still have to make it back on your own. When you surf the North Shore, you surf alone.

I felt the sea boil up behind me and prepared to leap to my feet. I asked Bodo afterwards if he'd seen what happened. He said, "You just didn't stand up, Andy." The lip tipped me through ninety degrees till I was perpendicular to the surface, like a spent rocket falling to earth, plunging down gravitic currents. Instead of swinging my feet under me, I was diving forwards, down with the exploding wave, down with the white curtain, down with my board, down until I kissed the Quigly and we tumbled around underwater, entwined in a hectic embrace.

KIDS

Seamus Heaney

Markings

I

We marked the pitch: four jackets for four goalposts,
That was all. The corners and the squares
Were there like longitude and latitude
Under the bumpy thistly ground, to be
Agreed about or disagreed about
When the time came. And then we picked the teams
And crossed the line our called names drew between us.

Youngsters shouting their heads off in a field
As the light died and they kept on playing
Because by then they were playing in their heads
And the actual kicked ball came to them
Like a dream heaviness, and their own hard
Breathing in the dark and skids on grass
Sounded like effort in another world . . .
It was quick and constant, a game that never need
Be played out. Some limit had been passed,
There was fleetness, furtherance, untiredness
In time that was extra, unforeseen and free.

II

You also loved lines pegged out in the garden,
The spade nicking the first straight edge along
The tight white string. Or string stretched perfectly
To mark the outline of a house foundation,
Pale timber battens set at right angles
For every corner, each freshly sawn new board
Spick and span in the oddly passive grass.
Or the imaginary line straight down
A field of grazing, to be ploughed open
From the rod stuck in one headrig to the rod
Stuck in the other.

III

All these things entered you
As if they were both the door and what came through it.
They marked the spot, marked time and held it open.
A mower parted the bronze sea of corn.
A windlass hauled the centre out of water.
Two men with a cross-cut kept it swimming
Into a felled beech backwards and forwards
So that they seemed to row the steady earth.

Geoffrey Willans and Ronald Searle

Criket

There is only one thing in criket and that is the STRATE BAT. Keep yore bat strate boy and all will be all right in life as in criket. So headmasters sa, but when my bat is strate i still get bowled is that an omen chiz. Aktually i usually prefer to hav a slosh: i get bowled just the same but it is more satisfactory.

For the reason that it is extremely dificult to hit the ball with a STRATE BAT or not criket matches are a bit of a strane. When you are a new bug or a junior in the 3rd game it is all right becos then you can sit around the boundary and keep the score in a notebook. When you get tired with that which is about 3 minits you can begin to tuough up your frendes and neighbours who look so sweet and angelic in their clean white criket shirts hem-hem. This is super. You look up long enuff to sa Good shot, grabber or Couldn't hit a squashed tomato and then back to the fray.

But it is a funy thing when you grow biger you always get into a criket team you canot avoid it chiz. Tremble tremble you arive and see the pitch which is 2388 miles approx from the pavilion. Captain win toss and choose to bat chiz chiz chiz chiz. Moan drone tremble tremble you sit with white face and with everybode's knees knoking together it sound like a coconut shy. Wot is the pleasure of it eh i would like to kno. Give me a thumbscrew or slo fire every time.

When your turn come the folowing things can hapen
A) You loose your bat.
B) You fante dead away.
C) Your trousis fall down.
D) You trip over your shoe laces.

Captain then come up to you and sa BLOCK EVERYTHING molesworth and do not slosh we need 6 to win. When he sa this all the things above hapen all at once. They revive you with a buket of water and drive you out to the wicket. This is not as you guessed 2388 miles away it is 6000 now and they hav men with gats covering all the exits so you canot run away.

AT THE WICKET

Of course it is the fast blower you hav to face he is wating there at the other end of the pitch looking very ferce. Umpire is v. kind he can aford to be he hav not got to bat. He sa

We are very pleesed to see you do make yourself at home. Of course you would like guard what guard would you like us to give you?

Squeak.

Come agane?

Squeak squeak.

i will give you centre hold your bat up strate to you a trifle now away agane. That is centre. Your position is 120 miles NNE of beachy head you may come in and land. There are 5 balls to come. At the 5th pip it will be 4. 2 precisely. Able Baker Out.

PLAY!

Fast blower retreat with the ball mutering and cursing. He stamp on the grass with his grate hary feet he beat his chest and give grate cry. Then with a trumpet of rage he charge towards you. Quake quake ground tremble birdseed fly in all directions if only you can run away but it is not done. Grit teeth close eyes. Ball hit your pads and everyone go mad.

OWSATSIR OW WASIT EHOUT!

Umpire look for a long time he is bent double at last he lift one finger.

He is a difrent man now from the kindly old gentleman who made you feel at home. His voice is harsh.

Out. No arguments. Get cracking. Take that xpresion off your face. On course at 20000 feet return to base. Out.

Distance back to pavilion is now 120000 miles and all the juniors sa ya boo sucks couldn't hit a squashed tomato. It is no use saing you were not out by a mile team give you the treatment behind the pav just the same. There is only one consolation you can give it up when you grow up. Then you rustle the paper and sa Wot a shocking show by m.c.c. most deplorable a lot of rabits ect. ect. Well, you kno how they go on. Enuff.

Donna Tartt

Basketball Season

The year I was a freshman cheerleader, I was reading *1984*. I was fourteen years old then and failing algebra and the fact that I was failing it worried me as I would worry now if the Mafia was after me, or if I had shot somebody and the police were coming to get me. But I did not have an awful lot of time to brood about this. It was basketball season then, and there was a game nearly every night. In Mississippi the schools are far apart, and sometimes we would have to drive two hundred miles to get to Panola Academy, Sharkey-Issaquena, funny how those old names come back to me; we'd leave sometimes before school was out, not get home till twelve or one in the morning. I was not an energetic teenager and this was hard on me. Too much exposure to the high-decibel world of teen sports—shrieking buzzers; roaring stomping mobs; thunderous feet of players charging up the court— kept me in a kind of perpetual stunned condition; the tin-roof echo of rural gymnasiums rang through all my silences, and frequently at night I woke in a panic, because I thought a player was crashing through my bedroom window or a basketball was flying at me and about to knock my teeth out.

I read *1984* in the back seats of Cadillacs, Buicks, Lincoln Town Cars, riding through the flat wintry Delta with my saddle oxfords off and my schoolbooks piled beneath my feet. Our fathers—professional men, mostly, lawyers and optometrists, prosperous local plumbers— took turns driving us back and forth from the games; the other cheerleaders griped about this but though I griped along with them, I was secretly appalled at the rowdy team bus, full of boys who shouted things when you walked by their table in the cafeteria and always wanted to copy your homework. The cars, on the other hand, were wide, spacious, quiet. Somebody's mother would usually have made cookies; there were always potato chips and old issues of *Seventeen*. The girls punched listlessly at the radio; applied Bonne Bell lip gloss; did their homework or their hair. Sometimes a paperback book would make the rounds. I remember reading one book about a girl whose orphaned cousin came to live with her, gradually usurping the girl's own position in the household and becoming homecoming queen and family favorite. ("'Why can't *you* be more like Stephanie?' yelled Mom, exasperated.") It turned out that Stephanie was not the girl's real cousin at all, but a witch: a total surprise to the nincompoop parents, who had not noticed such key signs as Stephanie failing to show up in photographs, or the family dog ("Lady") and the girl's horse ("Wildfire") going crazy every time Stephanie came within fifty feet.

Now that I think about it, I believe I read *Animal Farm* before *1984*. I read it in the car, too, riding through monotonous cottonfields in the weak winter afternoon, on the way to a tournament at Yalobusha Academy. It upset me a little, especially the end, but the statement "All Animals are Equal, but Some Animals are more Equal than Others" echoed sentiments which I recognized as prevalent in the upper echelons of the cheerleading squad. Our captain was a mean senior girl named Cindy Clark. She talked a lot about spirit and pep, and how important it was we work as a team, but she and her cronies ostracized the younger girls and were horrible to us off the court. Cindy was approximately my height and was forced to be my partner in some of the cheers, a circumstance which displeased her as much as it did myself. I remember a song that was popular around that time—it had lyrics that went:

> We are family
> I've got all my sisters with me

This had for some reason been incorporated into one of the chants and Cindy and I were frequently forced to sing it together: arms around each other, leaning on each other like drunks, beaming with joy and behaving in every way like the sisters which we, in fact, were most certainly not.

Though there was a sharp distinction between the older girls and the younger ones, we were also divided, throughout our ranks and regardless of age, into two distinct categories: those of snob and slut. The snobs had flat chests, pretty clothes, and were skittish and shrill. Though they were always sugar-sweet to one's face, in reality they were a nasty, back-biting lot, always doing things like stealing each other's boyfriends and trying to rig the elections for the Beauty Revue. The sluts were from poorer families, and much better liked in general. They drank beer, made out with boys in the hallways, and had horrible black hickeys all over their necks. Our squad was divided pretty much half and half. Physically and economically, I fell into the category of snob, but I did poorly in school and was not gung-ho or clubbish enough to fit in very well with the rest of them. (To be a proper snob, one had always to be making floats for some damn parade or other, or organizing pot-luck dinners for the Booster Club.) The sluts, I thought, took a more sensible view of such foolishness; they smoked and drank; I found them, as a rule, much nicer. Being big girls generally, they were the backbones of the stances, the foundations from which the pyramids rose and, occasionally, fell; I, being the smallest on the squad, had to work with them rather closely, in special sessions after the regular cheerleading practices, since they were the ones who lifted me into the air, who spotted me in gymnastics, upon whose shoulders I had to stand to form the obligatory pyramid. They all had pet names for me, and—though vigorously heterosexual—babied me in what I am sure none of them realized was a faintly lecherous way: tickles and pinches, slaps on the rump, pulling me into their laps in crowded cars and crooning stupid songs from the radio into my ear. Most of this went on in the afterschool practices. At the games they completely ignored me, as every fiber of their attention was devoted to flirting with—and contriving to make out with—various boys. As I was both too young to be much interested in boys, and lacking in the fullness of bosom and broadness of beam which would have made them much interested in me, I was excluded from this activity. But still they felt sorry for me, and gave me tips on how to make myself attractive (pierced ears, longer hair, tissue paper in the bra)—and, when we were loitering around after practices, often regaled me with worldly tales of various sexual, obstetric, and gynecological horrors, some of which still make my eyes pop to think about.

The gymnasiums were high-ceilinged, barnlike, drafty, usually in the middle of some desolate field. We were always freezing in our skimpy plaid skirts, our legs all goose pimples as we clapped and stamped on the yellowed wooden floor. (Our legs, being so much exposed, were frequently chapped from cold, yet we were forbidden to put lotion on them, Cindy and the older girls having derived a pathological horror of "grease" from—as best as I could figure—the Clearasil ads in *Tiger Beat* and *Seventeen*—this despite the fact that grease was the primary element of all our diets.) Referee's whistle, sneakers squealing on the varnish. "Knees together," Cindy would hiss down the line, or "Spit out that gum," before she hollered "Ready!" and we clapped our hands down to our sides in unison and yelled the response: "O-Kay!" At halftime there were the detested stances, out in the middle of the court,

which involved perilous leaps, and complex timing, and—more likely
than not—tears and remonstrations in the changing rooms. These were
a source of unremitting dread, and as soon as they were over and the
buzzer went off for third quarter the younger girls rushed in a greedy
flock to the snack bar for Cokes and French fries, Hershey bars,
scattering to devour them in privacy while Cindy and her crew slunk
out to the parking lot to rendezvous with their boyfriends. We were all
of us, all the time, constantly sick—coughing, blowing our noses, faces
flushed with fever—a combination of cold, bad food, cramped conditions, and yelling ourselves hoarse every night. Hoarseness was, in
fact, a matter of pride: we were accused of shirking if our voices
weren't cracked by the end of the evening, the state to which we
aspired being a rasping, laryngitic croak. I remember the only time the
basketball coach—a gigantic, stone-faced, terrifying man who was also
the principal of the school and who, to my way of thinking, held
powers virtually of life or death (there were stories of his punching
kids out, beating them till they had bruises, stories which perhaps were
not apocryphal in a private school like my own, which prided itself on
what it called "old-fashioned discipline" and where corporal punishment was a matter of routine); the only time this coach ever spoke to
me was to compliment me on my burnt-out voice, which he overheard
in the hall the morning after a game. "Good job," he said. My
companions and I were struck speechless with terror. After he was
gone they stared at me with awestruck apprehension and then, one by
one, drifted gently away, not wishing to be seen in the company of
anyone who had attracted the attention—even momentarily—of this
dangerous lunatic.

There were pep squads, of a sort, in George Orwell's Oceania. I read
about them with interest. Banners, processions, slogans, games, were
as popular there as they were at Kirk Academy. Realizing that there
were certain correspondences between this totalitarian nightmare and
my own high school gave me at first a feeling of smug superiority, but
after a time I began to have an acute sense of the meaninglessness of
my words and gestures. Did I really care if we won or lost? No matter
how enthusiastically I jumped and shouted, the answer to this was
unquestionably no. This epiphany both confused and depressed me.
And yet I continued—outwardly at least—to display as much pep as
ever. "I always look cheerful and I never shirk anything," says Winston
Smith's girlfriend, Julia. "Always yell with the crowd, that's what I say.
It's the only way to be safe." Our rival team was called the Patriots. I

remember one rally, the night before a big game, when a dummy Patriot was hanged from the gymnasium rafters, then taken outside and burned amid the frenzied screams and stomps of the mob. I yelled as loud as anybody even though I was suffused by an airy, perilous sense of unreality, a conviction that—despite the apparently desperate nature of this occasion—that none of it meant anything at all. In my diary that night—a document which was as secretive and, to my mind at least, as subversive as Winston's own—I noted tersely: "Hell's own Pep Rally. Freshmen won the spirit stick. Rah, rah."

It was on the rides home—especially on the nights we'd won—that the inequity of not being allowed on the team bus was most keenly felt by the cheerleaders. Moodily, they stared out the windows, dreaming of back seats, and letter jackets, and smooching with their repulsive boyfriends. The cars smelled like talcum powder and Tickle deodorant and—if we were with one of the nicer dads, who had allowed us to stop at a drive-in—cheeseburgers and French fries. It was too dark to read. Everyone was tired, but for some reason we were all too paranoid to go to sleep in front of each other; afraid we might drool, perhaps, or inadvertently scratch an armpit.

Whispers, giggles, sighs. We rode four to a car and all four of us would be crammed in the back seat; bare arms touching, goosebumped knees pressed together, our silences punctuated by long ardent slurps of Tab. The console lights of the Cadillac dashboards were phosphorescent, eerie. The radio was mostly static that time of night but sometimes you could get a late-night station coming out of Greenwood or Memphis; slow songs, that's what everyone wanted, sloppy stuff by Olivia Newton-John or Dan Fogelberg. (The cheerleaders had a virtual cult of Olivia Newton-John; they tried to do their hair like her, emulate her in every possible way, and were fond of speculating what Olivia would or would not do in certain situations. She was like the ninth, ghost member of the squad. I was secretly gratified when she plummeted—with alarming swiftness—from favor because someone heard a rumor that she was gay.)

Olivia or not, the favorite song that winter hands down was "You Light Up My Life" by Debby Boone. It must have been number one for months; at least, it seemed to come on the radio just about every other song, which was fine with everybody. When it came on the girls would all start singing it quietly to themselves, staring out the window, each in their own little world; touching the fogged window-glass gently with their fingertips and each thinking no one could hear them, but all their

voices combined in a kind of low, humming harmony that blended
with the radio:

> So many nights
> I sit by my window
> Waiting for someone
> To sing me his song . . .

Full moon; hard frost on the stubbled cottonfields. They opened up
on either side of the car in long, gray spokes, like a fan.

Robert Lipsyte

Is Connors a Killer?

Sixteen years ago, in a motel room in Orlando, I tried to watch a telecast of George Foreman fighting five opponents in a row, but I never got to see more than a minute at a time because Angelo Dundee, the great boxing trainer, kept switching the channel. He wanted to watch Jimmy Connors fight John Newcombe.

"Connors is a killer," said Angelo. "He's got timing, guts, he knows just when to come in and dig. Would've made a helluva fighter."

Connors the Killer has been both the beacon and the aberration of the Great Yuppie Carnival at Flushing Meadows these past two weeks. Contemporary tennis players have been built out of junk bonds and downtown art, hyped, inflated, driven, sponsored, and most of them seem whiney (see Aaron Krickstein's blood blister) or silly (Monica Seles complaining about her seventeen-year-old life's "distractions") or a bit grand (the Croatian patriot Goran Ivanisevic declaring, "My racquet is my gun") compared with someone as elemental as Jimmy Connors. His age is only relevant because so many in the crowd have seen him play for longer than Aaron or Monica or Goran have lived; it is not his longevity but his neediness that sucks the gallery dry, his willingness to give up body and soul for their attention and love. Jimmy is a child; not an adolescent like most athletes, but a child. Say, two years old, when everything is gorgeously, hilariously, maddeningly naked.

But after Connors, the emotional pickings have been slim. John McEnroe is not emotional, he is tortured, and the agony of the artist at work is exciting only when it leaks out on the ceiling of the Sistine Chapel. McEnroe has been fingerpainting on velvet lately. Martina seems gallant enough, but she has become more interesting as a person than as an athlete. Her description of her bisexuality to Barbara Walters on TV recently was one of the most provocatively intelligent I've heard. Martina said, in effect, that she could go to bed with either sex, but preferred to wake up with a woman. She found women more emotionally satisfying as companions. It was all said so matter-of-factly that it raised the level of that particular dialog. Then again, when sports figures get serious—Billy Sunday, Muhammad Ali, Bill Bradley—they can be very direct.

While most athletes, particularly pro team sports athletes, follow fashion, tennis players have always been in the avant-garde of popular culture. Perhaps it is because they began as the intimate servants, like hairdressers, of the rich and tanned. No wonder independents like Jack Kramer and Pancho Gonzalez and Billie Jean King preferred to be paid like grownups even if the life was harder.

"We're on the edge of culture shock," Billie Jean King liked to say in the 70s, even as she was experimenting with bicoastal marriage, bisexual relationships and, in what became the feminist equivalent of invading Grenada, the victory over Bobby Riggs.

It was in tennis that we first met Western Euro-trash, beautiful, delightful, cynical, jaded, and it was in tennis we met the first wave of East Europeans yearning for the freedom to buy condos in Marina del Rey. But the Romanians, the Russians and the Czechoslovaks who came to play tennis rather than play art could not coast on the adoration of claques and collectors. They had to win. Even now, when tennis players are ranked, like golfers and stockbrokers, by money earned, they still have to step into cockpits like the stadium at Flushing Meadows and show us what they've really got.

Like art, tennis has the capacity to stop your heart and leave the indelible memory of a moment in which a human flew. And, like the art media, the tennis media is largely scandalous or sycophantic, shoveling out words that have no meaning and that muddy memories. In tennis, such words as "courage," "tragedy" and "heroism" should never be applied to yuppies trying to stick more billboards on their racquets or shoes or shirts. Somewhere under all that gear may be a human being, but it's hard to tell. The healthiest will never let us find out what really makes them tick, because then we will try to take them apart to see for ourselves.

Yet who can deny the pleasure that these children give us, these pampered, hypochondriacal egomaniacs. No wonder David Dinkins, elected to be Mayor Dad, divided his time among Crown Heights, the Union Square Station and Flushing Meadows. People are killed in New York every day; the playpen is Open but once a year.

And Connors reminds us all how much we have given up by growing up. Lucky Jimmy. If only we could once again stop the party in the living room, make all the grownups applaud our naughty words, dance through the hors d'oeuvres, posture and preen and be a Terrible Two, the only time when a human being will be loved for conquering the world while crying.

WHAT'S IT
WORTH?

Hugh McIlvanney

The Best Years of Our Lives

It is two decades since George Best walked out of football at the highest level. Yet he remains a potent symbol of what we have lost from the fabric of our lives and from the spirit of our national game. Hugh McIlvanney, who witnessed the player's rise to greatness in the 60s, catches up with the errant Irishman and discusses his life, his loves and where he and football went wrong.

George Best had come in along the goal line from the corner-flag in a blur of intricate deception. Having briskly embarrassed three or four challengers, he drove the ball high into the net with a fierce simplicity that made spectators wonder if the acuteness of the angle had been an optical illusion.

'What was the time of that goal?' asked a young reporter in the Manchester United press box. 'Never mind the time, son,' said an older voice beside him. 'Just write down the date.'

The date was in the 60s and by 1974 Best had walked out of first-class football at the age of twenty-seven and headed into another life shaped by a painful and continuing struggle with alcoholism. Yet when I accompanied him to a Tottenham Hotspur–Manchester United match recently, he stirred more excitement in the main lounge at White Hart Lane afterwards than any contemporary player other than Paul Gascoigne could have expected to generate. 'I never do this, but I'll do it with him,' one middle-aged Spurs supporter said as he joined the polite scramble for autographs. 'That,' he told his son, 'is the best player that ever lived.'

The assertion is a shade excessive. Pelé, the Brazilian phenomenon who had a stunning impact on the World Cup Finals of 1958 as a seventeen-year-old and was the orchestrator of the best team I ever saw when his country won the Cup again in 1970, has irresistible claims to being considered the supreme footballer of all time. Diego Maradona would be a popular nomination as the principal challenger and another, very different Argentine of an earlier generation, Alfredo Di Stefano, would have his advocates, as would the elegant, swift and cerebral Dutchman Johan Cruyff. But Best could run Pelé as close as any of them. Where the Brazilian was superior (leaving aside his extraordinary longevity as a player) was in his far broader awareness of the imperatives of team play and in the humility with which he deployed vast abilities, his refusal to do anything complicated where something simple would cause more damage.

Yet even Best's extravagances were a joy, so long as you weren't Denis Law making a killer run, only to find that the ball had not arrived because Georgie had opted to beat the same defender twice. He was most likely to inflict such humiliation on desperadoes who had threatened to break his leg.

With feet as sensitive as a pickpocket's hands, his control of the ball under the most violent pressure was hypnotic. The bewildering repertoire of feints and swerves, sudden stops and demoralizing spurts, exploited a freakish elasticity of limb and torso, tremendous physical strength and resilience for so slight a figure and balance that would have made Isaac Newton decide he might as well have eaten the apple. It was Paddy Crerand (whose service from midfield was so valued that Best says the Glaswegian's was the first name he looked for on the Manchester United team-sheet) who declared that the Irishman gave opponents twisted blood. He was an excellent header of the ball and a courageous, effective challenger when the opposition had it, and he reacted to scoring chances with a deadliness that made goalkeepers dread him.

That was an attribute emphasized by Alex Ferguson, the present United manager, when he talked to me about the stupidity of likening his impressive young winger, Ryan Giggs, to Best. 'He'll never be a Best,' said Ferguson. 'Nobody will. George was unique, the greatest talent our football ever produced – easily! Look at the scoring record: 137 goals in 361 League games, a total of 179 goals for United in 466 matches played. That's phenomenal for a man who did not get the share of gift goals that come to specialist strikers, who nearly always had to beat men to score … Here at Old Trafford they reckon Bestie had double-jointed ankles. Seriously, it was a physical thing, an extreme flexibility there. You remember how he could do those 180-degree turns without going through a half-circle, simply by swivelling on his ankles. As well as devastating defenders, that helped him to avoid injuries, because he was never really stationary for opponents to hurt him. He was always either riding or spinning away from things.'

Best, of course, was always capable of hurting himself, with help from the girls who were constantly willing to accompany him all the way through long boozy evenings and sexually hectic nights. Apart from the lithe grace of his body, his attractiveness had much to do with colouring, with the vivid blue eyes set wide in a dark, mischievous face framed by luxuriant black hair. 'If I had been born ugly,' he once said to me, 'you would never have heard of Pelé.' In fact, he was never remotely as vain as the joke makes him out to be.

The warmth felt towards him by so many old players is not merely a tribute to a man who embodied a beautiful fulfilment of the dreams they all started out with. It is a recognition of the extent to which, for all his pride in his gifts and his certainty that they were unique, he remained essentially unspoilt. My own memories of many hours spent in his company contain nothing but proof of how unaffected he was by finding himself the first British footballer to be treated like a pop star.

One fresh image is of a night when, after a European Cup match at Old Trafford, a bunch of us gathered in the Brown Bull, a pub near the Granada television studios. No one had given much thought to dinner but, by the time the after-hours session was under way, hunger was a problem. At least it was until Best went round taking fish and chips orders from everyone in the bar, then disappeared. He returned half-an-hour later, not merely with all the orders accurately filled but with plates, knives and forks for everybody. The waiter seemed less like a superstar than the appealing boy who had worked small miracles with a tennis ball on the streets of the Cregagh housing estate in East Belfast.

For those who witnessed Best's brief zenith in the 60s, the effect went beyond the realization that we were seeing the world's most popular game played better than all but two or three men in its long history have ever played it. Sport at its finest is often poignant, if only because it is almost a caricature of the ephemerality of human achievements, and Best's performances were doubly affecting for some of us because they coincided with an uneasy suspicion that football was already in the process of separating itself from its roots. It would be dishonest to claim that we foresaw the pace and extent of the separation that was to occur over the ensuing twenty years. How could we? The true working-class foundations of the game were still incarnated and articulated all around us by managers like Bill Shankly, Bill Nicholson, Matt Busby, Jock Stein and, regardless of what happened to his accent,

Alf Ramsey. English football still contained dozens of highly gifted players (that would have been an insulting description of Bobby Charlton, Bobby Moore, Denis Law, Jimmy Greaves, Ray Wilson, John Giles and Gordon Banks) and they, like the managers, were bonded by shared background with the mass of ordinary supporters on the terraces.

From the vantage point of such an era no one could accurately predict the hurtling decline in standards and the cynical distortion of priorities that have brought us to the lamentable mediocrity of the Premier League, a competition in which an unreconstructed hod-carrier called Vinny Jones not only qualifies for first-team wages but is enough of a roughneck celebrity to promote a video that purports to be a macho-man's guide to dirty tricks. Plenty of hod-carriers made it in football in the past but they had to learn to play first. The elevation of the plainest of the Joneses is, however, a lot less remarkable than it would have seemed two decades ago.

In the intervening years a shameless emphasis on speed and muscle, on making the field claustrophobic with clattering bodies, has established his kind of negative physicality as a viable commodity. Well over £2 million has been spent on his transfers between clubs.

The self-proclaimed hard case happens to be linked by the laying on of hands (an unapostolic grabbing of the testicles, actually) to the one player constantly put forward as comparable with any seen in English football before the current blight descended. Paul Gascoigne would undoubtedly have been recognized as an immense talent in any period. His feet are wonderfully deft, whether dribbling or passing the ball; he has the alertness and imagination to see and exploit openings of which others have no inkling; he shoots with dramatic power and accuracy; and in the application of his skills he has more balls than a bully like Jones could ever hope to crush.

But Gascoigne's qualities have to be weighed against an immaturity that has effortlessly survived his twenty-fifth birthday. However, even if the likeable man-boy from the North-east did not have these problems, the messianic status accorded him would be an alarming confirmation of the scarcity of exceptional performers in our national sport. If the midfields of England were peopled, as they once were simultaneously, by Charlton, Giles, Martin Peters, Colin Bell, Billy Bremner, Alan Ball, Alan Hudson, Paddy Crerand, Charlie Cooke and a few others nearly as distinguished, a Gascoigne would still be outstanding but he could not possibly have been singled out for the idolatry that was lavished on him before he moved to Italy. And mention of Best, of course, introduces another dimension altogether.

Many will dismiss such speculation as an offensive lurch into nostalgia. But the real offence is perpetrated by those who try to persuade us everything in football is as good as it ever was, for that is an attempt to cheapen an experience that enriched millions of lives. What they are telling us is that the excitement and sense of aesthetic pleasure stirred in us by the football of that other time might, if we were unprejudiced, be just as readily created by the banalities encountered on an average day in the Premier League. It is a kind of mad sporting structuralism, the equivalent of suggesting that you can get as much from McGonagall as you can from Yeats.

Of course, English football has not become an absolute wasteland. There are still skilled and entertaining players, matches that offer more than clamorous vigour, and apologists believe the fact that these are desperately rare must be set against evidence of a worldwide drop in standards. Italia 90 provided much the poorest World Cup finals most of us who attended had ever seen.

But blaming global conditions for the technical impoverishment of England's domestic game is about as valid as making the same excuse for the state of the nation's economy. Diagnosis must start with the twisted values on and off the field.

The Premier League itself is an unsightly symptom. Having instantly reneged on the original concept of reducing the number of clubs to raise the quality of play, the founders blithely trampled on the interests of their traditional public by selling television rights to a satellite company. Nothing they have done since – least of all their internecine squabbling over the spoils – has obscured the truth that their overwhelming priority is profit. Long after Thatcherism has been discredited, they appear happy to inhabit its mores.

As the corporate entertainment boxes multiply in grandstands, and the cost of following football climbs almost as dramatically as the unemployment figures, the regular fans feel betrayed, left out on the edge of the sport their commitment built. They have good reason to fear that their game is being taken away from them. Rogan Taylor, a former chairman of the Football Supporters' Association who now works at the Centre for Football Research at Leicester University, defined the fear when he said that the current packaging was apparently designed to appeal to some imagined Home Counties family in which the husband would say to his wife on a Saturday morning: 'Well, darling, is it to be the golf club today – or is it the Arsenal?'

In such a time of poverty on the field, and threat from the indifference of the legislators, people who have grown up with football as a vital adjunct to their lives can hardly avoid a yearning for happier days. The longing does not have to reach back as far as the prime of George Best and his contemporaries.

Long after he had made his disenchanted exit, Liverpool produced a team worth cherishing, constructed around Hansen, Souness, Dalglish and Rush. A later version, with Barnes, Beardsley and Whelan prominent, was rather memorable, too, and Brian Clough's Nottingham Forest did their bit to sustain the morale of the discerning. But as we lament what has gone from our football, perhaps forever, it is inevitable that Best, the greatest player ever bred in these islands, should be the most potent symbol of the loss.

Within the legend, a life has to be lived. Since the Brown Bull days, Best has owned the odd bar and nightclub and helped to pay for dozens of others, he has known a lot more bad times than good and the grey that is taking over his beard is not the only sign of what the world (often at his invitation) has done to him.

When we went to that Spurs–Manchester United game two or three weeks back, the rendezvous, predictably, was in a pub. But it was one in which his celebrity brought no hazards. His home is in a street off the King's Road, Chelsea, and the pub, tucked around a quiet corner a few hundred yards away, is used by locals who regard him as one of them.

Having tried drying out in clinics, attending meetings of Alcoholics Anonymous and taking alcohol-deterrent drugs, both orally and by having them implanted in his body, he has convinced himself that the best compromise he can manage in his efforts to cope with his drink problem is an attempt to shorten the binges and lengthen the periods when the craving is under control.

'I'd be sitting in AA meetings longing for them to end, so I could get to a bar,' he admits. 'When I was supposed to be swallowing those tablets that make you allergic to alcohol – I was married to Angela, the mother of my son, at the time – I was sometimes hiding them behind my teeth and getting rid of them later. And even when I had the implants, I was saying to myself: when the effect of these pellets wears off, I'll have a good drink. So those therapies didn't have much chance of working. Now I have a drink when I feel like it and concentrate on preventing things from getting out of hand. The better times are getting longer and longer, whereas a few years ago they were getting shorter and shorter.' The fear that this is another of the convenient rationalizations in which alcoholics become expert is at least partially allayed by some corroboration from Mary Shatila, who has been with him for five and a half years in a relationship that is the strongest mooring he has ever had since childhood. After all the years of frantic bedding, of lurching hazily from one brief embrace to the next, after the Miss Worlds and the actresses and a marriage that began drunkenly in Las Vegas and was too ill-starred to be saved by the birth eleven years ago of his son, Calum, he finds himself at forty-six with an attractive, caring woman who has the intelligence, the tolerance and, perhaps most crucially, the stamina to go on trying to reduce the hurtful chaos into which he has habitually plunged himself.

Mary Shatila has been matured by deep sadness in her own life. When her marriage in Lebanon broke up she brought her daughter, Layla, back to England but in 1988 her husband snatched the child away and Mary has not seen her since.

She and Best both talk frequently of the children who are separated from them by thousands of miles, one in Beirut, the other in California. Best went to America in 1975 and stayed until 1981, combining his football-playing commitments in Los Angeles, Fort Lauderdale and San Jose with spells on this side of the Atlantic with Fulham and Hibernian, in Edinburgh. But the talent, not unnaturally, was suffering premature erosion, and the drinking became cataclysmic. When he returned to Britain he was met with a tax bill for £16,000. He offered £10,000 immediately and the rest in six months but was told that was not acceptable. The result was a marathon wrangle which, he estimates, cost him ten times the original debt, and made him a bankrupt. It was a tunnel without the smallest glimmer of light until he was introduced recently to Bryan Fugler, a solicitor who acts for Tottenham Hotspur. Fugler quickly made sense of the tax muddle and reached an agreement with the revenue men. With the help of £72,000 raised by a testimonial match and dinner in Belfast, Best was able at last to lift a shadow that had darkened his spirits for more than a decade. ('The people of Belfast have sorted my whole life out,' he says emotionally.)

He is no longer a bankrupt and last June he was able to open a bank account for the first time since he was in the US. The account will not be threatened, as it once would have been, by betting fever. Though he claims he was never really a heavy hitter, that £50 was a big wager, there was a steady volume of activity. And two or three spectacular wins (like the night when he and a business partner were £17,000 down in a Manchester casino and then held the dice for an hour and forty minutes and finished up cashing chips worth £26,000, or the £22 Yankee on the horses that brought Best more than £12,000) merely ensured that he stayed keen enough to be a long-term loser. 'These days if I lose a fiver on a horse, I want to go into the toilet and throw up,' he told me. Quality-paper crosswords have more interest for him now than the racing pages.

His name is still a passport to lucrative employment. He works regularly as an analyst on LBC radio's coverage of the Premier League, has been in demand lately for appearances on Sky Television and makes occasional sorties to the Middle East, where expatriates pay him handsomely for some coaching and a bit of chat about the great years. He can still turn out in celebrity matches but his right leg, ravaged by cartilage trouble and the thrombosis that gave him a major fright in the early 70s, cannot withstand much strain. Strain of another kind is involved in his speaking engagements on the sporting dinner circuit. Though he is highly intelligent and the possessor of nuggets of knowledge on an unlikely range of subjects (like many drinkers, he is liable to be reading when others are sleeping), being publicly articulate has never been easy for him. The lifetime of headlines notwithstanding, he is shy. When he was a boy at Manchester United and travelled to the ground by bus, he had to make a change at a point that put him on the route driven by Matt Busby each morning, and the Boss was always eager to give him a lift. But Best, embarrassed by the need to make conversation, used to hide until the car went past. So rising to make a speech is an ordeal. 'Going out to perform in front of a hundred thousand in a stadium never worried me, because I was doing something that nobody could do better, but standing in front of an audience of two or three hundred to say a few words could frighten me to death.' However, in pursuit of solvency, he has overcome his nervousness, helped recently by the formation of a double-act with Denis Law.

As the negotiator of his fees and organizer of his schedule, Mary has her share of difficulties. An obvious one is her man's reputation for failing to keep appointments. She insists there has been a substantial improvement of late but her armoury of excuses has to be in constant readiness. Of a booking he should have skipped, the infamous appearance on *Wogan* in 1990, she says (perhaps with more love than logic) his descent from controlled behaviour beforehand to lolling, swearing drunkenness in the studio was so abrupt that she wonders if someone doctored his pre-show drinks as a malicious joke. A persistent commercial handicap is the widespread assumption that Best's contracts are still handled by Bill McMurdo, the Scottish agent with whom he became associated after his return from the States. In fact, Best has been bitterly estranged from McMurdo for years and the bad feeling will not be diminished by the fact that the agent, on the basis of an idiosyncratic interpretation of share arrangements in a company they formed, is seeking to lay claim to the Chelsea flat.

When he mentions McMurdo, Best's eyes take on the combative hardness that he once showed in action but the Scotsman's high tackle will be dealt with by Bryan Fugler. 'Now that we've made a breakthrough with the taxman, Mr McMurdo will be our next port of call,' the solicitor told me.

Best believes he has mellowed sufficiently to be disciplined by a diary well filled with entries that will earn money. In keeping with a long-established habit, he reacts to any disfiguring increase in weight by going to a health farm. There was a time when his first move on arrival was to set up an escape committee, but when I went to see him at Henlow Grange in Bedfordshire he and Mary were leaving their VIP room only to exercise or take the treatments. Admittedly, she made herself busier than he did but his visits to the gym were rather more serious. Back in a tracksuit, and with four days of abstinence already removing the smudged look from his features, he evoked moving echoes of his youth. He was always a voracious trainer, proudly torturing himself to keep pace with less indulgent teammates. 'I knew I had to be fit to avoid being battered by some of the guys who were after me on a Saturday. I wouldn't have stayed out of hospital very long if I'd been stumbling around with a hangover.'

He has been through so many awful scenes, sometimes as the befuddled, brawling offender, often as the malevolently chosen victim, that a capacity for gallows humour was a necessary protection. Sober after an evening at the cinema, he slipped into a pub near Piccadilly Circus that was run by an elderly couple he knew would let him use the telephone to order a Chinese takeaway. As he was making the call, the mirror in front of him suddenly accommodated the nightmare vision of a drunken customer, a man he had never seen before, raising a heavy pint mug above his head. When the glass crashed into Best's skull ('I can still see the whole thing in detailed slow-motion'), the wound was so terrible that bar towels had to be stuffed into it. At the hospital, a doctor told him a brain scan was indicated. 'Don't bother with that,' said Best. 'I'm Irish.'

After failing to appear in court on a drunk-driving charge in 1984, he was violently arrested at his home by a posse of police formidable enough to round up the Dalton Gang. When he eventually went to Southwark Crown Court to appeal against a prison sentence imposed earlier at Bow Street, his counsel somehow reasoned that it would be of assistance if Jeff Powell of the *Daily Mail* and I turned up as character witnesses. In the court canteen, I told George that having us on his side might make him the first man to be hanged for a driving offence. But such feeble efforts at cheering him up were soon stifled by the realization that he was probably going to jail (he did, for two months), and before long everybody was staring into the bottom of the coffee cup, with nothing to say. Then he glanced across at me with a smile. 'Well, I suppose that's the knighthood fucked,' he said.

He thinks he can specify the day when his career at the top reached a similar condition. It was in January 1974, on a Saturday when Manchester United were at home to Plymouth Argyle in the FA Cup. Best, following the most prolonged of several defections from the club, had been persuaded into one more comeback by Tommy Docherty, the latest hopeful to step through the revolving door that appeared to have been fitted to the manager's office at Old Trafford. Having fought to regain a respectable percentage of his former fitness, the great footballer was beginning to feel the penetrative surge returning to his play, and he was sure the limited resistance of Plymouth would give him the chance to put on a show. Then he missed a morning's training in midweek. He went in and punished himself the same afternoon and, when Docherty made no complaint, assumed the lapse had been forgiven. But shortly before the kick-off (it had to be then, because Best never arrived early) he was called into the referee's room and told by Docherty that he would not be playing. He tried to remonstrate but Docherty was adamant.

'When he and Paddy Crerand left me, I sat in that room and cried my eyes out,' Best recalled at Henlow Grange. 'Then after the match I went up into the empty stands and sat on my own for about an hour. I knew I had ceased to be a part of Manchester United and it was a desperate feeling.'

Considering that he was attached to United before he was properly into his adolescence, that the club was his world through the most exciting and fulfilling years of his life, the reaction was inevitable. Equally natural, perhaps, is his vehement assertion that disenchantment was entirely responsible for the shortening of his career. 'It had nothing to do with women and booze, car crashes or court cases. It was purely and simply football. Losing wasn't in my vocabulary. I had been conditioned from boyhood to win, to go out and dominate the opposition. When the wonderful players I had been brought up with – Charlton, Law, Crerand, Stiles – went into decline, United made no real attempt to buy the best replacements available. I was left struggling among fellers who should not have been allowed through the door at Old Trafford. I was doing it on my own and I was just a kid. It sickened me to the heart that we ended up being just about the worst team in the First Division and went on to drop into the Second.'

His conviction must be respected but the case is an over-simplification. Had his life and his personality not been in such confusion, he might have withstood those miseries on the field and refused to let the mediocrities who had invaded Manchester United drive him away from the most important means of expression he would ever know. His rationalization of his departure at twenty-seven is no more convincing than the argument of those who tell us that disillusionment with football provides a total explanation of his alcoholism.

There is no doubt that great sportsmen are immensely vulnerable when their gifts, and the drama they create, begin to fade, when the rest of their lives may loom like a dreary anticlimax. But alcoholism is a complicated disease, one not readily susceptible to simplistic cause-and-effect analysis. Recent research suggests that there may well be a relationship between heredity and alcoholism and, whatever other factors have been at work in the case of George Best, there could be significance in the sad fact that his mother died an alcoholic.

Best loved his mother, just as he loves his father, Dickie, a spirited, engaging little man who was an iron turner in the Harland and Wolff shipyard. They gave him a warm, carefree childhood. It was a Protestant upbringing but that was in the 40s and 50s and, though there were plenty of Catholics on the Cregagh council estate, he was not troubled by sectarian bitterness. His lack of bigotry shows in consistent advocacy of a united Ireland on the football field. He is proud of his origins and has a dream of having a house that would enable him to be near his father.

There is another dream, one that comes to him repeatedly in his sleep. 'The theme is always basically the same,' he says. 'I am the age I am now but I have been brought back to play for Manchester United, along with some of the players from my own time and others of the present day. Sir Matt's in charge and he's put me in the previous week and I've played well. But I've been away for a while – well, I have, haven't I? – and I am worried about whether he will pick me. Bryan Robson of the current squad is often involved, and big Steve Bruce and young Giggs. And Paddy and Denis are nearly always there.'

If George Best concentrates hard in his dream, he may see quite a few of us on the sidelines, straining to catch a glimpse of a footballer whose like we may never look upon again.

Eamon Dunphy

Saturday Nights in Hell

15 November

I was watching one of the apprentices this morning. He is a young boy who has been at the club a couple of years as an apprentice, and has just signed as a professional. But he has got absolutely no chance of making it. He really is the butt of everything. You get such lads in every club, who haven't got a lot of ability possibly. They have a fair amount, enough to get taken on in the first place, but not enough to look like they are ever going to make it. And they have no way of compensating for that by being one of the lads or being particularly good at anything.

They get it during the week in the five-a-sides. Everyone gets at them. You get a lad who is last pick every morning. You pick up sides. And it ends up with the same two lads standing there for the last two places. And it is the same every morning of their lives. There is a moment of complete rejection every day, their fellow professionals saying, 'I don't want you in my side.' That is a comment on their whole career. And when the game starts, if things start going wrong, everyone blames them. Everyone slags them off.

This particular boy is dead honest, a nice lad. He works really hard at the game. He never shirks anything, he gets involved as best he can. But it all comes to the same in the end. He has got absolutely no chance of making it. He is a certainty to get a free transfer at the end of the season. And there are lots of lads like that. They come in at fifteen from school, and you get maybe one out of every ten who is going to make a League player. And for the rest the next three years is going to be one long agony. A long-drawn-out process of not making it at a crucial time in their lives. A time when your confidence can either grow so that you can grow into being a man, or when you can be really destroyed if the wrong things happen to you.

And football clubs are notoriously insensitive to people's feelings. Because it is a whole group thing, and at times pretty brutal. Being a footballer means that some marvellous things happen to you. But for those who don't do so well, agonizing things can happen too. And there is nobody around in a football club to say, 'Never mind, son,' or to try and understand how they feel.

The way the game treats young players is a disgrace. It is one of the really shameful aspects of the game. Not only that they are not doing well as players, but that they aren't getting any preparation for the inevitable end when they are eighteen or nineteen or twenty. When they are kicked out or given a free transfer. They aren't given any education, they aren't prepared for any trade. They are on the streets. And worst of all really, the kind of lifestyle they have is completely undisciplined. The day finishes at lunchtime, so they arse around for the rest of the day in betting shops, or watching TV or whatever. The whole thing, far from being a preparation for going out into life, is a complete negation of everything you will have to be when you have got to go to a nine-to-five job. The shock they experience must be frightful. And coming on top of all the abuse they have had to suffer and all the shattered dreams they have had, it is a very crushing process.

Sometimes you see the dad and family and friends at reserve-team matches. And the kid might not know what is going on, but the families must know. There is no progress to report. Their greatest day is the day they sign on. Every day after that it is getting worse and worse.

I remember seeing a kid break down and cry. He was seventeen. Because the moment of truth for them is on their seventeenth or eighteenth birthday, when they have to be signed or released. This is the moment they have built up to ever since they signed as an apprentice. The moment they have worked for. At a club like Millwall they don't get any preparation. They get no coaching, very little assistance. The whole thing at Millwall throughout the years I've been there has been geared to one thing only – the first team. And the thing is, not only will the lads suffer in a personal sense, and feel the bitter rejection, but the club will suffer. There is nothing surer than that the club will decline because of a lack of young players coming through. That may seem a silly thing to say when people like Stevie Brown and Mickey Kelly are in the first team. But those youngsters illustrate it too. They have got plenty of talent, but they have been developed in the wrong environment. They haven't had the leadership, the coaching, or the right environment to grow in. So I don't believe they will make it. They haven't been developed as players, and they haven't been exposed to the right values. So everyone suffers from this policy of expediency, of looking after the immediate thing, the first team.

And it is so wasteful. Because all the time there is this fantastic raw material. No matter what anybody says, once kids are good enough to be signed on, a lot of them are good enough to make it. The difference between making it and not making it is the amount of time spent with them, the amount of effort put into helping them to become players. And the amount of opportunity they are given. So it is not as if you are discarding people who wouldn't be any use to you. Because they could save you hundreds of thousands of pounds in the end.

This kid I saw crying had just been up in the office with Benny, and Benny had had to tell him that he was being released. Benny did not like doing it, I know. He is quite a kind-hearted man in his way. But the kid was sitting out on the wall by the touchline, crying. I just happened to go out and saw him. I tried to tell him this was not the end of the road, and he could still have a decent life, that football is only a game, and so on. But it meant nothing to him at the time. In the end I got him fixed up with a catering class at the college. I think he was going to try and become a chef. I don't know whether it worked out or not. You don't. They just go, and that is the last you see of them.

It is desolation for them. And it is a commentary on some of the attitudes in football. You rarely get through to people in football if you start talking about this kind of thing. People say, 'Yes, but they know what they are doing when they come into it.' But do they? At fifteen, I didn't know what I was doing when I went into it. You come from a working-class home with no future except as factory fodder. No real education and no real choices available to you. So if someone comes along and says, 'Would you like to be a footballer?', of course you would. But is that a choice? It is something that you fall into.

And who is responsible? The parents obviously have a certain responsibility. But I think the game does too. Because if you want to be a big deal, which we do, which we claim, then along with being a big deal goes having big responsibilities. And we do not meet them for young people at all.

A lot of the flash guys going around now, who have made it in the First Division and who shame the game with their behaviour, are that way because they came out of this kind of mess. And if we are ever going to have a decent game, present a decent image, we are going to have to start working with the young people in the game. Giving them a sense of responsibility to the club and to the game. And that can only come when you have a sense of responsibility towards them.

I was at a function last night. Tommy Sampson was there. And all the first team. We were all in a group. And this guy came up, a supporter. He was a bit drunk. And he said to Tommy, 'You are Brian Clark, aren't you?' 'No,' said Tommy. 'My name is Tommy Sampson.' 'Oh, yes,' said the supporter. 'You've never really made it, have you?' Tommy hasn't, yet. He is a good lad. He still has a chance. He has been a bit unlucky. Luckier than some, unluckier than most. But this supporter just crushed him. Dreadful. We all laughed at the time. Tommy laughed too. But it was a terrible thing.

Paul Solotaroff

The Power and the Gory

Half the world was in mortal terror of him. He had a sixty-inch chest, twenty-three-inch arms, and when the Anadrol and Bolasterone backed up in his bloodstream, his eyes went as red as the laser scope on an Uzi. He threw people through windows, and chased them madly down Hempstead Turnpike when they had the temerity to cut him off. And in the gym he owned in Farmingdale, the notorious Mr. America's, if he caught you looking at him while he trained, you generally woke up, bleeding, on the pavement outside. Half out of his mind on androgens and horse steroids, he had this idea that being looked at robbed him of energy, energy that he needed to leg-press two thousand pounds.

Nonetheless, one day a kid walked up to him between sets and said, "I want to be just like you, Steve Michalik. I want to be Mr. America and Mr. Universe."

"Yeah?" said Michalik in thick contempt. "How bad do you think you want it?"

"Worse than anything in the world," said the kid, a scrawny seventeen-year-old with more balls than biceps. "I can honestly say that I would die for a body like yours."

"Well, then you probably will," snorted Michalik. "Meet me down at the beach tomorrow at six a.m. sharp. And it you're like even half a minute late . . ."

The kid was there at six a.m. pronto, freezing his ass off in a raggedy hood and sweats. "What do we do first?" he asked.

"Swim," grunted Michalik, dragging him into the ocean. Twenty yards out, Michalik suddenly seized the kid by his scalp and pushed him under a wave. The kid flailed punily, wriggling like a speared eel. A half-minute, maybe forty-five seconds, passed before Michalik let the kid up, sobbing out sea water. He gave the kid a breath, then shoved him down again, holding him under this time until the air bubbles stopped, whereupon he dragged him out by the hood and threw him, gasping, on the beach.

"When you want the title as bad as you wanted that last fucking breath," sneered Michalik, "then and only then can you come talk to me."

For himself, Michalik only wanted two things any more. He wanted to walk on stage at the Beacon Theater on November 15, 1986, professional bodybuilding's Night of Champions, and just turn the joint out with his 260 pounds of ripped, stripped, and shrink-wrapped muscle. And then, God help him, he wanted to die. Right there, in front of everybody, with all the flash bulbs popping, he wanted to drop dead huge and hard at the age of thirty-nine, and leave a spectacular corpse behind.

The pain, you see, had become just unendurable. Ten years of shotgunning steroids had turned his joints into fish jelly and spiked his blood pressure so high he had to pack his nose to stop the bleeding. He'd been pissing blood for months, and what was coming out of him now was *brown*, pure protoplasm that his engorged liver hadn't the wherewithal to break down. And when he came home from the gym at night, his whole body was in spasm. His eight-year-old boy, Steve Junior, had to pack his skull in ice, trying to take the top 10 percent off his perpetual migraine.

"I knew it was all over for me," Michalik says. "Every system in my body was shot, my testicles had shrunk to the size of cocktail peanuts. It was only a question of which organ was going to explode on me first.

"See, we'd all of us [professional bodybuilders] been way over the line for years, and it was like, suddenly, all the bills were coming in. Victor Faizowitz took so much shit that his brain exploded. The Aldactazone [a diuretic] sent his body temperature up to 112 degrees, and he literally melted to death. Another guy, an Egyptian bodybuilder training for the Mr. Universe contest, went the same way, a massive hemorrhage from head to toe—died bleeding out of every orifice. And Tommy Sansone, a former Mr. America who'd been my very first mentor in the gym, blew out his immune system on Anadrol and D-ball [Dianabol], and died of tumors all over his body.

"As for me, I couldn't wait to join 'em. I had so much evil in me from all the drugs I was taking that I'd go home at night and ask God why he hadn't killed me yet. And then, in the next breath, I'd say, 'Please, I know I've done a lot of terrible things—sold steroids to kids, beaten the shit out of strangers—but please don't let me go out like a sucker, God. Please let me die hitting that last pose at the Beacon, with the crowd on its feet for a second standing O.'"

Michalik's prayers might better have been addressed to a liver specialist. Two weeks before the show, he woke up the house at four in the morning with an excruciating pain beneath his rib cage. His wife, Thomasina, long since practiced at such emergencies, ran off to fetch some ice.

"Fuck the ice," he groaned. "Call Dr. Ludwig."

Dr. Arthur Ludwig, a prominent endocrinologist who had been treating Michalik on and off for a number of years, was saddened but unsurprised by the call. "Frankly," he told Michalik, "I've been expecting it now for ages. Your friends have been telling me lately how bad you've been abusing the stuff, especially for the last five years."

That he certainly had. Instead of cycling on and off of steroids, giving his body here and there a couple months' recuperation, Michalik had been juicing pretty much constantly since 1976, shooting himself with fourteen different drugs and swallowing copious amounts of six or seven others. Then there was all the speed he was gulping—Bennies, black beauties—to get through his seven-hour workouts, and the handful of downs at night to catch four hours of tortuous sleep.

There, at any rate, Michalik was, doubled over in bed at four in the morning, his right side screaming like a bomb had gone off in it.

"You'd better get him to New York Hospital as fast as you can," Ludwig told Michalik's wife over the phone. "They've got the best liver specialist on the East Coast there. I'll meet you in his office in an hour."

At the hospital, they pumped Michalik full of morphine and took a hasty sonogram upstairs. The liver specialist, a brusque Puritan who'd been apprised of Michalik's steroid usage, called him into his office.

"See this?" He pointed to the sonogram, scarcely concealing a sneer. "This is what's left of your liver, Mr. Michalik. And these"—indicating the four lumps grouped inside it, one of them the size of a ripe grapefruit—"these are hepatic tumors. You have advanced liver cancer, sir."

"I do?" grinned Michalik, practically hugging himself for joy. "How long you think I've got?"

"Mr. Michalik, do you understand what I'm telling you?" snapped the doctor, apparently miffed that his news hadn't elicited operatic grief. "You have cancer, and will be dead within weeks or days if I don't operate immediately. And frankly, your chances of surviving surgery are—"

"Surgery!" blurted Michalik, looking at the man as if he were bonkers. "You're not coming near me with a knife. That would leave a *scar*."

The doctor was with perfect justice about to order Michalik out of his office when Ludwig walked in. He took a long look at the sonogram and announced that surgery was out of the question. Michalik's liver was so compromised, he would undoubtedly die on the table. Besides, Ludwig adjudged, those weren't tumors at all. They were something rarer by far but no less deadly: steroid-induced cysts, or thick sacs of blood and muscle, that were full to bursting—and growing.

He ordered Michalik strapped down—the least movement now could perforate the cysts—and wheeled upstairs to intensive care. The next twenty-four hours, he declared, would tell the tale. If, deprived of steroids, the cysts stopped growing, there was a small chance that Michalik might come out of this. If, on the other hand, they fed on whatever junk he'd injected the last couple of days—well, he'd get his wish, at any rate, to die huge.

Michalik knew it was the liver, of course. He might have been heedless, but he was hardly uninformed. In fact, he knew so much about steroids that he'd written a manual on their use, and gone on the *Today* show to debate doctors about their efficacy. Like the steroid gurus of southern California, Michalik was a self-taught sorcerer whese laboratory was his body. From the age of eleven, he'd read voraciously in biochemistry, obsessed about finding out what made people big. He walked the streets of Brooklyn as a teenager, knocking on physicians' doors, begging to be made enlightened about protein synthesis. And years later he scoured the *Physicians' Desk Reference* from cover to cover, searching not for steroids but for other classes of drugs whose secondary function was to grow muscle.

Steroids, Michalik knew, were a kind of God's play, a way of rewriting his own DNA. He'd grown up skinny and hating himself to his very cell level. According to Michalik, his father, a despotic drunk with enormous forearms, beat him with whatever was close to hand, and smashed his face, for fun, into a plate of mashed potatoes.

"I was small and weak, and my brother Anthony was big and graceful, and my old man made no bones about loving him and hating me," Michalik recalls. "The minute I walked in from school, it was, 'You worthless little shit, what are you doing home so early?' His favorite way to torture me was to tell me he was going to put me in a *home*. We'd be driving along in Brooklyn somewhere, and we'd pass a building with iron bars on the windows, and he'd stop the car and say to me, 'Get out. This is the home we're putting you in.' I'd be standing there, sobbing on the curb—I was maybe eight or nine at the time— and after a while he'd let me get back into the car and drive off laughing at his little joke."

Fearful and friendless throughout childhood—even his brother was leery of being seen with him—Michalik hid out in comic books and Steve Reeves movies, burning to become huge and invulnerable. At thirteen, he scrubbed toilets in a Vic Tanny spa just to be in the presence of that first generation of iron giants—Eddie Juliani and Leroy Colbert, among others. At twenty, stationed at an Air Force base in Southeast Asia, he ignored sniper fire and the 120-degree heat to bench-press a cinder-block barbell in an open clearing, telling the corps psychiatrist that he couldn't be killed because it was his destiny to become Mr. America. And at thirty-four, years after he'd forgotten where he put all his trophies, he was still crawling out of bed at two in the morning to eat his eighth meal of the day because he *still* wasn't big enough. As always, there was that fugitive inch or two missing, that final heft without which he wouldn't even take his shirt off on the beach—for fear that everyone would laugh.

And so, of course, there were steroids. They'd been around since at least the mid-1930s, when Hitler had them administered to his SS thugs to spike their bloodlust. By the 50s, the Eastern Bloc nations were feeding them to schoolkids, creating a generation of bioengineered athletes. And in the late 60s, anabolics hit the beaches of California, as U.S. drug companies discovered that there was a vast new market out there of kids who'd swallow anything to double their pecs and their pleasure.

The dynamics of anabolic steroids have been pretty well understood for years. Synthetic variations of the male hormone testosterone, they enter the bloodstream as chemical messengers and attach themselves to muscle cells. Once attached to these cells, they deliver their twofold message: grow, and increase endurance.

Steroids accomplish the first task by increasing the synthesis of protein. In sufficient quantities, they turn the body into a kind of fusion engine, converting everything, including fat, into mass and energy. A chemical bodybuilder can put on fifty pounds of muscle in six months because most of the 6,000 to 10,000 calories he eats a day are incorporated, not excreted.

The second task—increasing endurance—is achieved by stimulating the synthesis of a molecule called creatine phosphate, or CP. CP is essentially hydraulic fluid for muscles, allowing them to do more than just a few seconds' work. The more CP you have in your tank, the more power you generate. Olympic weightlifters and defensive linemen have huge stockpiles of CP, some portion of which is undoubtedly genetic. The better part of it, though, probably comes out of a bottle of Anadrol, a popular oral steroid that makes you big, strong, and savage—and not necessarily in that order.

Over the course of eleven years, Michalik had taken ungodly amounts of Anadrol. If his buddies were taking two 50 mg tablets a day, he took four. Six weeks later, when he started to plateau, he jacked the ante to eight. So, too, with Dianabol, another brutal oral steroid. Where once a single 5 mg pill sufficed, inevitably he was gulping ten or twelve of them a day, in conjunction with the Anadrol.

The obstacle here was his immune system, which was stubbornly going on about its business, neutralizing these poisons with antibodies and shutting down receptor sites on the muscle cells. No matter. Michalik, upping the dosage, simply overwhelmed his immune system, and further addled it by flooding his bloodstream with other drugs.

All the while, of course, he was cognizant of the damage done. He knew, for instance, that Anadrol, like all oral steroids, was utter hell on the liver. An alkylated molecule with a short carbon chain, it had to be hydralized, or broken down, within twenty-four hours. This put enormous stress on his liver, which had thousands of other chemical transactions to carry out every day, not the least of which was processing the waste from his fifty pounds of new muscle. The *Physicians' Desk Reference* cautions that the smallest amounts of Anadrol may be toxic to the liver, even in patients taking it for only a couple of months for anemia:

WARNING: MAY CAUSE PELIOSIS HEPATIS, A CONDITION IN WHICH LIVER TISSUE IS REPLACED WITH BLOOD-FILLED CYSTS, OFTEN CAUSING LIVER FAILURE.... OFTEN NOT RECOGNIZED UNTIL LIFE-THREATENING LIVER FAILURE OR INTRA-ABDOMINAL HEMORRHAGE OCCURS.... FATAL MALIGNANT LIVER TUMORS ARE ALSO REPORTED.

As lethal as it was, however, Anadrol was like a baby food compared to some of the other stuff Michalik was taking. On the bodybuilding black market, where extraordinary things are still available, Michalik and some of his buddies bought the skulls of dead monkeys. Cracking them open with their bare hands, they drank the hormone-rich fluid that poured out of the hypothalamus gland. They filled enormous syringes with a French supplement called Triacana and, aiming for the elusive thyroid gland, *shot it right into their necks.* They took so much Ritalin before workouts to psych themselves up that one of Michalik's training partners, a former Mr. Eastern USA, ran out of the gym convinced that he could stop a car with his bare hands. He stood in the passing lane of the Hempstead Turnpike, his feet spread shoulder-width apart, bracing for the moment of impact—and got run over like a dog by a Buick Skylark, both his legs and arms badly broken.

Why, knowing what he knew about these poisons, did Michalik continue taking them? Because he, as well as his buddies and so many thousands of other bodybuilders and football players, were fiercely and progressively addicted to steroids. The American medical community is currently divided about whether or not the stuff is addictive. These are the same people who declared, after years of thorough study, that *steroids do not grow muscle.* Bodybuilders are still splitting their sides over that howler. Michalik, however, is unamused.

"First, those morons at the AMA say that steroids don't work, which anyone who's ever been inside a gym knows is bullshit," he snorts. "Then, ten years later, they tell us they're deadly. Oh, now they're deadly? Shit, that was like the FDA seal of approval for steroids. C'mon, everybody, they *must* be good for you—the AMA says they'll kill you!

"Somehow, I don't know how, I escaped getting addicted to them the first time, when I was training for the Mr. America in 1972. Maybe it was because I was on them for such a short stretch, and went relatively light on the stuff. Mostly, all it amounted to was a shot in the ass once a week from a doctor in Roslyn. I never found out what was in that shot, but Jesus, did it make me crazy. Here I was, a churchgoing, gentle Catholic, and suddenly I was pulling people out of restaurant booths and threatening to kill them just because there were no other tables open. I picked up a 300-pound railroad tie and caved in the side of some guy's truck with it because I thought he'd insulted my wife. I was a nut, a psycho, constantly out of control—and then, thank God, the contest came, and I won it and got off the juice, and suddenly became human again. I retired, and devoted myself entirely to my wife for all the hell I'd put her through, and swore I'd never go near that shit again."

A couple of years later, however, something happened that sent him back to the juice, and this time there was no getting off it. "I'd bought Thomasina a big house in Farmingdale, and filled it with beautiful things, and was happier than I'd ever been in my life. And then one day I found out she'd been having an affair. I was worse than wiped out, my soul was ripped open. It had taken me all those years to finally feel like I was a man, to get over all the things my father had done to me . . . and she cut my fucking heart out."

Michalik went back to the gym, where he'd always solved all his problems, and started seeing someone we'll call Dr. X. A physician and insider in the subculture, for two decades Dr. X had been supplying bodybuilders with all manner of steroids in exchange for sexual favors. Michalik hit him up for a stack of prescriptions, but made it clear that he couldn't accommodate the doctor sexually, to the latter's keen disappointment. The two, however, worked out a satisfactory compromise. Michalik, the champion bodybuilder who was constantly being consulted by young wannabes, directed some of them posthaste to the tender governance of Dr. X.

"They had to find out sooner or later that the road to the title went through Dr. X's office," Michalik shrugs. "Nobody on this coast was gonna get to be competition size unless they put out for him—that, or they had a daddy in the pharmaceutical business. The night Dr. X first tried to seduce me, he showed me pictures of five different champions that he said he'd had sex with. I checked it out later and found out it was all true. Nice business, isn't it, professional bodybuilding? More pimps and whores than Hollywood."

Michalik didn't care about any of that, however. Nor did he care if he went crazy or got addicted to steroids. "I didn't care if I fucking died from 'em. All I cared about was getting my body back. I was down to one hundred fifty pounds, which was my natural body weight, and no one in the gym even knew who I was. Big guys were screaming at me, 'Get off that bench, you little punk, I wanna use it!' Three months later, I'm two hundred pounds and bench-pressing four hundred, and the same guys are coming over to me, going, 'Hey, aren't you Steve Michalik? When did you get here?' And I'd tell 'em, 'I've been here for the last three months, motherfucker. I'm the guy you pushed offa that bench over there, remember?'"

By that third month, he recalls, he was hopelessly hooked on steroids, unable to leave the house without "gulping three of something, and taking a shot of something else. I'd get out of bed in the morning feeling weak and sick, and stagger around, going, 'Where's my shit?' I was a junkie and I knew it and I hated myself for it. But what I hated much, much more was not getting to Dr. X's office. He had the *real* hot shit—Primobolan, Parabolin—that you couldn't get anywhere else. They were so powerful you felt them *immediately* in your muscles, and tasted them for hours on your lips. My heart would start pounding, and the blood would come pouring out of my nose, but he'd just pack it with cotton and send me on my way.

"Suddenly, all I was doing was living and dying for those shots. I was totally obsessed about seeing him, I'd have terrible panic attacks on the subway, my brain would be racing—was I going to make it up to his office before I fell down? I was throwing people out of my way, shoving 'em into poles, practically knocking the door down before we pulled into the station.

"Understand, there was no justification for the things I did; not my wife's affair, not what had happened to me as a kid—nothing. I was an adult, I knew what I was doing, at least at the beginning, and when you add it all up, I deserve to have died from it.

"But I want you to understand what it's like to just completely lose yourself. To get buried in something so deep that you think the only way out is to die. Those ten years, it was like I was trapped inside a robot body, watching myself do horrible things, and yelling, 'Stop! Stop!' but I couldn't even slow down. It was always *more* drugs, and *more* side effects, and *more* drugs for the side effects. For ten years, I was just an animal on stimulus-response."

He flew to London in the fall of 1975 for the Mr. Universe show, already so sick from the steroids and the eight meals a day that he could scarcely make it up the stairs to the stage. "I had a cholesterol level of over 400, my blood pressure was 240 over 110—but, Jesus Christ, I was a great-looking corpse. No one had ever seen anything like me on stage before, I had absolutely *perfect* symmetry: nineteen-inch arms, nineteen-inch calves, and a fifty-four-inch chest that was exactly twice the size of my thighs. The crowd went bazongo, the judges all loved me—and none of it, not even the title, meant shit to me. Joy, pride, any sense of satisfaction—the drugs wiped all of that out of me. The only feeling I was capable of anymore was deep, deep hatred."

Michalik went home, threw his trophy into a closet, and began training maniacally for the Mr. Olympia show, bodybuilding's most prestigious event. He'd invented a training regimen called "Intensity/ Insanity," which called for *seventy* sets per body part instead of the customary ten. This entailed a seven-hour workout and excruciating pain, but the steroids, he found, turned that pain into pleasure, "a huge release of all the pressure built up inside me, the rage and the energy."

And with whatever rage and energy he had left, he ran his wife's panicked lover out of town, and completed his revenge by impregnating her "so that there'd be *two* Steve Michaliks in the world to oppress her." Spotlessly faithful to her for the first ten years of their marriage, he began nailing everyone he could get his hands on now, thanks in no small part to his daily dosage of Halotestin, a steroid whose chief side effect was a constant—and conspicuous—erection. He was also throwing down great heaps of Clomid and HCG, two fertility drugs for women that, in men, stimulate the production of testosterone.

"Bottom line, I was insatiable, and acting it out all over the place. I had girlfriends in five different towns in Long Island, and one day I was so hormone-crazed I fucked 'em all, one right after the other. Suddenly, I saw why there was so much rampant sex in this business, why the elite bodybuilders always had two or three girls in their hotel room, or were making thousands of dollars a weekend at private gay parties. In fact, one of my friends in the business, a former Mr. America, used to get so horny on tour that he'd fuck the Coke machine in his hotel. Swear to God, he'd stick his dick right in the change slot and bang it for all he was worth. I'm telling you, my wife saw him do this, she can vouch for it. He fucked those machines from coast to coast, and even had ratings for them. I seem to remember the Chicago Hyatt's being pretty high up there on the list."

Hot, in any event, off his win in the Mr. Universe, and absolutely galactic now at 250 pounds, he was the consensus pick among his peers to put an end to Arnold Schwarzenegger's reign as Mr. Olympia and begin a five- or six-year run of his own. He had even prepped himself to follow Ahnuld into show business, taking two years of acting lessons and a year of speech at Weiss-Baron Studios in Manhattan. One of the networks approached him about hosting a science show. George Butler and Charles Gaines filmed him extensively for *Pumping Iron,* the definitive bodybuilding flick that put Schwarzenegger on the map in Hollywood.

And then, driving himself to the airport for the Mr. Olympia show that November, Michalik suddenly ran into something bigger than steroids. A tractor-trailer driver, neglecting to check his mirror, veered into Michalik's lane on Route 109 and ran right over the hood of his Mustang. Michalik was dragged twenty yards into an embankment; the Mustang crumpled up around him. When they finally sawed him out of it two hours later, he had four cracked discs and a torn sciatic nerve, and was completely paralyzed from the waist down.

The bad news, said the surgeon after a battery of X-rays, was that Michalik would never walk again. The good news was that with a couple of operations, the pain could be substantially mitigated. Michalik told him to get the fuck out of his room. For months he lay in traction, refusing medication, and with his free arm went on injecting himself with testosterone, which he'd had with him in a black bag at the time of the accident, and which the hospital had so thoughtfully put on his bedside table.

"It was hilarious. The idiot doctors kept coming in and going, 'Gee, your blood pressure seems awfully high, Mr. Michalik,' and I'd just lay there with a straight face and go, 'Well, I *have* been very tense, you know, since the accident.'

"Meanwhile, for the one and only time in my life, the steroids were actually helping me. They speeded up the healing, which is actually their medical purpose, and kept enough size on me so that the nurses used to fight over who was supposed to wash me every day. I started getting a little sensation back in my right leg, enough so that when the doctor told me he'd send me home if I could stand up, I managed to fake it by standing on one leg."

There, however, the progress halted, and Michalik, unspeakably depressed, lay in bed for a year, bloating on steroids and chocolate chip cookies. He got a call from the TV people, telling me that they'd hired Leonard Nimoy to replace him on the science show. He got another one from the producers of *Pumping Iron,* informing him that he'd been all but cut out of the film. Worst of all, his friends and training partners jumped ship on him, neither calling nor coming by to see him.

"So typical of bodybuilders," he sneers. " 'Hey, Michalik's crippled,

I gotta go see him—nah, it's Tuesday, chest-and-back day. Fuck him.'
But the *real* reason, I think, was they couldn't stand to see one of their
own hurt. In order to keep on doing what they're doing—the drugs,
the binge eating, the sex-for-money—they've gotta keep lying to
themselves, saying, 'I can't be hurt, I can't get sick. I'm Superman.
Cancer is *afraid* to live in my body.'"

About the only person who didn't abandon him was his kid brother,
Paulie, an adopted eight-year-old who utterly worshiped Michalik. "He
used to come into my room every day and massage my legs, going,
'You feel anything yet? You feel it?' He's stubborn like me. He just
refused to give up, he kept saying, 'You're a *champion*, Steve, you're
my hero, you're gonna be back.'

"And then one day we're watching TV, and a pro bodybuilding
show comes on. This was 1978, and the networks had started up a
Grand Prix tour to cash in on the fad after *Pumping Iron*. I'm watching
all the guys and just going crazy, wishing I could just get up on stage
against 'em one more time, and Paulie goes, 'You *can* do it, Steve. You
can come back and whip those guys. I'll help you in the gym.'"

Aroused, Michalik called an old friend, Julie Levine, and begged
him for the keys to his new gym in Amityville. The next night, he got
out of bed at 2 a.m. and scuttled to the window, where Paulie assisted
him over the sash. Crawling across the lawn to his wife's car, Michalik
got in the driver's seat and pushed his dead legs back, making room
for his little brother beneath the steering wheel. As he steered, Paulie
worked the gas and brake pedals with his hands, and in this manner
they accomplished the ten miles to Amityville.

In the gym, Paulie dragged him from machine to machine, helping
him push the weight stacks up. Michalik's upper body responded
quickly—muscle has remarkable memory—but his legs, particularly
the left one, lay there limp as old celery. After several months, however,
the pain started up in them. Sharp and searing, it was as if someone
had stuck a fork in his sciatic nerve. Michalik, a self-made master of
pain, couldn't have been happier if he'd hit the lottery.

"The doctors all told me it would be ten years, if ever, for the nerve
to come back, and here it was howling like a monster. I kicked up the
dosages of all the stuff I was taking, and started *attacking* the weights
instead of just lifting 'em. Six months later, the pain was so bad I still
could barely straighten up—but I was leg-pressing seven hundred and
eight hundred pounds, and my thighs were as big as a bear's."

And a year after that, he walked on stage in Florida, an unadvertised guest poser at the end of a Grand Prix show. The crowd, recognizing a miracle when it saw one, went berserk as Michalik modeled those thirty-four-inch thighs, each of which was considerably wider than his twenty-seven-inch waist. Shwarzenegger, in the broadcast booth doing color for ABC, was overwhelmed. "I don't believe what I am seeing," he gasped. "It's Steve Michalik, the phantom bodybuilder!"

There Michalik should have left it. He was alive, and ambulatory, and his cult status was set. Thanks to Arnie, he would be forever known as the Phantom Bodybuilder, a tag he could have turned into a merchandizing gold mine, and retired.

But like a lot of other steroid casualties, Michalik couldn't stop pushing his luck. He had to keep going, had to keep *growing*, testing the limits of his skeleton and the lining of his liver. If he'd gotten galactic, he figured, on last year's drugs, there was no telling how big he could get on this year's crop. A new line of killer juice was coming out of southern California—Hexalone, Bolasterone, Dehydralone—preposterously toxic compounds that sent the liver into warp drive but which grew hard, mature muscle right before your very eyes. Sexier still, there was that new darling of the pro circuit, human growth hormone, and who knew where the ceiling even *began* on that stuff?

Instead of pulling over, then, Michalik put the hammer down. He joined the Grand Prix tour immediately after the show in Florida and began the brutal grind of doing twelve shows annually. Before the tour, top bodybuilders did five shows a year, tops—the Mr. Olympia, the Night of Champions, and two or three others in Europe—which gave them several months to recuperate from the drugs and heavy training. Now, thanks to TV, they had to do a show a month. The pace was quite literally murderous.

"Not only did guys have to peak every month, they had to keep getting *better* as the year went on. No downtime, no rest from the binging and fasting—you could see guys turning green from all the shit in their systems. As you might expect, some of them were falling by the wayside, one guy from arrythmia, another guy from heart attacks.

"As for me, all I knew was that I was spending every dime I had on drugs. It cost me $25,000 that first year just to keep up, and that was *without* human growth hormone, which I couldn't even afford. The sport had become like an arms race now. If you heard that some guy was using Finajet, then *you* had to have it, no matter what it cost or where you had to go to get it. It actually paid to fly back and forth to

France every couple of months, where you could buy the crap off the shelves of some country pharmacy and save yourself thousands of bucks.

"Needless to say, those five years on the tour were the most whacked-out of my life. My cognitive mind went on like a permanent stroll, and I became an enormous, lethal caveman. The only reason I didn't spend most of that time in jail was because two-thirds of the cops in town were customers of mine. They belonged to my gym, and bought their steroids from me, and when I got into a little beef, which was practically every other day, they took care of it on the QT for me.

"Once I was on Hempstead Turnpike, on my way to the gym, when some guy in a pickup gave me the finger. That's it, lights out. I chased him doing ninety in my new Corvette, and did a three-sixty in heavy traffic right in front of him. I jumped out, ripped the door off his truck, and caved in his face with one punch. The other guy in the cab, who had done nothing to me, jumps out and starts running down the divider to get away from me. I chased him on foot and was pounding the shit out of him on the side of the road when the cops pulled up in two cruisers. 'Michalik, get outta here, ya crazy fuck,' they go, 'this is the last goddamn time we're lettin' you slide.'"

Word quickly got around town that Michalik was to be avoided at all costs. That went double for the wild-style gym he opened, which did everything but hang a sign out saying, STEROIDS FOR SALE HERE. There were plaques on the walls that proclaimed, UP THE DOSAGE! and pictures not of stars but of twenty-gauge syringes.

As for the clientele, it ran heavily toward the highly crazed. There was the seven-foot juice freak who stomped around muttering, "I'll kill you all. I'll rip your guts out and eat them right here." There was the mob hit man who drove up in a limo every day and checked his automatic weapons at the door. There was the herpetologist who came in with a python wrapped around him, trailing a huge sea turtle, for good measure, on a leash. There was the former Mr. America who was so distraught when his dog died that he had it stuffed, and dragged it around the gym from station to station.

"I had every freak and psycho within a 300-mile radius," Michalik recalls. "At night, there'd be all these animals hanging around outside my gym, slurping protein shakes and twirling biker chains—and every single one of 'em was afraid of me. That was the only way I kept 'em in line. As crazy as they all were, they knew I was crazier, and that I'd just as soon kill 'em as re-enroll 'em."

If that sounds like dubious business practice, consider that a year after opening, Michalik was so successful that he had to move to a location twice the size. But for all the money he was making, and for all the scams he was running—selling "Banana Packs," a worthless mixture of rotten bananas and egg powder, as his "secret muscle formula" for $25 a pop; passing himself off as a veterinarian to get cases of human growth hormone at wholesale for his "clinical experiments"—he was still being bankrupted by his skyrocketing drug bills.

The federal heat had begun to come down on the steroid racket, closing out the pill-mill pharmacies where Michalik was filling his scrips. The national demand, moreover, for the high-octane stuff—Hexalone, Bolasterone, etc.—was going through the roof, which meant that Michalik, like everybody else, had to get on line, and pay astronomical prices for his monthly package from Los Angeles.

Constantly broke, and going nowhere fast on the Grand Prix tour—"where in the beginning I'd been finishing third or fourth in the shows, by 1983 I was coming in like eleventh or twelfth"—Michalik began caving in emotionally and physically. He'd come home from the gym at night, dead-limbed and nauseous, and suddenly burst into tears without warning. Cut off from everyone, even the stouthearted Thomasina, who had finally thrown up her hands and stopped caring what he did to himself, he sat alone in a dark room, hearing his joints howl, and dreamed about killing himself.

"I was just lost, gone, in a constant state of male PMS—the hormones flying around inside, my mood going yoyo. I just wanted an end to it; an end to all the pain I was in, and to the pain I was causing others.

"I mean, of course I had tried to get off the drugs, and always it just got worse. The depression got deeper, the craving was incredible, and those last couple of years, I was worse than any crackhead. As crazed as I was, I'd've killed to keep on going, to get my hands on that next shipment of Deca or Maxibolin."

As for his body, it was finally capitulating to all the accumulated toxins. By 1983, he was bleeding from everywhere: his gums, kidneys, colon, and sinuses. The headaches started up, so piercing and obdurate that he developed separate addictions to Percodan and Demerol. And worst of all (by Michalik's lights), his muscles suddenly went soft on him. No matter how he worked them or what he shot into them, they lost their gleaming, osmotic hardness, and began to pooch out like $20 whitewalls.

His last two years on the tour were a run-on nightmare. He almost dropped dead at a show in Toronto, collapsing on stage in head-to-toe convulsions; the promoters, disgraced, hauled him off by the ankles. There was a desperate attempt in 1985, after his cholesterol hit 500, to wean himself from steroids once and for all. His testosterone level plummeted, however, his sperm count went to zero, and all the estrogen in his body, which had been accruing for years, turned his pecs into soft, doughy breasts. Such friends as he still had pointed out that his ass was plumping like a woman's, and tweaked him for his sexy new hip-swishing walk.

He ran to one endocrinologist after another, begging them for something to reverse the condition. To a man, each pointed to Michalik's liver reading and showed him out of his office. Leaving, he had the distinct feeling that they were laughing at him.

And so, after weighing his options—a bleak, emasculated life off steroids or a slam-bang, macho death on them—Michalik emphatically chose the latter. He packed a bag, grabbed his weight belt, and caught a plane for L.A., winding up for nine months in the valley, where all the chemical studs were training.

Just up the freeway, a cartel of former med students were minting drugs so new they scarcely had names for them yet. The stuff ran $250, $300 a bottle, but pumped you up like an air hose and kept you that way. It also made you violently sick to your stomach, but Michalik didn't have time to worry about that. He simply ran to the bathroom to heave up his guts, then came back and ripped off another thirty sets.

His hair fell out in heavy clumps; a dry cough emanated from his liver, wracking him. Every joint was inflamed; it was excruciating even to walk now. But at night, in bed and in too much pain to sleep, it cheered him to think that he would finally be dead soon, and that it would take eight men to carry his casket.

He came back to New York in the fall of 1986, on his last legs but enormous and golden brown. All along, he'd targeted the Night of Champions, to be held that November at the Beacon Theater, as his swan song. It was the Academy Awards show of bodybuilding. Everyone would be there, all the stars and cognoscenti, and it would consolidate his legend to show up one last time, coming out of a coffin to the tune of Elton John's "Funeral for a Friend." Of course, it would really help matters if he could drop dead on stage, but that seemed too much to hope for. All that mattered, finally, was that he go out with twenty-five hundred people thundering their approval, drowning out, once and for all, his old man's malediction that he'd never amount to shit.

And then, two weeks before the show, he woke up at four in the morning with his liver on fire, and that was the end of all that.

Happily afloat on morphine and Nembutol, Michalik drifted for seventy-two hours, dreaming that he was dead. In the course of those three days, however, his extraordinary luck held up. The huge cysts in his liver stabilized and began to shrink, though they'd so eviscerated the organ already that there was practically nothing left of it. Short of a transplant, it would be months before he could so much as sit up and take nourishment. His bodybuilding career, in any case, was finished.

When Michalik awoke in intensive care, he was inconsolable. Not only was he still unaccountably alive, his beautiful body was dissolving and going away from him. His muscles, bereft of steroids and the five pounds of chicken he ate a day, decomposed and flowed into his bloodstream as waste. In three weeks, he lost more than a hundred pounds, literally pissing himself down to 147 from a steady weight of 255.

Predictably, his kidneys began to fail, functioning at 60 percent, then 40, then 20. His black hair turned gray, and the skin hung off him in folds. His father came in and told him, with all his customary tact, that he looked like an eighty-five-year-old man.

In the few hours a day that he was lucid, Michalik wept uncontrollably. Out of the unlikeliest materials—bad genes, a small bone structure, and a thoroughly degraded ego—he had assembled this utterly remarkable thing, a body that no less than Arnold Schwarzenegger once venerated as the very best in the world. Now he was too weak to lift his head off the pillow. He lay there inert for months and months, the very image, it seemed to him, of his old man's foretelling.

"I was just like Lyle Alzado, who I went to high school in Brooklyn with: weak and broken-down, leaning on my wife to keep me alive. She came and fed me every day through a straw, and swiped the huge bunch of pills I was saving to kill myself. To thank her for still being there after everything, I sold the gym and gave her all the money from it. I didn't want any of it, I didn't want anything. I just wanted to lie in bed and be miserable by myself. I was so depressed I could hardly move my jaws to speak."

Finally, by the spring of 1988, he'd recovered sufficiently to get out of bed for short stretches. Possessed by the sudden urge to atone for his sins, Michalik called every promoter he knew, begging them to let him go on stage in his condition and dramatize the wages of steroids. Surprisingly, several of them agreed to the idea. They brought Michalik out, a bag of bones in a black shirt, and let him turn the place into a graveyard for ten minutes.

"All these twenty-year-olds would be staring up at me with their jaws hanging open, and I'd get on the mike and say, 'You think this can't happen to you, tough guy? You think you know more about steroids than I do? Well, I wrote the book on 'em, buddy, and they *still* ate me up. I'm forty years old and I'm finished. Dead.'"

The former proselytizer for steroids got some grim satisfaction out of spreading the gospel against them. He dragged himself out to high schools and hard-core juice gyms, using himself as a walking cautionary tale. But whatever his good works were doing for his soul, they weren't doing a damn thing for his body. He still woke up sick in every cell, poisoned by the residue of all the drugs. The liver cysts, shrunk to the size of golf balls but no further, sapped his strength and forced him to eat like a sparrow, subsisting on farina and chicken soup. His hormones were wildly scrambled—a blood test revealed he had the testosterone level of a twelve-year-old *girl*—and it had been two years since he'd had even a twinge of an erection. Indeed, his moods were so erratic that he had his wife commit him to a stretch in a Long Island nut bin.

"I wasn't crazy, but I didn't know what else to do. All day long I just sat there, consumed with self-hatred: 'Why did you do this? Why did you do that?' I mean, even when I was huge, I never had what you would call the greatest relationship with myself, but now it was, 'You're *weak!* You're *tiny!* You're *stupid!* You're *worthless!*'—and what the hell was I going to say to shut it up? The only thing I'd ever valued about myself was my body, and I'd totally, systematically fucked it up. My life, as you can probably guess, was intolerable."

It was here, however, that fate stepped in and cut Michalik a whopping break. Halfway across the world, an Australian rugby player named Joe Reesh somehow heard about Michalik's plight and called to tell him about a powerful new detox program. It was a brutally arduous deal—an hour of running, then five hours straight in a 180-degree sauna, for a minimum of twenty-one days—but infallibly, it leeched the poisons out of your fat cells, where they'd otherwise sit, crystallized, for the rest of your life.

Utterly desperate, Michalik gave it a shot. He could scarcely jog around the block that first day, but in the sauna, it all started coming out of him: a viscous, green paste that oozed out of his eyes and nostrils. By the end of the first week, he reports, he was running two miles; by the end of the second, his ex-wife verifies, his gray hair had turned black again. And when he stepped out of the sauna after the twenty-third and final day, his skin was as pink and snug as a teenager's. Liver and kidney tests confirmed the wildly improbable: he was perfectly healthy again.

"Everything came back to me: my sense of humor, my lust for life—hell, my lust, *period*. Don't forget, it'd been almost three years since I'd gotten it up—I had some serious business to take care of. But the greatest thing by far was what *wasn't* there anymore. All the biochemical hatred I'd been walking around with for twelve years, it was like that all bled out of me with the green stuff, and I had this overpowering need to be with people again, especially my son, Stevie. I had tons of making up to do with him, and I've loved every minute of it. It kills me that I could've let myself get so sick that I was ready to die and leave him."

Michalik went to his wife and told her he was going back to bodybuilding. It was his life, his art, he couldn't leave it alone—only this time, he swore on Heaven, he was going to do it clean. She understood, or at least tried to, but said she couldn't go through with it again: the 2 a.m. feedings, the $500-a-week grocery bills. They parted amicably, and Michalik returned to the gym, as zealous and single-minded as a monk. In the last two years he's put on sixty pounds, and looks dense and powerful at 225, though he's sober about the realities.

"There are *nineteen-year-olds* clocking in now at two sixty-five," he says, shaking his head. "The synthetic HGH [human growth hormone] has evolved a new species in five years. By the end of the decade, the standard will be three-hundred-pounders, with twenty-three-inch necks that are almost as big as their waists.

"But all around the country, kids'll be dropping dead from the stuff, and getting diabetes because it burns out their pancreas. I don't care what those assholes in California say, there's no such thing in the world as a 'good' drug. There's only bad drugs and sick bastards who want to sell them to you."

Someone ought to post those words in every high school in the country. The latest estimate from a *USA Today* report is that there are half a million teenagers on juice these days, almost half of whom, according to a University of Kentucky study, are so naïve they think that steroids *without exercise* will build muscle. In this second Stone Age, the America of Schwarzkopf and Schwarzenegger, someone needs to tell them that bigger isn't necessarily better. Sometimes, bigger is deader.

Martin Amis

Tennis: The Women's Game

The emerging women's game can be imagined – perhaps with literal accuracy – as a transcontinental jumbo, with three classes. In First Class you find the top-ten ladies (or bobby-soxers or nymphets), with footrests up, harassed by the courtesies of the cabin stewards: Steffi is playing backgammon with her dad; Gaby is hunched under a Sony Walkman. In Club World, together with the shrinks and physios of the top-ten ladies, are the second-string ladies, all of them quite well attended, and wearing those special pairs of Club World slippers. In the chaos of Coach, wedged together in blocks of three and four, are the 'gym rats', the eternal aspirants of the modern tour, on yet another leg of their frazzled quest for ranking points, sponsors, backers. Nearly every girl on board has entrusted her schooling to the correspondence course. They are all enduring, or developing, a variety of injuries: 'always *something* hurts'. And they all have jet lag.

It is raining in Boca Raton, to the disgust of the entire resort. The PR machine is reshuffling flights, drivers and schedules; and the ladies are in the clubroom, playing snap and Scrabble. When the action resumes, Jo Durie will go out in the first round, foreclosing British interest in the event. But that's where all similarities to Wimbledon end. The crowd isn't cringing under umbrellas, smelling of damp dog. It is strolling the landscaped grounds, lightly clad and gorging itself on ice-cream and gooey pretzels. For we are in Florida, the global nursery of the women's game, where the girls can conveniently flit from condo to sports ranch to tournament, and to the stratospheric tendrils of mammoth Miami Airport. The county is still mopping its brow from Prince Charles's recent visit to Palm Beach; but lots of locals are rich and idle enough to turn out for the tennis. The heavy sun gives the young flesh of the players a sumptuously toasty tang, and turns the rest of us into various shades of peanut butter and hot-dog mustard.

'Nice place, don't you think,' said my driver as we approached, and then added, before I got any ideas, 'You have to be a millionaire to live here, though.' I believed him. Chris Evert lives here, or has a 'home' here anyway. This is polo-club America, with shaved grass, caddy-carts, rows of identical modern villas and fanatical security. I look in on the sodden press tent to collect my ID tag. But there is hardly time to sample the free Danish ('For MEDIA Only!'), and to be disabused of the idea that tennis journalism is a glamorous job, before we hear the rumour of play. The clouds clear and the voluptuous raindrops cease to fall. Soon the sky is wearing an outfit of faded denim; at dusk it will don a watermelon T-shirt. This is Florida, and even the sky is in questionable taste.

In the absence of Martina Navratilova (either injured or conserving herself for 'the Slams'), and in the absence of any hard gossip about burn-out, grasping parents or lesbian molestation, there was only one big story, one big question, at the Virginia Slims of Florida. The question was: can anybody beat Steffi Graf, who nowadays seems to be losing about one match a year? Pat Cash recently called women's tennis 'rubbish'. Yet many well-informed observers believe that the women's game is now more interestingly poised than the men's – as well as being better fun to watch. The men have entrained a power struggle of outsize athleticism, machismo and foul temper. It's all *rat-a-tat-tat*, or *rat-a-tat*, or, on fast courts, simply *rat*. Where is the pleasure in witnessing an ace? The women's game has become just as powerful while remaining significantly slower, so that the amateur has time to recognize the vocabulary of second-guessing and disguise. Although it's still a fight, it's a woman's fight, settled not by the muscles but by the subtler armaments with which women wage their wars. Women's tennis is *Dynasty* with balls, bright yellow fuzzy ones, stroked and smacked by the Fallons, Krystles and Alexises of the lined court.

The crowd wants something to talk about, and the press must have something to write about; so for the first few days attention fixes on the Latest Sensation – the latest double-fisted infant to be groomed for stardom, Monica Seles from Yugoslavia, who has just turned fourteen. The older girls hate playing the child wonders, and Helen Kalesi, the Canadian number one, is having a terrible time with Monica. 'Better than Steffi at that age,' a coach informs me. 'Look at her nerve. She *loves* the ball.' The contest looks elegant but sounds barbaric. Helen is a 'grunter', and Monica is a 'whoofer', emitting a duosyllabic shriek with each contact of ball and racket. 'Uhh!' 'Ugh-*eh*!' 'Uhh!' 'Ugh-*eh*!' Jimmy Connors started the grunting, with his legendary 'Hworf!' Then, as Clive James noted, Bjorn Borg responded with his own Nordic variant: 'Hwörjf!' The idea, supposedly, is to incorporate the strength of the stomach muscles; but the strength of the women all derives from their *timing*, in at least two senses. Prodigies can't happen in men's tennis because the physique develops later. Hence the money trap of the women's game, and one of its peculiar cruelties: as an earner, a girl can peak at puberty and be 'history' by the age of sixteen.

At the press conference after her shock win Monica looks like a startled elf in a Disney cartoon. Her charmingly nervous laugh reveals a garrison of orthodonture. 'What do you feel?' 'Very happy.' 'What is your goal?' 'To be number one.' Later, Steffi Graf strides into the tent, having briskly lunched on her first opponent. Asked about the child wonder, Steffi concedes with a shrug that Monica, while 'very skinny', is 'a good player'. She is especially haughty about Monica's reliance on the two-handed ground stroke, which Steffi clearly regards as a contemptible anachronism, like using your knickers to store the ball for the second serve. As befits a number one, Steffi is visibly impatient with questions about her rivals, and generally shows little interest in disguising her feelings. She quite lacks the PR burnish of the American girls, all of whom have impeccable media manners and a nice tidy image. It makes sense: they might want to diversify later on, like Pam Shriver. If you retire at twenty-five there are a lot of years ahead, and sportscasting may fill some of them.

The next evening, under the lights, little Monica plays Chris Evert, who knows a thing or two about child prodigies, having traumatized them by the dozen year after year. She was also one herself, and remains the only player in the modern game who has paced her hunger over two decades. Given a big build-up by the PR witch with the mike ('Ladies and gentlemin! ... Wimbledin ... the US Opin' etc., plus details of her career earnings), Chris steps forward sternly smiling, as straight and crisp as the pleats in her skirt, and shining with money dignity and hardened achievement. 'Mm,' says Chris as she strikes the ball (for Chris is no whoofer: more a gentle moaner). 'Mm.' 'Ugh-*eh*!' 'Mm.' 'Ugh-*eh*!' 'Mm.' Monica cuts a chastened figure at the post-match conference. She broke Chris's serve three times, but she failed to hold any of her own. No laughter now, poor mite. She looks as though she is longing for a refreshing weep with her mother, or five hours with her coach, rewiring that drive volley.

Now that the Latest Sensation is history for the time being, the public eye greedily swivels and fixes with an incredulous leer on Gabriela Sabatini. As she unveils herself for the first match, under the

sun's spotlight, a sigh of admiration and yearning wafts through the
crowd. Sabatini looks like a human racehorse, a (successful) experiment
in genetico-aesthetics, engineered, cultured and conditioned for opti-
mum gorgeousness. Her beauty alone scares the life out of her
opponents – because tennis is above all an expression of personal
power and, in the women's game, is closely bound up with how a
player looks, and how she feels she looks.

Up against Gabriela is the noble veteran Wendy Turnbull, with her
gym knickers and boyish bob. It is, perhaps, not too great a trespass
against gallantry to point out that Wendy is shaped like a Prince Pro
tennis racket. She plays a stubby game, too, while Gabriela, of course,
is pure motion sculpture on the court, with her balletic delay in the
service action and her bravura – her toreador – backhand. It looked
like a deeply thankless hour for Wendy, facing this bronzed hallucin-
ation of fluency and youth. She tried her 'old tricks' (block return,
chip-and-charge), but Gabriela's topspin was a torment to her ageing
legs. 'Time,' explained the umpire, every five minutes. 'Time. Time.'
And it's the operative word. To Monica it says, 'Not yet'; to Wendy,
'No longer.'

Soon, the Sabatini charisma is devastating the press tent. 'Still got
the red BMW, Gaby?' asks one tennis expert from the floor. 'This
Argentine singer friend – what's his name?' 'Elio Roza.' 'How do you
spell Elio?' 'E,l,i,o.' 'Great. How do you spell Roza?' What did you feel?
What will you buy? At the best of times the press tent is hardly a
fortress of shrewd enquiry, and when a superstar is near, the Sports
Department quickly collapses into Features or Lifestyles. All week the
girls troop in and tell the corps that they're crazy about their new
coach and are now doing ten thousand pull-ups a day and eating
nothing but alfalfa. It is an obligation, and a ritual. 'Have you dreamt
of this moment all your life?' 'Yes.' This exchange will go into the
paper as follows: 'I have dreamt of this moment all my life.' Thus a
cliché is thrown up by the press, and printed by the press. The closed
circle suits everybody. And if you put in a 'request' and secure a private
interview, if you try to look 'behind the scenes', then all you'll find is
another scene, another layer of press patter. This shouldn't surprise
anyone. And besides, it has never been a particularly fruitful business,
asking teenage girls *what they feel.*

'5 to 11 – Complimentary Champagne FOR ALL LADIES', says the sign,
rather desperately, in the bar of the official hotel. Needless to say, Gaby

and Steffi are not to be seen here, enjoying six hours of complimentary champagne. There used to be a few ravers among the better-known players; but tennis girls are compulsive types, and once they started raving, they soon stopped being among the better-known players. All that is of course out of the question these days. Fun and boys and free champagne, like everything else, is scheduled to happen 'later'.

Steffi and Gaby are not to be seen in the hotel. They are cordoned off elsewhere. Only the Coach Class players dwell here in Park Place. They wander around with their sausage bags. They drink milk with breakfast (suggesting childish tastes as well as sensible nutrition). They sleep three to a room and talk worriedly about how they will split the tab. They are not yet – and may never be – on the other side, the place where everyone is suddenly dying to give them money. Their numbers remorselessly dwindle as the week goes on.

For things are getting serious. The plucky underdogs and the eye-catchers are all falling away: Gigi Fernandez, with her vociferous flair and fecklessness; Rafaella Reggi, the glamorous grunter; squawlike Mary Joe Fernandez, the unforgiving baseliner; Sandra Cecchini, dynamically butch and spivvy; the Czech pylon Helena Sukova, borne everywhere on the shoulders of two little bodybuilders (which turn out to be her legs): the shriekers and whoofers and hworfers step aside, revealing the handful of players who are capable of winning it – or of worrying Steffi Graf. All week, as tickets get pricier, the seat allocations for the press have become more and more disadvantageous. For the final, a further spasm of sponsorial greed lofts us up into the bleachers. It is the match everyone wants to see: Graf v. Sabatini. Fräulein Forehand meets Bonita Backhand.

On the big day I breakfast within eavesdropping distance of the TV crew that has flown down for the match. 'Do we do a *pre*-match interview?' one of them asks. 'With Steffi? I don't know. She goes into like a trance before the start.' The upside of interviewing Steffi in mid-reverie – or of at least televising the trance – is briefly discussed. Can they *get* the pre-match interview? They think so. In no other sport will two individuals be given up to three hours of screen time, and TV is the fount of all the real tennis money. It is why each square inch of Steffi's shirt is worth a million dollars.

'Ladies and gentlemin!' Seen from on high, the demeanour of the show court clearly reflects the narrowing gap between top tennis and show business. The flags, the floodlights, the VIP boxes, the camera gantries, the officials in candy stripe (pompous Pancho Gonzalez lookalikes, fully convinced, like the TV people, of their vital contribution to the spectacle), the rock-hard PR girl with her interminable plugs and mentions and personal thanks to all the allegedly wonderful Dekes and Duanes and Sharons and Karens who have made all this possible. The crowd, too, is participatory in the American style. What kind of clothes do Americans wear when they watch tennis? Tennis clothes. And they join in with their aggressive questioning of calls, frequent demands to be reminded of the score, and continuous and deafening cries of 'Quiet!'

Steffi Graf is something unbelievable on the tennis court, a miracle of speed, balance and intense athleticism. She looks like a skater but she moves like a puck. During changeovers she gets up early from her chair, and she is always exasperated (hands on hips, head bowed) by any delay from opponent or ballboy. After a great shot she doesn't wait for the applause to start, let alone stop, before she is striding back to the baseline, twiddling her racket like a six-gun. She never smiles. She wants to win every set to love and get on with the next one. You feel that the only player she would enjoy facing is herself.

Today she is facing Gabriela, who has never beaten her in eleven meetings. And it looks like the same old story. Steffi's forehand is booming, and she is slicing her backhand under the breeze. Instead of retreating twenty feet for the high topspin (as Evert had done in the semi-final), Steffi adopts the ploy of jumping waist-high to make her drives. Steffi is one set up and serving at 3–2 in the second. The crowd (strongly Hispanic, or strongly Jewish and therefore anti-German) groans and sweats for the wilting, shamefaced Gaby. Then something happens. And we'll never know what. Steffi collapses in a blizzard of errors, losing all but one of the next eleven games. An instant after the last point Gaby has the snout of a TV camera in her face. Then a microphone in her hand ('It's hard to talk right now'). Soon she is in the press tent, being asked what she feels ('It's hard to say'). And then she is packing her rackets and heading down to Key Biscayne for the Lipton, where she will lose to Mary Joe Fernandez in the quarters, and where Steffi, as tennis writers say, will return to her winning ways.

The person to ask about modern tennis stardom is not a modern tennis star, who will probably be seventeen and speak little English, and who will have attended a course on how to handle herself with – or, more simply, how to handle – the media. The person to ask, if you can get past her agent, is Tatum O'Neal, who is married to John McEnroe and, more importantly, was herself a prodigy, a thoroughbred of the star system. The system prescribes a life of unique enclosure, in which every contact is featherbedded, insulated, mediated. Fixers, helpers, PR people, guys with guns everywhere: these extras are just part of the scenery for the gazelles and snow leopards of modern tennis, a protected species – priceless specimens – in their bijou theme park. Of course, for the virgin millionairesses there will be life after tennis. But there was no life before it – before they sank into the strange obscurity of stardom.

Colm Tóibín

Maradona

The Buenos Aires police came for him when he was still sleeping. Once they had the warrant to search the house, they had begun to ring around journalists and television crews: the address, they said, is Calle Franklin 869, and the raid will be between two and three in the afternoon. You might be interested, they said, because Diego Maradona is inside.

He had been up most of the night playing *chin-chon*, a local version of rummy, with two friends. Friends from the old days, who enjoyed his power and his money. One of them was known as El Soldado – the soldier – because he tended to do whatever Maradona wanted when they were out on the town. At some stage the previous evening, three young women had visited the apartment; two stayed and enjoyed themselves with Maradona and his friends, but the other left early.

She may or may not have been a police informer. She may or may not have phoned the police. But by the following morning the police knew who was in the apartment – and that there was cocaine, which those inside had been consuming that night.

That was Friday, 26 April 1991. On Monday, Argentina's main sports magazine, *El Grafico*, reported the police had found Maradona asleep in bed, naked beside one of his friends. That report caused much righteous indignation in Buenos Aires. But it was untrue. Maradona was alone in bed when the police came, and he was wearing underpants. He was asleep, curled up in a foetal position.

By the time the police entered the apartment, the evidence went, one of Maradona's companions had thrown a nylon packet of cocaine out of the window, and it had landed on the awning over the shop below. It contained two or three grams of cocaine. The police had a witness who said he saw it being thrown from the window of the apartment in which Maradona was sleeping. That such a witness was so easily found and so willing to come forward makes the raid on Calle Franklin 869 seem a set-up to get Maradona, and Buenos Aires buzzes with theories about the reasons for the raid: to distract the public from the scandals surrounding President Carlos Menem's wife's family; to impress the American Embassy, increasingly perturbed by evidence that Argentina, rich in private airstrips, is being used as a centre for cocaine distribution and that Menem's family is involved.

Maradona had been living it up since he slipped out of Italy on 1 April, using the diplomatic passport he had been given by President Menem before the 1990 World Cup. Suddenly, for the first time in his life, he was in Buenos Aires without any training schedule or daily routine. For three weeks, he had been free to do as he pleased. When he was arrested, his family had not seen him for two days.

Some of his soccer friends have remained intensely loyal. Sergio Batista, who played with him in the 1986 World Cup and shared a room with him in Italy during the 1990 tournament, turned up in court to support him, and has been seeing him and training with him since then. Batista believes Maradona has never come to realize fully what his name means, what being Maradona entails. He loves it, the fame, the adulation, but he has never fully understood, Batista says, just how limited the rest of his life would have to be.

Batista did not see much of Maradona during his first weeks back in the city, nor did Maradona see many of his close friends from sport. He hung around instead with people more interested in what Argentinians used to call *samba y caramba* than in keeping fit or playing football. There is, in Argentina, a deep disapproval of drug consumption, as there is a disapproval of alcohol (Maradona hardly touches alcohol). It is eminently possible, perhaps the most likely scenario, that Diego Maradona and his activities came to the attention of the police in Buenos Aires over and over again in the weeks before his arrest. It is entirely possible that there was no government-sponsored conspiracy to get him. It could be that he simply left himself wide open, innocently misunderstanding how far he could go in his home town.

The night of his arrest he was scheduled to attend a huge party to celebrate the National Day of Sport. Carlos Menem, ex-President Raúl Alfonsín and the entire Argentinian sports establishment would be there. He was the hero come home as victim. Up to his arrest, he had had everyone's sympathy.

But now you could watch him on television being led out of the flat by police. People remembered he had been involved in an anti-drugs advertising campaign just eighteen months before. He had suddenly joined the list of people whom Argentinians blame for the terrible despair that overwhelms their country.

*

'Who is representing whom?' Hans Henningson asked. It was early
1976, in the Sheraton Hotel in Buenos Aires. These two youngsters had
come to meet Henningson and Juan Carlos Cazaux to discuss sponsorship from Puma, for which both men worked. The two youngsters
were so small and raw. One was dark and open-faced; the other was
pudgy with curly fair hair. He was introduced as the *representante*; he
walked with a limp.

No Argentinian player had ever had an agent before. It was unheard
of. But even then it was clear that the player, the dark, open-faced one,
Diego Maradona, was exceptional; even then he stood out. Juan Carlos
Cazaux had first heard about him the previous year, but wasn't
interested in offering him sponsorship. Maradona was too young at
fifteen to be taken on.

And there were other reasons for not going to see him. He had
come to fame not as a footballer but as a performer. He was the small
boy who came out at half-time with a football and moved around the
pitch, to wild cheers and applause, keeping the ball in the air, using his
feet and his head with incredible skill, never letting the ball get beyond
his control. They loved this kid, he could do amazing things, and all the
time he moved so each side could see how prodigious his talent was.

Still Cazaux was not impressed; such kids had been around before,
had come and gone, but had never made it as footballers. But his
informer insisted: this *negrito* is something else, you must come and
see. The word *negrito* is important. In Argentina, it means someone
from the social margins, from the shanty towns beyond the city, with
Bolivian or Paraguayan blood, perhaps with Indian blood, but with
darker skin than the ruling class. That was the word Cazaux first heard
to describe Maradona.

Eventually, he went to see him and he loved him. He still remembers
the way Maradona dominated the ball, he still remembers his speed.
He knew he was watching a great player. He contacted him, invited
him to come to his office to accept a pair of shoes. Maradona came in
with his two younger brothers in an old Fiat 1600. They were shy, but
watchful, and they were well dressed, Cazaux remembers.

It was the first time he had given shoes to such a young player. But
the following year, as he watched Maradona's progress, he decided to
contact him and arranged to meet him at the Sheraton Hotel.
Maradona and his 'representative' came looking for sportswear, and
were very surprised when they were offered a contract from Puma for
fifty thousand dollars over four years. They signed.

The representative, the pudgy one (Cazaux refers to him as *el gordito)*, was to stay with Maradona as agent, friend and constant companion over the next ten years. He was to become Maradona's shadow. In 1980, they sent a joint Christmas card. They were like complete opposites: Maradona was talkative, Jorge Cyterszpiler (pronounced Seeterspeeler) was taciturn, much given to monosyllabic communication; Maradona was Catholic, of Italian origin; Cyterszpiler was Jewish, of Polish origin; Cyterszpiler's older brother, his hero as a child, had been a player with Argentinos Juniors, but he had died. For a few years as an adolescent, Cyterszpiler did not go near a pitch.

He was twelve, two years older than Maradona when they first met. Cyterszpiler had become interested in an under-age team called Los Cebollitas – 'the little onions' – in which Maradona played. Most of the kids lived in the shanty towns outside the city and had to travel long distances for games and practices. Some, including Maradona who lived miles out in a place called Fiorito, began to stay over on Friday and Saturday nights in Cyterszpiler's house, close to the Argentinos Juniors football grounds.

Oswaldo Lopez, a Juniors official, remembers Maradona hanging around the fringes of the club from the age of eight, first as a ballboy, then as a half-time performer and a member of Los Cebollitas. He remembers his playing style from the beginning as being without fear, without caution. No one else from Los Cebollitas ever made it into professional football, Lopez says, but it was clear that as soon as Maradona came of age he would be taken on by Argentinos Juniors.

Maradona's first contract was negotiated by Cyterszpiler, who demanded something which the Juniors had never given to a player, and have not since: a rented apartment near the grounds for Maradona and his family. So, at fifteen, Maradona was able to take his family out of the *villa miseria* of Fiorito and house them in a modest apartment near the centre of Buenos Aires.

Later, as his fame grew and his playing became more skilled, the club bought him and his family a house. His aim, he said, was to make enough money so that his father, who worked long hours in a mill for very little money, could give up his job. Cyterszpiler remembers that when Maradona was eighteen – in 1978 – he was making enough money to support his parents and most of his seven brothers and sisters.

That was the year of the World Cup in Argentina, and Maradona was bitterly disappointed to be one of the three dropped at the last minute by Cesar Menotti. He cried like a child, Cyterszpiler says. Juan Carlos Cazaux remembers his going outside on the day he heard the news and spending more than an hour with his elbows leaning on a fence, staring into the distance. He went over it in interview after interview, how he could never forgive Menotti. But his non-inclusion was an issue only for those who closely followed sport in Argentina; his status as national hero came about only the following year when he played in the Junior World Championship in Japan, and the entire country followed his playing on television.

From then on, he was public property; everyone who came across him in the subsequent years talks about how hard it was for him, so outgoing and extrovert but unable to walk the streets without being hassled for autographs. Sergio Batista talks about Maradona's acute consciousness now that he never had a youth, that from the age of nineteen he could never go anywhere without being noticed.

He began to give constant interviews and to keep a diary, which was published in *El Grafico*. In it, he portrayed himself as a small, innocent angel, protected by Menotti and Cyterszpiler, a youngster who trained hard, did what he was told and went to bed early at night. Over and over, he talked about his family, some of whom travelled with him wherever he went. When he scored a goal, he said, he thought of his mother. When he was away, he telephoned home all the time. In 1976, after his move from Fiorito he met Claudia Villafane and he wrote about how much he missed her when he was away.

He had no difficulty talking about his need for prayer, his love of his family or about how he cried after a match. He was, in the publicity surrounding him during his early years, goodness personified. He also began to portray himself as a victim and with good reason. He was so fast and inventive as a player that it was almost impossible to mark him. So players began to kick him. Kicking Maradona seemed to have become as much a part of the games in which he played as kicking the ball. 'All my rivals want to kick me,' he said.

During his trip to Ireland in 1980, he wrote in his diary not about the quality of the game, but about his fear that he would be kicked, and he records one particular kick from an Irish international. His Performance against England at Wembley in 1980 was triumphant, and the report in *The Sunday Times* was reproduced in the Argentinian press: 'Maradona kept possession of the ball for two minutes and ten seconds of continuous action,' it said.

Argentinians are obsessed with the view the outside world has of them, and Maradona's success abroad, especially at Wembley ('the home of football', he recorded in his diary), increased his hero status in an Argentina that was becoming known in the outside world for illegal detentions, disappearances and an ugly military regime.

From 1980 onwards, the talk was of Europe, and of which club would buy Maradona. By now, he had transferred from Argentinos Juniors to Boca, another local club. There were dark complaints in the Argentinian press about their best players leaving, and hope was expressed that something could be done to keep Maradona. But he was ready to go to the highest bidder, and so in 1982 he left Argentina to play for Barcelona. His best years were to be spent outside Argentina.

They ask you again and again: what do you think of Argentina? Do people in Europe think this is a banana republic? They feel abandoned by the world outside; they are, they keep telling you, Europeans; they built Buenos Aires to look like a European city; they are not South Americans; they never intermarried with the natives; why, look around you, there are no natives. (They murdered all the natives in the last years of the nineteenth century.) There is a sadness and a despair in the way they appeal to you to understand them and accept them. Look at the opera house the Teatro Colon; all the great singers came here, they tell you – Caruso, Galli-Curci, Joan Sutherland. They have the list at their fingertips. This was one of the richest countries in the world.

The great plain of Argentina was, even in the nineteenth century, a vast emptiness. The early Spanish settlers were looking for gold and silver, so they left the plain, the pampas, pure clay, to the natives. Until the first half of the nineteenth century, you could go and claim some of the richest land in the world.

At first, Argentina thrived by exporting wheat to Europe, but the country's real wealth came with the refrigerated ship. They produced the best beef in the world, and they built their capital city and their great pride out of the money they made from beef. In the last years of the nineteenth century and the first decades of the twentieth, they built mansions throughout Buenos Aires. But they never believed in Argentina and they invested their money elsewhere. They honeymooned and holidayed in Europe; they imported European furniture and fittings. Argentina was a cultural and spiritual exile.

The second wave of immigrants, from the south of Italy and northern Spain, came to service the new wealth, as labourers in the port, the mills and the slaughterhouses. They found work, but they found, too, that the wealth of the new country had already been divided up. Their sharp sense of exclusion would later take root in the Peronist movement once they had settled.

As the century progressed, the country's fabulous wealth began to evaporate. It had allowed too many outside interests to control its infrastructure. It had nothing to fall back on once Europe and the US adopted protectionist policies, nowhere else to send its beef and wheat and nothing else to send. It was destined to dream of former greatness, to grow old reminiscing about a glory turned to dust.

If you drive out from Buenos Aires to Fiorito in search of the house where Maradona was born, you move from that world of privilege and wealth and dreams to another world made up of immigrants who never shared in the wealth. You move from the planned centre of the city, with its long boulevards and expensive shops, to a township with unpaved roads and windowless shacks.

But it is not simply the contrast in architecture or streetscape that is striking. The people look different; some have Indian features, but most have darker skin, the skin of people who have been out in the sun. This is where the *negritos* live.

In Buenos Aires, people are dismissive about Fiorito; they talk about its inhabitants in racist terms and mention Maradona's Fiorito background as signalling a sort of reduced moral and intellectual fibre.

Although Sergio Batista expresses his delight at Maradona's wealth because he has come from such lowly origins, most feel that someone who comes from Fiorito cannot properly represent Argentina.

You turn off a road full of potholes on to a dirt road. Not all the people are badly dressed, but most look poor. All the houses are small, but some have been plastered and painted. There are mongrel dogs and horses everywhere. After a while there are no cars. and people sit outside the houses, staring at you as you pass. Everyone you ask can direct you to the house where Maradona was born, but the football pitch where he played as a child has been built on.

Maradona's house in Calle Azamor is big by Fiorito's standards; it is plastered and there is a window on each side of the door; there is a small yard in front, and a gate leading to the unpaved road. Its current owners are not at home, according to a young man two doors away. Yes, he says, like everyone else in the street he knew the family, he played football with Diego, but he doesn't want his name written down; everyone around here played football together. Diego's father was his godfather, he says. and he knows he could go and see them any time. but, he shrugs, he sees no reason to do so, they have moved away.

Journalists have come before, he says, and been told by a group of people who gathered on the corner that Maradona used to collect scraps and cardboard when he was a child, but that simply is not true. Maradona went to school, and in Fiorito that was important. Also, this street is a settled community, unlike other parts of Fiorito where people come and go. The young man thinks these distinctions important.

Maradona has not been back to Fiorito for five or six years, the man says. The last time he came with a friend, a singer, to play in a celebrity match, but the people couldn't leave him alone, couldn't stop coming up to him and wanting to touch him. It was clear he was exasperated and would not be in a hurry to come back. People from the street were not invited to his wedding in 1989.

There is still a football pitch close to the house, close, too, to a smouldering dump. The pitch has a clay surface, perfectly laid out and flattened. It is Saturday afternoon, and there is a match in progress. The players are young, but the game is being conducted with extraordinary speed, seriousness and ferocity. All of the players are decked out in decent sports gear, despite the poverty of the locality.

Football in Argentina comes from poverty. This is the world from which Maradona and most other Argentinian professional footballers come, the world he constantly refers to, the place where he was formed. When asked if he had ever been there, a senior figure in Argentina's football organization winced and pointed to his clothes and body and said of course he had never been there, he was from Buenos Aires.

Someone from out there could never become a gentleman. 'Look at Pelé,' a member of the old Argentinian bourgeoisie said. 'He came to Punte del Este [the posh seaside resort in Uruguay] last year and sat close to me in a restaurant. He was a gentleman [*un caballero*]. You could never imagine Maradona in such a place.'

The boy from Fiorito did not grow up to become a gentleman. He made no effort to join the bourgeoisie of Buenos Aires, he remained intensely loyal to his family and his childhood sweetheart and the friends he made when he moved out of Fiorito into the city. Even the house he bought for his parents in Calle Cantilo stands out in the street of quiet, detached houses as shiny and ostentatious.

His wedding was, in the words of one member of the establishment,

perhaps the most vulgar occasion ever held in Argentina. He invited
more than a thousand people, flying a plane-load from Europe. It was
held in the Luna Park and cost more than a million dollars. People
who were there, such as Oswaldo Lopez from Argentinos Juniors or
Daniel Arcacce from *El Grafico* magazine, had a great time, loved the
glitter of the occasion and point out that Maradona could have had
the whole event sponsored, but he chose to pay for everything himself.

Maradona had been going out with Claudia for fourteen years.
When asked why he was getting married, he said he wanted to have a
party, a really big one, and anyway his girlfriend's mother was being
asked all the time why her daughter wasn't getting married, and he
thought he should do the decent thing. He treated the whole thing as
a joke.

His first child had been born two years previously, and the journalist
Carlos Bonelli was invited to the huge party in the Harrods salon in
the centre of Buenos Aires. Maradona led his baby daughter into the
ceremony in a supermarket trolley. Antics like that, and the fact that
Maradona was the best-known Argentinian in the world, were an even
further humiliation for the rich of the city as inflation increased at
home and the value of their investments abroad lessened each year.

But the parties and the ostentatious wealth did not help Maradona's
popularity among the class he came from. He loved being photographed with stars and famous people. His visits to Buenos Aires were
becoming vast media events. In the beginning, he had come to
represent the outsiders in Argentina, just as General Perón had done,
but as he moved towards his thirtieth birthday his fame and his wealth
had placed him outside the world that produced him.

Even now, after all this time, Jorge Cyterszpiler grimaces when he hears
the Catalan language spoken by the management and most supporters
of the Barcelona football team. The two years Maradona spent in
Barcelona were not easy. The Catalans may cheer at a football match
on Sunday and passionately support their team, but the rest of the
week they work hard and stick to themselves.

Maradona brought with him hangers-on, 'the clan Maradona', who
peopled the nightclubs and fast-lane scene in the city. Barcelona has a
reputation for nightclubs and fancy bars, but there is a strict code of
laid-back, European behaviour. So a bunch of failed Argentinian
footballers with nothing to do all day stuck out in the city, and in the
newspapers became known as Maradona's Indians.

The more famous Maradona grew, the worse the physical attacks on him became. In Argentina before he left, the other players had begun to abuse him verbally as they marked him, taunting him for being worth millions of dollars. He did not learn to retaliate to physical attacks, unlike Pelé, who was not such easy prey. 'I can't learn,' he said, when asked if he was going to start defending himself. He also remarked that so much attention was paid to his behaviour on the pitch that if he elbowed an opponent it would be photographed and seen all over the world.

The most famous attack on him was in Barcelona in January 1984 when a Basque opponent, Goicoechea, gave him a vicious kick that severed a ligament in his ankle and caused him to have thirty stitches, putting him out of action for four months.

By the end of 1983, Maradona was known to be having personal problems with the club, which sees itself as a symbol for the Catalan nation and in 1984 he agreed to transfer to Naples.

He had felt uncomfortable in Barcelona, Jorge Cyterszpiler says, but he was not prepared for Naples. The Catalans tend to be very reticent; Maradona was not mobbed in the streets of Barcelona, and his house in the Pedralbes district offered him a good deal of privacy. Buenos Aires is a huge city with sprawling suburbs, and there are, Cytserszpiler points out, at least a hundred restaurants Maradona could go to. Naples, on the other hand, is tiny. That was Maradona's first Neapolitan shock: there were only ten restaurants to visit.

And the people did not have the natural reticence of the Catalans. Maradona was public property. He made his coming to Naples into a sort of homecoming. 'I want to make myself into the idol of the kids of Naples,' he said, 'as I was to the kids of Buenos Aires.' He loved the adulation and the openness, but soon he and Cyterszpiler realized that he would have no privacy in the city.

He was now worth a great deal of money, but was subsequently to tell an interviewer that at the age of twenty-five, around the time when he began playing for Naples, he hadn't got a penny. Cyterszpiler denies this, and says that one report has been quoted over and over. He adds that Maradona has recently told him that he never said he was broke at twenty-five.

And yet it does seem that certain foolish investments were made. The Argentinian journalist Carlos Bonelli did not believe that Maradona had invested money in the bingo business in Paraguay until he was in Asunción himself and saw a Maradona bingo hall in the most exclusive suburb of the city, two blocks away from where Somoza was assassinated and close to where government ministers were living. It was not doing good business.

In 1985, Maradona and Cyterszpiler split up in acrimony. Cyterszpiler went back to Argentina, and Maradona's new manager, Guillermo Cuppola, did not encourage Maradona to see him again. Cyterszpiler was not one of the thousand friends invited to Maradona's wedding in 1989. He dedicated himself, back in the old country, to furthering the career of an obscure Peronist politician called Carlos Menem and became chief of his campaign organization during the presidential elections, which Menem won. ('I'm thirty-two,' he says proudly, 'and I've managed Maradona and Menem.')

Cuppola was the exact opposite to Cyterszpiler. It would be almost impossible to imagine Cyterszpiler in a nightclub. Cuppola loved nightclubs: he was talkative, outgoing, he enjoyed the high life. He had been married to an actress and he liked being photographed with beautiful women. He had started from the bottom, as a messenger boy in a bank. He had begun to work on the side as a players' agent, and at one point he had almost two hundred Argentinian players and managers on his books.

Cuppola devoted his entire time to Maradona's career. He was now the most expensive player in the world, and Cuppola, it is said, handled his finances with great skill. But as Maradona changed the fortunes of his club, Naples itself became more and more of a nightmare. He was a prisoner in his apartment. Carlos Bilardo, the manager of the Argentinian football team from 1983 to 1990, says the effect on Maradona should not be underestimated. He couldn't go out on the street, Bilardo says, and if he was asked to sign an autograph and refused, news would spread that Maradona had insulted a fan.

On tour, Bilardo says, Maradona couldn't even go down to the hotel lobby. If the rest of the team went to a restaurant with Maradona, they knew their meal would be constantly interrupted, so Maradona tended not to go out with them.

Opponents continued to kick him. Puma's Cazaux spoke to a doctor who had seen him after a match and remarked that his body was covered in bruises. In his seven seasons with Napoli, the club won two Italian titles, one UEFA Cup and one Italian Cup. In Maradona's first season alone, the club easily recouped his purchase price by increased ticket sales. He was treated like royalty as long as he continued to deliver.

But every move he made was subjected to scrutiny. A woman claimed he was the father of her child. There were other claims that he was seeing unsavoury people and hiring prostitutes. The problem for him and for Cuppola was when and how to leave Naples. Clearly, in retrospect, had he left in 1990, he would have become a great myth and a hero in Naples, but his contract demanded that he stay on, so he stayed.

Last November, for reasons that have never been explained, Cuppola retired as his manager – he has since denied in the magazine *Somos* that he ever saw Maradona taking cocaine – and so Maradona was left in Naples between then and April without an essential piece of his protection. Once he ceased to deliver, once his erratic behaviour became a hindrance to Napoli's (his team) fortunes, he was defenceless in the city. It would be easy to make him a scapegoat. He lacked the guile and watchfulness to save himself.

Last November, Maradona refused to travel with Napoli to Moscow for a European Championship game. He made no secret of the fact that he had been out the previous night having a good time. Napoli were eliminated from the tournament, which cost the club a great deal of money in potential ticket sales. A few months later, Maradona was subjected to a cocaine test, which he failed, and suspended from soccer for fifteen months by FIFA, the world soccer association.

There is a terrible sadness about Buenos Aires now. Its glory has departed; the great singers no longer come to the Teatro Colon; all the cars are old.

Everything has been tried to get the economy working again. In the 1970s, the generals who took over from Isabel Perón decided to borrow money to keep the value of the currency artificially high. They hoped Argentinian industry would import machinery at low cost. Instead, the Argentinians, on discovering their pesos were worth a fortune outside Argentina, began to travel. They bought anything they could lay their hands on in France, in Spain, in the US. Taxi drivers, it is said, could afford to take their holidays in Tokyo.

This period is now referred to as *la epoca de la plata dulce*, the years of the sweet money, and it did not last long. It was to become the Indian summer of the Argentinian dream. They are still paying back the money. It was in Europe and the US that they first heard of the disappearances, how people were being picked up by the police and the army and never seen again, and this was happening in their own country. Many of them still do not believe it ever happened, although there are at least ten thousand names unaccounted for.

They are proud of Argentina, they love its flag and its national anthem. They were outraged when the Italians booed the anthem during the 1990 World Cup. They are loyal to the army, whose generals are members of the old aristocracy, and so the defeat in the Falklands War is an unmentionable event, a trauma that has not yet been exorcized.

For ordinary people, democracy means you can feel free to say what you please and that is good. Except what people say is that wages are not keeping up with massive inflation, that you need two jobs to live and that there is no sign that things are going to improve. In 1985, the peso was replaced by the austral; now the austral has become debased.

The presidency of Raúl Alfonsín, who took over from the generals in 1983, was a period of great industrial strife, which often crippled Buenos Aires and did not help the Argentinian economy. But at least Alfonsín was an honest and stabilizing influence. His successor, Carlos Menem, the obscure politician whom Jorge Cyterszpiler helped to power, the man who made Maradona Argentina's ambassador for sport, has provided Argentina with a soap opera that may have amused the outside world but has done nothing for Argentina's great pride.

His difficult relationship with his wife, their public rows, her eviction from the presidential palace became part of the daily news in his first year. Since then, the allegations against Menem and his wife and his wife's family have become more serious. They include the accusation that Menem's sister-in-law carried suitcases of drug money – each said to contain a million dollars – into Argentina and was let through customs at the airport in Buenos Aires by her ex-husband, an airport official. Argentina's Vice-President, Eduardo Duhalde. remarked that Menem's wife's family 'are making the government look like a situation-comedy show.'

The Argentinians' nightmare is that people all over the world will laugh at them. Menem is one aspect of their shame; now Diego Maradona is back in the city in disgrace, after admitting that over the past three years he has been taking cocaine. He is seeing psychiatrists and keeping a low profile. Recently, while out running in the suburbs, he met a group of joggers. He said he would run with them as long as they did not ask him to talk. His lawyers have made it clear he must say nothing.

Jorge Cyterszpiler has begun to see him again, after a break of more than five years. Sergio Batista has missed practice with his team to go and train with Maradona, who has a private football pitch and sports complex outside the city. He is living quietly, Batista says, and, more than anything else, he feels shame for what he has done.

People speak well of him now that he is back. Carlos Bilardo speaks of him as the most perfect and well-behaved player he has ever known. For the many companies who have sponsored him, it is vital that his reputation be salvaged in some way, that the parties, cocaine and women are seen as a thing of the past.

His family still adores him. His photograph has pride of place in the hallway of his parents' house. The journalist Carlos Bonelli accompanied him on a trip to Cuba several years ago with members of his family, including his mother and two sisters. He remembers how Maradona basked in their adulation. He loves being loved.

On that trip to Cuba, Bonelli remembers Maradona on the beach, how he could not sit still, how he played all day with a football, tossing it in the air, running with it. He can't stop performing. Carlos Bilardo believes that he will play again, and Sergio Batista hopes that he will. But over the past few weeks, Batista says, Maradona himself has been insisting he will not return to the game, that he is ready now to begin to live and wants to retire from football.

Most observers in Buenos Aires agree he will not be sent to jail, if he is convicted as a result of the 26 April raid, but be given some sort of suspended sentence. It will be hard for him, Batista says, to settle down after all the adulation, all the fame and glory. 'It's very difficult,' Batista says. 'He lost his youth. He didn't have a youth. He says he doesn't want to play again.'

Matthew Engel

Sweeping Death Under the Carpet

Bill Smith, Chairman of the Auto Cycle Union, and I were standing in a garden belonging to a lovely lady called Beryl, waiting for the riders to come by in the Supersport 400 event, the third race of the Isle of Man TT week. We were on Bray Hill in Douglas, which to the untutored eye appears to be a street of detached and semi-detached 1930s houses like thousands of others in the British Isles, though the TT course guide talks instead about 'an ultra-fast right-left hander with a sadistic bump just out of sight over the crest'.

Smith was apologetic. 'They're not very quick, the 400s.' Suddenly, the first rider came by, a flash of man and motorbike. He was doing 130 miles an hour on a line precisely seven feet from Beryl's front gate.

The rest streaked through at intervals of a few seconds, silencing conversation and birdsong, whooshing past Armleigh and Monaveen, past the pebble-dash garages and the rock gardens and the bird tables and the rose trellises, down past the newsagents and the beauty salon, up the next hill and out of sight.

It does not require much imagination to work out what the attitude of most people in similar streets in Dorking or Doncaster would be if motorbikes were doing such speeds seven feet from their front gate at five in the morning. I asked Beryl what she thought. 'Oh, love it,' she said.

Beryl spoke for everyone. On the Isle of Man and among the motorcycling fancy the TT Races are a matter of huge interest, intense pride and no controversy. The TT made the island famous; otherwise, there are only cats, kippers and the birch. The races are the basis of a tourist trade which in other respects has been in steady decline, but the TT ceased to be part of the Grand Prix circuit fifteen years ago. The top track riders no longer come here, nor do most sportswriters.

Non-Manxmen and non-bikers now hear little except the statistics: of the 535 competitors entered in this year's TT, four are already dead – Ian Young, Petr Hlavatka from Czechoslovakia, a father of three,

Frank Duffy and Roy Anderson. This brings the total killed on the course over the past eighty years to 160. For reasons we shall come to, this is a strictly unofficial figure.

The event, however, is not declining. It has turned into the world's greatest bike-festival: 40,000 enthusiasts flock here, bringing with them 14,000 motorbikes. But two of the fans have also been killed this year, one of them on an occasion known, with reason, as Mad Sunday, when anyone can ride round the course. No one knows how many people, competitors and others, have been injured, crippled or rendered senseless over the years. But an informed source estimated that there are between twenty and fifty major injuries – broken legs and worse – during the fortnight every year. These are subjects which no one on the island wants to discuss. They want to talk about Steve Hislop's chances of winning the big race today and whether he might push the lap record to over 125 m.p.h. It is not exactly a conspiracy of silence, but there is a conspiracy to talk as quietly as possible.

Forty per cent of the Isle of Man's declining tourist industry depends on motor-sport events; the Manx weekly papers did not even name all the dead riders. There must be Manxmen who oppose the whole business, but they keep quiet and take their holidays when the TT is on. For motorcyclists the island is a haven of tolerance in a hostile world and they hate the bad publicity as much as their hosts. *Motor Cycle News* shoved the deaths very quietly on page two.

People here – nice, helpful, friendly people – begin to shuffle uneasily when they meet a journalist who does not want to write about the torque ratios on the 750 Honda. In the early 1970s in the United States, 30 people were killed every year playing American football; last year no one was. Grand Prix racing drivers used to die with horrific regularity; the last death, touch wood, was in 1982.

There is a modern obsession with avoiding risk of any kind: James Dean and Jim Morrison are modern icons but no longer role models. Most westerners now want to grow old. The Isle of Man prides itself on being behind the times.

Roy Anderson, the fourth rider to die this year, was a Scot. At once a Scottish Labour MP, Tony Worthington, demanded that the whole thing be banned, as Labour MPs are prone to do when they know nothing about a subject.

'He wants to mind his own business,' said Michael Jopling, the former Conservative Chief whip and agriculture minister who is president of the Auto Cycle Union. The Isle of Man is not part of the

United Kingdom. They make their own laws and they are grown-up boys. It really is nothing to do with Westminster MPs.'

Is this so? Well, up to a point. The Isle of Man is a 'Crown dependency' like Jersey and Guernsey. Its parliament, Tynwald, existed when the Saxons and Celts on the two big islands nearby were running about in woad. If its 70,000 people did send an MP to Westminster it would undoubtedly be someone not unlike Michael Jopling.

The TT – which stands for Tourist Trophy – started here in 1907 because Westminster even then refused to countenance the idea of closing public roads for racing. It fits into the island's prevailing philosophy, which might be defined as selective libertarianism.

The tax laws are famously generous. There is no breathalyser and no general speed limit. Seat-belts are not compulsory. On the other hand, hanging and birching are still on the statute books, homosexuals can, theoretically, be locked up for life and a TT fan from Nuneaton was jailed this week after disembarking from the ferry with the grand total of 1.3 grams of cannabis.

In practice the laws are less draconian than they sound. The lad with the dope will be released when the races are over, the police do not charge into homosexuals' bedrooms, and no one will ever be hanged or birched again – quiet pressure from Westminster sees to that.

Manxmen just like to maintain the pretence that they could do it if they wanted, and that their strictness keeps them free of the modern world's impurities. This is total rubbish, as even the island's Minister of Tourism, Alan Bell, admitted: 'We kid ourselves that we have the moral high ground. We have exactly the same problems for our size as any rural community anywhere.'

But when it comes to road safety, the island is different. Driving down the hill to Creg Ny Baa on Tuesday, which was not a race day, we were overtaken by a motorcyclist doing at least 140. He was committing no offence.

Everyone admits that the race kills people. The famous Mountain Course, almost 38 miles round the centre of the island and along the fringe of lovely Snaefell, has been in use since 1911. Victor Surridge was killed on Creg Willey's Hill that year, when the machines were little more than pushbikes with engines attached and the fastest lap was clocked at 50 m.p.h. Competitors have been dying ever since, but there is no discernible pattern. Victims include brilliant riders and other riders who should never have been there. They have died through their own errors and mechanical failure. They have died in obvious danger spots and on the most ordinary stretches.

Safety measures have improved over the years and injured riders are now picked up by helicopter and rushed to hospital much faster. But the motorbikes keep getting faster too. Obvious hazards are cushioned with bags of hay, but on a course of thirty-eight miles and 400 bends it is not possible to soften every tree, telegraph pole and stone wall.

'I would have to accept that the TT is dangerous,' said Bill Smith of the ACU. 'Bloody dangerous. There is no doubt about that. I think people accept the risks.'

Not everyone does. Among the race's most forceful critics is the former world champion, Barry Sheene. 'It is totally impossible to make the course even reasonably safe,' says Sheene, who raced here once and never came back.

The islanders are scornful. 'It's easy to go on a bike and ride round a track five or ten times with plenty of spin-off areas,' says Paul Quine, who lives just by Bray Hill. 'It takes a motorcyclist to ride this. Barry Sheene wasn't man enough to ride the course.'

The arguments of the TT's supporters become a bit repetitive. They endlessly claim that other sports are just as dangerous. They have been known to argue that considering the number of riders and the miles they travel, the race is really rather safe.

The most astute point was made by Peter Sheen of the Motor-Cycle Industry Association, who said the course was such a superb test that it contributed hugely to bike development and thus saved lives elsewhere.

One enthusiast was talking less intelligently: 'Look at all the rugby players in Stoke Mandeville. Compare it to other sports. I think it's safe.'

'I've covered a lot of sports,' I said. 'I don't think it is.'

He sighed. 'Well, that's what makes it. I'll tell you what. You put handrails up Mount Everest, you'll get ice picks in your back.'

And that's the point, of course. Even seat-belted, low-fat, look-after-yourself modern man has a deep-seated urge to test himself. Among road racers it just lurks nearer the surface.

'These marvellous young men queue up to come here because they want to,' said Jopling. 'The vast majority of these nice guys who ride round the track lose money. It is inherently dangerous. People go into it because they know it is dangerous. I think the world is a more vigorous, interesting and exciting place when young men have the opportunity to meet this sort of challenge.'

The challenge of saying this loudly and meeting the objectors head-on is something the event's supporters find more daunting. If the ACU does keep a record of the deaths and injuries, it has never made it public. The figure of 160 comes from a little green notebook kept since 1965 by a Manx journalist, Terry Cringle, who discovered that no list existed and set out to compile one, he says, out of youthful enthusiasm and bloody-mindedness.

'I'm seen as a TT wrecker. Nothing could be further from the truth,' says Cringle. 'The only thing that annoyed me was that they kicked death under the carpet. These men had died and they dishonoured them. At one time they were really obstructive about giving out information on deaths. Now they do at least give it out in a professional way.'

But not very professionally. For a major sporting event, the TT is rather shambolic; that is part of its charm. There is none of the commercialized, security-conscious slickness of most modern sports events.

It is easy to drive up to the Grandstand and wander round. It is an event for fans, even in the press room. When Steve Hislop came in on Monday, he had more requests for autographs than interviews.

The organizers do care about the deaths, but they are bikers and bikers know the score. Could they do more? 'Not a lot, to be honest,' said Smith, 'not a lot.' But there are dangers that are obvious to the most casual observer.

At Creg Ny Baa, where the riders scream down the hill at 160-plus and take a right-hander with their right knees almost scraping the tarmac, they straighten up and take a line a few feet from kids dangling their feet over a bank. A mistake there could kill not just the rider but many spectators. I mentioned this to an official.

'Sore point,' he said. 'I've told them.'

The TT's appeal, however, lies not only in its challenge to competitors but in the freedom it offers spectators. Bike fans love to ride up to their own favourite spots, watch the racing, then get together with like-minded people afterwards.

On Douglas seafront the horse trams clip-clop incongruously past thousands of bikers of both sexes and a remarkable range of ages, caressing their machines and lovingly pointing out to new friends the twin-cams on their Kawasaki ZX-10 or something. Later they will earnestly discuss the Suzuki's cooling system over a pint of Okell's before revving up to go to the BMW Owners' Rally, say, or the nightly Miss Wet TT-shirt competition. About 6,000 of the visitors come from Germany. Everyone gets on famously. There is hardly any violence.

Motorcyclists see themselves as an oppressed minority. Other road users hate them. In their space gear they look frightening. Old ladies cower and imagine them all as Hell's Angels. In fact, they are often shy and solitary, which is why they ride motorbikes.

'It's an opportunity for motorcyclists to come somewhere in complete freedom where they're not hassled,' said Bell. 'They can go into the bars at the Palace Hotel and the Empress in their leathers and they're more than welcome.'

The TT offers freedom on many levels. Smith rode for twenty-seven years, losing many good friends but doing no damage to himself until his gearbox locked in 1982 and he broke both arms, both legs and his back. But the thrill has never vanished for him.

'The early morning practice is the best, climbing the mountain on a clear morning. Even on the bike you can see the five kingdoms – England, Scotland, Ireland, Wales and Man. It's the best feeling you could have in your life. Better than sex. A lot of the guys used to say they would sing when they were riding, they were so elated.'

And at the start line next day, you could see the current generation lined up, eyes intense behind their helmets, at ease with their machine but anxious to get going. The first away was number two, Brian Morrison.

There was no number one. Number one was meant to be Ian Young, and Ian Young was dead.

Joyce Carol Oates

On Boxing

I ain't never liked violence.
—Sugar Ray Robinson
former welterweight and middleweight
champion of the world

To the untrained eye most boxing matches appear not merely savage but mad. As the eye becomes trained, however, the spectator begins to see the complex patterns that underlie the "madness;" what seems to be merely confusing action is understood to be coherent and intelligent, frequently inspired. Even the spectator who dislikes violence in principle can come to admire highly skillful boxing—to admire it beyond all "sane" proportions. A brilliant boxing match, quicksilver in its motions, transpiring far more rapidly than the mind can absorb, can have the power that Emily Dickinson attributed to great poetry: you know it's great when it takes the top of your head off. (The physical imagery Dickinson employs is peculiarly apt in this context.)

This early impression—that boxing is "mad," or mimics the actions of madness—seems to me no less valid, however, for being, by degrees, substantially modified. It is never erased, never entirely forgotten or overcome; it simply sinks beneath the threshold of consciousness, as the most terrifying and heartrending of our lives' experiences sink beneath the level of consciousness by way of familiarity or deliberate suppression. So one knows, but does not (consciously) know, certain intransigent facts about the human condition. One does not (consciously) know, but one *knows*. All boxing fans, however accustomed to the sport, however many decades have been invested in their obsession, know that boxing is sheerly madness, for all its occasional beauty. That knowledge is our common bond and sometimes—dare it be uttered?—our common shame.

To watch boxing closely, and seriously, is to risk moments of what might be called animal panic—a sense not only that something very ugly is happening but that, by watching it, one is an accomplice. This awareness, or revelation, or weakness, or hairline split in one's cuticle of a self can come at any instant, unanticipated and unbidden; though of course it tends to sweep over the viewer when he is watching a really violent match. I feel it as vertigo—breathlessness—a repugnance beyond language: a sheerly physical loathing. That it is also, or even primarily, self-loathing goes without saying.

For boxing really isn't metaphor, it is the thing in itself. And my predilection for watching matches on tape, when the outcomes are known, doesn't alter the fact that, as the matches occurred, they occurred in the present tense, and for one time only. The rest is subterfuge—the intellectual's uneasy "control" of his material.

Impossible to see the old, early fights of Dempsey's and not to feel this *frisson* of dread, despite the poor quality of the films, the somewhat antic rhythms of the human figures. Or, I would guess, the trilogy of Zale–Graziano fights about which people speak in awe forty years later. For one man of my acquaintance it was a fight of Joe Louis's, against a long-forgotten opponent. For another, one of the "great" dirty matches of Willie Pep and Sandy Saddler—"little white perfection / and death in red plaid trunks" as the poet Philip Levine has written of that infamous duo. There was Duk Koo-Kim, there was Johnny Owen, in an earlier decade luckless Benny Paret, trapped in the ropes as referee Ruby Goldstein stood frozen, unable to interfere—

And Paret? Paret died on his feet. As he took those eighteen punches something happened to everyone who was in psychic range of the event. Some part of his death reached out to us. One felt it hover in the air. He was still standing in the ropes, trapped as he had been before, he gave some little half-smile of regret, as if he were saying, "I didn't know I was going to die just yet," and then, his head leaning back but still erect, his death came to breathe about him. He began to pass away. He went down more slowly than any fighter had ever gone down, he went down like a large ship which turns on end and slides second by second into its grave. As he went down, the sound of Griffith's punches echoed in the mind like a heavy ax in the distance chopping into a wet log.

—NORMAN MAILER, "Ten Thousand Words a Minute"

For one friend of mine it was a bloody fight fought by the lightweight contender Bobby Chacon that filled him with horror—though, ironically, Chacon came back to win the match (as Chacon was once apt to do). For another friend, a fellow novelist, enamored of boxing since boyhood, it was the Hagler–Hearns fight of 1985—he was frightened by his own ecstatic participation in it.

At such times one thinks: What is happening? Why are we here? What does this mean? Can't this be stopped? My terror at seeing Floyd Patterson battered into insensibility by Sonny Liston was not assuaged by my rational understanding that the event had taken place long ago and that, in fact, Patterson is in fine health at the present time, training an adopted son to box. (Liston of course has been dead for years—he died of a heroin overdose, aged thirty-eight, in "suspicious" circumstances.) More justified, perhaps, was my sickened sense that boxing is, simply, wrong, a mistake, an outlaw activity for some reason under the protectorate of the law, when, a few weeks ago in March 1986, I sat in the midst of a suddenly very quiet closed-circuit television audience in a suburban Trenton hall watching bantamweight Richie Sandoval as he lay flat and unmoving on his back ... very likely dead of a savage beating the referee had not, for some reason, stopped in time. My conviction was that anything was preferable to boxing, anything was preferable to seeing another minute of it, for instance standing outside in the parking lot for the remainder of the evening and staring at the stained asphalt ..."

A friend who is a sportswriter was horrified by the same fight. In a letter he spoke of his intermittent disgust for the sport he has been watching most of his life, and writing about for years: "It's all a bit like bad love—putting up with the pain, waiting for the sequel to the last good moment. And like bad love, there comes the point of being worn out, when the reward of the good moment doesn't seem worth all the trouble ..."

Yet we don't give up on boxing, it isn't that easy. Perhaps it's like tasting blood. Or, more discreetly put, love commingled with hate is more powerful than love. Or hate.

The spectacle of human beings fighting each other for whatever reason, including, at certain well-publicized times, staggering sums of money, is enormously disturbing because it violates a taboo of our civilization. Many men and women, however they steel themselves, cannot watch a boxing match because they cannot allow themselves to see what it is they are seeing. One thinks helplessly, This can't be happening, even as, and usually quite routinely, it *is* happening. In this way boxing as a public spectacle is akin to pornography: in each case the spectator is made a voyeur, distanced, yet presumably intimately involved, in an event that is not supposed to be happening as it is happening. The pornographic "drama," though as fraudulent as professional wrestling, makes a claim for being about something absolutely serious, if not humanly profound: it is not so much about itself as about the violation of a taboo. That the taboo is spiritual rather than physical, or sexual—that our most valuable human experience, love, is being desecrated, parodied, mocked—is surely at the core of our culture's fascination with pornography. In another culture, undefined by spiritual-emotional values, pornography could not exist, for who would pay to see it?

The obvious difference between boxing and pornography is that boxing, unlike pornography, is not theatrical. It is not, except in instances so rare as to be irrelevant, rehearsed or simulated. Its violation of the taboo against violence ("Thou shalt not kill" in its primordial form) is open, explicit, ritualized, and, as I've said, *routine*—which gives boxing its uncanny air. Unlike pornography (and professional wrestling) it is altogether real: the blood shed, the damage suffered, the pain (usually suppressed or sublimated) are unfeigned. Not for hemophobics, boxing is a sport in which blood becomes quickly irrelevant. The experienced viewer understands that a boxer's bleeding face is probably the least of his worries, and may, in fact, mean nothing at all—one thinks of Rocky Marciano's garishly bloodied but always triumphant face, Marvin Hagler's forehead streaming blood even as he outfought Thomas Hearns. The severely bleeding boxer and his seconds are anxious not about his cut face but about the possibility of the fight being stopped, which means a TKO victory for the opponent. Recall Ray "Boom Boom" Mancini in his second match with Livingstone Bramble, in which he desperately tried to wipe away with his gloves blood pouring from inch-long cuts in his eyelids: twenty-seven stitches were needed to sew up the cuts afterward. (Bramble, pragmatic like all boxers, naturally worked Mancini's damaged eyes as frequently as he could. Of 674 blows struck by Bramble 255 struck him in the face.)

Just as the boxer is trained to fight until he can't go on, so he is trained, or is by nature equipped, to fight unconscious on his feet. The image is indelibly imprinted in my memory of the doomed South Korean lightweight Duk Koo-Kim struggling to rise from the canvas after a blow of Mancini's burst a blood vessel in his brain—as if his body possessed its own demonic will even at the threshold of death. It is said that Joe Louis, badly stunned by Max Schmeling in their first fight, fought unconscious for several rounds—his beautifully conditioned body performing its trained motions like clockwork. (And it was during this losing bout that Louis's prodigious talent for endurance, and therefore for great boxing, manifested itself.) So customary is this sort of "fearless" boxing that the behavior of heavyweight Jesse Ferguson in his February 1986 match with Mike Tyson—clinching, holding on to Tyson's gloves, refusing in effect to fight—struck the eye as unnatural when of course it was utterly natural, the way the average man would behave in so desperate a situation. But boxing is contrary to nature.

One of the paradoxes of boxing is that the viewer inhabits a consciousness so very different from that of the boxer as to suggest a counterworld. "Free" will, "sanity," "rationality"—our characteristic modes of consciousness—are irrelevant, if not detrimental, to boxing in its most extraordinary moments. Even as he disrobes himself ceremonially in the ring the great boxer must disrobe himself of both reason and instinct's caution as he prepares to fight.

THE MOMENT

Nick Hornby

The Greatest Moment Ever

Liverpool v. Arsenal 26.5.89

In all the time I have been watching football, twenty-three seasons, only seven teams have won the First Division Championship: Leeds United, Everton, Arsenal, Derby County, Nottingham Forest, Aston Villa and, a staggering eleven times, Liverpool. Five different teams came top in my first five years, so it seemed to me then that the League was something that came your way every once in a while, even though you might have to wait for it; but as the 70s came and went, and then the 80s, it began to dawn on me that Arsenal might never win the League again in my lifetime. That isn't as melodramatic as it sounds. Wolves fans celebrating their third championship in six years in 1959 could hardly have anticipated that their team would spend much of the next thirty years in the Second and Third Divisions; Manchester City supporters in their mid-forties when the Blues last won the League in 1968 are in their early seventies now.

Like all fans, the overwhelming majority of the games I have seen have been League games. And as most of the time Arsenal have had no real interest in the First Division title after Christmas, nor ever really come close to going down, I would estimate that around half of these games are meaningless, at least in the way that sportswriters talk about meaningless games. There are no chewed nails and chewed knuckles and screwed-up faces; your ear doesn't become sore from being pressed up hard against a radio, trying to hear how Liverpool are getting on; you are not, in truth, thrown into agonies of despair or eye-popping fits of ecstasy by the result. Any meanings such games throw up are the ones that you, rather than the First Division table, bring to them.

And after maybe ten years of this, the Championship becomes something you either believe in or you don't, like God. You concede that it's possible, of course, and you try to respect the views of those who have managed to remain credulous. Between approximately 1975 and 1989 I didn't believe. I hoped, at the beginning of each season; and a couple of times – the middle of the 86/7 season, for example, when we were top for eight or nine weeks – I was almost lured out of my agnostic's cave. But in my heart of hearts I knew that it would never happen, just as I knew that they were not, as I used to think when I was young, going to find a cure for death before I got old.

In 1989, eighteen years after the last time Arsenal had won the League, I reluctantly and foolishly allowed myself to believe it was indeed possible that Arsenal could win the Championship. They were top of the First Division between January and May; on the last full weekend of the Hillsborough-elongated season they were five points clear of Liverpool with three games left to play. Liverpool had a game in hand, but the accepted wisdom was that Hillsborough and its attendant strains would make it impossible for them to keep winning, and two of Arsenal's three games were at home to weaker teams. The other was against Liverpool, away, a game that would conclude the First Division season.

No sooner had I become a born-again member of the Church of the Latterday Championship Believers, however, than Arsenal ground to a catastrophic halt. They lost, dismally, at home to Derby; and in the final game at Highbury, against Wimbledon, they twice threw away the lead to draw 2–2 against a team they had destroyed 5–1 on the opening day of the season. It was after the Derby game that I raged into an argument with my partner about a cup of tea, but after the Wimbledon game I had no rage left, just a numbing disappointment. For the first time I understood the women in soap operas who have been crushed by love affairs before, and can't *allow* themselves to fall for somebody again: I had never before seen all that as a matter of choice, but now I too had left myself nakedly exposed when I could have remained hard and cynical. I wouldn't allow it to happen again, never, ever, and I had been a fool, I knew that now, just as I knew it would take me years to recover from the terrible disappointment of getting so close and failing.

It wasn't quite all over. Liverpool had two games left, against West Ham and against us, both at Anfield. Because the two teams were so close, the mathematics of it all were peculiarly complicated: whatever score Liverpool beat West Ham by, Arsenal had to halve. If Liverpool won 2–0, we would have to win 1–0, and so on. In the event Liverpool won 5–1, which meant that we needed a two-goal victory; 'YOU HAVEN'T GOT A PRAYER, ARSENAL', was the back-page headline of the *Daily Mirror.*

*

I didn't go to Anfield. The fixture was originally scheduled for earlier in the season, when the result wouldn't have been so crucial, and by the time it was clear that this game would decide the Championship, the tickets had long gone. In the morning I walked down to Highbury to buy a new team shirt, just because I felt I had to do something, and though admittedly wearing a shirt in front of a television set would not, on the face of it, appear to offer the team an awful lot of encouragement, I knew it would make me feel better. Even at noon, some eight hours before the evening kick-off, there were already scores of coaches and cars around the ground, and on the way home I wished everyone I passed good luck; their positiveness ('3–1,' '2–0, no trouble', even a breezy '4–1') on this beautiful May morning made me sad for them, as if these chirpy and bravely confident young men and women were off to the Somme to lose their lives, rather than to Anfield to lose, at worst, their faith.

I went to work in the afternoon, and felt sick with nerves despite myself; afterwards I went straight round to an Arsenal-supporting friend's house, just a street away from the North Bank, to watch the game. Everything about the night was memorable, right from the moment when the teams came on to the pitch and the Arsenal players ran over to the Kop and presented individuals in the crowd with bunches of flowers. And as the game progressed, and it became obvious that Arsenal were going to go down fighting, it occurred to me just how well I knew my team, their faces and their mannerisms, and how fond I was of each individual member of it. Merson's gap-toothed smile and tatty soul-boy haircut, Adams's manful and endearing attempts to come to terms with his own inadequacies, Rocastle's pumped-up elegance, Smith's lovable diligence ... I could find it in me to forgive them for coming so close and blowing it: they were young, and they'd had a fantastic season and as a supporter you cannot really ask for more than that.

I got excited when we scored right at the beginning of the second half, and I got excited again about ten minutes from time, when Thomas had a clear chance and hit it straight at Grobbelaar, but Liverpool seemed to be growing stronger and to be creating chances at the end, and finally, with the clock in the corner of the TV screen showing that the ninety minutes had passed, I got ready to muster a brave smile for a brave team. 'If Arsenal are to lose the Championship, having had such a lead at one time, it's somewhat poetic justice that they have got a result on the last day, even though they're not to win

it,' said co-commentator David Pleat as Kevin Richardson received
treatment for an injury with the Kop already celebrating. 'They will see
that as scant consolation, I should think, David,' replied Brian Moore.
Scant consolation indeed, for all of us.

Richardson finally got up, ninety-two minutes gone now, and even
managed a penalty-area tackle on John Barnes; then Lukic bowled the
ball out to Dixon, Dixon on, inevitably, to Smith, a brilliant Smith
flick-on ... and suddenly, in the last minute of the last game of the
season, Thomas was through, on his own, with a chance to win the
Championship for Arsenal. 'It's up for grabs now!' Brian Moore yelled;
and even then I found that I was reining myself in, learning from
recent lapses in hardened scepticism, thinking, Well, at least we came
close at the end there, instead of thinking, Please Michael, please
Michael, please put it in, please God let him score. And then he was
turning a somersault, and I was flat out on the floor, and everybody in
the living room jumped on top of me. Eighteen years, all forgotten in
a second.

What is the correct analogy for a moment like that? In Pete Davies's
brilliant book about the 1990 World Cup, All Played Out, he notices
that the players use sexual imagery when trying to explain what it feels
like to score a goal. I can see that sometimes, for some of the more
workaday transcendent moments. Smith's third goal in our 3–0 win
against Liverpool in December 1990, for example, four days after we'd
been beaten 6–2 at home by Manchester United – that felt pretty good,
a perfect release to an hour of mounting excitement. And four or five
years back, at Norwich, Arsenal scored four times in sixteen minutes
after trailing for most of the game, a quarter of an hour which also had
a kind of sexual otherworldliness to it.

The trouble with the orgasm as metaphor here is that the orgasm,
though obviously pleasurable, is familiar, repeatable (within a couple
of hours if you've been eating your greens), and predictable, particularly for a man – if you're having sex then you know what's coming, as
it were. Maybe if I hadn't made love for eighteen years, and had given
up hope of doing so for another eighteen, and then suddenly, out of
the blue, an opportunity presented itself ... maybe in these circumstances it would be possible to recreate an approximation of that
Anfield moment. Even though there is no question that sex is a nicer
activity than watching football (no nil–nil draws, no offside trap, no
Cup upsets, and you're warm), in the normal run of things, the feelings

it engenders are simply not as intense as those brought about by a once-in-a-lifetime last-minute Championship winner.

None of the moments that people describe as the best in their lives seem analogous to me. Childbirth must be extraordinarily moving, but it doesn't really have the crucial surprise element, and in any case lasts too long; the fulfilment of personal ambition – promotions, awards, what have you – doesn't have the last-minute time factor, nor the element of powerlessness that I felt that night. And what else is there that can possibly provide the *suddenness*? A huge pools win, maybe, but the gaining of large sums of money affects a different part of the psyche altogether, and has none of the *communal* ecstasy of football.

There is then, literally, nothing to describe it. I have exhausted all the available options. I can recall nothing else that I have coveted for two decades (what else *is* there that can reasonably be coveted for that long?), nor can I recall anything else that I have desired as both man and boy. So please, be tolerant of those who describe a sporting moment as their best ever. We do not lack imagination, nor have we had sad and barren lives; it is just that real life is paler, duller, and contains less potential for unexpected delirium.

When the final whistle blew (just one more heart-stopping moment, when Thomas turned and knocked a terrifyingly casual back-pass to Lukic, perfectly safely but with a coolness that I didn't feel) I ran straight out of the door to the off-licence on Blackstock Road; I had my arms outstretched, like a little boy playing aeroplanes, and as I flew down the street, old ladies came to the door and applauded my progress, as if I were Michael Thomas himself; then I was grievously ripped off for a bottle of cheap champagne, I realized later, by a shopkeeper who could see that the light of intelligence had gone from my eyes altogether. I could hear whoops and screams from pubs and shops and houses all around me; and as fans began to congregate at the stadium, some draped in banners, some sitting on top of tooting cars, everyone embracing strangers at every opportunity, and TV cameras arrived to film the party for the late news, and club officials leaned out of windows to wave at the bouncing crowd, it occurred to me that I was glad I hadn't been up to Anfield, and missed out on this joyful, almost Latin explosion on my doorstep. After twenty-one years I no longer felt, as I had done during the Double year, that if I hadn't been to the games I had no right to partake in the celebrations; I'd done the work, years and years and years of it, and I belonged.

Frank Keating

Another Time, Another Planet

On 6 July, between the first and second Tests, the Lions came to Wellington to play the rated New Zealand Universities side. Barry had played In seven games so far, but in this, his eighth, he needed only six points to equal Brand's mark. Within twenty minutes he had kicked two penalty goals to equal it, then cast around (one can only presume) in his subconscious for something suitable to festoon in colourful gift-wrapping the record itself.

Now it so happened that 'the subconscious' was, you might say, on Barry's mind that day. The night before, after supper John had fallen into a 'nice, deep-rooted philosophical discussion and disputation' with Carwyn and that grand and deep-thinking Irish prop forward Ray McLoughlin, who was defending his insistence (and probably his position at the sharp, business end of the scrum) that in sport, taking ball-playing skills, balance and fitness for granted, then down-to-earth pragmatism and technical and mechanical excellence were all that was required – and only inside those parameters, plus the unknown variables of luck, bounce and rub-of-green, were some men winners, some losers.

As Barry listened, intrigued, Carwyn begged to differ with Ray – sport, he said, was made up of all those things the Irishman had listed; but then there could be more, much more – in seemingly straight-forward rugby, too, as well as possibly more obviously cerebral sports and pastimes. 'Instinct, intuition, call it what you like, and a player can be nervous in the extreme at the precise moment, or ice cold and calculating, but suddenly, unpractised, an almost "accidental profundity" can invade his mind in a split-atom fraction of a second and he will do something he had never thought himself capable of had he planned it for a century.'

That, insisted Carwyn in his turn, was what helped transcend sport to an art form. 'That's what makes one actor, say, or one piece of journalism, or one spouting politician seem streets ahead of the other who has just as much, even more, technical and well-coached ability – *spiritual, subconscious, transcendental, unknowing-where-it-came-from ruddy instinctive intuition.*'

Look at Muhammad Ali, the boxer, said Carwyn, 'he trains for all *conscious* eventualities, sure, but his greatest moments are when his *instinct* takes over, and afterwards he cannot remotely explain why he did what he did; all he knows is he's won dramatically'. In a way, he did what he did so conclusively just because 'the spirit was with him'. Did Ted Dexter walk out at Lord's a few years ago knowing he was going to take on the deadly West Indian fast bowlers Hall and Griffith and scatter them to all points? It wasn't a *plan*. It wasn't predetermined; the state of the game needed, if anything, a long and sober innings. But suddenly the spirit, the unnamed force, the 'adrenalin' got hold of him, and he had laid them to waste in half an hour. Did Richard Sharp know that try might be 'on' against Scotland before the scrum-half gave him the ball at Twickenham that day? Had he planned those three dummies as he caught the ball, or even one of them? Of course he hadn't. It was beyond his sphere of experience – till the moment it happened. 'Even more than the Scots defenders, in a way, did Richard Sharp *not* quite know what was going to happen next,' says Carwyn.

And so on and so forth, into a pleasant New Zealand night. Ray was not wholly convinced. Barry saw what Carwyn meant, and after another G-and-T or two they all went off to bed.

Next afternoon, Barry in no time kicked his two penalties to level Brand's record. Nothing so mundane as another penalty to break it, surely? After about half an hour, there was a set scrum, midfield, on the Universities' twenty-five. The Lions heeled. The reserve scrum-half, the popular Chico Hopkins, shovelled it out to Barry, who caught the ball, stood stock-still for a split second, then feinted to drop for goal – the obvious thing.

The loose forwards moved in desperately to charge down the 'pot'. Instead, John glided outside their desperate lunge by an inch or two and made as if to link up with his centres, Dawes and Gibson. He 'showed' the next defender the ball, which gave him that split second to come strongly off his left foot and leave the fellow crash-tackling thin air. Every man-jack of the cover was now either on his heels or on precisely the wrong foot, and as four or five of them screeched either to stop, turn or alter gear, like floundering and cursing cartoon cats, John tiptoed delicately through each of these hair-tearing tulips to pop the ball down over the line.

The *Sunday Telegraph* rugby correspondent, John Reason, who had seen no end of 'special' tries in his long experience, told his readers the following weekend how every man on either team – not only the mesmerized defenders, who had been turned to stone – had been as transfixed in wonder as the crowd: 'The try on Tuesday left the crowd at Athletic Park absolutely dumbfounded. John had touched the ball down between the posts and was trotting back to take the conversion himself before the realization of what had happened sent the applause crashing round the ground. John confessed afterwards that he thought there must have been an infringement. "I thought Chico must have put the ball in crooked, or something," he said, "I couldn't understand why the crowd was so quiet."'

Many years later, the moment was still vivid for its perpetrator – for he remembered particularly the conversation with Carwyn and Ray the night before. 'Looking back, I know that try owes a lot to that first feint to drop a goal. To this day I don't know why I didn't go for it, I had enough room to pop it over. But from then on I could just "sense intuitively" that not one of the opposition around or ahead of me was balanced and sort of "ready" for me. So I just continued on – outside one, inside the other – all the way to the posts. I know it's funny, but it was all as if I was in a dream, that I had "placed" the defenders exactly where I wanted them, like poles in the garden to practise swerving. I don't know what you call it? "Transcendental"? "Metaphysical"? I don't really know the exact definition of those words, but it was just marvellously weird, like I was down there re-enacting the slow-motion replay before the actuality itself had happened. As if I was in a dreamy state of *déjà vu*, that I was in a game, and doing something that had already taken place at another time.'

Perhaps it had – the night before in the bar – and Barry recalls that as soon as he had dapped the ball down over the line, up in the grandstand at the windy Athletic Ground, Ray McLoughlin, who was a few seats away from Carwyn James, had stayed standing till Carwyn caught his eye. And when he did, he waved acknowledgement to the coach that, OK, he did now fully understand what he had been unable to grasp the night before.

Whether they witnessed that try or not, fully ten years after it the authors of *Fields of Praise*, in their triumphant panegyric to John and the deft, poised, fragile illusion of his running, memorably conjured again the image of that day in Wellington by describing him as 'the dragonfly on the anvil of destruction, who ran in another dimension of time and space'. And fully twenty years after it, Barry over-dined, and certainly over-wined, me in his favourite Chinese restaurant in Cardiff's Tiger Bay. Even well into the happy night, he was still eerily crystal-clear about the day in New Zealand when he scored his try 'in another time, another place' to prove Carwyn's point about a sportsman's instinct and intuition.

I wonder how the experience of such an 'ultimate' vision subconsciously helped John's decision to retire. For within nine months he had gone. Just like that, at the age of twenty-seven and at the height of his sublime powers, as well as the adulation that went with it.

Richard Williams

The Death of Ayrton Senna

There is another Brazilian word that takes some explaining in English: *ginga*. The first *g* soft, the second hard, it defines a certain quality of grace in movement. In a woman, it is usually summoned to suggest a kind of sensuality. In a businessman, it can be a gift for tricky, perhaps devious, negotiation. It has to do with equilibrium, but also with originality and flair. A *capoeira* dancer, performing a sort of martial art with knives attached to his heels, needs plenty of *ginga*: nimbleness, balance, fluidity, continuity, a sort of arrogant courage.

There were Brazilian world champions in Formula 1 before Ayrton Senna, but he was the one who brought to it the quality of the *capoeira* dancer. Nigel Mansell and Alain Prost probably would not have put a name to it, but that was what they faced on numerous occasions when they raced head to head with Senna and came off worst – Mansell at Spa in 1987, Prost at Estoril in '88 and Suzuka in 1990, or Mansell again at Adelaide in '92.

These were incidents through which the very nature of Grand Prix racing was changed utterly, and probably for good; and since Senna was not only their common denominator but also their catalyst, we can say that he was responsible for this great and disturbing change – by which a sport which had always depended on the inherent chivalry of its participants suddenly came to accommodate the possibility of the systematic application of controlled violence.

All of these individual incidents are worth examination, but the one at Adelaide in 1992 was the last such of Senna's career. It was the final round of the season, with the championship already Mansell's, and the decision taken that the Englishman would be leaving for America at the end of the season, removed from his seat with the Williams team by Prost's subtle backstage manoeuvres. Mansell wanted to end his Formula 1 career and his championship season with a win, and he jumped straight into the Iead, with Senna on his tail. But on lap nineteen something happened, and the McLaren went into the back of the Williams, both cars spinning off the track and out of the race. Mansell ran away from the scene, straight across the track towards the pits; afterwards he told reporters that he'd done it to stop himself punching Senna. 'All I know is that someone hit me up the back when I was turning into the corner,' Mansell said. 'It seems that certain people in Formula 1 can get away with anything. I didn't go near him afterwards because if I had there would have been a big fight and I don't think that's the right way to leave Formula 1.' For his part, Senna claimed that Mansell knew he was close behind, but had braked early for no apparent reason.

Commentating for BBC television, James Hunt immediately took Mansell's side. 'Nigel Mansell is absolutely the innocent party,' the former world champion announced as the cameras lingered on the two ruined cars. Back home, Mansell's huge informal fan club rose up in fury against the wicked South American whose characteristic trickery had ended their man's chance of closing his Grand Prix career with another champagne shower.

But what else did they expect? It was, after all, just like Senna. Remember Spa, when he pushed Mansell off the track, and the burly Nigel grabbed the slight Senna by the throat in the pits afterwards, and had to be dragged away by three mechanics? Or Estoril, when Senna had made his car lunge across the track at Prost (his teammate, for goodness' sake) while they were both doing 190 m.p.h. in their McLarens down the main straight, right in front of the pits? Or Suzuka, where he rammed Prost from behind at 100-plus in the first corner, knowing the Frenchman had to win the race to keep alive his hope of the world title? So when Senna crunched his McLaren into the back of Mansell's Williams at Adelaide, it simply seemed like part of the Brazilian's established pattern of behaviour. The extension of this line of reasoning was a stab at guessing Senna's motivation. Perhaps he just wanted to deprive Mansell of the satisfaction of ending his world championship season with a win. Perhaps he wanted to hoist a signal for the next season, one announcing that while he might have lost his title, he was nevertheless still not a man to trifle with.

But that's not how all Englishmen saw it. 'Mansell ran away because he knew it was his fault,' Dave Coyne said the next morning. 'He'd given Senna a brake test. It's the kind of thing only another driver could see. The stewards wouldn't have a clue.'

Rick Morris agreed. 'Mansell braked early,' he said. 'Of course, in a situation like that it has to be the fault of the guy who's behind if he hits the guy in front. But at 170 miles an hour, if someone's that close

behind and you lift your foot even a hair, there's nothing he can do.
And if he hadn't been that close, he wouldn't have been Senna.'

Dave Coyne and Rick Morris are not household names in motor
racing. What made them different from most other middle-aged Home
Counties motor traders rewinding the video of the Australian Grand
Prix was that they had both raced against Ayrton Senna before the
world knew about him. And each of them could fit the events of
Adelaide into another, perhaps truer pattern of behaviour.

'I've had accidents with Senna,' Coyne said, remembering the 1981
season, when he and Morris competed with the Brazilian in the British
Formula Ford championships. 'He was always aggressive. He had a
very strong belief in himself. He believed he was the best. His life was
100 per cent motor racing.'

At the time Coyne was twenty-three, hoping for a career as a top-
line driver; Senna was twenty, and just out of go-karts. Morris, on the
other hand, was thirty-four, a comparative veteran, and he remembered with special clarity an accident on the opening lap of a race at
Oulton Park in Cheshire that year. 'I was on pole position, considerably
the quickest in practice,' he said. 'At Oulton, you go up the hill and
into a right-hander with a double apex. It's not one of the accepted
passing places, and going into it on the first lap I thought I had a good
lead when suddenly he came up and banged me out of the way. I got
back on the track in tenth place. He won the race.' It was one of twelve
wins in twenty starts for Senna that year, his maiden season in racing
cars. As early as that, people were talking about his talent in a special
tone of voice, but to some the incident with Morris and several others
like it seemed to set the mould for his future behaviour. Senna, it
appeared, thought he had a divine right to win, and woe betide anyone
who got in his way; even when, like Mansell at Adelaide, his opponent
had a faster car.

Right from the beginning, Senna had what they call natural speed,
but the ability to drive a car round a circuit faster than anyone else
isn't the hardest part of being a racing driver. What is more difficult is
the bit that actually makes it racing as opposed to high-speed driving:
the overtaking. And although Senna's sixty-five pole positions in 161
Grands Prix attested to his pure speed, the overtaking was what he was
best at. Better, perhaps, than any man who ever sat behind the wheel
of a racing car.

During successive seasons graduating through the junior single-
seater categories – Ford 1600, Ford 2000 and Formula 3 – other drivers

quickly became accustomed to giving Senna room. When they didn't –
as his Formula 3 rival Martin Brundle refused to on several occasions
during 1983 – they often ended up on the grass or in the sand trap.
Nor did it take the world of Formula 1 long to get the idea. Right
from the occasion of his début in a Toleman-Hart at Rio de Janeiro in
1984, Senna made it clear that he wasn't scared to hold the inside line
of a corner against pressure from more experienced men. Once he had
established himself as a front-runner, slicing past dozing backmarkers
became a particularly emphatic component of his repertoire. Some
slow men kept an eye on their mirrors, and knew to get out of the way
when the yellow helmet showed up; when he came across one who
wasn't paying attention, he showed an astonishing gift for getting by
without wasting time. He never held back, and most of the time he
brought his manoeuvres off. It was a form of psychological pressure:
other drivers got used to moving over when they saw that helmet.
Whether they would admit it to themselves or not, they had done half
of his job for him. 'He took no prisoners,' Brundle was to say ten years
after their Formula 3 duels. 'He had that brightly coloured helmet, and
you could clearly see him coming up behind you. He left you to decide
whether or not you wanted to have an accident with him. What you
did depended on how badly you wanted to finish the motor race.'

All this was to become most starkly evident during the course of the
1989 and 1990 seasons, when Alain Prost, his chief rival, was so
emasculated by the Brazilian's superiority – no, not just by that
superiority but by an unhesitating willingness to brandish it before the
world's audience, a willingness that would have seemed sadistic had it
not been self-evidently the product of his conception of destiny – that
he seemed to lose the capacity to overtake not just Senna but anyone
at all.

Motor racing, at whatever level, takes the competitive urge to an
extreme further than any other sport. It might not dismantle a player's
psyche in public in the naked and sometimes unbearably protracted
way that a tennis match can do; it might not take him as far beyond
his physical limits as a third consecutive day in the Alps during the
Tour de France, when drugs become less of a method of gaining an
unfair advantage than a necessity to deaden the pain; it might not
require the mad courage of a downhill skier, who throws himself out
of the start-hut and down a glass wall without any form of protection;
barring accidents, it will certainly not hurt as much as any run-of-the-
mill boxing match. More than any of these, however, motor racing,

head to head and in hot blood, presents a test of manhood. Uniquely, the car becomes a weapon: encasing the driver, armour-plating him, it responds exactly to his bidding. Its capabilities are a direct reflection of his power – either his purchasing power, in the case of a road car, or the power of his talent and reputation, in the case of a Formula 1 car. Even after a century of motoring, and in an era when all sensible people recognize the internal combustion engine's threat to the environment, the car remains the clearest and most potent symbol of selfhood. And if such factors can lead the drivers of saloon cars in the morning rush hour to mad rage, with nothing at stake beyond momentary pride, it does not take much to imagine the degree of emotional intensity involved when the contest – the race – becomes the whole point of existence.

Usually these rivalries, whether momentary or long term, are clear enough to the observer. But sometimes they are expressed in the form of hidden trials-within-trials whose existence is known only to the participants. Not even a James Hunt, with all his privileged insider's understanding of the men and the event, could be certain to spot it. Which is where Dave Coyne's 'brake test' came in.

The informal brake test is something you can see in its mundane form on an overcrowded motorway: two men in company cars travelling too close together in the fast lane, jousting, getting over-heated, and the one in front dabs the brake pedal just to give the other a fright. At ninety on a public road it's stupid and dangerous; at 190 on a racetrack it sometimes becomes a tactic.

There are two reasons why a racing driver might use it. The first, a bit like the speedsters on the motorway, is to teach someone a lesson – usually a novice obstructing a faster man, who then cuts in front and gives his opponent a character-forming experience to ensure that he makes room next time. The second is less blatant but more profound in intention. In a fight between equals, what it may do is force the close pursuer to lift his own foot off the throttle in response, which unsettles the balance of his car. Executed in the run-up to a corner, before the accepted braking zone, it can make the second man lift, brake, accelerate and then brake again for the corner: four improvised decisions whose effect might cost the driver a vital length or two at a time when he could have been positioning himself to come out of the slipstream and overtake. Done with cunning, as Coyne suggested, it can be undetectable to the naked eye in the grandstands (or the stewards' observation window), its effect known only to the victim.

Misjudged, it can at best give the pursuer a clear overtaking opportunity; at worst it can end with two cars tangling and spinning off the
track.

Both Coyne and Morris mentioned it in connection with the
incident between Senna and Mansell in Adelaide, and a voice from
another era added his support to the view. 'The one thing Senna
wanted to do was beat Mansell in Nigel's last race,' Stirling Moss said.
'The fact that he was so close shows how hard he was racing. But it's a
business in which things can happen very fast. Maybe Nigel lifted off
early. I don't know. Since that kind of accident must always be the
fault of the man who was behind, I guess it was Senna's fault – but I
don't think he was to blame, if you see what I mean.'

Why might Mansell have used it? To throw Senna off balance,
perhaps. Or maybe he had braked early simply out of a sudden excess
of caution, as Prost may have done when he threw the title away at
Suzuka in 1990. More likely he was thinking back five months, to the
Monaco Grand Prix. In this, a race Mansell had never won, the
Englishman led by a comfortable half-minute until, with eight laps to
go, a puncture brought him into the pits. There ensued a chase of brief
but nevertheless epic proportions, culminating in a final lap throughout
which the Williams, on fresh tyres, seemed to be trying to climb over
the McLaren, which was getting no grip from its tired rubber.
Somehow, against all probability even on a track notorious for making
overtaking difficult, pitting his wits against a car that was probably
three or four seconds a lap quicker at that point, Senna held Mansell
off, to win by a length. And much later the vanquished driver
explained, without rancour, how his rival had done it. 'Ayrton will
sometimes slow up on a short straight just to make you back off,' he
said. Looking at the video of that last lap, paying particular attention
to the sequence around the swimming-pool complex, where the cars
turn left, right and left again before approaching the last corner, you
can see, without the benefit of telemetry, that this is exactly what the
McLaren is doing. 'Ayrton was perfectly entitled to do what he did,'
Mansell said immediately after the race. But memories are long in
motor racing, and the Englishman – who may have yielded nothing to
Senna in terms of guts but never commanded anything like the same
degree of tactical finesse – may just have been indulging an ill-judged
and ultimately expensive desire to show the Brazilian that he hadn't
forgotten that particular episode in their long and semi-private battle.

An alternative and rather more intellectually satisfying explanation

came from another man who raced against Senna in the early days.
Back in 1983, Davy Jones was an eighteen-year-old American prodigy
competing for the British Formula 3 title. At home in Nevada, between
races for Jaguar in a US sports car series, he chuckled as he replayed
the Adelaide video, remembering the time he sat back and watched as
Senna and Brundle landed on top of each other at Oulton Park when
the Brazilian tried a run down the inside and found the door locked.
After paying the customary tribute to Senna's mental toughness, Jones
said something very interesting: 'I wonder,' he said, 'if his thinking in a
race isn't so far advanced that his mind is not relating to the incident
that's actually happening. Maybe if Nigel lifted a bit early, Ayrton just
wasn't prepared for it, because his mind was already two or three
corners ahead. You know, when you take a corner, your mind goes to
the turn-in, then to the apex, then the exit. You're always a step ahead
of what you're actually doing. But maybe Senna is always three steps
ahead. Maybe that was it. And maybe that's why he's such a great
champion.'

But was that great champion responsible for bringing the hooligan
tactics of Formula Ford to the more sophisticated and refined world of
Formula 1? Did he turn Grand Prix racing into a contact sport?

'It's not slot-car racing, after all,' Rick Morris said. 'It's not a non-
contact sport. It's supposed to be a spectacle.' And he stated that he
didn't think Senna was any more to blame for the changes in etiquette
than Prost or Mansell or anybody else.

Stirling Moss agreed, but added that the term 'brake test' hadn't
existed in his day; nor had the concept. 'If someone had tried it on
me,' he said, 'I'd have gone and punched him in the face.' Davy Jones
said wistfully that he wished he'd been racing in the 60s, against Moss
and Jim Clark and Jackie Stewart: 'There's a lot of money involved
now, and teams have to do well to justify and hang on to their
sponsorship. That's certainly changed the ethics. Some of the moves
you have to make now ... well, in the old days they'd probably have
taken a second thought.'

There was never a more contemplative Grand Prix driver than
Ayrton Senna, nor one more obviously concerned with the philosophical questions raised by his occupation. Once he was in the car,
however, he didn't go in for second thoughts; not about the dimension
of his own talent, not about going for a pass at the first and slightest
hint of an opportunity. He knew that this willingness to work in the
margins was what gave him the advantage over those who were more

inclined to pause, even for a microsecond, to check the odds and evaluate the risk.

Thinking back to the Formula Ford days, Dave Coyne got to the heart of it. 'I knew he was hard,' he said, 'and he knew I was hard. Once one of you gives way, it's all over. And once you have that edge, you've got to hold on to it.' Senna got it, and was in the very act of trying to hold on to it when he died.

ALI, ALI

José Torres

Sting Like A Bee

Muhammad Ali: Was there always a band traveling in his wake as he rolled through the cities of the 60s? A prince of his time and one of the great artists of the instrument known as the media. If you were alive during his time, you knew about him. Knew the handsome face, knew the voice moving from loudness to mock modesty to a kind of irony. He was American in a way that few others were American, because in him there was always the possibility of tragedy. He was a romantic, a man who believed in possibilities; if you believed hard enough, you could become the Olympic champion, the world's heavyweight champ, you could have the expensive houses, the Cadillacs, and you could do it all without losing anything, without compromising, without being damaged, without being hurt.

Muhammad Ali: black prince. His dignity always with him. And when it seemed to end on the night when he finally lost his championship, there was a sign in the 125th Street Station of the A train in New York. It said, quite simply, "Ali lives."

October 25, 1970: The day before the Ali–Quarry fight. It is almost midnight. The streets of Atlanta are quiet. The people who work in the fancy stores on Peachtree Street have vanished to the suburbs and we are in a wild and laughing knot of human beings coming out of a Loew's movie house as if they are part of a parade. At the head is a tall, good-looking man who is obviously the leader. His name: Muhammad Ali.

"That's right, man," he yells to the crowd. "The real champ is gonna show the world who is the greatest. So get to the fight early. The man might fall in one."

"What round, Ali?" someone asks, as if they listen to him but don't listen to him.

He starts to shadowbox and the crowd steps back to watch. "I'm feeling better than ever," he screams. "Better than ever."

"I hear that the fight won't take place," says a young girl. "Will you be disappointed?"

"Ask Jerry Quarry," Ali says. "I'm used to worse things."

Now we are at the Ali–Quarry fight headquarters at the ultramodern Regency-Hyatt House Hotel. "Here I am," he yells extending both arms as if to embrace the heavens. "The king is here." Smiles. "You see that," he says, pointing to the largely black crowd. "That's my people coming in from all over the country. Came to see the king ... the real champion."

Blacks move through the lobby of the Regency-Hyatt. They are wearing multicolored outfits. Some have rims on their hats so large they look like small umbrellas. They have arrived in psychedelic-colored Cadillacs, Mercedes-Benzes, Rolls-Royces. Some are equipped with white chauffeurs. Blonde whores from New York and from Chicago walk hand-in-hand with their rich black pimps, displaying super-mini skirts. Their cars are comfortably double-parked on the streets of Atlanta.

Black language reverberates all over the city that Scarlett O'Hara once knew, the city that is now 51 percent black. Blacks are still arriving at the nation's fourth busiest airport by way of seven airlines. They are coming in on the seven bus lines that serve Atlanta. Many of the rich ones who are afraid to fly, or apprehensive of the long drives, sent their chauffeurs with their cars and travel instead by one of the thirteen rail lines.

In the middle of the hotel lobby is a bar which looks like a giant sea shell suspended in the air. It's the fanciest hotel I've ever seen. The language of the place is special. "Man, we own this place," says Ali, regarding the parade of blacks in this lobby. Some of the laughter is wild. As a black from Watts says, some of the people are talking "Harlem language." Throughout the week preceding the fight the Southern whites, who ran the bar, were puzzled by the blacks with the fancy clothes. "We can't allow no one here without a tie," said a bartender to a young black from New York.

"You just," he was told, "can't wear a tie with *this* outfit. C'mon, my man, don't spoil my fashion."

Now people are drinking without being worried about ties or jackets. "You know," someone tells Ali, "the hotel changed the rules. We don't need special clothes anymore."

Now after three-and-a-half years of such inactivity, still engaged in a series of legal wrangles, most of his money gone and, with prison facing him, his name a synonym for controversy, Muhammad Ali is

coming back. Walking with him in the Atlanta night, it is still difficult
to believe, even for Ali himself.

"I'm thinking about this fight," he says more than once. "I need the
money and I need security for my family. I don't want to spoil this
fight by getting involved politically. I'm a fighter, period." But it is
hard for Ali to keep away from the political vibrations that fill the air
every time he holds a press conference. It is common knowledge that
the fight is opposed by Georgia's governor, Lester Maddox.

One remembers Maddox as the man who earned his first public
reputation by chasing black men out of his restaurant with a pistol in
one hand, an ax handle in the other. (He claimed later that the press
had lied: "It was really a pick handle," Lester Maddox said.) The night
before the fight, we are all conscious of where we are. It may be
Atlanta, "the oasis of the South," but it is still very much the South.

"What do you think about the Governor's announcement declaring
the day of your fight with Quarry a day of mourning?" a reporter asks.

"A day of what?" Ali answers.

"A day of mourning—m-o-u-r-n-i-n-g."

"I don't know what that means."

"You know, a sad day . . . a *black* day."

"Oh, that! Yes, *that* we gonna have."

But Atlanta's young Jewish Mayor, Sam Massell, has answered
Maddox's statement. Aware that in addition to the Ali–Quarry fight,
Atlanta is also having important pro and college football games as well
as a pro basketball game, the Mayor makes *his* announcement: "Next
week," he says, "will be Sport *Spectacular* week." It is the semifinal:
Massell versus Maddox. Does Ali enjoy these white men and their
sparring?

"No more popping off, no more boasting," Ali pronounces. "I don't
want no more trouble. Just the fight with Quarry."

But, in fact, until this last evening before the fight, his public mood
has not been happy; on the contrary, it has been sullen, it has been
stern and almost frozen—a strange role for ebullient Ali. But in some
ways he doesn't seem to be thinking of Quarry. In fact, Ali seems
obsessed with a hard-punching black man named Joe Frazier. Watching
him work. I am thinking about myself as well as him.

After all, Muhammad Ali is a complicated man and so am I. We
both have gone through many of the same experiences. We both
became world champions. But Ali has aroused the minds of many

people, mine included. I never did. Still, some of the experiences that made Ali a fighter made me a fighter. The details might be considerably different, but the ingredients are not. So, I'm watching him and thinking about him. I'm either better equipped or worse equipped to understand him than anybody else.

October 18, 1970: The week before the fight. We are in the Sports Arena, an old boxing gymnasium on the Southwest side of Atlanta, a mixed neighborhood.

Ali is sparring in the ring and looks fast. His legs get him out of trouble with the speed which has won him the label of "the fastest heavyweight of all time." His jab is coming fast and hard, perhaps even harder than before his exile. He is hitting with accuracy and concentrating on punching with more power. His combination punches carry speed and authority. His performance is consistent, his breathing normal. Trainers Angelo Dundee and Drew Bundini Brown are both satisfied. But one thing seems to be worrying them: Ali's thinking. The trainers can't figure out what's on Ali's mind. And he's not doing much talking.

"I'm not predicting this time," he says from the ring after finishing eight rounds of boxing.

"Do you think you'll be able to *perform* in the fight as well as you look in the gym?" I ask Ali. (Fighters rate themselves on performance. If they were usually no good in school, now they score themselves 60 percent, 80 percent, 95 percent.)

"That's a good question," he says and he smiles. A long pause. "You are not as dumb as you look."

My imagination is taking me into a boxing ring with Ali. There I think my thoughts, while also trying to think his. I throw punches (questions). Ali counters them (answers). Then I react by faking that I was not hit (when, in fact, I was). Or else I pretend I'm punching harder (when, in fact, I'm not).

Of course, Muhammad Ali is aware that workouts in gymnasiums are one thing; actual fights another.

What is involved is a basic transition; in the gym a champion knows he's the superior man. The guy in front of him is being paid to get his employer in top condition.

Both fighters, the employer and the employee, wear big gloves and headguards. A round can be stopped at any time by the trainers in charge. The sparring partner, the employee, is not usually well-known; the employer is, in most cases, a champion or leading contender.

So, sparring partners have a special respect for champions. A champ has the psychological advantage. There are no pressures on the champ. The objective, impersonal, cold attitude a professional champion must have is, almost always, not used in the gym. A champ becomes unprofessional. He takes it easy with his sparring partner. Usually, a champ gets hit much more often in the gym than he does in the actual fight. (But not as hard.) In fights a champ uses every ingredient which supposedly has made him a champ. And one of the ingredients is fear. Fear is nonexistent in the gym. But in fights it comes to your rescue, or at least it does when you can control it.

Now, Ali's trainers and many of his supporters see in Ali a different man. Nobody can be certain he has the old, positive confidence which had made him a great fighter.

The training is over. Ali stares at the ceiling of the dressing room for minutes. It gets his people nervous.

"What are you thinking about?" one of them asks. There is no answer, and the trainer says: "Are you thinking about Quarry?"

"Quarry?" Ali answers ironically. "Who's he?" His eyes are still fixed on the ceiling. Ali is distracted by thoughts not connected with the fight. His body looks in great shape, but his mind seems off.

I'm looking at Ali. He's a new man—how much, I have to think has he been affected and influenced by newspaper articles and by all the opinions of people other than Elijah Muhammad? That simple time when only one man knew the truth and that man was the Prophet of God and the leader of the Black Muslims is gone, that time is gone. There are worried looks on the faces of those close to Ali.

Of course, most of the sportswriters have picked Ali to win. As far as I'm concerned, they've done so for the wrong reasons. They go by how Ali looks in the gym, as opposed to how Quarry looks in the gym. Not me. I saw Quarry throwing a lot of leather. I saw him getting hit with shots by opponents who were faster than him. But I also saw Quarry pressing at all times. I saw him maintain a pressure which I didn't like a bit. Furthermore, I saw a fantastic enthusiasm in his attitude.

But the writers here only see when he gets hit, when he throws the "crazy" punches, when he begins to breathe hard after boxing two or three rounds. They are not aware of the pressure, they can't realize that Ali has been off for a long time, perhaps during his prime, and that consistent pressure by Quarry could produce the biggest upset in boxing history. If Ali's physical ability has been deteriorated by the three-and-a-half-year absence, I still think he has enough confidence to overcome that factor. That's why I pick Ali to win. I pick him because I think that Ali has enough confidence and enough will to overcome whatever superior physical ability Quarry should have for all these years of fighting while Ali was inactive.

Naturally, many people are praying for a Quarry victory. Besides being the recognized number one contender, Quarry is white. He has become a sophisticated version of those old "White Hopes" they used to bring in against Jack Johnson when he was the first black heavyweight champion.

Three-and-a-half years of exile in his own land probably taught Ali more than Jack Johnson ever learned. With Elijah Muhammad to reinforce the rhetoric of his religion, he has grown up. In press conferences he is more subdued. He doesn't brag or laugh with the same intensity as when he was a young champion. Sometimes he jokes and makes newsmen laugh, but he always evades political or social subjects. Not once does he mention Black Muslims. Ali is not what he was during his preparations for the 1964 Championship fight against Sonny Liston, when he had screamed, insulted and threatened his opponent. Nor is he the same Ali who, during the weigh-in ceremonies for that fight, was so out of control that doctors diagnosed him as "running scared."

October 26, 1970: George Plimpton spends the day in Ali's quarters in the suburban home of the man responsible for bringing the fight to Atlanta, Georgia, State Senator Leroy Johnson. "I was trying to talk to Ali and it was impossible," says Plimpton. "He was either on the phone, watching films, or busy with a lot of friends who went to him for fight tickets." I decide it is a good sign. It reminds me of the old unconventional Ali.

As the day moves into the hour for the fight, as in all of his previous fights, he does not "rest" enough.

Minutes before he is supposed to go to the Atlanta City Auditorium, he goes downtown and stands in front of the Regency-Hyatt, stage-managing bus accommodations for his army of followers, then waiting for the notoriously tardy Mrs. Martin Luther King, Jr. Having held the crowd for over thirty minutes, he finally gives up and steps into a car with Dundee, Bundini, Plimpton and a few close friends and leaves for the arena.

Walking toward the back entrance of the Auditorium, Ali can't evade the screaming crowd in the streets. He stops and shakes hands with a few and tells them to get in on time.

"You better get there early," Ali yells, "you might be too late."

"What round?" the crowd wants to know. No answer.

Fogs of nicotine, and the crowd vibrating like a motor with small roars of expectation. The crowd, with the exception of hundreds of reporters from all over the world, is almost all black.

Up in the balcony are blacks from Atlanta and poor blacks who hitched in from other states. At ringside are the prosperous.

They are black and beautiful. Men in full-length ermine coats, mink hats, diamond pins and velvet, dressed as beautifully as the women. Everyone models his clothes for the crowd, the cameras and the press. In fact, those in the press aren't without their little vanities, too.

Autograph-seekers surround the black celebrities that only Ali could bring to his fights. Diana Ross sits near Ali's corner. Bill Cosby is in the front press row, commenting on the fight for closed-circuit TV and alternately clowning for the crowd. And spread around the first row behind the press in ringside seats are Sidney Poitier, Whitney Young, Julian Bond, The Supremes, Mrs. Martin Luther King, Jr., the Rev. Ralph Abernathy, Henry Aaron and Donn Clendenon among others. Everyone from the black ticket-takers to the black announcer (who later handed the microphone over to New York's Johnny Addie) makes this a "Black Day" indeed in Atlanta history.

The motif even carries over into the singing of "The Star Spangled Banner," when rock singer Curtis Mayfield delivers the lyrics in the style of José Feliciano.

Beneath this brilliance of the surface, there is, however, a large lack of preparation. It is a complete reflection of the expectation that the fight would never happen, plus the unprofessionalism of many of those involved in putting it on. For Atlanta has not had a fight of any major proportions since 1939. No one in the city seems to have any idea of how to put this one on. The day before the fight I was laughing as I watched some of the executives of Sports Action, the promoters, working and sweating to help the carpenters finish the tiers of press seats. Just minutes before the preliminaries start, handlers are running all over ringside looking for nonexistent corner stools (which had to be purchased at the neighborhood hardware store after the prelims started and which still bore their price tags ($3.98) when brought into the ring). Even the gloves for the Ali–Quarry fight have been left at the airport! One of the fight promoters takes a cab to get them. What a sweat! Harold Conrad, the public relations man, is going crazy. He tries to organize. The man at the ticket door is having an argument with a local reporter. "I want my ticket right now," yells the reporter. "There is no ticket here for you," responds the man at the window. "Get Conrad," demands the reporter.

Now someone comes to Harold. "Mr. Conrad," the messenger says to the publicist. "A famous reporter is at the window without ticket."

"Fuck him."

"But . . ."

"Fuck him," repeats Conrad and keeps walking.

Preliminary fights are over. Johnny Addie is now in the middle of the ring. He introduces the celebrities. Bill Cosby is called up. He goes into the ring and begins shadowboxing. Sidney Poitier jumps in and begins doing the same in the opposite corner. People now seem relaxed. Poitier and Cosby are killing time before closed-circuit TV goes on the air for the real show.

Now the ring empties. Only announcer Addie and referee Tony Perez, both from New York, are in the ring.

Suddenly there is a rush of sound. Heads turn toward the south side of the Auditorium. Coming is Jerry Quarry. He is moving nervously toward the ring with his trainer, Teddy Bentham, in front of him.

His face is shining from the grease his trainers have put on to protect him from cuts. Quarry seems to hold the hard, determined attitude he had displayed during his gym workouts. He is dressed in a robe that covers his blue trunks. Bentham is whispering something in his ear.

Last-minute instructions are always necessary. Not simply because the fighter is really listening to them, but because it gives a sort of psychological satisfaction. If there is a flaw that Quarry or Bentham has just discovered, it is too late to correct it.

They reach the ring and Bentham goes up first to get in between the second and the last rope so Quarry can get in without effort. All eyes are on Quarry, who is now throwing punches at an invisible opponent. He walks toward a neutral corner and begins rubbing his white and red striped boxing shoes over grains of resin, to prevent him from slipping.

Now the crowd stands up and begins to scream hysterically.

Muhammad Ali is making his entrance. Ali has not heard this kind of noise for three-and-a-half years. He walks through the wild and screaming crowd, throwing punches at the air. Angelo Dundee is ahead of him while Bundini Brown follows from the rear. Atlanta's police surround them. The volume of the cheering increases as Ali steps into the ring and he acknowledges it by doing the "Ali shuffle," crisscrossing his legs like lightning and then coming up with a left jab. The screaming can be heard all over Atlanta.

Now both fighters are in the ring. In one corner Tony Perez waits for the announcer to introduce the fighters. After weeks of the wildest rumors of intervention by Maddox, the American Legion, the super patriots, the KKK and the Daughters of the Confederacy, nothing seems able to stop the fight now. For the first time since the announcement of the fight, there is the final confidence that there is a fight.

From the south side of the Auditorium, movie and television cameras move from one side of the ring to the other, focusing on the fighters. The fight is going to be seen in more countries than any other fight yet put on. Even Russia is interested in watching it.

Announcer Johnny Addie picks up the microphone. Ringside celebrities are introduced. Then Addie introduces Quarry, who receives a good ovation. But when the announcer tries to introduce Ali to the waiting crowd, they yell and scream so loudly no one hears his name. Ali is not introduced as a champion. But everyone there knows he is the real champion. Income from the fight is expected to be more than anything ever earned by Joe Frazier.

Referee Tony Perez signals both fighters to the middle of the ring for the traditional instructions. The audience is now quiet. Ali comes into the middle of the ring with trainers Angelo Dundee and Drew Bundini Brown. Quarry steps forward. Suddenly, we see Ali's lips moving—then Quarry's.

"You are in trouble, man. I'm going to get rid of you, fast," Ali says through his mouthpiece.

"Shut up and fight," is Quarry's answer. By now Perez is able to control the situation again. Ordering the fighters to remain quiet, the referee repeats the instructions.

The fighters begin to move to their respective corners and in the noise of the crowd, we hear the sound of the bell. It is the first second of the first round of Ali's return.

Hugh McIlvanney

He's Only a Human. My Guy Ain't

The short, humid days are shaped around the midday training sessions and the long, cool evenings are filled with talk, with an atmosphere of propaganda as reassuringly familiar as the odours of home cooking. But the hours are peeling away like layers of insulation and soon Muhammad Ali will have to grasp the bare wire of what Wednesday morning could mean to him and the extraordinary cast of helpers and hangers-on who have ridden first class on his dream for more than a decade.

A great tremor will pass through the whole of sport if he falls to George Foreman, and afterwards the landscape will be slightly dimmer for most of us. For those who have, over the years, been allotted some real or illusory role in his professional activities, trauma will be much more acute. They have made identities for themselves by travelling with the circus and when the big top comes down their egos and their standards of living are likely to collapse with it. Considering what they have at risk, these men – an unlikely collection ranging from the Woolworth's witch doctor Bundini Brown to a Pennsylvania Irishman called Gene Kilroy who styles himself business manager – are bound to offer some guidance to the balance of optimism and apprehension in Ali's camp. Of course, it would be foolish to equate their spirits with his, but the throb of misgiving that can be detected in their strident predictions of success has a more honourable echo in the realism that steals into his own utterances during his few quiet and thoughtful moments.

The other day he talked of how he would react if Foreman hit him hard enough to knock him down and possibly scramble his senses. He would, he insisted, neither cower like Ken Norton nor stumble into the mouth of the cannon like Joe Frazier. 'I'll be jabbin' and dancin', whuppin' and movin' till my head comes cool again,' he said. 'I'll run if I have to, rassle if I have to. I won't be out at the end of George's arms makin' a target. That's too much to ask if you are in there with me. But shit, the man ain't gonna knock me down.' For emphasis, he rose to demonstrate how to be hurtfully elusive, bouncing around the vast lounge that helps to rank his accommodation with the most luxurious available in the government complex at N'Sele, forty miles from Kinshasa. As an encore he reached for Angelo Dundee (who is no larger than a trainer has to be) and hugged him roughly off his feet.

'Son of a bitch,' says Dundee every time a tearing pain in the ribs reminds him of the horseplay. 'It kills me if I laugh now and it was laughing that kept me sane through the six weeks we've been here. Since the postponement most of us have been quietly going bananas. Muhammad is the only one who ain't affected. Every day is like a new toy to him. Foreman must have suffered more from the waiting than he has, even if the eye-cut has healed as well as it seems to have done. He's only a human. My guy ain't.

'George is going to find out about his own human limitations here. He wants to pull you onto punches or push you out by the shoulders to a convenient range but he won't be able to do that with my guy. George likes opponents who fight as if they are on rails, advancing in a straight line like Frazier or running in a straight line like Norton. You can kill him with angles. Ali will be either inside or outside the arc of the heavy stuff, and all the time that jab will be jumping into Foreman's face. This could be a repeat of the Liston job. Foreman is vulnerable to mobility and variety. Muhammad will knock him out.'

It is a nice script and in trying to stick to it Muhammad Ali will be able to call on a magnificent will and the substantial residue of the greatest athletic talent boxing has ever seen. He has appeared to shed the years with the surplus weight as he has sweated impressively in the conference hall that has been turned into a gymnasium at N'Sele. Now his torso is a wedge of flexible muscle and his face might belong to a film actor in his middle twenties rather than a boxer of thirty-two who has been a professional for fourteen years. His own declaration that already he weighs less than 15 stone is clearly absurd but he is trim enough to suggest he will enter the ring encouragingly close to the 15 st 2 lb he weighed when he won the world championship from Sonny Liston ten years ago.

After training, Ali sits on the ring apron in his white robe and fantasizes aggressively about the wonders he will perform in the 'Greatest eeee-vent in the history of the world'. His miracle will, he promises specifically, be the most remarkable since the resurrection of Christ. (It is hard to reconcile the need for such a feat with his dismissal of Foreman as an executioner of nobodies.) Having ranted, Ali gives his associates heart failure by leaping five feet from the ring to the floor, then joins the Californian negro who has been skilfully slapping some bongo drums in a corner of the hall. Ali pounds furiously on the drums, shouting: 'War ... war ... war,' before striding out into the burning glare of the day.

By comparison, Foreman almost slips into the gym. Each afternoon the world champion leaves his hotel – where he is shut off from the press and public most of the time – and is driven away from Kinshasa's tall buildings to the air-conditioned modernity of N'Sele. He comes to work, not to hold court, and pummels the heavy bag with all the ebullience of a lifer breaking stones. Once every few days he plants himself in front of journalists to answer questions. He does so civilly, but refuses to reciprocate Ali's insults. 'He's a fine man in many ways and I like him a lot. I don't mind all his talk. Talkin' is fun, a lot more fun than what we will be doin' Wednesday. Maybe Ali won't find that too pleasant.' Looking at George Foreman, at the vast, bare cliffs of shoulder that spread out from the straps of his denim dungarees, it is easy to share this last suspicion. The Zaïrese audiences, who are captivated by Ali, laugh at Foreman's clumsiness in the gym but most men who have faced him in earnest have wished they had an ejector seat instead of a corner stool. He has fallen on them like an avalanche and, despite what Angelo Dundee says, it will not be easy for Ali to stay clear of trouble.

Muhammad Ali is almost certain to fight in flurries, staying away to jab and cross when he can, falling into smothering clinches when the dancing has to stop. Foreman's biggest mistake would be to attempt a calculating fight. If he gives away the initiative he may never regain it. The twenty-five-year-old world champion should set out to be brutal from the first bell, to hunt and destroy, to batter the grace and elasticity and confidence out of a man who would surely be his master if both were in their prime. All this makes for a grim picture and I fear it is the one we are likely to see on Wednesday. As we go to the stadium at that unreal hour we shall be hoping for a miracle but dreading a calamity. Whatever happens those of us who have marched under Ali's banner will not be let down, for he is brave as well as beautiful.

Norman Mailer

The Fight

Right-hand leads

George would. George was certainly going to hit him in the belly. What a battle was to follow. If the five-minute warning had just been given, it passed in a rush. There was a bathroom off the dressing room and to it Ali retired with his manager, the son of Elijah Muhammad, Herbert Muhammad, a round-faced benign-looking man whose features offered a complete lack of purchase—Herbert Muhammad gave the impression nobody would know how to take advantage of him too quickly. He was now dressed in a priestly white robe which ran from his shoulders to his feet, a costume appropriate to his function as a Muslim minister, for they had gone into the next room to pray and their voices could be heard reciting verses of the Koran—doubtless such Arabic was from the Koran. In the big room, now empty of Ali, everybody looked at everyone and there was nothing to say.

Ferdie Pacheco returned from Foreman's dressing room. "Everything's O.K.," he stated. "Let's roll." In a minute Ali came out of the bathroom with the son of Elijah Muhammad. While he shadowboxed, his manager continued to pray.

"How are things with Foreman?" someone asked Pacheco, and he shrugged. "Foreman's not talking," he said. "They got him covered with towels."

Now the word came down the line from the stadium outside. "Ali in the ring, Ali in the ring."

Solemnly, Bundini handed Ali the white African robe which the fighter had selected. Then everybody in the dressing room was on their way, a long file of twenty men who pushed and were hustled through a platoon of soldiers standing outside the door and then in a gang's rush in a full company of other soldiers were racing through the gray cement-brick corridors with their long-gone echoes of rifle shots and death. They emerged into open air, into the surrealistic bliss and green air of stadium grass under electric lights, and a cheer of no vast volume went up at the sight of Ali, but then the crowd had been waiting through an empty hour with no semifinal to watch, just an empty ring, and hours gone by before that with dancers to watch, more dancers, then more tribal dancers, a long count of the minutes from midnight to four. The nation of Zaïre had been awaiting this event for three months, now they were here, some sixty thousand, in a great oval of seats far from that ring in the center of the soccer field. They must be disappointed. Watching the fighters would prove kin to sitting in a room in a housing project studying people through a window in another housing project on the other side of a twelve-lane freeway. The fighters would work under a big corrugated-tin shed roof with girders to protect the ring and the twenty-five hundred ringside seats from tropical downpour, which might come at any minute on this night so advanced already into the rainy season. Heavy rains were overdue by two weeks and more. Light rain had come almost every afternoon and dark portentous skies hung overhead. In America that would speak of quick summer storms, but the clouds in Africa were patient as the people and a black whirling smoky sky could shift overhead for days before more than a drop would fall.

Something of the weight of this oncoming rain was in the air. The early night had been full of oppression, and it was hot for so early in the morning, eighty degrees and a little more. Thoughts, however, of the oncoming fight left Norman closer to feeling chill. He was sitting next to Plimpton in the second row from the ring, a seat worth traveling thousands of miles to obtain (although counting two round trips, the figure might yet be twenty-five thousand miles—a barrel of jetlag for the soul). In front of them was a row of wire-service reporters and photographers leaning on the apron of the ring; inside the ropes was Ali checking the resin against his shoes, and offering flashes of his shuffle to the study of the crowd, whirling away once in a while to throw a kaleidoscope-dozen of punches at the air in two seconds no more—one-Mississippi, two-Mississippi—twelve punches had gone by. Screams from the crowd at the blur of the gloves. He was all alone in the ring, the Challenger on call for the Champion, the Prince waiting for the Pretender, and unlike other fighters who wilt in the long minutes before the titleholder will appear, Ali seemed to be taking royal pleasure in his undisputed possession of the space. He looked unafraid and almost on the edge of happiness, as if the discipline of having carried himself through the two thousand nights of sleeping without his title after it had been taken from him without ever losing a contest—a frustration for a fighter doubtless equal in impact to writing

A Farewell to Arms and then not being able to publish it—must have been a biblical seven years of trial through which he bad come with the crucial part of his honor, his talent, and his desire for greatness still intact, and light came off him at this instant. His body had a shine like the flanks of a thoroughbred. He looked fully ready to fight the strongest meanest man to come along in heavyweight circles in many years, maybe the worst big man of all, and while the Prince stood alone in his ring, and waited out the minutes for the Champion to arrive and had his thoughts, whatever they were, and his private communion with Allah, however that might feel, while he stood and while he shuffled and while he shadowboxed the air, the Lord Privy Seal, Angelo Dundee from Miami, went methodically from ring post to ring post and there in full view of ringside and the stadium just as methodically loosened each of the four turnbuckles on each post which held the tension of each of the four ropes, and did it with a spoke and a wrench he must have put in his little carrying bag back at N'Sele and transported on the bus and carried from the dressing room to this ring. And when the ropes were slack to his taste, loose enough for his fighter to lean way back, he left the ring and returned to the corner. Nobody had paid any particular attention to him.

Foreman was still in his dressing room. Later Plimpton learned a detail from his old friend Archie Moore. "Just before going out to the ring, Foreman joined hands with his boxing trust—Dick Sadler, Sandy Saddler, and Archie—in a sort of prayer ritual they had practiced (for every fight) since Foreman became champion in Jamaica," Plimpton wrote. "Now they were holding hands again in Zaïre, and Archie Moore, who had his head bowed, found himself thinking that he should pray for Muhammad Ali's safety. Here's what he said: 'I was praying, and in great sincerity, that George wouldn't *kill* Ali. I really felt that was a possibility.'" So did others.

Foreman arrived in the ring. He was wearing red velvet trunks with a white stripe and a blue waistband. The colors of the American flag girded his middle and his shoes were white. He looked solemn, even sheepish, like a big boy who as Archie said "truly doesn't know his own strength." The letters GF stood out in embossed white cloth from the red velvet of his trunks. GF—Great Fighter.

The referee, Zack Clayton, black and much respected in his profession, had been waiting. George had time to reach his corner, shuffle his feet, huddle with the trust, get the soles of his shoes in resin, and the fighters were meeting in the center of the ring to get instructions. It was the time for each man to extort a measure of fear from the other. Liston had done it to all his opponents until he met Ali who, then Cassius Clay at the age of twenty-two, glared back at him with all the imperative of his high-destiny guts. Foreman, in turn, had done it to Frazier and then to Norton. A big look heavy as death, oppressive as the closing of the door of one's tomb.

To Foreman, Ali now said (as everybody was later informed), "You have heard of me since you were young. You've been following me since you were a little boy. Now, you must meet me, your master!"— words the press could not hear at the time, but Ali's mouth was moving, his head was twelve inches from Foreman's, his eyes were on the other. Foreman blinked, Foreman looked surprised as if he had been impressed just a little more than he expected. He tapped Ali's glove in a move equal to saying, "That's *your* round. Now *we* start."

The fighters went back to their corners. Ali pressed his elbows to his side, closed his eyes and offered a prayer. Foreman turned his back. In the thirty seconds before the fight began, he grasped the ropes in his corner and bent over from the waist so that his big and powerful buttocks were presented to Ali. He flexed in this position so long it took on a kind of derision as though to declare: "My farts to you." He was still in such a pose when the bell rang.

The bell! Through a long unheard sigh of collective release, Ali charged across the ring. He looked as big and determined as Foreman, so he held himself, as if *he* possessed the true threat. They collided without meeting, their bodies still five feet apart. Each veered backward like similar magnetic poles repelling one another forcibly. Then Ali came forward again, Foreman came forward, they circled, they feinted, they moved in an electric ring, and Ali threw the first punch, a tentative left. It came up short. Then he drove a lightning-strong right straight as a pole into the stunned center of Foreman's head, the unmistakable thwomp of a high-powered punch. A cry went up.

Whatever else happened, Foreman had been hit. No opponent had cracked George this hard in years and no sparring partner had dared to.

Foreman charged in rage. Ali compounded the insult. He grabbed the champion around the neck and pushed his head down, wrestled it down crudely and decisively to show Foreman he was considerably rougher than anybody warned, and relations had commenced. They circled again. They feinted. They started in on one another and drew back. It was as if each held a gun. If one fired and missed, the other was certain to hit. If you threw a punch, and your opponent was ready, your own head would take his punch. What a shock. It is like seizing a high-voltage line. Suddenly you are on the floor.

Ali was not dancing. Rather he was bouncing from side to side looking for an opportunity to attack. So was Foreman. Maybe fifteen seconds went by. Suddenly Ali hit him again. It was again a right hand. Again it was hard. The sound of a bat thunking into a watermelon was heard around the ring. Once more Foreman charged after the blow, and once more Ali took him around the neck with his right arm, then stuck his left glove in Foreman's right armpit. Foreman could not start to swing. It was a nimble part of the advanced course for tying up a fighter. The referee broke the clinch. Again they moved through invisible reaches of attraction and repulsion, darting forward, sliding to the side, cocking their heads, each trying to strike an itch to panic in the other, two big men fast as pumas, charged as tigers—unseen sparks came off their moves. Ali hit him again, straight left, then a straight right. Foreman responded like a bull. He roared forward. A dangerous bull. His gloves were out like horns. No room for Ali to dance to the side, stick him and move, hit him and move. Ali went back, feinted, went back again, was on the ropes. Foreman had cut him off. The fight was thirty seconds old, and Foreman had driven him to the ropes. Ali had not even tried to get around those outstretched gloves so ready to cuff him, rough him, break his grace, no, retreating, Ali collected his toll. He hit Foreman with another left and another right.

Still a wail went up from the crowd. They saw Ali on the ropes. Who had talked of anything but how long Ali could keep away? Now he was trapped, so soon. Yet Foreman was off his aim. Ali's last left and right had checked him. Foreman's punches were not ready and Ali parried, Ali blocked. They clinched. The referee broke it. Ali was off the ropes with ease.

To celebrate, he hit Foreman another straight right. Up and down the press rows, one exclamation was leaping, "He's hitting him with *rights*." Ali had not punched with such authority in seven years. Champions do not hit other champions with right-hand leads. Not in the first round. It is the most difficult and dangerous punch. Difficult to deliver and dangerous to oneself. In nearly all positions, the right hand has longer to travel, a foot more at least than the left. Boxers deal with inches and half-inches. In the time it takes a right hand to travel that extra space, alarms are ringing in the opponent, counterattacks are beginning. He will duck under the right and take off your head

with a left. So good fighters do not often lead with their right against
another good fighter. Not in the first round. They wait. They keep the
right hand. It is one's authority, and ready to punish a left which
comes too slowly. One throws one's right over a jab; one can block the
left hook with a right forearm and chop back a right in return. Classic
maxims of boxing. All fight writers know them. Off these principles
they take their interpretation. They are good engineers at Indianapolis
but Ali is on his way to the moon. Right-hand leads! My God!

In the next minute, Ali proceeded to hit Foreman with a combination rare as plutonium: a straight right hand followed by a long left
hook. Spring-zing! went those punches, bolt to the head, bolt to the
head; each time Foreman would rush forward in murderous rage and
be caught by the neck and turned. His menace became more impressive
each time he was struck. If the punches maddened him, they did not
weaken him. Another fighter would be staggering by now. Foreman
merely looked more destructive. His hands lost no speed, his hands
looked as fast as Ali's (except when he got hit) and his face was
developing a murderous appetite. He had not been treated so disre-
spectfully in years. Lost was genial George of the press conferences. His
life was clear. He was going to dismember Ali. As he kept getting hit
and grabbed, hit and grabbed, a new fear came over the rows at
ringside. Foreman was awesome. Ali had now hit him about fifteen
good punches to the head and not been caught once in return. What
would happen when Foreman finally hit Ali? No heavyweight could
keep up the speed of these moves, not for fourteen more rounds.

But then the first was not even over. In the last minute, Foreman
forced Ali to the ropes, was in on him, broke loose, and smashed a
right uppercut through Ali's gloves, then another. The second went
like a spear through the top of Ali's skull. His eyes flew up in
consternation, and he grabbed Foreman's right arm with his left,
squeezed it, clung to it. Foreman, his arm being held, was still in a
mood to throw the good right again, and did. Four heavy half-
smothered rights, concussive as blows to the heavy bag, went up to the
head, then two down to the body, whaling on Ali even as he was held,
and it was apparent these punches hurt. Ali came off the ropes in the
most determined embrace of his life, both gloves locked around the
back of Foreman's neck. The whites of Ali's eyes showed the glaze of a
combat soldier who has just seen a dismembered arm go flying across
the sky after an explosion. What kind of monster was he encountering?

Foreman threw a wild left. Then a left, a right, a left, a left and a right. Some to the head, some to the body, some got blocked, some missed, one collided with Ali's floating ribs, brutal punches, jarring and imprecise as a collision at slow speed in a truck.

With everybody screaming, Ali now hit Foreman with a right. Foreman hit him back with a left and a right. Now they each landed blows. Everybody was shaking their head at the bell. What a round!

Now the press rows began to ring with comment on those right-hand leads. How does Ali dare? A magnificent round. Norman has few vanities left, but thinks he knows something about boxing. He is ready to serve as engineer on Ali's trip to the moon. For Ali is one artist who does not box by right counter to left hook. He fights the entirety of the other person. He lives in fields of concentration where he can detect the smallest flicker of lack of concentration. Foreman has shown himself a lack of quiver flat to the possibility of a right. Who before this had dared after all to hit Foreman with a right? Of late his opponents were afraid to flick him with a jab. Fast were Foreman's hands, but held a flat spot of complacency before the right. He was not ready for a man to come into the ring unafraid of him. That offered its beauty. But frightening. Ali cannot fight every round like this. Such a pace will kill him in five. Indeed he could be worried as he sits in the corner. It has been his round, but what a force to Foreman's punches. It is true. Foreman hits harder than other fighters. And takes a very good punch. Ali looks thoughtful.

There is a sound box in the vicinity, some small loudspeaker hooked into the closed circuit, and on it Norman can hear David Frost, Jim Brown, and Joe Frazier talking between rounds, an agreeable sense of detachment thereby offered for they are on the other side of the press rows. Listening to them offers the comfort of a man watching a snowstorm from his fireplace. Jim Brown may have said last night that Ali had no chance, but Brown is one athlete who will report what he sees. "Great round for Muhammad Ali," he comments. "He did a fantastic job, although I don't think he can keep up this pace."

Sullenly, Joe Frazier disagrees. "Round was even . . . very close."

David Frost: "You wouldn't call that round for Ali?"

Joe is not there to root Ali home, not after Ali called him ignorant. "It was very close. Ali had two or three good shots to the face while George been landing body shots."

Foreman sits on his stool listening to Sadler. His face is bemused as if he has learned more than he is accustomed to in the last few minutes and the sensation is half agreeable. He has certainly learned that Ali can hit. Already his face shows lumps and welts. Ali is also a better wrestler than any fighter he has faced. Better able to agitate him. He sits back to rest the sore heat of his lungs after the boil of his fury in the last round. He brings himself to smile at someone at ringside. The smile is forced. Across the ring, Ali spits into the bowl held out for him and looks wide awake. His eyes are as alive as a ghetto adolescent walking down a strange turf. Just before the bell, he stands up in his corner and leads a cheer. Ali's arm pumps the air to inspire the crowd, and he makes a point of glowering at Foreman. Abruptly, right after the bell, his mood takes a change.

As Foreman comes out Ali goes back to the ropes, no, lets himself be driven to the corner, the worst place a fighter can be, worst place by all established comprehension of boxing. In the corner you cannot slip to the side, cannot go backward. You must fight your way out. With the screech that comes up from a crowd when one car tries to pass another in a race, Foreman was in to move on Ali, and Ali fought the good rat fight of the corner, his gloves thrown with frantic speed at Foreman's gloves. It became something like a slapping contest—of the variety two tall kids might show when trying to hit the other in the face. It is far from orthodox practice, where you dart out of a corner, duck out of a corner, or blast out. Since Ali kept landing, however, and Foreman did not, George retreated in confusion as if reverting to memories of fights when he was ten years old and scared—yes, Ali must have made some psychological choice and it was well chosen. He got out of the corner and held Foreman once again by the head in a grip so well applied that Foreman had the pensive expression of a steer being dogged to the ground by a cowboy.

Once the referee separated them, Ali began to back up across the ring. Foreman was after him throwing fast punches. "Show him," George's corner must have instructed, "that your gloves are as fast as his." Suddenly Foreman hit Ali with a straight hard right. Ali held on to Foreman to travel through the shock. After the fight he would say that some of Foreman's punches went right down to his toes, and this must have been one of them. When the fighters were separated, Foreman chased Ali to the ropes, and Ali pulled out a new trick, his full inch and a half of reach. He held his arms in Foreman's face to keep him off. The round was almost a minute gone before Ali got in his first good punch, another right. But Foreman charged him and pushed him, driving down on Ali's gloves with his own gloves, stalking him back and back again, knocking Ali's gloves away when he didn't like the character of their moves. Foreman was beginning to dictate how the fight should be. If a bully, he was a master bully. He did not react to the dictation of others, liked his own dictation. The force he sought in serenity had locked him on a unilinear road; it was working now. Ali kept retreating and Foreman caught him again. Hard! Once more, Ali was holding on with both hands, back of the neck, back of the bicep, half writhing and half riding with the somewhat stifled punches Foreman kept throwing. Foreman had begun to dominate the action to the point where Ali's best course seemed to be obliged to take what was left of each punch after the attempt to smother it. He kept trying to wrestle Foreman to a stop.

But then Ali must have come to a first assessment of assets and weaknesses, for he made—somewhere in the unremarked middle of the round—he must have made a decision on how to shape the rest of the fight. He did not seem able to hurt Foreman critically with those right-hand leads. Nor was he stronger than Foreman except when wrestling on his neck, and certainly he could not afford any more of those episodes where he held onto Foreman even as George was hitting him. It was costly in points, painful, and won nothing. On the other hand, it was too soon to dance. Too rapid would be the drain on his stamina. So the time had come to see if he could outbox Foreman while lying on the ropes. It had been his option from the beginning and it was the most dangerous option he had. For so long as Foreman had strength, the ropes would prove about as safe as riding a unicycle on a parapet. Still what is genius but balance on the edge of the impossible? Ali introduced his grand theme. He lay back on the ropes in the middle of the second round, and from that position he would work for the rest of the fight, reclining at an angle of ten and twenty degrees from the vertical and sometimes even further, a cramped near-tortured angle from which to box.

Of course Ali had been preparing for just this hour over the last ten years. For ten years he had been practicing to fight powerful sluggers who beat on your belly while you lay on the ropes. So he took up his station with confidence, shoulders parallel to the edge of the ring. In this posture his right would have no more impact than a straight left but he could find himself in position to cover his head with both gloves, and his belly with his elbows, he could rock and sway, lean so far back Foreman must fall on him. Should Foreman pause from the fatigue of throwing punches, Ali could bounce off the ropes and sting him, jolt him, make him look clumsy, mock him, rouse his anger, which might yet wear Foreman out more than anything else. In this position, Ali could even hurt him. A jab hurts if you run into it, and Foreman is always coming in. Still, Ali is in the position of a man bowing and ducking in a doorway while another man comes at him with two clubs. Foreman comes on with his two clubs. In the first exchange he hits Ali about six times while Ali is returning only one blow. Yet the punches to Ali's head seem not to bother him; he is swallowing the impact with his entire body. He is like a spring on the ropes. Blows seem to pass through him as if he is indeed a leaf spring built to take shock. None of his spirit is congested in his joints. Encouraged by the recognition that he can live with these blows, he begins to taunt Foreman. "Can you hit?" he calls out. "You can't hit. You push! Since his head has been in range of Foreman's gloves, Foreman lunges at him. Back goes Ali's head like the carnival boy ducking baseballs. Wham to you, goes Ali, catapulting back. Bing and sting! Now Foreman is missing and Ali is hitting.

It is becoming a way to fight and even a way to live, but for Ali's corner it is a terror to watch. In the last thirty seconds of this second round, Ali hits out with straight rights from the ropes fast as jabs. Foreman's head must feel like a rivet under a riveting gun. With just a few seconds left, Foreman throws his biggest punch of the night, an express train of a left hook which leaves a spasm for the night in its passing. It has been a little too slow. Ali lets it go by in the languid unhurried fashion of Archie Moore watching a roundhouse miss his chin by a quarter of an inch. In the void of the effort, Foreman is so off-balance that Ali could throw him through the ropes. "Nothing," says Ali through his mouthpiece. "You have no aim." The bell rings and Foreman looks depressed. There has been premature desperation in that left. Ali shakes his head in derision. Of course that is one of Ali's basic tricks. All through his first fight with Frazier he kept signaling to the crowd that Joe failed to impress him. All the while Ali was finding himself in more trouble.

The man in the rigging

It seems like eight rounds have passed yet we only finished two. Is it because we are trying to watch with the fighters' sense of time? Before fatigue brings boxers to the boiler rooms of the damned, they live at a height of consciousness and with a sense of detail they encounter nowhere else. In no other place is their intelligence so full, nor their sense of time able to contain so much of itself as in the long internal effort of the ring. Thirty minutes go by like three hours. Let us undertake the chance, then, that our description of the fight may be longer to read than the fight itself. We can assure ourselves: It was even longer for the fighters.

Contemplate them as they sit in their corners between the second and third rounds. The outcome of the fight is not yet determined. Not for either. Ali has an enormous problem equal to his enormous confidence. Everybody has wondered whether Ali can get through the first few rounds and take Foreman's punch. Now the problem has been refined: Can he dismantle Foreman's strength before he uses up his own wit?

Foreman has another problem; he may not be as aware of it as his corner. There is no fear in his mind that he will fail to win the fight. He does not think about that any more than a lion supposes it will be unable to destroy a cheetah; no, it is just a question of catching Ali, a maddening frustration. Still the insult to his rage has to worry his corner. They can hardly tell him not to be angry. It is Foreman's rage after all which has led him to knock out so many fighters. To cut it off is to leave him cowlike. Nonetheless he must contain his anger until he catches Ali. Otherwise he is going to wear himself out.

So Sadler works on him, rubs his breasts and belly, Sadler sends his fingers into all the places where rage has congested, into the meat of the pectorals and the muscle plating beneath Foreman's chest. Sadler's touch has all the wisdom of thirty-five years of black fingers elucidating comforts for black flesh, sensual are his fingers as he plucks and shapes and shakes and balms, his silver bracelet shining on his black wrist. When Sadler feels the fighter is soothed, he begins to speak, and Foreman takes on the expression of a man whose head is working slowly. He has too much to think about. He spits into the bowl held before him and nods respectfully. He looks as if he is listening to his dentist.

In Ali's corner, Dundee, with the quiet concern of a sommelier, is bringing the mouth of the adhesive-taped water bottle to Ali's lips, and does it with a forefinger under the neck so the bottle will not pour too much as he tips it up. Ali rinses and spits with his eyes off on the serious calculation of a man weighing grim but necessary alternatives.

Joe Frazier: "George is pounding that body with shots. He's hurting the body. Ali shouldn't stay on that rope ... If he don't move or cut

George, George will walk him down. He need to move. He don't need
to stay on that rope. For what reason's he on the *rope?*" Frazier sounds
offended. Even the sound of the word worries him. Joe Frazier would
consider himself *gone* if he had to work there. Rope is an ugly and
miserable kuntu.

Jim Brown replies: "Ali is punishing George Foreman even *though*
he's on the rope. He's getting some tremendous blows in and"—the
wisdom of the professional football player—"at some point that can
tell."

The bell. Once more Ali comes out of the corner with a big and
threatening face as if this round for certain he will bring the attack to
Foreman and once again sees something wrong in the idea, profoundly
wrong, shifts his plan instantly, backs up and begins to play the ropes.
On comes Foreman. The fight has taken its formal pattern. Ali will go
by choice to the ropes and Foreman will chase him. Now in each round
Ali will work for thirty or forty seconds or for so much even as a
minute with his back no more than a foot or two from the top rope,
and he is on the rope as often as not. When the strength of the mood,
or the logic of the clinch suggests that the virtue of one set of ropes
has been used up, be will back off across the ring to use another set.
He will spend on an average one-quarter of each round on each of the
four sides of the ring. He might just as well be drawing conscious
strength from the burial gods of the North, the West, the East, and the
South. Never has a major fight been so locked into one pattern of
movement. It appears designed by a choreographer who knows nothing
about the workings of legs and is endlessly inventive about arms. The
fight goes on in exactly this fashion round after round, and yet it is
hardly boring, for Ali appears in constant danger, and is, and is not.
He is turning the pockets of the boxing world inside out. He is
demonstrating that what for other fighters is a weakness can be for
him a strength. Foreman has been trained to cut instinctively from side
to side in such a way as to spoil Ali's ability to circle, Foreman has
learned how to force retreat to the ropes. But Ali makes no effort to
get away. He does not circle, neither does he reverse his circle. Instead
he backs up. Foreman's outstretched arms become a liability. Unable
to cuff at a dancing target, he must probe forward. As he does, Ali
keeps popping him with straight lefts and rights fast as karate strokes.
But then Ali's wife has a black belt in karate.

Sooner or later, however, Foreman is always on him, leaning on
him, banging him, belting away with all the fury George knows how to

bring to the heavy bag. Ali uses the ropes to absorb the bludgeoning. Standing on one's feet, it is painful to absorb a heavy body punch even when blocked with one's arms. The torso, the legs, and the spine take the shock. One has to absorb the brunt of the punch. Leaning on the ropes, however, Ali can pass it along; the ropes will receive the strain. If he cannot catch Foreman's punches with his gloves, or deflect them, or bend Forman's shoulder to spoil his move, or lean away with his head, slip to the side, or loom up to hug Foreman's head, if finally there is nothing to do but take the punch, then Ali tightens his body and conducts the shock out along the ropes, so that Foreman must feel as if he is beating on a tree trunk which is oscillating against ropes. Foreman's power seems to travel right down the line and rattle the ring posts. It fortifies Ali's sense of relaxation—he has always the last resort of composing himself for the punch. When, occasionally, a blow does hurt, he sticks Foreman back, mean and salty, using his left and right as jabs. Since his shoulders are against the ropes, he jabs as often with his right as his left. With his timing it is a great jab. He has a gift for hitting Foreman as Foreman comes in. That doubles or triples the force. Besides he is using so many right jabs Foreman must start to wonder whether he is fighting a southpaw. Then comes the left jab again. A converted southpaw? It has something of the shift of locus which comes from making love to a brunette when she is wearing a blonde wig. Of course, Ali has red wigs too. At the end of the round, Ali hits Foreman with some of the hardest punches of the fight. A right, a left, and a right startle Foreman in their combination. He may not have seen such a combination since his last street fight. Ali gives a look of contempt and they wrestle for a few seconds until the bell. For the few extra seconds it takes Foreman to go to his corner, his legs have the look of a bedridden man who has started on a tour of his room for the first time in a week. He has almost stumbled on the way to his stool.

In the aisle, Rachman Ali began to jeer at Henry Clark. "Your man's a chump," Rachman said. "Ali's going to get him." Clark had to look worried. It was hardly his night. First his own fight had been postponed, then called off, now he was watching George from a crate in the aisle. Since he had a big bet on George, this last round offered its woes.

In the corner Sadler was massaging Foreman's right shoulder and George was gagging a bit, the inside of his lips showing a shocking frothy white like the mouth of an overgalloped horse.

Nonetheless, he looked lively as he came out for the bell. He came right across the middle of the ring to show Ali a new kind of feint, a long pawing movement of his hands accompanied by short moves of his head. It was to a different rhythm as if to say, "I haven't begun to show what I know."

He looked jaunty, but he was holding his right hand down by the waist. Fatigue must have lent carelessness to what he did, for Ali immediately answered with an insulting stiff right, an accelerating hook, and another right so heavy to Foreman's head that he grabbed for a clinch, first time in the fight. There, holding on to Ali while vertigo collided with nausea, and bile scalded his breath, he must have been delivered into a new awareness, for George immediately started to look better. He began to get to Ali on the ropes and hit him occasionally, and for the first time in a while was not getting hit as much himself. He was even beginning to jam a number of Ali's rhythms. Up to now, whenever Ali took a punch, he was certain to come off the ropes and hit Foreman back. A couple of times in this round, however, even as Ali started his move, George would jam his forearm into Ali's neck, or wrestle him to a standstill.

All the while Ali was talking. "Come on, George, show me something," he would say. "Can't you fight harder? That ain't hard. I thought you was the champion, I thought you had punches," and Foreman working like a bricklayer running up a pyramid to set his bricks would snort and lance his arms in sudden unexpected directions and try to catch Ali bouncing on the rope, Ali who was becoming more confirmed every minute in the sinecure of the rope, but at the end of the round, Foreman caught him with the best punch he had thrown in many a minute, landing just before the bell, and as he turned to leave Ali, be said clearly, "How's that?"

It must have encouraged him, for in the fifth round he tried to knock Ali out. Even as Ali was becoming more confident on the ropes, Foreman grew convinced he could break Ali's defense. Confidence on both sides makes for war. The round would go down in history as one of the great rounds in heavyweight boxing; indeed it was so good it forged its own frame as they battled. One could see it outlined forever in lights: *The Great Fifth Round of the Ali–Foreman fight!*

Like much of greatness, the beginnings were unremarked. Foreman ended the fourth round well, but expectation was circling ringside that a monumental upset could be shaping. Even Joe Frazier was admitting that George was "not being calm." It took John Daly to blurt out cheerfully to David Frost, "Ali is winning all the way for me and I think he's going to take it within another four rounds!"

Foreman didn't think so. There had been that sniff of victory in the fourth, the good punch which landed—"How's that?" He came out in the fifth with the conviction that if force had not prevailed against Ali up to now, more force was the answer, considerably more force than Ali had ever seen. If Foreman's face was battered to lumps and his legs were moving like wheels with a piece chipped out of the rim, if his arms were beginning to sear in the lava of exhaustion and his breath come roaring to his lungs like the blast from a bed of fire, still he was a prodigy of strength, he was *the* prodigy, he could live through states of torture and hurl his cannonade when others could not lift their arms, he had been trained for endurance even more than execution and back in Pendleton when first working for this fight had once boxed fifteen rounds with half a dozen sparring partners coming on in two-round shifts while Foreman was permitted only thirty seconds of rest between each round. He could go, he could go and go, he was tireless in the arms, yes, could knock down a forest, take it down all by himself, and he set out now to chop Ali down.

They sparred inconclusively for the first half-minute. Then the barrage began. With Ali braced on the ropes, as far back on the ropes as a deep-sea fisherman is braced back in his chair when setting the hook on a big strike, so Ali got ready and Foreman came on to blast him out. A shelling reminiscent of artillery battles in World War I began. Neither man moved more than a few feet in the next minute and a half. Across that embattled short space Foreman threw punches in barrages of four and six and eight and nine, heavy maniacal slamming punches, heavy as the boom of oaken doors, bombs to the body, bolts to the head, punching until he could not breathe, backing off to breathe again and come in again, bomb again, blast again, drive and steam and slam the torso in front of him, wreck him in the arms, break through those arms, get to his ribs, dig him out, dig him out, put the dynamite in the earth, lift him, punch him, punch him up to heaven, take him out, stagger him—great earthmover he must have sobbed to himself, kill this mad and bouncing goat.

And Ali, gloves to his head, elbows to his ribs, stood and swayed and was rattled and banged and shaken like a grasshopper at the top of a reed when the wind whips, and the ropes shook and swung like sheets in a storm and Foreman would lunge with his right at Ali's chin and Ali go flying back out of reach by a half-inch, and half out of the ring, and back in to push at Foreman's elbow and hug his own ribs and sway, and sway just further, and lean back and come forward from the ropes and slide off a punch and fall back into the ropes with all the calm of a man swinging in the rigging. All the while, he used his eyes. They looked like stars, and he feinted Foreman out with his eyes, flashing white eyeballs of panic he did not feel which pulled Foreman through into the trick of lurching after him on a wrong move, Ali darting his expression in one direction while cocking his head in another, then staring at Foreman expression to expression, holding him in the eye, soul to soul, muntu to muntu, hugging his head, peeking through gloves, jamming his armpit, then taunting him on the edge of the ropes, then flying back as Foreman dove forward, tantalizing him, maddening him, looking for all the world as cool as if he were sparring in his bathrobe, now banishing Foreman's head with the turn of a matador sending away a bull after five fine passes were made, and once when he seemed to hesitate just a little too long, teasing Foreman just a little too long, something stirred in George like that across-the-arena knowledge of a bull when it is ready at last to gore the matador rather than the cloth, and like a member of a cuadrilla, somebody in Ali's corner screamed, "Careful! Careful! Careful!" and Ali flew back and just in time for as he bounced on the ropes Foreman threw six of his most powerful left hooks in a row and then a right, it was the center of his fight and the heart of his best charge, a left to the belly, a left to the head, a left to the belly, a left to the head, a left to the belly, another to the belly, and Ali blocked them all, elbow for the belly, glove for the head, and the ropes flew like snakes. Ali was ready for the lefts. He was not prepared for the right that followed. Foreman hit him a powerful punch. The ring bolts screamed. Ali shouted, "Didn't hurt a bit." Was it the best punch he took all night? He had to ride through ten more after that. Foreman kept flashing his muscles up out of that cup of desperation boiling in all determination, punches that came toward the end of what may have been as many as forty or fifty in a minute, any one strong enough to send water from the spine to the knees. Something may have finally begun to go from Foreman's n'golo, some departure of the essence of absolute rage, and Ali reaching over the barrage would give a prod now and again to Foreman's neck like a housewife sticking a toothpick in a cake to see if it is ready. The punches got weaker and weaker, and Ali finally came off the ropes and in the last thirty seconds of the round threw his own punches, twenty at least. Almost all hit. Some of the hardest punches of the night were driven in. Four rights, a left hook and a right came in one stupendous combination. One punch turned Foreman's head through ninety degrees, a right cross of glove and forearm that slammed into the side of the jaw; double contact had to be felt; once from the glove, then from the bare arm, stunning and jarring. Walls must begin to crack inside the brain. Foreman staggered and lurched and glared at Ali and got hit again, zing-bing! two more. When it was all over, Ali caught Foreman by the neck like a big brother chastising an enormous and stupid kid brother, and looked out to someone in the audience, some enemy or was it some spiteful friend who said Foreman would win, for Ali, holding George around the neck, now stuck out one long white-coated tongue. On the other side of the ropes, Bundini was beaming at the bell.

"I really don't believe it," said Jim Brown. "I really don't believe it. I thought he was hurt. I thought his body was hurt. He came back. He hit Foreman with everything. And he winked at *me.*" Did he wink or stick out his tongue?

In the aisle, Rachman was screaming at Henry Clark. "Your fighter's a chump. He's an amateur. My brother is killing him. My brother is showing him up!"

The executioner's song

So began the third act of the fight. Not often was there a better end to a second act than Foreman's failure to destroy Ali on the ropes. But the last scenes would present another problem. How was the final curtain to be found? For if Foreman was exhausted, Ali was weary. He had hit Foreman harder than he had ever hit anyone. He had hit him often. Foreman's head must by now be equal to a piece of vulcanized rubber. Conceivably you could beat on him all night and nothing more would happen. There is a threshold to the knockout. When it comes close but is not crossed, then a man can stagger around the ring forever. He has received his terrible message and he is still standing. No more of the same woe can destroy him. He is like the victim in a dreadful marriage which no one knows how to end. So Ali was obliged to produce still one more surprise. If not, the unhappiest threat would present itself as he and Foreman stumbled through the remaining rounds. There is agony to elucidate even a small sense of the aesthetic out of boxing. Wanton waste for an artist like Ali to lose then the perfection of this fight by wandering down a monotonous half-hour to a dreary unanimous decision.

A fine ending to the fight would live in legend, but a dull victory, anticlimactic by the end, could leave him in half a legend—overblown in reputation by his friends and contested by his enemies—precisely that state which afflicted most heroes. Ali was fighting to prove other points. So he said. So Ali had to dispose of Foreman in the next few rounds and do it well, a formidable problem. He was like a torero after a great faena who must still face the drear potential of a protracted inept and disappointing kill. Since no pleasure is greater among athletes than to overtake the style of their opponent, Ali would look to steal Foreman's last pride. George was an executioner. Ali would do it better. But how do you execute the executioner?

The problem was revealed in all its sluggish intricacies over the next three rounds. Foreman came out for the sixth looking like an alley cat with chewed-up brows. Lumps and swellings were all over his face, his skin equal to tar that has baked in the sun. When the bell rang, however, he looked dangerous again, no longer a cat, but a bull. He lowered his head and charged across the ring. He was a total demonstration of the power of one idea even when the idea no longer works. And was immediately seized and strangled around the neck by Ali for a few valuable and pacifying seconds until Zack Clayton broke them. Afterward, Foreman moved in to throw more punches. His power, however, seemed gone. The punches were slow and tentative. They did not reach Ali. Foreman was growing glove-shy. His fastest moves were now in a nervous defense that kept knocking Ali's punches away from his own face.

At this point Ali proceeded to bring out the classic left jab everyone had been expecting for the first round. In the next half-minute, he struck Foreman's head with ten head-ringing jabs thrown with all the speed of a good fencer's thrust, and Foreman took them in apathy to compound the existing near-apathy of his hopes. Each time his head snapped back, some communciation between his mind and his nerves must have been reduced. A surgical attack.

Yet something in Foreman's response decided Ali to give it up. Perhaps no more than his own sense of moderation. It might look absurd if he kept jabbing Foreman forever. Besides, Ali needed rest. The next two minutes turned into the slowest two minutes of the fight. Foreman kept pushing Ali to the ropes out of habit, a dogged forward motion that enabled George to rest in his fashion, the only way he still knew, which was to lean on the opponent. Ali was by now so delighted with the advantages of the ropes that he fell back on them like a man returning home in quiet triumph, yes, settled in with the weary pleasure of a working man getting back into bed after a long day to be treated to a little of God's joy by his hardworking wife. He was almost tender with Foreman's laboring advance, holding him softly and kindly by the neck. Then he stung him with right and left karate shots from the shoulder. Foreman was now so arm-weary he could begin a punch only by lurching forward until his momentum encouraged a movement of the arm. He looked like a drunk, or rather a somnambulist, in a dance marathon. It would be wise to get him through the kill without ever waking him up. While it ought to be a simple matter to knock him down, there might not be enough violence left in the spirit of this ring to knock him out. So the shock of finding himself on the floor could prove a stimulant. His ego might reappear: once on the floor, he was a champion in dramatic danger of losing his title—that is an unmeasurable source of energy. Ali was now taking in the reactions of Foreman's head the way a bullfighter lines up a bull before going in over the horns for the kill. He bent to his left and, still crouched, passed his body to the right under Foreman's fists, all the while studying George's head and neck and shoulders. Since Foreman charged the move, a fair conclusion was that the bull still had an access of strength too great for the kill.

Nonetheless, Foreman's punches were hardly more than pats. They were sufficiently weak for any man in reasonable shape to absorb them. Still, Foreman came on. Sobbing for breath, leaning, almost limping, in a pat-a-pat of feeble cuffs, he was all but lying over Ali on the ropes. Yet what a problem in the strength of his stubbornness itself. Endless powers of determination had been built out of one season of silence passing into another. The bell rang the end of the sixth. Both men gave an involuntary smile of relief.

Foreman looked ready to float as he came to his corner. Sandy Saddler could not bring himself to look at him. The sorrow in Foreman's corner was now heavier than in Ali's dressing room before the fight.

In his corner Ali looked thoughtful, and stood up abstractedly before the bell and abstractedly led a cheer in the stadium, his arm to the sky.

The cheer stirred Foreman to action. He was out of his corner and in the middle of the ring before the bell rang. Ali opened his eyes wide and stared at him in mock wonder, then in disdain as if to say, "Now you've done it. Now you're asking for it." He came out of his corner too, and the referee was pushing both men apart as the bell rang.

Still it was a slow round, almost as slow as the sixth. Foreman had no speed, and in return Ali boxed no faster than he had to, but kept shifting more rapidly than before from one set of ropes to another. Foreman was proving too sluggish to work with. Once, in the middle of the round, Foreman staggered past Ali, and for the first time in the fight was literally nearer the ropes. It was a startling realization. Not since the first five seconds of the fight had Ali crossed the center of the ring while moving forward. For seven rounds his retreating body had been between Foreman and the ropes except for the intervals when he traveled backward from one set of ropes to another. This time, seeing Foreman on the ropes instead, Ali backed up immediately and Foreman slogged after him like an infantryman looking at the ground. Foreman's best move by now might be to stand in the center of the ring and invite Ali to come to him. If Ali refused, he would lose the luster of his performance, and if he did come forward it would be George's turn to look for weaknesses. While Foreman waited for Ali, he could rest. Yet George must have had some unspoken fear of disaster if he shifted methods. So he would drive, thank you very much, into the grave he would determine for himself. Of course, he was not wholly without hope. He still worked with the idea that one punch could catch Ali. And with less than a minute left, he managed to drive a left hook into Ali's belly, a blow that indeed made Ali gasp. Then Foreman racked him with a right uppercut strong enough for Ali to hold on in a clinch, no, Foreman was not going to give up. Now he leaned on Ali with one extended arm and tried to whale him with the other. He looked like he was beating a rug. Foreman had begun to show the clumsiness of a street fighter at the end of a long rumble. He was reverting. It happened to all but the most cultivated fighters toward the exhausted end of a long and terrible fight. Slowly they descended from the elegance of their best style down to the knee in the groin and the overhead punch (with a rock in the fist) of forgotten street fights.

Ali, half as tired at least, was not wasting himself. He was still graceful in every move. By the end of the round he was holding Foreman's head tenderly once more in his glove. Foreman was becoming reminiscent of the computer Hal in *2001* as his units were removed one by one, malfunctions were showing and spastic lapses. All the while something of the old panache of Sadler, Saddler, and

Moore inserted over those thousands of hours of training still showed in occasional moves and gestures. The weakest slaps of his gloves, however, had begun to look like entreaties. Still his arms threw punches. By the end of the seventh he could hardly stand: yet he must have thrown seventy more punches. So few were able to land. Ali had restricted himself to twenty-five—half at least must have gone to target. Foreman was fighting as slowly as a worn-out fighter in the Golden Gloves, slow as a man walking up a hill of pillows, slow as he would have looked if their first round had been rerun in slow motion, that was no slower than Foreman was fighting now, and thus exposed as in a film, he was reminiscent of the slow and curving motions of a linebacker coiling around a runner with his hands and arms in the slow-motion replay—the boxing had shifted from speed and impact to an intimacy of movement. Delicately Ali would cradle Foreman's head with his left before he smashed it with his right. Foreman looked ready to fall over from exhaustion. His face had the soft scrubbed look of a child who has just had a dirty face washed, but then they both had that gentle look boxers get when they are very tired and have fought each other very hard.

Back in the corner, Moore's hands were massaging Foreman's shoulders. Sandy Saddler was working on his legs. Dick Sadler was talking to him.

Jim Brown was saying, "This man, Muhammad Ali, is *unreal.*" When Jim used the word, it was a compliment. Whatever was real, Jim Brown could dominate. And Frazier added his humor, "I would say right now my man is not in the lead. I got a feeling George is not going to make it."

On the aisle, Rachman was still calling out to Henry Clark. Henry, admit it, your man is through, he's a chump, he's a street fighter. Henry, admit it. Maybe I'm not a fighter, I know I'm not as good as you, but admit it, admit it, Muhammad has whipped George."

Except he hadn't. Not yet. Two rounds had gone by. The two dullest rounds of the fight. The night was hot. Now the air would become more tropical with every round. In his corner, Ali looked to be in pain as he breathed. Was it his kidneys or his ribs? Dundee was talking to him and Ali was shaking his head in disagreement. In contrast to Foreman, his expression was keen. His eyes looked as quick as the eyes, indeed, of a squirrel. The bell rang for the eighth round.

Working slowly, deliberately, backing up still one more time, he hit Foreman carefully, spacing the punches, taking aim, six good punches, lefts and rights. It was as if he had a reserve of good punches, a numbered amount like a soldier in a siege who counts his bullets and so each punch had to carry a predetermined portion of the work.

Foreman's legs were now hitched into an ungainly prance like a horse high-stepping along a road full of rocks. Stung for the hundredth time with a cruel blow, his response was to hurl back a left hook that proved so wild he almost catapulted through the ropes. Then for an instant, his back and neck were open to Ali, who cocked a punch but did not throw it, as though to demonstrate for an instant to the world that he did not want to flaw this fight with any blow reminiscent of the thuds Foreman had sent to the back of the head of Norton and Roman and Frazier. So Ali posed with that punch, then moved away. Now for the second time in the fight he had found Foreman between himself and the ropes and had done nothing.

Well, George came off the ropes and pursued Ali like a man chasing a cat. The wild punch seemed to have refreshed him by its promise that some of his power was back. If his biggest punches were missing, at least they were big. Once again he might be his own prodigy of strength. Now there were flurries on the ropes which had an echo of the great bombardment in the fifth round. And still Ali taunted him, still the dialogue went on. "Fight hard," said Ali, "I thought you had some punches. You're a weak man. You're all used up." After a while, Foreman's punches were whistling less than his breath. For the eighteenth time Ali's corner was screaming, "Get off the ropes. Knock him out. Take him home!" Foreman had used up the store of force he transported from the seventh to the eighth. He pawed at Ali like an infant six feet tall waving its uncoordinated battle arm.

With twenty seconds left to the round, Ali attacked. By his own measure, by that measure of twenty years of boxing, with the knowledge of all he had learned of what could and could not be done at any instant in the ring, he chose this as the occasion and lying on the ropes, he hit Foreman with a right and left, then came off the ropes to hit him with a left and a right. Into this last right hand he put his glove and his forearm again, a head-stupefying punch that sent Foreman reeling forward. As he went by, Ali hit him on the side of the jaw with a right, and darted away from the ropes in such a way as to put Foreman next to them. For the first time in the entire fight he had cut off the ring on Foreman. Now Ali struck him a combination of punches fast as the punches of the first round, but harder and more consecutive, three capital rights in a row struck Foreman, then a left, and for an instant on Foreman's face appeared the knowledge that he was in danger and must start to look to his last protection. His opponent was attacking, and there were no ropes behind the opponent. What a dislocation: the axes of his existence were reversed! He was the man on the ropes! Then a big projectile exactly the size of a fist in a glove drove into the middle of Foreman's mind, the best punch of the startled night, the blow Ali saved for a career. Foreman's arms flew out to the side like a man with a parachute jumping out of a plane, and in this doubled-over position he tried to wander out to the center of the ring. All the while his eyes were on Ali and he looked up with no anger as if Ali, indeed, was the man he knew best in the world and would see him on his dying day. Vertigo took George Foreman and revolved him. Still bowing from the waist in this uncomprehending position, eyes on Muhammad Ali all the way, he started to tumble and topple and fall even as he did not wish to go down. His mind was held with magnets high as his championship and his body was seeking the ground. He went over like a six-foot sixty-year-old butler who has just heard tragic news, yes, fell over all of a long collapsing two seconds, down came the champion in sections and Ali revolved with him in a close circle, hand primed to hit him one more time, and never the need, a wholly intimate escort to the floor.

The referee took Ali to a corner. He stood there, he seemed lost in thought. Now he raced his feet in a quick but restrained shuffle as if to apologize for never asking his legs to dance, and looked on while Foreman tried to rouse himself.

Like a drunk hoping to get out of bed to go to work, Foreman rolled over, Foreman started the slow head-agonizing lift of all that foundered bulk God somehow gave him and whether he heard the count or no, was on his feet a fraction after the count of ten and whipped, for when Zack Clayton guided him with a hand at his back he walked in docile steps to his corner and did not resist. Moore received him. Sadler received him. Later, one learned the conversation.

"Feel all right?"

"Yeah," said Foreman.

"Well, don't worry. It's history now."

"Yeah."

"You're all right," said Sadler, "the rest will take care of itself."

In the ring Ali was seized by Rachman, by Gene Kilroy, by Bundini, by a host of black friends old, new, and very new, who charged up the aisles, leaped on the apron, sprang through the ropes, and jumped near to touch him. Norman said to Plimpton in a tone of wonder like a dim parent who realizes suddenly his child is indeed and indubitably married, "My God, he's champion again!" as if one had trained oneself for years not to expect news so good as that.

In the ring Ali fainted.

It occurred suddenly and without warning and almost no one saw it. Angelo Dundee circling the ropes to shout happy words at reporters was unaware of what had happened. So were all the smiling faces. It was only the eight or ten men immediately around him who knew. Those eight or ten mouths which had just been open in celebration now turned to grimaces of horror. Bundini went from laughing to weeping in five seconds.

Why Ali fainted, nobody might ever know. Whether it was a warning against excessive pride in years to come—one private bolt from Allah—or whether the weakness of sudden exhaustion, who could know? Maybe it was even the spasm of a reflex he must have refined unconsciously for months—the ability to recover in seconds from total oblivion. Had he been obliged to try it out at least once on this night? He was in any case too much of a champion to allow an episode to arise, and was back on his feet before ten seconds were up. His handlers having been lifted, chastened, terrified, and uplifted again, looked at him with faces of triumph and knockdown, the upturned mask of comedy and the howling mouth of tragedy next to each other in that instant in the African ring.

David Frost was crying out: "Muhammad Ali has done it. The great man has done it. This is the most joyous scene ever seen in the history of boxing. This is an incredible scene. The place is going wild. Muhammad Ali has won." And because the announcer before him had picked the count up late and was two seconds behind the referee and so counting eight when Clayton said ten, it looked on all the closed-circuit screens of the world as if Foreman had gotten up before the count was done, and confusion was everywhere. How could it be other? The media would always sprout the seed of confusion. "Muhammad Ali has won. By a knockdown," said Frost in good faith. "By a knockdown."

Back in America everybody was already yelling that the fight was fixed. Yes. So was *The Night Watch* and *Portrait of the Artist as a Young Man.*

Thomas Hauser

Muhammad Ali: His Life and Times

Muhammad Ali: "He's no Liston. He's no Foreman. He's no Frazier. He's only Larry Holmes, and he's nothin'. He's just the man between me and my fourth title, and I'm going to beat him so bad it's going to be a total mismatch. You think I'd come back now and go out a loser? You think I'd be that stupid? Everybody else goes out loser, but not this one. Four-time champion, how does that sound?"[1]

Larry Holmes: "That's the same old broken record I've been hearing as long as I can remember. That kind of talk don't win no fights. It might convince Ali and it might convince some people, but the guy he's got to convince is Larry Holmes. If Ali stays in front of me, he's gonna get knocked out early. If he's still there after eight rounds, he's lucky. I feel better than I ever felt. I've had four fights in the last year, and what was he doing? Blowing up past 250 pounds."[2]

Muhammad Ali: "I'm the underdog. Great! I love that. I need a fight like this to motivate me. I've been off two years, no activity, thirty-eight years old, and I promise you, this will be no contest. I'll be supremely superior. I'm serious. I was 252 pounds when I started training. Now I'm 227, and I hope to fight around 222. I predict a miracle."[3]

Larry Holmes: "I don't believe in miracles, and I'm sure none is gonna happen that night. To me, Ali isn't a god. He's a human being, just like you and me. He got his weight down, and he thinks that will make him young again, but it won't. Ali can't turn back the clock; no one can. Just about everybody he fought was old. Now he's going to find out how it feels to be an old man fighting a good fast young man. I really believe I'll knock him out."[4]

Muhammad Ali: "Holmes must go. I'll eat him up. I'll hit him with jabs and right crosses. He can't dance; I'm gonna dance fifteen rounds. This old man will whup his butt. Pow! Pow! Pow! I see it all now. He's exhausted. Bam! The right hand over the tired jab. And Holmes is down! Ali goes to a neutral corner. Seven, eight, nine, ten! And for the world-record-setting never-to-be-broken fourth time, Muhammad Ali is the heavyweight champion of the world."[5]

Larry Holmes: "Ali was a great fighter, but he stepped out of his time into my time. I know all there is to know about how he fights. Whatever he tries, I'll beat him. At a distance, I'll out-jab him. If he covers up, I'll break his ribs or murder his kidneys. If he wants to rassle, I'll show him a few holds. I'll beat him to death. He's in trouble. You know it; everybody knows it. They just feel sorry for the old man. He thinks he can pull a rabbit out of a hat, but there's no more rabbits. His ass is grass, and I'm the lawnmower."[6]

MIKE KATZ: "Before Ali–Holmes, the biggest prefight story was, how would Larry Holmes handle the pressure, which was enormous on anyone who fought Ali. But Ali couldn't get under Larry's skin. In fact, he complained to me one day; he said, 'I can't do anything with Larry, because he's been around me too much. He knows my lines before I finish them.' And it was true. Ali would start a line, and Larry could finish it. Larry kept his cool. He was very calm, very professional. In fact, I remember a week or so before the fight, some nut was going to jump a motorcycle over the fountain at Caesar's Palace. It wasn't Evel Knievel; it was some other lunatic. Ali was talking about it, saying how this was another example of someone doing the impossible. He'd done the impossible against Sonny Liston; people were going to the moon, which was impossible; and he was going to beat Holmes, which was impossible. Anyway, I asked Larry if he was going to watch the jump. And Larry told me, 'No way; I measured it. I know motorcycles, and the guy can't make it.' And of course, the guy didn't make it. He wound up breaking a bunch of bones. But that was Larry Holmes; he was into realism. He knew what was possible and what wasn't."

As the fight approached, public interest grew, with an ever-increasing number of people giving Ali a legitimate chance to win. The odds, which had once been three-to-one, dropped to thirteen-to-ten in Holmes's favor. Pat Putnam of *Sports Illustrated* wrote, "Whatever happens when Ali meets Larry Holmes, one irrefutable fact will stand out. Ali will be in better physical and mental condition than at any time since he battled George Foreman. His face is slim and firm. So is his body. It's as if he has turned the clock back to 1971, when he was twenty-nine."[7]

But Ali's appearance was a mirage. His hair was black only because dye covered the gray. His reflexes were slower than they'd ever been. His followers thought that beating Larry Holmes wouldn't be any more extraordinary than beating Sonny Liston. But in reality, Ali had no chance at all. He was an aging fighter about to face a very good champion. And along with everything else, Ali's physical condition was worsening. Not only wasn't he ready to fight, he wasn't in condition to shadowbox for fifteen rounds.

The true nature of Ali's health wasn't known to the public, nor was the most immediate cause—medication that had been improperly prescribed and abused. In mid-September, several weeks before the fight, Ali had been visited by Herbert Muhammad's personal physician, Dr. Charles Williams. Williams advised Ali that he was suffering from a hypothyroid condition, and gave him one hundred tablets of a drug called Thyrolar. Among its many side effects, Thyrolar speeds up the body's metabolism and interferes with its self-cooling mechanisms. Thus, Ali continued to lose weight, and began to feel fatigued and sluggish. But internally, even more dangerous changes were occurring.

"When Ali left Deer Lake after training," Gene Kilroy recalls, "he was in great shape. His spirits were good; he was ready. Then in Vegas, he started taking those drugs. I was in the room with him at Caesar's Palace when Dr. Williams came in and said, 'Ali, I have something for you that will make you strong.' I told Ali, 'This is crazy. It's the worst thing in the world; don't fool with it.' But Ali took it, and afterward he was dehydrated and urinating all the time. He couldn't run; he was losing weight like mad. And the closer the fight came, the worse it got. I was worried but I wanted to build him up, so I told him, 'You're gonna win. I'm betting everything on you.' And Ali told me, 'No, don't do it. Something is wrong.'"

MIKE KATZ: "I remember watching Ali spar right before he fought Larry Holmes. And outside the ring, maybe he looked magnificent. But in it, he had nothing at all. I mean nothing; he was an empty shell. I told Angelo he looked awful, and Angelo said, 'I know, I know; but he always looks awful in the gym.' Which was true. Ali's idea of training, especially late in his career, was to let sparring partners hit him. There were a couple of times when he hit back for real, but mostly, even if there was an obvious opening, he wouldn't do anything more than tap whoever he was in with. He didn't believe in beating on his sparring partners. The heavy-bag was where he sharpened his combinations.

But even knowing how Ali trained, what I saw in the gym before Holmes was awful.

"Ali was sparring with a heavyweight named Marty Monroe, who was a decent fighter. He would be a cruiserweight today. And Monroe was beating the shit out of him. Ali was trying as hard as he could, and not only couldn't he keep Monroe off, he couldn't get out of the way of his punches. Monroe was landing everything he threw. And you know, Angelo thinks every one of his fighters is going to win before a fight. So he was telling me, 'Yeah, Ali looks bad now, but his most important piece of equipment is the mirror. Every morning, he stands in front of the mirror and admires how good he looks. It gives him confidence, and that's what he needs to pull something out of the bag to beat Holmes.'

"And that's what a lot of people thought. There were people, some of them far more knowledgeable than I am, who actually gave Ali a chance because they had this incredible faith in the man and were sure he'd find a way to win. Even Angelo was hoping against hope; but I told him, and I think he knew, 'Angelo, you don't beat Larry Holmes with mirrors.'"

GENE DIBBLE: "I've known Ali a long time, since before he fought Sonny Liston. I know when he's happy; I know when something is bothering him. And before Holmes, things just weren't right. He was slow and debilitated physically. He couldn't run. Hell, he could hardly stay awake. My brother and I saw him the day before the fight. And my brother, who's a physician, took one look at Ali and said there was no way he should fight. That was enough for me. I said, 'Ali, why don't you postpone this thing?' But he shrugged it off, and said there were people coming from all over the world to watch him. Then he stood up and threw a few jabs, shadowboxing like he usually does, but he wasn't his regular self. After that, I talked to Bingham; I talked to Kilroy. I talked to everyone I could, trying to stop the fight. But what it came down to was, there was only one person who could tell Ali not to fight, and that was Herbert Muhammad. So I went to Herbert. I saw him in the lobby of the hotel, and I told him I didn't think Ali should fight. And Herbert told me I didn't know what I was talking about."

JERRY IZENBERG: "A day or two before the fight, I had a talk with Larry Holmes. Larry was saying, 'This is going to be terrible. Ali has nothing left.' And then he asked me, 'What would you think if I came out hard, just to establish something, and then eased off? Would that be wrong?' And he wasn't asking in terms of what he should or shouldn't do to win the fight. He was worried about hurting Ali. And it was eerie, because I had a feeling of *déjà vu* with Ali and Cleveland Williams, except this time Ali was the fighter who was shot. I kept thinking about Manila, and how Eddie Futch had stepped in to keep Joe Frazier from taking more punishment. And I wondered, if it came down to that, who would come out of Ali's corner? That's what worried me most about that night. And when fight night finally arrived; well, I tried to be professional. But then, that round when Holmes unloaded and landed that awful hook to the kidneys, when Ali stood there covering his face with his hands; I died, I felt horrible. I said to myself, 'Please, don't let him get hurt.' And I started shouting, 'Stop it! Stop the fight!' I was very sad that night; and I guess, relieved when it was over, because Ali got out alive. And you know, I've seen that happen too in boxing."

On October 2, 1980, Muhammad Ali and Larry Holmes entered a temporary arena constructed in the parking lot at Caesar's Palace in Las Vegas. The 24,740 fans in attendance paid $5,766,125, breaking the previous record for a live gate set in Ali's most recent bout against Leon Spinks. Ali weighed 217 pounds, the lightest he'd been since facing George Foreman. Holmes weighed in at 211.

It wasn't a fight; it was an execution. Most of the world might have been rooting for Ali, but in the ring, like every other fighter, he was alone. "Every fighter has the same nightmare," Ali had said years before. "You dream you've boxed six or seven fast rounds, and then you get tired, exhausted. You have nothing left. It's all gone. You have to quit."[8]

Against Holmes, that nightmare became a reality, except Ali had nothing from the opening bell on. Each judge awarded Holmes every round, until the slaughter was stopped at the end of ten rounds.

RICHIE GIACHETTI: "Larry and I were confident going in. We'd seen Ali both times against Spinks, and knew there was nothing left. The only problem I saw was, mentally it would be a hard fight for Larry because of how he felt about Ali. When Larry was a kid, he'd idolized Ali, and when he got to know him, he loved him.

"I thought they should have stopped it in the sixth round. After that, there was no point in going on, and that's when the mental thing started to get to Larry. He didn't want to hurt Ali, and began backing off because Ali wouldn't go down. After that, he'd come back to the corner and say, 'What am I supposed to do with this guy?' And I told him, 'Larry, this guy is trying to take away everything you have. The best thing you can do is knock him out, for him and for yourself.'"

"I sat next to Herbert Muhammad during the fight," Dave Kindred, then with *The Washington Post*, remembers. "Herbert never said a word. Mostly, he just hung his head and looked like he was in pain. Right before the fight ended, he signaled to someone. I don't know who it was, but Herbert shook his head and Angelo stopped it. Herbert must have missed half the fight, the way he was looking down. And it was awful; the worst sports event I ever had to cover. Ali had that great fighter's heart, boundless courage, all that pride. And he got his brains beat out by Holmes. It was like watching an automobile accident that kills someone you love. Round after round, he kept going out. And if they'd let him, he would have gone out for more."

In the ninth round, Holmes stunned Ali with an uppercut that draped the challenger against the ropes. Turning away involuntarily, Ali covered his face with his gloves, and the champion followed with a right hand to the kidney that caused Ali to cringe and double over in pain. Round ten was more of the same—"Like watching an autopsy on a man who's still alive," Sylvester Stallone said later.

And then at last it was over. Herbert Muhammad gave his signal, and Angelo Dundee told referee Richard Greene, "That's all."

"One more round," Bundini pleaded, grabbing onto Dundee's sweater.

"Fuck you! No!" Dundee shouted. "I'm the chief second. The ballgame's over."

MUHAMMAD ALI: "Before the fight started, I thought I could win. I wouldn't have fought if I didn't think I'd beat him. But after the first round, I knew I was in trouble. I was tired, nothing left at all. A couple of times before, when I had hard fights, in the middle of the fight I'd ask myself, 'What am I doing here?' With George Foreman in Zaïre, against Joe Frazier in Manila, I told myself I had to be crazy. But when the fights were over, it always seemed worth it, except when I fought Holmes. I didn't want Angelo to stop it. I wanted to go the fifteen rounds. But I guess what he did was right, because if it had gone on, maybe I would have gotten hurt more."

LARRY HOLMES: "After the fight, I went to Ali's room in the hotel and told him, 'You're still the greatest; I love you.' I meant it; and I felt awful. I felt terrible before I went to his room, and when I got there I felt worse. Even though I won, I was down. And Muhammad saw it, so he said to me, 'Man, now you got me mad. I took care of you; I fed you; I taught you how to fight. And look what you did to me. I'm coming back again to whup your ass.' And that made me feel better, listening to him say, 'I want Holmes; gimme Holmes.' And the only other thing I want to say is, I want people to know I'm proud I learned my craft from Ali. I'm prouder of sparring with him when he was young than I am of beating him when he was old."

Four days after he fought Larry Holmes, Ali checked into the UCLA Medical Center. "His condition was bad," Howard Bingham remembers. "He was sitting around at home, real tired, worse than I'd seen him ever. And he didn't want to go. He didn't want people reading in the newspaper that Larry Holmes put him in the hospital. But we told him it was better reading that Holmes put him in the hospital than it would be reading that Holmes killed him."

Ali underwent two days of tests at UCLA, after which the outline of what had occurred emerged. Several weeks before the fight, he'd been visited by Dr. Charles Williams, who was Herbert Muhammad's personal physician. Dr. Williams advised Ali that he was suffering from a hypothyroid condition, and prescribed one tablet of Thyrolar (three grains) per day. The doctor's diagnosis was speculative and apparently incorrect. Moreover, Thyrolar is a potentially lethal drug, and no one on Thyrolar should engage in a professional fight. Also, Ali was not advised of the drug's side effects, and there was no subsequent verification whether he was taking the proper dosage. Ali then compounded the problem by taking three tablets a day, because in his words, he "thought the pills would be like vitamins." Tests administered at UCLA also revealed the presence of Benzedrine in Ali's system. Benzedrine is a stimulant, and when it wears off, the user is more fatigued than he otherwise would have been. The use of these drugs over a period of several weeks was consistent with Ali's condition immediately before, during, and after the fight. In the fight itself, according to the medical history taken from Ali at UCLA, he felt weak, fatigued, and short of breath from round one on. His body wasn't able to cool itself properly, and his temperature rose. That, Dr. Williams later acknowledged, "led to heat exhaustion that went into heat stroke with an intermediate period of slight stupor and maybe delirium. I may have placed him in jeopardy inadvertently.[9]

Or, phrased differently, the medication given to Ali before the fight, in conjunction with the fight itself, had the potential to kill him. Dr. Williams explains his actions.

DR. CHARLES WILLIAMS: "I was Elijah Muhammad's doctor. He had confidence in me, and then Herbert got confidence in me and asked if I'd like to go to Japan with Ali as a guest for the Mac–Foster fight. After that, they invited me to be one of the doctors in the group on most of the trips, although Pacheco was the main doctor. Each time, it was a fantastic journey. I'd never been treated like anything other than a nigger in my life, and now we're on this big plane up in the sky, and we'd have the front of it, the whole first-class section, and in back was where all the white people sat. It thrilled me that black people could reach up that high. And I did whatever Herbert and Ali wanted me to do. I wanted to be the best servant of all.

"It was right before the second Spinks fight that I learned Ali's thyroid wasn't working properly. This is the first time I've told anybody about that. Ali told me things weren't quite right. I noticed a little slowing down, and Herbert was worried. So I took some samples of Ali's blood and urine over to the Oschner Clinic. That's a famous clinic in New Orleans. Ali never went there himself, but the pathologist at the clinic knew it was Ali's specimen. They did a battery of tests to check his thyroid function. And the pathologist told me his thyroid function was far below normal, so I corrected it. I won't say how. I only had a day or two to correct it. Let's just say I corrected it, and Ali whupped Leon Spinks. But based on that, I knew his internal environment wasn't being regulated like it should by the body. The equilibrium in the body wasn't being maintained.

"Then after that, we had the Holmes fight, and I knew Ali had something wrong with his thyroid. He gained a huge amount of weight. He went up to about 260 pounds. I saw him on TV and said, 'Jesus Christ, his thyroid is way out of line.' And it was made worse by all the stress he was under. The effect of stress on the human body is poorly known by most doctors. I probably know more about stress than any doctor in America. But Herbert didn't call me until two weeks before the fight, so it forced me to correct things in too short a period of time. It was just too much. Ali's metabolism had to be increased to normal, plus he was getting older; too old, really. My job, as I interpreted it, was to do the best I could. The contracts were signed, Ali fights the fight; he conforms to the stipulations of the contract; and he gets paid. I didn't worry about whether he was going to win. It was stupid to think he was going to win. I just wanted to get him in good enough shape, and sure enough, he looked good. What the hell; he was almost thirty-nine. He'd fought a million fights. He'd already proved himself three times world champion, and I knew it had to end sometime. Don King showed me something that said, 'See the great man fight; his last tango.' I said to myself, 'Well, people aren't expecting him to win. People are just coming to see the great Ali fight.' He was always interesting whether he won or lost.

"Anyway, I only had a few weeks to get Ali ready, and I was in a dilemma. So I told him, 'Well, try this.' And as soon as I gave him just a little bit of Thyrolar, whoom, he shot back up. He felt like he could whip a gorilla. He responded well; he was looking good. People were saying I really knew what I was doing, and as soon as he lost, they started blaming it on me. At UCLA, when they checked Ali, they didn't find any evidence of a thyroid problem but that's because I'd corrected it. I'm positive I was correct. I don't take a back seat to any doctor. When I told Ali something, I'd put my life on it. And if I had it to do over again, I'd do exactly the same thing. I know I've been criticized for the way I treated him, but when you know you're right you just accept that."

Dr. Williams's statement raises numerous questions. Several days before the Spinks fight in New Orleans, Ali had in fact complained of weariness. However, tests showed that his blood was low in salt, iron, and potassium. There was no mention of a thyroid deficiency. Dennis Cope, who supervised Ali's stay at the UCLA Medical Center and continues to monitor Ali's health, casts further doubt on Williams's evaluation. "The thyroid extract was given to Muhammad because, in the opinion of Dr. Williams, he looked hypothyroid," Dr. Cope states. "Unfortunately, there wasn't any testing done to verify that this was actually the case. I don't know for sure, but I can infer that prior to medical intervention, Muhammad's thyroid gland was functioning properly, because since then without medication it has functioned properly. And when a person's thyroid gland malfunctions, it's usually a long-term problem."

FERDIE PACHECO: "Ali is lucky he lived through the Holmes fight. And as far as Charles Williams is concerned, I don't like to talk badly about another doctor, but I think the facts speak for themselves.

"I first became aware of Charles Williams in Zaïre, when he announced that Ali was tired because he had hypoglycemia. That means low blood sugar. Now for starters, you can't diagnose hypoglycemia without a battery of tests—glucose tolerance and things like that—none of which were performed in Africa. But worse than Dr. Williams's diagnosis was his proposed cure. There's a delicate needle in the pancreas that determines how much insulin is released into the blood to burn how much sugar. And what happens with hypoglycemia is, the needle goes crazy and releases too much insulin when you take in sugar. Now what does the body do with that excess insulin? It goes to the brain and makes you groggy. That's hypoglycemia, pure and simple. It's not a killer; it's something you can adjust. The endocrine system is an interlinking of several glands, and everything can be balanced out so the insulin is kept within a certain limit. It's not a big thing. It's just something that requires a little attention on the part of an internist or endocrinologist. But the one thing in red letters that you cannot in any way, shape, or form do is give someone with hypoglycemia more sugar. That's the last thing you do unless you're trying to kill them, because whatever additional amount of sugar you put in, you'll get that much more insulin proportionally. And if you put enough sugar in, the patient will go into an insulin coma. You'd get thrown out of medical school if you reached third year and didn't know that.

"So there we were in the heart of Africa, and here's Charles Williams telling Ali he has hypoglycemia. And his cure was for Ali to eat a peach cobbler with ice cream right before the fight. In other words, his blood sugar was supposedly low, so we'll put some more sugar in. Let's fill his tank up with gas. And it was a problem. I wasn't sure what to do. I knew what I couldn't do, which was give Ali more sugar. But here's a doctor; he treats Herbert. I can't tell him he's an ignoramus. So what I said was, 'Look, this is a boxer; he's not a regular patient. He can't eat a peach cobbler right before the fight, because the possibility exists that George Foreman will punch him in the stomach. So what we'll do is, fill a bottle with orange juice and sugar; make sort of an orange syrup, and give that to Ali between rounds.' Williams said, 'Great!' We mixed the bottle. And that bottle is still out in the jungle somewhere between N'Sele and Kinshasa.

"Then came the Holmes fight. And as you know, I wasn't with Ali by then. But one thing I can tell you with great certainty is, in the absence of appropriate laboratory tests, you can't diagnose a hypothyroid condition. Ali had just been to the Mayo Clinic, with no evidence at all of a thyroid problem. To my knowledge, the condition never surfaced in any physician's evaluation of Ali other than Charles Williams's before or after Larry Holmes. And beyond that, if a fighter needs Thyrolar, it's like Russian roulette for him to be in the ring. His heart rate accelerates; his basic metabolism changes; his muscles are affected, because muscle tissue as well as fat is burning off. He can't sweat; he's debilitated by loss of water.

Thyrolar has never been given to another fighter in the history of boxing that I know of. And I don't know of anybody who ever had a thyroid condition who fought.

"Ali was a walking time bomb in the ring that night. He could have had anything from a heart attack to a stroke to all kinds of bleeding in the head. It's not up to me to make a judgment as to whether Charles Williams is competent to practice medicine. That's up to a medical board in the state of Illinois, where he practices. He's got his credentials, and that's that. But Ali–Holmes was a horrible end for a great champion, and years later, I'm still pissed off about it."

But the questions about Ali–Holmes go beyond Charles Williams. And foremost among them is why the fight ever happened. Why were contracts signed to begin with? And why was the bout allowed to proceed given the sudden marked deterioration of Ali's physical condition?

Ali himself is partly to blame for a fight that should never have taken place. He wanted the glory, he wanted a platform for his views, and he wanted the money. And in pursuit of those ends, he deceived himself, massively. "Getting ready for Holmes," says Ferdie Pacheco, "Ali was like a vain actress who's forty and wants to look twenty again. Maybe he looked young, but he was past his age in terms of his physical condition."

In the end, none of Ali's prefight objectives were realized. Once the bout began, glory was replaced by pain and humiliation. "I embarrassed myself," Ali acknowledged afterward. "I felt embarrassed for all my fans. I fought like an old man who was washed up."[10] Rather than give Ali a platform for future crusades, the fight diminished his credibility. And as in the past, the money he earned was siphoned into many hands. Herbert Muhammad took his one-third share. Taxes, training expenses, and the entourage ate up a significant amount. There were gifts, more bad business ventures, and ultimately a short paycheck from Don King.

MICHAEL PHENNER: "The contract for the fight called for Ali to receive eight million dollars. It had a clause saying there could be no amendment except in writing, and that was that. Ali was entitled to eight million dollars. Then, maybe a week before the fight, King started complaining about financial problems, and claimed Ali had agreed orally to fight for seven million. He had a lawyer chasing me all over Caesar's Palace trying to get me to amend the contract, and I refused. I was Ali's lawyer. My job was to protect Ali, not bail Don King out of financial trouble. Then, after the fight, when it was clear King had done quite well, I talked with Ali and we agreed the contract should be enforced the way it was written—that we'd go after Don for the million dollars, which he was refusing to pay. It was an open-and-shut lawsuit; summary judgment. But about a month later, I saw Ali. He was very chagrined. He told me he'd met with Don King; that King had put fifty thousand dollars in cash on the table in front of him. And fifty thousand dollars in cash looks like a lot of money, so Ali had taken it and signed a release. When I heard that, a tear rolled down my cheek. Here we were, trying to get Ali set financially. He'd just taken a horrible beating, in large part for the money. And then he'd gone and signed a piece of paper that cost him $950,000."

But Ali isn't the only person who should shoulder responsibility for the fight. The Nevada State Athletic Commission had a copy of the Mayo Clinic report. It also supposedly gave Ali its own physical examination just before the bout. By then, Ali was showing the effects of Thyrolar. Indeed, two days before the fight, he'd tried to do his usual roadwork, but been so fatigued after a half-mile that he'd had to stop. Yet the Nevada commission, whose first mission is to protect fighters within its jurisdiction, let the fight go on.

Herbert Muhammad also bears responsibility for Ali–Holmes. He's the manager who made the fight. "On things like that," says Howard Bingham, "Ali might not have listened to other people, but he always listened to Herbert. If Herbert had told him not to fight, that fight wouldn't have happened."

Moreover, it's hard to understand why Herbert wasn't aware of his fighter's deteriorating physical condition after Ali began taking Thyrolar. "I watched Ali the day of the fight," Bernie Yuman remembers. "And he was debilitated, terribly slow. You've got to understand, there was a difference between Ali being slow and Ali being serene. Ali had a serenity about him right before his fights; it was a mind-over-matter sort of thing. Everybody else could be freaking out in the heat of the moment, and he'd be incredibly peaceful and serene. But this was different. He wasn't peaceful; he was slow. He wasn't serene; he was drugged out. He was a sick man."

The charge most often made against Herbert Muhammad with regard to Ali–Holmes is that he sold Ali out for the money—one-third of Ali's purse, plus the possibility of more. Herbert Muhammad responds.

HERBERT MUHAMMAD: "I wasn't in boxing for the money. I was in boxing because my father put the obligation on me to look after Ali, and that's what I did. Other fighters constantly contacted me to manage them. Even now, I'm contacted by fighters who are having problems with managers or promoters, and I turn them all down. I once even had paper in Larry Holmes. When he was sparring with Ali, I had him on paper as manager, but I never did pursue it. I never managed but one fighter, and that's the only one I wanted.

"As far as Ali fighting Holmes, I believed he could beat Larry. That's not the fight I was worried about. The fight where I was worried was against George Foreman in Zaïre. Before that fight—and I shouldn't tell you this, because people will take it and twist it around—but before that fight, one of our people went to Zack Clayton, the referee, with my knowledge. He offered him five thousand dollars cash, and told him, 'This is for one thing, and one thing only. If Ali gets in trouble, stop the fight. Don't let Foreman keep beating on him if he's hurt.'*

"And against Holmes, I was the one who stopped the fight. Most of the time at Ali's fights, I sat in the front row, right by Ali's corner. Usually I didn't look at the fight, unless it was clear there was no danger. I didn't like seeing Ali get hit. Usually I'd be praying with my head down. When he fought Frazier, the time he lost, I almost fainted. And against Holmes; well, I was watching, and I wondered what was

---

* Herbert Muhammad maintains that he doesn't know if Clayton accepted the money or for that matter if it was ever actually offered to him. The $5,000 was never returned by the member of Ali's entourage who was authorized to make the offer.

wrong with Ali. He was getting hit and not hitting back. I started talking with Lloyd Wells, and Lloyd thought it should be stopped. So I didn't leave my seat, but I sent word to Angelo. I sent Lloyd and Pat Patterson to say, 'If there's one more round like this, stop it. If it looks like this at the end of the next round, throw the towel in.' And that's what happened. The next round, Ali was still getting beat, so I made the sign for them to stop the fight."

The decision to approve Ali–Holmes will be debated well into the next century, but one thing is clear. The fight was significant for a lot of people and affected many careers. For most of the past hundred years, whoever controlled the heavyweight champion controlled the lion's share of professional boxing. When Tex Rickard controlled Jack Dempsey, when Mike Jacobs controlled Joe Louis, when James Norris controlled Rocky Marciano, they turned that position into an empire. Herbert Muhammad never did that with Ali; he didn't want to control boxing. But the man who promoted Ali–Holmes did. Don King was Larry Holmes's exclusive promoter. It was very much in his interest for Holmes to fight and beat Ali. Once that occurred, King was well on his way to achieving a stranglehold on the heavyweight division, and that translated into a massive amount of money for anyone who had a share.

MIKE KATZ: "I don't know what happened behind the scenes in Vegas. I just know that it was essential to Don King for Ali to go ahead with the fight. This was one of the few times King had his own money on the line, as opposed to someone else's. If Ali–Holmes had fallen through or failed at the gate, King would have been in trouble. And of course, it was clearly in Don's interest to have Holmes win. He was Larry s exclusive promoter. And from beginning to end, Don was able to play Larry like a violin. He reeled him in with his black-brother line, jerked him around, and paid him millions of dollars less than Larry could have gotten from another promoter. When Ali and Frazier fought the first time, Frazier was champ, Ali was the draw, and Frazier got parity. When Ali fought Foreman, Foreman was champ, again Ali was the draw, and Foreman got parity. But when Holmes fought Ali, even though Larry was champ, he got five million dollars less than Ali. Who do you think got the five million? And it happened again when Larry fought Gerry Cooney. Larry was champ; he was at the peak of his career. But Cooney got nine million dollars, and Larry, if he was lucky, got half as much. And I felt for Larry, because I thought he was basically an O.K. guy and a great fighter. But I felt more for Ali. I was crying, literally crying, when the two of them fought. Tears were rolling down my cheeks. There was a total emptiness inside me. All I could see was Ali slumped on his stool, and I was like listening to echoes. 'Ali! Ali!' "

1. September 29, 1980, *Sports Illustrated*; August 28, 1980, *New York Times*.
2. August 27, 1980, *New York Times*.
3. August 28, 1980, *New York Times*; Big Fights, Inc., film archives.
4. September 28, 1980, *New York Times*; September 29, 1980, *Sports Illustrated*.
5. Big Fights, Inc., film archives; September 29, 1980, *Sports Illustrated*.
6. Hugh McIlvanney, *McIlvanney on Boxing*, p. 176; Big Fights, Inc. film archives.
7. September 29, 1980, *Sports Illustrated*.
8. September 16, 1974, *New York Daily News*.
9. October 8, 1980, *New York Daily News*; October 8, 1980, *New York Times*.
10. October 8, 1980, *New York Post*.

Acknowledgements

PREFACE

Extract from *The Real Thing*, copyright © Tom Stoppard 1982, 1983, 1986, reprinted by permission of Faber and Faber Ltd.

ON REFLECTION

'The Window' from *Beyond a Boundary*, copyright © Executor to the estate of C. L. R. James 1963, reprinted by permission of Serpent's Tail Ltd.

Extract from 'The High Life' from *The Dogs*, copyright © Laura Thompson 1994, reprinted by permission of Random House UK Ltd.

Extract from *Haunts of the Black Masseur: The Swimmer as Hero*, copyright © Charles Sprawson 1992, reprinted by permission of Random House UK Ltd.

'Hutton and the Past' from *Collected Poems and Prose*, copyright © Harold Pinter 1978, reprinted by permission of Faber and Faber Ltd.

'Charlie Cook' from the *Independent*, copyright © Roddy Doyle 1992, reprinted by permission of the author.

FANS' NOTES

'The Silence' from *Late Innings: A Baseball Companion*, Ballantine Books, copyright © Roger Angell 1982, reprinted by permission of International Creative Management Inc.

Extract from *A Fan's Notes: A Fictional Memoir*, copyright © Frederick Exley 1968, reprinted by permission of the Peters, Fraser & Dunlop Group Ltd.

'In Off the Post: Chelsea 1973/4' from *My Favourite Year: A Collection of New Football Writing*, copyright © Giles Smith 1993, reprinted by permission of the author.

'A New Yorker's Derby' from *The Best of A. J. Liebling*, copyright © A. J. Liebling 1938, 1944, 1947, 1952, 1953, 1958, 1961, 1962, 1963, reprinted by permission of the *Observer*.

HOW IT LOOKS

'Hutton, Hobbs and the Classical Style' from *Cricket All the Year*, copyright © Neville Cardus 1952, reprinted by permission.

'Iron Mike and the Allure of the "Manly Art"' by Tom Callahan from *Come Out Writing: A Boxing Anthology*, Queen Anne Press, edited by Bill Hughes and Patrick King, copyright © Bill Hughes and Patrick King 1991, reprinted by permission.

'Cardus and the Aesthetic Fallacy' from *The Willow Wand: Some Cricket Myths Explored*, Sportspages, copyright © Derek Birley 1979, reprinted by permission of the author.

BEING THERE

'England v West Indies (1963)' from *Harpers and Queen* 1963, copyright © V. S. Naipaul 1963, reprinted by permission of Aitken, Stone & Wylie.

'Ahab and Nemesis' from *The Sweet Science*, Sportspages, copyright © A. J. Liebling 1951, 1952, 1953, 1954, 1956, reprinted by permission of A. M. Heath & Company Ltd.

Extract from 'The Beautiful Game: England–West Germany' from *All Played Out: The Full Story of Italia '90*, William Heinemann Ltd copyright © Pete Davies 1990, reprinted by permission of Reed Consumer Books Ltd.

MEANWHILE, SOMEWHERE ELSE . . .

'It Occurs to Me . . .' from *Arlott on Cricket*, William Collins Sons & Co Ltd copyright © John Arlott 1984, reprinted by permission of John Pawsey.

'Golf Caddies' from *The Best of Plimpton*, Simon & Schuster Ltd, copyright © George Plimpton 1991, reprinted by permission of Simon & Schuster.

'Keith Boyce: head groundsman' from *Cricket Voices: Interviews with Mihir Bose*, the Kingswood Press, copyright © Mihir Bose 1990, reprinted by permission of Reed Consumer Books Ltd.

'Under the Lights' from *Broken Vessels*, Picador, copyright © Andre Dubus 1991, reprinted by permission of David R. Godine, Publishers.

'The Referee' from *The Football Man: People and Passions in Soccer*, Penguin Books 1971, copyright © Arthur Hopcraft 1968, reprinted by permission.

DOING IT

Extract from *Faster* from *The Norton Book of Sports* edited by George Plimpton, W. W. Norton & Co, copyright © Jackie Stewart and Peter Manso), reprinted by permission of IMG.

Extract from *Shadow Box*, Andre Deutsch Ltd, copyright © George Plimpton 1977, reprinted by permission of Andre Deutsch Ltd.

Extract from *The Game*, Sportspages, copyright © Ken Dryden 1983, reprinted by permission of Simon & Schuster.

Extract from *Native Stones: A Book About Climbing*, Secker and Warburg Ltd. copyright © David Craig 1987, reprinted by permission of Rogers, Coleridge & White Ltd.

'My Aintree Nightmare' from *Front Runners: More of the best of Brough Scott*, Victor Gollancz Ltd, copyright © Brough Scott 1991, reprinted by permission of Victor Gollancz Ltd.

'Great Sporting Moments: The Treble' from *Kid*, Faber and Faber Ltd, copyright © Simon Armitage 1992, reprinted by permission of Faber and Faber Ltd.

Extract from *Walking on Water*, John Murray Ltd, copyright © Andy Martin 1991, reprinted by permission of John Murray (Publishers) Ltd.

THE MOMENT

'The Greatest Moment Ever' from *Fever Pitch*, Victor Gollancz Ltd, copyright © Nick Hornby 1992, reprinted by permission of the author.

Extract from 'Another Time, Another Planet' from *The Great Number Tens*, Transworld Publishers Ltd, copyright © Frank Keating 1993, reprinted by permission of the author.

Extract from *The Death of Ayrton Senna*, Viking, copyright © Richard Williams 1995, reprinted by permission of Penguin UK Ltd.

ALI, ALI

Extract from *Sting Like A Bee: The Muhammad Ali Story*, Sportspages, copyright © José Torres and Bert Randolph Sugar 1971, reprinted by permission.

'He's Only a Human. My Guy Ain't' from *McIlvanney On Boxing: An Anthology*, Stanley Paul & Co. Ltd copyright © Hugh McIlvanney 1982, reprinted by permission of the *Observer*.

Extract from *The Fight*, Penguin Books Ltd, copyright © Norman Mailer 1975, reprinted by permission of Aitken, Stone & Wylie.

Extract from *Muhammad Ali: His Life and Times*, Robson Books Ltd, copyright © Thomas Hauser and Muhammad Ali 1991, reprinted by permission of Robson Books.